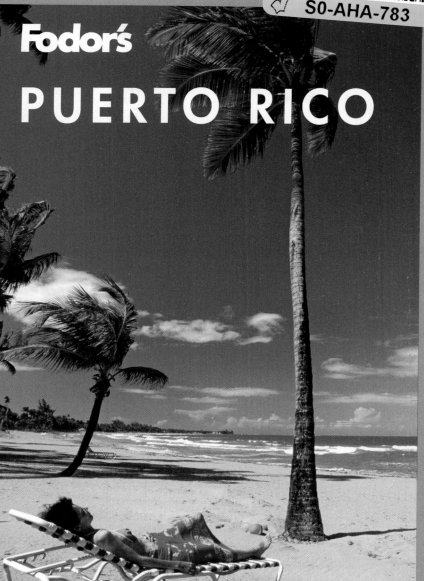

Fodor's

PUERTO RICO

WELCOME TO PUERTO RICO

It's easy to have a Caribbean vacation on Puerto Rico, but this tropical island offers much more than sun and sand. In the exciting city of San Juan, you're sure to find your scene whether it's art museums, posh boutiques, or trendy bars. Nearby, the lush El Yunque rain forest provides a peaceful retreat from urban diversions. Colonial towns such as Ponce and San Germán bring history to life in centuries-old churches and plazas. Nighttime is always right for salsa dancing and piña coladas, and no matter where you stay, you're never far from the beach of your dreams.

TOP REASONS TO GO

★ **Dining:** From Nuevo Latino restaurants to simple spots serving comida criolla.

★ **Old San Juan:** Cobblestone streets, cafés, and boutique hotels in a charming neighborhood.

★ **Beaches:** From lively resort-fronted strands to remote coves with calm waters.

★ **El Yunque:** The only tropical rain forest managed by the U.S. Forest Service.

★ **History:** Sixteenth-century fortifications such as El Morro and La Muralla still stand.

★ **Vieques and Culebra:** Laid-back islands with unspoiled beauty and quiet towns.

Fodor's PUERTO RICO

Publisher: Amanda D'Acierno, *Senior Vice President*

Editorial: Arabella Bowen, *Editor in Chief*; Linda Cabasin, *Editorial Director*

Design: Fabrizio La Rocca, *Vice President, Creative Director*; Tina Malaney, *Associate Art Director*; Chie Ushio, *Senior Designer*; Ann McBride, *Production Designer*

Photography: Melanie Marin, *Associate Director of Photography*; Jessica Parkhill and Jennifer Romains, *Researchers*

Maps: Rebecca Baer, *Senior Map Editor*; Henry Colomb and Mark Stroud, Moon Street Cartography; David Lindroth, Inc. *Cartographers*

Production: Linda Schmidt, *Managing Editor*; Evangelos Vasilakis, *Associate Managing Editor*; Angela L. McLean, *Senior Production Manager*

Sales: Jacqueline Lebow, *Sales Director*

Marketing & Publicity: Heather Dalton, *Marketing Director*; Katherine Punia, *Senior Publicist*

Business & Operations: Susan Livingston, *Vice President, Strategic Business Planning*; Sue Daulton, *Vice President, Operations*

Fodors.com: Megan Bell, *Executive Director, Revenue & Business Development*; Yasmin Marinaro, *Senior Director, Marketing & Partnerships*

Copyright © 2015 by Fodor's Travel, a division of Random House LLC

Writers: Heather Rodino, Paulina Salach, Julie Schwietert Collazo

Editor: Eric B. Wechter
Production Editor: Evangelos Vasilakis

8th Edition

ISBN 978-0-8041-4266-3

ISSN 1531–0396

All details in this book are based on information supplied to us at press time. Always confirm information when it matters, especially if you're making a detour to visit a specific place. Fodor's expressly disclaims any liability, loss, or risk, personal or otherwise, that is incurred as a consequence of the use of any of the contents of this book.

SPECIAL SALES

This book is available at special discounts for bulk purchases for sales promotions or premiums. For more information, e-mail specialmarkets@randomhouse.com

PRINTED IN THE UNITED STATES OF AMERICA

10 9 8 7 6 5 4 3 2 1

CONTENTS

Fodor's Features

CONTENTS

ABOUT
THIS GUIDE

Fodor's Recommendations
Everything in this guide is worth doing—we don't cover what isn't—but exceptional sights, hotels, and restaurants are recognized with additional accolades. **Fodor's**Choice★ indicates our top recommendations; and **Best Bets** call attention to notable hotels and restaurants in various categories. Care to nominate a new place? Visit Fodors.com/contact-us.

Trip Costs
We list prices wherever possible to help you budget well. Hotel and restaurant price categories from $ to $$$$ are noted alongside each recommendation. For hotels, we include the lowest cost of a standard double room in high season. For restaurants, we cite the average price of a main course at dinner or, if dinner isn't served, at lunch. For attractions, we always list adult admission fees; discounts are usually available for children, students, and senior citizens.

Hotels
Our local writers vet every hotel to recommend the best overnights in each price category, from budget to expensive. Unless otherwise specified, you can expect private bath, phone, and TV in your room. For expanded hotel reviews and current deals, visit Fodors.com.

Restaurants
Unless we state otherwise, restaurants are open for lunch and dinner daily. We mention dress code only when there's a specific requirement and reservations only when they're essential or not accepted. To make restaurant reservations, visit Fodors.com.

Credit Cards
The hotels and restaurants in this guide typically accept credit cards. If not, we'll say so.

Top Picks
★ Fodor'sChoice

Listings
⊠ Address
✉ Branch address
☎ Telephone
🖷 Fax
⊕ Website
✎ E-mail
🎫 Admission fee
☉ Open/closed times
Ⓜ Subway
⊹ Directions or Map coordinates

Hotels & Restaurants
🏨 Hotel
🛏 Number of rooms
†◯† Meal plans
✕ Restaurant
☞ Reservations
🎩 Dress code
▭ No credit cards
Ⓢ Price

Other
⇨ See also
☞ Take note
⛳ Golf facilities

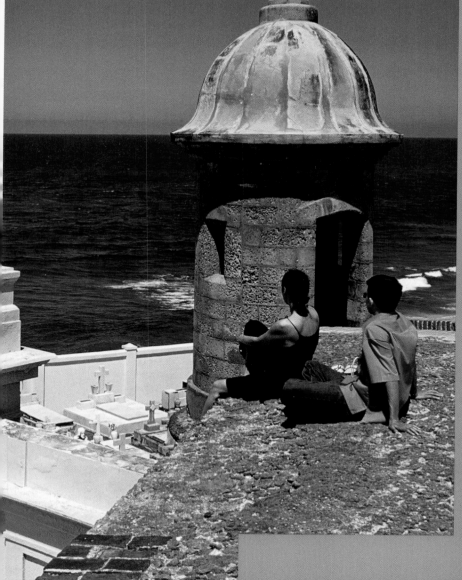

EXPERIENCE
PUERTO RICO

WHAT'S WHERE

2 San Juan. Old San Juan's a visual delight of cobbled streets, cathedrals, forts, and convents dating back centuries. Hotels concentrate in the beach-lined Condado and Isla Verde districts, where the nightlife sizzles. San Juan has tremendous museums, a vivacious bar scene, restaurants from earthy to trendy, plus fabulous boutiques and galleries.

3 El Yunque and the Northeast. El Yunque is the most popular day trip from San Juan: hiking trails that snake through this tropical rain forest lead to hidden pools and mountaintop *miradores* (lookouts). Luquillo has one of the island's best-known beaches, Luquillo Beach, aka Balneario La Monserrate. Westward, Reserva Natural las Cabezas de San Juan teems with wildlife in

several distinct ecosystems, including mangroves. Fajardo is a base for exploring exquisite offshore cays, including Isla Palomino and Isla Palominito.

4 Vieques and Culebra. Once used by the U.S. armed forces for military exercises, this pair of sand-fringed isles is now famous for their jaw-dropping beaches. Boutique hotels and trendy eateries have popped up alongside beachy bars.

Old San Juan

SAN JUAN

Cataño · Loíza

Reserva Nat. Las Cabezas de San Juan

Bayamón

Carolina

Canóvanas

Luquillo

Cayo Icacos

Pta. de Molinos

Dewey

CULEBRA

El Yunque

SIERRA DE LUQUILLO

Fajardo

Pasaje de San Juan

Ceiba

Sonda de Vieques

Caguas

El Toro

Cidra

San Lorenzo

Naguabo

Punta Puerca

Punta Lima

Punta Santiago

Humacao

Punta Este

Isabel Segunda

Ruta Panorámica

Cayey

SIERRA DE CAYEY

Esperanza

VIEQUES

Pasaje de Vieques

Yabucoa

Patillas

Maunabo

Lobos

Guayama

Caribbean Sea

0   10 mi

0   10 km

Ecotourism is big, with popular activities including snorkeling, diving, kayaking, and visits to the stunning bioluminescent bay in Vieques.

5 Ponce and the Porta Caribe. The southern coast is studded with tropical dry forests, such as Bosque Estatal de Guánica, a destination for hikers and birders. The colonial center of Ponce has one of the finest art museums in the Caribbean.

Offshore, "The Wall" gives scuba divers raptures of the deep.

6 Rincón and the Porta del Sol. The jagged coastline of the west is renowned for world-class surfing centered on Rincón, where dozens of beaches beckon those who like to hang 10. Cabo Rojo offers great birding. Architecture buffs appreciate the grandeur of downtown Mayagüez and the charms of San Germán, a colonial hilltop town.

7 The Ruta Panorámica. The rugged mountain spine that runs the width of the isle is festooned with forest. The roads of the scenic Panoramic Route wend through this tangled, lush terrain, linking yesteryear towns and indigenous sites. Several nature reserves along this rewarding drive provide delightful hiking jaunts.

PUERTO RICO PLANNER

Health

Few visitors experience health problems, and inoculations aren't required. There's no malaria, but as a precaution against dengue fever, a mosquito-borne disease, use an insect repellent with DEET and wear clothing that covers your arms and legs.

Tap water on the island is generally fine for drinking, but avoid it after storms (when the water supply can become mixed with sewage). Thoroughly wash or peel produce you buy in markets.

Most medical centers have English-speaking medical staff, and many large hotels have an English-speaking doctor on call.

Safety

San Juan, Mayagüez, and Ponce, like most other big cities, have their share of crime, so guard your wallet or purse in crowded areas; handbags should be worn bandolier style (across one shoulder and your chest). Avoid walking anywhere alone at night. Always lock your car, and do not leave any valuables in sight.

When to Go

Puerto Rico is a tropical island, so temperatures don't vary much. When considering what time of year to visit, think about the "dry" and "rainy" seasons. Dry season runs from mid-December through mid-April. Hotel rates can be as much as 25% higher than the rest of the year, and hotels tend to be packed. This doesn't mean that rooms won't be available, but if you plan to beat that winter sleet in Duluth, make arrangements for flights and accommodations as far in advance as possible. A less expensive time to visit is during the "shoulder" seasons of fall and spring, when discount rates may be available, the weather is still perfect, and the tourist crush is less intense.

The best bargains are in the slower summer season, when temperatures are hotter, it's rainier, and hurricanes are a slim possibility. Puerto Rico can be an excellent hurricane-season option for the Caribbean for last-minute flight and hotel deals, when you'll be able to watch the weather report and know a storm isn't about to strike.

However, business travel—not to mention the fact that San Juan serves as a major hub for connecting flights to the rest of the Caribbean—keeps flights to Puerto Rico fairly full on weekdays all year long.

Climate

Puerto Rico's weather is moderate and tropical year-round, with an average temperature of about 82°F (26°C). There are no big seasonal changes, although winter sees cooling (not cold) breezes from the north, and temperatures in higher elevations drop by as much as 20 degrees. The rainier summer months are hurricane season in the Caribbean, which runs July through November. (Historically, August and September present the greatest risk for hurricanes.) The southwest is relatively dry year-round, while the region around El Yunque can be deluged at any time of year, feeding the lush rain forest.

Festivals and Events

January: Fiestas de la Calle San Sebastián (*San Sebastián Street Festival*). The annual Fiestas de la Calle San Sebastián in January feature four nights of live music as well as food festivals and *cabezudos* parades, where folk legends are caricatured in oversize masks. ⊕ *www.seepuertorico.com/en/what-to-do/events.*

February–early March: Carnival. In the days preceding Lent, Ponce celebrates Carnival with flamboyant costumes, parades, and music. ⊕ *www.visitponce.com.* **Casals Festival.** San Juan's annual Casals Festival honors world-renowned cellist Pablo Casals, who lived in Puerto Rico for nearly three decades until his death. Classical music performances feature the Puerto Rico Symphony Orchestra, as well as soloists, trios, and quartets from the island and around the world. ☎ *787/918–1106.*

April: Saborea Puerto Rico. Puerto Rico's largest culinary event, Saborea Puerto Rico, is a three-day extravaganza held at Escambrón Beach in San Juan. It includes presentations by island and international chefs, and food from local restaurants, as well as beer, wine, and rum tastings. ⊕ *http://saboreapuertorico.com.*

May: Puerto Rico Restaurant Week. PRRW is a one-week, island-wide dining celebration held every May. It's the perfect opportunity to visit top restaurants and enjoy specially priced pre-fixe menus lunch and dinner menus. ⊕ *www.prrestaurantweek.com.*

June: SoFo Culinary Festival. For several days in both June and December, Old San Juan's Calle Fortaleza is closed to traffic for the SoFo Culinary Festival, when many restaurants set up shop on the cobblestone street. **Heineken JazzFest.** The annual Heineken JazzFest attracts some 15,000 aficionados to San Juan for four days of outdoor concerts by the likes of Spyro Gyra and George Benson. ⊕ *http://prheinekenjazz.com/.*

Late June–early July: Aibonito Flower Festival. This popular festival displays incredible tropical foliage, including countless varieties of colorful orchids and ginger plants. There's also plenty of food and music.

September: Puerto Rico Symphony Orchestra. The annual season of the PRSO begins in San Juan with classical and pop performances by the island's finest orchestra. ⊕ *www2.pr.gov.*

December: Festival de las Máscaras. The annual Festival de las Máscaras honors the mask-making traditions of Hatillo, where colorful masks used in religious processions have been crafted for centuries.

What to Pack

Although "casual" is the operative word for vacation clothes, Puerto Ricans dress up to go out, particularly in the cities. Pack some dressy-casual slacks and shirts, summer skirts for women, casual clothes for the resort, at least two bathing suits, and sturdy shoes for walking. A light sweater or jacket is also a good idea. If you're planning on visiting nature reserves, pack long-sleeve shirts and long pants to guard against mosquitoes.

Visitor Information

In addition to Puerto Rico Tourism Company's magazine, *¡Qué Pasa!,* pick up the Puerto Rico Hotel and Tourism Association's *Bienvenidos* and *Places to Go* for information about the island and its activities. All are free and available at tourism offices and hotel desks. The Puerto Rico Tourism Company has information centers at the airport, and in Old San Juan, Ponce, Aguadilla, and Cabo Rojo. Most towns also have a tourism office, usually in the city hall.

Contacts Puerto Rico Tourism Company ☎ *800/866–7827, 787/721–2400* ⊕ *www.seepuertorico.com.*

PUERTO RICO
TOP ATTRACTIONS

San Juan National Historic Site

(A) The U.S. National Park Service maintains this huge colonial military complex, which includes Castillo San Felipe del Morro and Castillo San Cristóbal. A visit to Old San Juan is not complete without exploring these twin fortresses. Park rangers offer fascinating tours of the tunnels, cannon batteries, and barracks, which today feature museum pieces recalling a once-glorious past.

El Yunque National Forest

(B) Pack your raingear and hike the crown jewel of Puerto Rico—carpeting the slopes of the rugged Luquillo Mountain Range. From El Portal Visitor Center the Sendero El Yunque climbs 1,365 feet through an eerie cloud forest. This 2.6-mile trail puts you atop the summit at 3,496 feet. When it's clear, the 360-degree views are spectacular. Add a twist to your return hike by diverting along Forest Road 10 to the Mt. Britton observation tower, resembling

a castle turret. A spiral staircase leads to a viewing platform.

Playa Flamenco

(C) Puerto Rico's best beach? Ask the thousands of *sanjuaneros* who fly or ferry out to the isle of Culebra on weekends and holidays. Long and broad enough to absorb the masses, this visual stunner tempts disbelief with its bright white sands and waters of Maxfield Parrish blues and greens. Snorkeling is tops, thanks to an offshore reef, and when the wind is up surfers are thrilled by the action.

Parque de las Cavernas del Rio Camuy

(D) Puerto Rico has some of the deepest and longest caves in the world, and it's a special thrill to rappel down a cliff face to enter Cueva Camuy. Donned in life jacket and lamped helmet, you'll never forget the 250-foot rope descent, Spider-Man style, into the gaping mouth of Angeles Cave. Dripstone formations take on surreal forms in the cool, moist depths, where you slide down mud chutes and body raft in the care of experienced guides. Aventuras Tierra Adentro offers trips. Less adventurous travelers can take a tram tour of the caves.

Bioluminescent Bay, Vieques

(E) A remarkable natural wonder, Vieques's world-famous Mosquito Bay's surreal glowing waters inspire childlike delight in all who visit. Microscopic organisms that live in the lagoon light up around your kayak, enveloping you in a neon-like spectral glow. Choose a moonless pitch-black night for best effect. The experience is well worth the journey to Vieques, even if you do nothing else here. Several operators on the island offer trips.

Arecibo Observatory

(F) If this space-age facility deep in the mountains of northwest Puerto Rico looks like something from a sci-fi movie, it is. *Contact*, with Jodie Foster, was filmed here. The view over the 1,000-ft.-wide dish (the largest such telescope ever built) is a jaw-dropper. The visitor center doubles as a superb museum on astronomy and the atmosphere.

The Ruta Panorámica

(G) Puerto Rico's interior is a beautiful mountainous region with cooler climes and splendid climbs. The Ruta Panorámica is a network of roads that snake through the entire region. Some are nicely maintained, others less so. But the "Panoramic Route" lives up to its name, providing eye-catching vistas around every bend of the road. It's an exciting journey that reveals an enthralling vision of Puerto Rico undisclosed to those who don't venture beyond the city and shores.

HISTORY YOU CAN SEE

Precolonial Puerto Rico

The Taínos were the indigenous group that populated the island prior to its "discovery" by Christopher Columbus during his second trip to the New World in 1493. The Taínos' name for the island was Borinquen, and even today Puerto Ricans honor their Taíno heritage by referring to themselves as *boricuas*.

What to See: The island's two main ceremonial centers—**Tibes** and **Caguana**—have preserved the limited artifacts of Taíno culture that have been discovered over the years. At Tibes, just north of Ponce, visitors can see reproductions of the *bohíos* in which Taínos lived, as well as fields believed to be the sites of ceremonial events.

Closer to San Juan, those curious to get a window into the Taíno world can visit **La Cueva de María de la Cruz**, a cave in Loíza where archaeologists discovered Taíno artifacts in the mid-20th century. As of this writing, entry to the cave was free; there are no officials on-site.

Colonial Puerto Rico

Columbus arrived in 1493, and the Spanish crown controlled the island—though with a determinedly laissez-faire approach—until the Spanish-American War of 1898 ended with the concession of Puerto Rico to the United States. The first Spanish governor of the island was Juan Ponce de Léon, the explorer famous for his tireless pursuit for the elusive fountain of youth. Spain's Queen Isabella charged de Léon with the task of "compel[ling] and forc[ing] the Indians to work for the Christian inhabitants." According to the late historian and archaeologist Ricardo Alegría, the Taínos were decimated, refusing to resist the Spanish conquistadores because they believed that Spaniards were immortal; thus, taking up arms against them was futile.

By the 1530s, Africans had been brought to the island for slave labor; they built San Juan's two biggest fortresses, Castillo San Felipe del Morro and Castillo San Cristóbal, massive construction projects that took more than 250 years of intense, arduous labor. Slavery in Puerto Rico was finally abolished in 1873.

What to See: Built in 1521, **Casa Blanca** was the intended home of Juan Ponce de Léon, who never actually lived here. His descendants, however, called the Old San Juan property home for 250 years. It's fresh from a recently completed renovation.

Castillo San Felipe del Morro and **Castillo San Cristóbal** aren't San Juan's only forts—there's also Fortín San Gerónimo del Boquerón, located just behind the Caribe Hilton, and the Fortín El Cañuelo on Goat Island, visible across San Juan Bay—but they're certainly the largest and most impressive. Both offer commanding views of the Atlantic from their upper levels.

Built between 1533 and 1540, **La Fortaleza** was intended to serve as a perch from which the Bay of San Juan could be monitored and protected. Its strategic limitations were soon discovered, though, and the UNESCO-recognized structure is home to Puerto Rico's governor, as it has been since the late 16th century. Guided tours allow the public to glimpse how the governor lives.

A predominantly Afro–Puerto Rican town, **Loíza** was founded in 1719 and was populated by escaped slaves. Separated from the mainland by the Río Grande, the town remained geographically and socially isolated until the mid 1970s, allowing many Afro–Puerto Rican traditions to be preserved. Called the "capital of tradition," Loíza is home to popular *bomba* and *plena* (music and dance) and is famous for coconut masks, or *vejigantes*, used during annual festivals *(see also the "Masks of Puerto Rico" feature in Chapter 5)*. Though it's most lively during early July, when the Santiago Apóstol festival is under way, a visit at any other time of year should include a stop at **San Patricio**, one of the island's oldest churches and home to what may be the only black St. Patrick statue in the world.

The Transition to the Commonwealth

In 1898 Puerto Rico became a U.S. territory. Although few would argue that life was better under the Spanish, many have had misgivings about the transfer. As Puerto Rican historians Kal Wagenheim and Olga Jiménez de Wagenheim remarked, "The invasion of Puerto Rico [by the U.S.] ended four centuries of oppressive Spanish colonial rule, only to replace it with a more subtle brand of colonialism."

Although the island was now part of the U.S., Puerto Ricans were without formal citizenship for more than a decade. The educational system underwent frequent upheavals, as did the structure of the government, as the U.S. imposed policies reflecting evolving defense and economic interests. Even when U.S. citizenship was conferred in the 1917 passage of the Jones–Shafroth Act, the development did little to resolve the ambiguous relationship between Puerto Rico and the U.S. Citizenship for Puerto Ricans was not, after all, conferred with all the rights and privileges enjoyed by mainland citizens. In 1952 the island became a commonwealth (or a "free associated state"), though this did little to change the day-to-day lives of inhabitants.

Fierce debates continue among Puerto Ricans about the status of the island. Of the three major political parties, one is in favor of statehood, one prefers being a commonwealth, and the third advocates independence.

What to See: Built between 1919 and 1929, Puerto Rico's Beaux-Arts–style **Capitolio** building is an often-overlooked site that shouldn't be missed. Its rotunda is inlaid with colorful mosaic tiles depicting the major periods of Puerto Rican history, and the Puerto Rican Constitution is displayed in glass cases. Busts of important Puerto Rican politicians are also on display. Visitors will often encounter protesters on the Capitolio steps; citizens gather here frequently to peacefully protest government policies.

Las Mercedes Cemetery, located in Ponce, is the final resting place of some of Puerto Rico's most important and celebrated politicians, among them Don Luis A. Ferré, former governor and founder of the Museo de Arte in Ponce. The grand tombstones and mausoleums in this cemetery are photo worthy, as are the bones resting within your reach in open crypts at the back of the cemetery. ■ TIP➔ Every town has its own culture trolley, offering a historic guided tour of the area's highlights. The trolleys are often free. Stops can generally be found in the town's plaza, in front of the city hall.

CRUISING TO PUERTO RICO

San Juan is a home base for many cruise ships and a staple of itineraries for cruise ships sailing from Florida. It's an excellent way for first-time visitors to sample Puerto Rico, as most cruise companies offer excursions beyond Old San Juan. Some itineraries begin or end here—a chance for more extensive exploration.

Arriving in San Juan

Most cruise ships dock within a couple of blocks of Old San Juan; however, there is a second cruise pier across the bay at Isla Grande. If your ship docks here you'll need a taxi to get anywhere on the island. The Paseo de la Princesa, a tree-lined promenade beneath the city wall, is a nice place for a quick stroll—you can admire local crafts and stop at the refreshment kiosks. Fortunately, major sights in the Old San Juan area are just a short walk from the piers. Two major tourist information booths are within one block of the cruise-terminal area.

Carnival Cruises. They call themselves "fun ships" for good reason, with lots of entertainment and youthful things to do aboard. Singles, couples, children, and even older folks will enjoy these cruises. Kids' programs earn rave reviews. ☎ 888/227–6482 ⊕ www.carnival.com.

Celebrity Cruises. Celebrity's focus is on service, and it shows. Every aspect of your trip has been well thought out. They cater to adults more than children, so this may not be the best line for families. ☎ 800/647–2251 ⊕ www.celebritycruises.com.

Holland America. The grande dame of cruise lines, Holland America has a reputation for service and elegance. This company includes San Juan on its itineraries departing from Fort Lauderdale and Tampa. ☎ 877/932–4259 ⊕ www.hollandamerica.com.

Norwegian Cruise Line. Billing its relatively relaxed, family-friendly cruises as "freestyle," NCL was one of the earliest companies to specialize in the Caribbean. It boasts the youngest fleet on the planet. ☎ 866/234–7350 ⊕ www.ncl.com.

Princess Cruises. Princess strives to offer affordable luxury. Its prices start out a little higher, but you get more bells and whistles (more affordable balcony rooms, nice decor, more restaurants, personalized service). It has a wide range of itineraries departing from Fort Lauderdale and San Juan. It draws a slightly older crowd. ☎ 800/774–6237 ⊕ www.princess.com.

Regent Seven Seas. Aiming for the high-end market with deluxe staterooms, noteworthy speakers, and performance troupes, this company's ships are among the most sophisticated afloat. ☎ 877/505–5370 ⊕ www.rssc.com.

Royal Caribbean. Royal Caribbean is known for its spacious and stylish mega-liners. In keeping with its reputation for being all things for all people, Royal Caribbean offers a huge variety of activities and services on board and more shore excursions than any other cruise line. ☎ 866/562–7625 ⊕ www.royalcaribbean.com.

Silversea. Silversea serves deluxe cruisers with small vessels renowned for exquisite decor and attentive service. Expect classical performers among the entertainers. ☎ 877/276–6816 ⊕ www.silversea.com.

Although Puerto Rico is a U.S. territory and no passport is required for U.S. citizens, you'll still need yours for ports of call in other Caribbean islands.

Almost all of the ship's shore excursions can be arranged more cheaply with local tour operators. Taxis are also available near the dock. Within the city, metered cabs charge an initial $1.75; after that, it's 10¢ for each additional 1/19 mile or every 25 seconds of waiting time. There's a $1 charge for each piece of luggage. You can negotiate with taxi drivers for specific trips, and you can hire a taxi for as little as $36 per hour for sightseeing tours. You can also prearrange a rental car if you'd prefer to drive yourself, but leave plenty of time to return it before your ship sails.

Most mainland cell phones work in Puerto Rico, but that is not usually the case while at sea. Check with the cruise company before setting out.

SAN JUAN BEST BETS

Castillo San Felipe del Morro. Explore the giant labyrinthine fort.

El Yunque National Forest. This rain forest east of San Juan is a great half-day excursion.

Casa Bacardí. Rum lovers can jump on the public ferry and then taxi over to the factory.

Old San Juan. Walk the cobblestone streets of Old San Juan.

Shopping. Within a few blocks of the port there are plenty of factory outlets and boutiques.

WEDDINGS AND HONEYMOONS

Many other Caribbean destinations make a big pitch as wedding destinations, and Puerto Rico often gets overlooked. But it has all the ingredients of a spectacular place to wed and/or honeymoon. Gorgeous beaches dissolving into warm turquoise waters and a sensual tropical climate induce romance, and many an enamored couple has tied the knot here on the spur of the moment.

Choosing the Perfect Place

You can be as stylish or as informal as you wish. Although Puerto Rico has fewer ritzy beach resorts than many other islands, there's no shortage of exquisite boutique hotels with just the right ambience to inspire "I do." In San Juan, Villa Herencia and El Convento have just the right romantic style. In Rincón the Horned Dorset Primavera exudes honeymoon chic, and the Hix Island House on Vieques will suit honeymooners seeking a reclusive escape. Also on Vieques, the W Retreat & Spa has all the hip sophistication perfectly suited to young newlyweds, including sexy rooms and a holistic spa. Also consider Copamarina Beach Resort, which has spa- and diving-themed packages for honeymooners. Many larger hotels have their own wedding planners to take care of all arrangements—a distinct advantage over smaller hotels if you're seeking to wed on the island.

Getting Your Licenses

You must get an application from the Demographic Registry Office, which is in the Plaza las Americas Mall in the Hato Rey neighborhood of San Juan. There are no special residency requirements, but U.S. citizens must produce a birth certificate, as well as a driver's license or other state-issued photo identification. Non-U.S. citizens must produce a valid passport for identification purposes. Medical certificates that conform to the requirements for marriage in your state of residence are required; these can be completed by your own doctor, but must be valid for 10 days beyond their issue date.

Both you and your intended must appear together at the office to purchase a marriage license; the cost is $20. A judge or any member of the clergy may then perform your ceremony. The fee is usually between $150 and $350. Most large hotels on the island have marriage coordinators who can explain the necessary paperwork and help you complete it on time for your marriage ceremony.

STATE OF THE ARTS
IN PUERTO RICO

Puerto Rico's visual arts have long been shaped by the influences of its African, Spanish, and indigenous roots. Though the history of Puerto Rican art can be categorized into several predominant thematic preoccupations, a close examination of seminal Puerto Rican works reveals the persistence of these diverse cultural influences.

The indigenous Taíno people were living on the island at the time of Columbus's arrival in the late 15th century; their art consisted primarily of petroglyphs and daily-use or ceremonial objects made of ceramic or wood. Little survived Spanish colonization, but we know about its existence thanks to written accounts of Spanish priests like Fray Ramón Pané, who described Taíno *cemíes*—ceremonial figures—in extensive detail. The few remaining Taíno objects are largely preserved in private collections, although small collections of representative pieces and some examples of petroglyphs can be seen at the **Parque Ceremonial Indígena de Tibes** (Tibes Indigenous Ceremonial Center) in Ponce and the **Parque Ceremonial Indígena de Caguana** (Caguana Indigenous Ceremonial Center) in Utuado.

The arrival of the Spanish also resulted in the introduction of new art forms. According to art historian Osiris Delgado, much of the art from the early colonial period was religious in nature and function, the most representative examples being the *santos*—saint figurines carved of wood, an art form that endures on the island to this day *(see also the "A Guide to Puerto Rico's Carved Saints" feature in chapter 5)*. It wasn't until the mid- to late-18th century that the "fine" arts began in earnest, the works of José

Campeche (1751–1809) being the most representative.

Campeche became known for his exceptional oil portraits of religious figures and the social elite; his renown was particularly noteworthy considering that he was a self-taught artist with little formal education. Campeche's seminal works, such as *Dama a caballo* (*Lady on Horseback*), can be seen at the **Museo de Arte in Ponce (MAP)** and at the **Museo de Arte de Puerto Rico (MAPR)** in San Juan.

Campeche was followed by Francisco Oller (1833–1917), a painter who remains a central figure in the narrative of Puerto Rican art. Also working primarily in oils, Oller turned his brush toward a realistic treatment of Puerto Rican life as he observed it. His paintings can be grouped into one of two broad categories: landscapes (*paisajes*) and folkloric images of daily life. *La ceiba de Ponce* (*The Ponce Ceiba Tree*) and *Hacienda Aurora* (*Aurora Hacienda*) are cornerstones in the permanent collection at the MAP and help viewers understand why Oller has been called "a realist of impressionism." *El Velorio* (*The Wake*), his most powerful and enduring work, is on display in the **Museo de Historia, Antropología y Arte**, on the main campus of the University of Puerto Rico.

Oller not only established the subjects and styles that would dominate Puerto Rican art throughout most of the 20th century, but he also played a significant role in creating a community of artists and an artistic culture on the island. He opened Puerto Rico's first gallery in Old San Juan around 1870, exhibiting the work of local artists. His influence is visible in the works of many 20th-century artists who are shown alongside Campeche and Oller in the permanent collections at the MAP and the MAPR. An appreciation for rural landscapes and lifestyles, as well as the signature figure the *jíbaro*—a poor, humble, hard-working mountain man—became the stamp of Puerto Rican identity.

In the 1940s the government started supporting the arts, and art institutions began to flourish, with the **Museo de la Universidad de Puerto Rico** opening in 1946.

During the 1950s artists turned their interests toward social justice and the urban proletariat, focusing on slums and poverty. The evolution of these motifs is evident in the work of Ramón Frade and Rafael Tufiño, whose works are on display in San Juan's **Galería Nacional**.

The Instituto de Cultura Puertorriqueña (Institute of Puerto Rican Culture) was established in 1955 to promote Puerto Rican artists; today the agency oversees many of the island's museums and art programs. In 1959 the MAP was founded by former governor, philanthropist, and passionate art collector Luis A. Ferré. MAP houses a collection of more than 4,500 works from the 14th through 19th centuries, including paintings by El Greco, Goya, Rubens, Cranach, Murillo, and Delacroix. The collection is particularly strong in Italian baroque and Pre-Raphaelite works, with good representation by Latin American and Puerto Rican artists from the 18th century to the present, including Myrna Baéz, Julio Rosado del Valle, and Antonio Martorell.

In the 1960s, as the art world moved away from socially committed art, Puerto Rican artists still struggled with nationalism and identity issues. Locally, this struggle resulted in a battle between abstraction—with artists such as Julio Rosado Del Valle, Olga Albizu, and Luis Hernández Cruz—and avant-garde expressionism that favored figurative and socially minded art considered "genuinely" Puerto Rican.

In the 1980s abstract expressionists and other stylistic experimenters were granted a place at the table of Puerto Rican identity. These years opened art to the irreverent humor of Carmelo Sobrino, to the environmental activism of Carlos Marcial, and to aspects of the fantastic, as in the works of Marta Pérez, Jorge Zeno, and Rafi Trelles. Zeno's whimsical sculptures, often fusing human and animal elements, are on permanent display in front of the Hotel El Convento in Old San Juan.

By 1988 a group of artists, professors, critics, collectors, and other art lovers came together to establish the **Museo de Arte Contemporáneo de Puerto Rico** (Museum of Contemporary Art of Puerto Rico). The collection is composed mostly of works donated by the artists. Private collectors continued to expand their sphere of influence in the art world throughout the late 1980s and into the 1990s. Most notable among them are Diana and Moisés Berezdivin, whose collection became so extensive the museum acquired a space for part of the work and opened it to the public in 2005. Their **Espacio 1414** is dedicated to cultivating the visual arts in Puerto Rico, and is one of the most interesting places on the island to see art.

A robust, homegrown art scene continues to thrive today, and increasingly, Puerto Rican artists are showing their work abroad, engaging audiences in a more nuanced dialogue about what, exactly, Puerto Rican art is and what it's becoming.

FLAVORS OF PUERTO RICO

Puerto Rican cuisine has been experiencing a boom of sorts, with innovative, gourmet restaurants opening around the island. Today more chefs and restaurateurs are developing menus in the line of a Nuevo Latino cuisine. Joyfully departing from traditional Continental and Puerto Rican recipes, these chefs nevertheless include traditional ingredients and update old favorites. Standard meats like chicken, pork, and lamb are given added zest by sauces made from such tropical fruits as tamarind, mango, or guava. Take your palate out for a few adventures. Puerto Rican cuisine may surprise and delight you with both new and old tastes.

Cocina Criolla

The origins of contemporary Puerto Rican cuisine can be traced to the Taíno people, the island's native inhabitants. Taíno staples still used today include yuca, peppers, and corn. The Taíno are also believed to have grown guava, pineapple, and soursop.

Cocina criolla—literally, creole cooking—is an aggregate of Caribbean cuisines, sharing basic ingredients common to Cuban, Dominican, and to some extent even Brazilian culinary traditions. Still, it has its own distinct flavorings.

When the Spaniards arrived on the island, they brought olives, eggplant, onion, garlic, rice, and cilantro. Wheat would not grow on the island, so yuca remained a staple, as did rice. Regional culinary specialties from Spain, such as *paella*, came out of the Spanish-influenced kitchen. These specialties played an important role in the development of Puerto Rican recipes, recognizable today in such dishes as *arroz con pollo*. Lacking olive oil, early Puerto Ricans often used lard as a fat. African slaves brought by the Spanish

from Guinea and the Gold Coast of Africa during the 16th century to toil in the sugar fields also left their mark on the Puerto Rican table. The slaves brought plantains, bananas, pigeon peas, okra, and yams. The Taíno used corn husks to wrap foods, but the Africans replaced them with plantain leaves. The African population developed a variety of coconut-based dishes and preferred frying foods to stewing them.

Local Seafood

Puerto Rico is home to an abundance of freshwater and saltwater fish, both native and introduced, and the island is readily associated with big-game fishing. Off the coast of Culebra, fishermen catch bonefish, tuna, blue and white marlin, and dolphin fish, otherwise known as mahimahi. Surprisingly, however, the commercial fishing industry is small, and the catch is unpredictable. San Juan restaurant owners will apologetically explain that it's often difficult for them to find fresh local fish. For that, head to the informal restaurants on the coast, where you can often sit on the waterfront, local beer in hand, and feast inexpensively on octopus-stuffed *mofongo* or fried snapper served with *mojo isleño*, a sauce made with olive oil, onions, red bell pepper, capers, tomato sauce, and vinegar. The seafood shacks of Joyuda are so well regarded that patrons travel from as far away as Ponce and San Juan. In Boquerón, customers line up at pushcarts to sample oysters on the half shell. (Hot sauce is optional.)

Indigenous Fruits and Vegetables

Tropical fruits often wind up at the table in the form of delicious juices or shakes called *batidas*. A local favorite is pineapple juice from crops grown in the north of the island. Coconut, mango, papaya, lime, and tamarind are also popular. Puerto Rico is home to lesser-known fruits that are worth trying if you find them; these include the *caimito* (which is also called a star apple and has a mild, grapelike flavor), *quenepa* (also called a Spanish lime, with a yellow sweet-tart pulp surrounded by a tight, thin skin), and *zapote* (a plum-size fruit that tastes like a combination of peach, avocado, and vanilla). The Plaza del Mercado in the Santurce sector of San Juan is a good place to look for these fruits.

Spices

Puerto Rican dishes often feature pepper, lime rind, cinnamon, cloves, fresh ginger, garlic, and the juice of the sour orange. Three popular herb seasonings are oregano, cilantro, and culantro (known locally as *recao*). These ingredients, along with small sweet peppers, called *ajíes dulces*, are commonly used to flavor soups, beans, and meats. Conventional wisdom says the real secret of *cocina criolla* depends on the use of *sofrito* (a sauce that may include tomatoes, onion, garlic, peppers, cumin, and cilantro), *achiote* (the inedible fruit of a small Caribbean shrub whose seeds are sometimes ground as a spice), lard, and the *caldero* (cooking pot).

Plantains and Mofongo

Plátanos, or plantains, are related to bananas but are larger and starchier. They are served mostly as side dishes and may be eaten green (as *tostones*, which are salty) or ripe (as *amarillos or maduros*, which are sweet). They can be fried, baked, boiled, or roasted, and served either whole or in slices. Sometimes whole amarillos are served with cinnamon as a dessert. *Pasteles*, similar to tamales, are wrapped in plantain leaves and boiled.

Traditionally a Christmas specialty, they can be eaten anytime.

Of all the delicious plantain preparations, one of the tastiest is also the simplest: *mofongo*. Green plantains are mashed with a wooden *pilón* (mortar and pestle), mixed with garlic and other flavorings, and fried in a pan. Served plain, it's often a side dish. But when it's stuffed with chicken, beef, or some other meat, mofongo becomes one of Puerto Rico's signature entrées.

In the center of the island it's often made with pork. On the coast, however, mofongo is almost always stuffed with fresh fish or shellfish. Some restaurants are even known for what they put in their plantains. A neon sign outside Tino's, one of a long line of seafood restaurants in Joyuda, touts its signature dish: an earthenware goblet overflowing with plantains and seafood.

Rice

Rice is omnipresent on the Puerto Rican plate. It can be served "white" with kidney beans, or prepared with *gandules* (pigeon peas) or garbanzos (chickpeas); most often, rice is simply served with *habichuelas rosadas* or *blancas* (pink or white beans). Whatever the case, the accompaniment for rice is almost always some kind of bean, always richly seasoned. Crispy rice stuck to the pot, known as *pegao*, is the most highly prized, full of all the ingredients that have sunk to the bottom.

Rum

As you enjoy your piña colada—a cocktail served in nearly every bar on the island—lift your glass to Christopher Columbus. Although the explorer didn't invent the fruity cocktail, he did bring sugarcane to the Caribbean on his second voyage in 1493. Sugarcane is native to Southeast

Asia, but it was cultivated in Spain at the time, and Columbus thought it would do well in the tropical "New World." Juan Ponce de Léon, the island's first governor, planted vast fields of the stuff. The first sugar mill was opened in 1524, leading to the distillation of what was then called *brebaje*. Although rum was first exported in 1897, it took a bit longer for it to become the massive industry it is today. The Bacardí family, after fleeing Cuba, set up shop near San Juan in 1959. Their company's product, lighter-bodied than rums produced by most other distilleries, gained favor around the world. Today Puerto Rico produces more than 35 million gallons of rum a year. You might say it's the national drink.

ON THE MENU

Adobo: a seasoning made of salt, oregano, onion powder, garlic powder, and ground black pepper.

Ájili-mójili: a dressing combining garlic and sweet, seeded chili peppers, flavored with vinegar, lime juice, salt, and olive oil.

Alcapurrias: yuca croquettes stuffed with beef or pork.

Amarillos: fried ripe, yellow plantain slices. Also called *maduros*.

Arepas: fried corn or bread cakes.

Batida: a tropical fruit-and-milk shake.

Bacalaítos: deep-fried salt cod fritters.

Chimichurri: an herb sauce of finely chopped cilantro or parsley with garlic, oil, and lemon juice or vinegar.

Empanadillas: turnovers, bigger than *pastelillos,* filled with beef, crabmeat, conch, or lobster.

Lechón: seasoned, spit-roasted whole pig.

Mofongo: a deep-fried mix of plantains mashed with garlic, olive oil, and salt in a *pilón*, the traditional Puerto Rican mortar and pestle.

Mojo or Mojito Isleño: a sauce made of olives and olive oil, onions, red bell pepper, capers, tomato sauce, vinegar, garlic, and bay leaves.

Pasteles: yuca or other mashed root vegetable stuffed with various fillings and wrapped in a plantain leaf.

Pastelillos: deep-fried cheese and meat turnovers; a popular fast-food snack.

Picadillo: spicy ground meat used for stuffing or eaten with rice.

Pique: a condiment consisting of hot peppers soaked in vinegar, sometimes with garlic or other spices added.

Tembleque: a coconut custard, usually sprinkled with cinnamon or nutmeg.

Tostones: sliced and crushed fried green plantains.

GREAT ITINERARIES

COLONIAL TREASURES

More than almost any other island in the Caribbean except Cuba, Puerto Rico has a trove of well-preserved colonial cities. Old San Juan is the best known, and it's a must-see for anyone interested in the region's rich history. But the southern coast also has some gems, from the graceful square in Coamo to the churches of San Germán, to the heady mix of neoclassical and art deco masterpieces in Ponce.

Day 1: Old San Juan

If you truly want to experience Old San Juan, make sure you stay within the city walls. El Convento, once a Carmelite convent, is one of Old San Juan's most luxurious lodgings. **Gallery Inn**, whose mascot is a cockatoo named Campeche, has the most personality, while **Da House** is cheap and funky. After you drop off your suitcases, hit the cobblestone streets. Make sure to stroll along the city walls and visit one of the forts—most people pick **Castillo San Felipe del Morro**, but the nearby **Castillo San Cristóbal** is equally impressive. Old San Juan isn't just for historical sightseeing, though. When the sun goes down the streets of the historic district light up, becoming one of the city's nightlife centers. For dinner, head to Calle Fortaleza, where you'll find some of the city's best restaurants. Then you can while away the night at one of the happening bars or clubs.

Logistics: Believe us when we tell you that you don't want the headache of parking in Old San Juan. At San Juan's Aeropuerto Internacional Luis Muñoz Marín, take a *taxi turístico* (tourist taxi) to your hotel. The streets here were made for walking, and that's just what you'll do. Wait and pick up your car when you're ready to leave town for the countryside.

Day 2: Coamo

Head south from San Juan, and if you get an early enough start, take a short detour to Guayama, where you'll find the gorgeous **Casa Cautiño**. This 19th-century manor house, transformed into a museum, is one of Puerto Rico's most beautifully restored colonial-era structures. Continue west to Coamo, known for its thermal springs. On Coamo's lovely main square is the gleaming white **Iglesia Católica San Blás**, one of the island's oldest churches. In terms of distance, Coamo isn't so far from San Juan—only about 60 miles (96 km)—so you don't have to leave at the crack of dawn to have most of a day to explore the town.

Logistics: Ponce is reached via Route 52, a toll road that heads south from San Juan. Exit Route 52 and follow Route 15 to Guayama. Then take Route 3 west to Santa Isabel; turn north on Route 53 for Coamo.

Day 3: Ponce

Your destination on your third day is Ponce, the "Pearl of the South." You'll know you've arrived when you drive through the massive letters spelling the name of the city. The main square, the Plaza de las Delicias, is a delight. Here, you'll find the **Catedral de Nuestra Señora de Guadalupe**, a church dating from 1835, and **Parque de Bombas**, a firehouse from 1882, painted in bold red-and-black stripes. There are several museums around the city, but the most interesting is the small **Casa Wiechers-Villaronga**, a house built in 1911. In a city filled with neoclassical confections, this is one of the most elaborate. Strolling the downtown streets, you'll also marvel at neoclassical and art deco architecture. Don't miss the **Museo de**

Arte de Ponce, one of the Caribbean's best art museums.

Logistics: Ponce is reached by Route 14 from Coamo. To get downtown, take Route 1.

Day 4: San Germán

Less than an hour west of Ponce is San Germán, a must-see for anyone interested in the colonial era. The best place to start a tour of San Germán is Plazuela Santo Domingo, the small park in the center of the historic district, which itself is listed on the National Register of Historic Places. At the eastern edge of the park is the **Capilla de Porta Coeli.** This chapel, at the top of some steep stone steps, is now a museum of religious art. Stroll west past the delightful assemblage of buildings of every architectural style from mission to Victorian. Make sure to see the other gorgeous church, the **Iglesia de San Germán de Auxerre,** a few blocks north.

Logistics: San Germán is easy to reach—simply take Route 2 west of Ponce. When you reach Route 122, head south.

Day 5: San Juan

If you have time on your way back to San Juan, stop for lunch at one of the open-air eateries near Guavate, off Route 52.

TIPS

If you're staying in Old San Juan, pick up your rental car at one of the hotel desks. You'll avoid an expensive taxi ride to the airport.

Pack comfortable shoes for exploring these colonial-era cities. You'll be glad you brought sneakers after a few hours traipsing around on cobblestone streets.

Old San Juan is hillier than it first appears, and in Ponce avoid walking to Castillo Serallés—a steep hike through an unsavory area. Take advantage of free trolleys, which depart from main plazas and will take you to the most popular tourist sites in both cities.

You can try the famous *lechón,* whole pig roasted on a spit.

Logistics: From San Germán take Route 2 until you reach Ponce. Exit onto Route 52; a toll road takes you all the way to San Juan.

ISLAND HOPPING

If you have a week for your trip, this itinerary will give you a taste of each of eastern Puerto Rico's highlights.

Day 1: El Yunque

East of San Juan is El Yunque, the undulating rain forest that covers much of the eastern edge of the island. It's a highlight of any trip to Puerto Rico, and you can still have a memorable time if you have only one day to spend there. Several of the trails can be hiked in an hour or less, including one leading to the spectacular waterfalls called the **Cascada La Mina**. Spend the night in Río Grande; our favorite hotel along this stretch of shoreline is the luxurious **St. Regis Bahia Beach Resort**, known for its Robert Trent Jones golf course, beautiful private beach, and first-rate service.

Logistics: Take Route 3 east of San Juan; then head south on Route 191, which leads through El Yunque.

Day 2: Reserva Natural Las Cabezas de San Juan

Head to Fajardo, on the northeastern tip of the island. Drop your stuff off at your hotel—we prefer the smaller ones like **Fajardo Inn**—and then head out for a prearranged tour of the mangrove forests of **Reserva Natural Las Cabezas de San Juan**. However, exploring this area isn't just a daytime experience. You may also want to head out at night to get a very different view of Las Cabezas; you can paddle through the bioluminescent bay here in a kayak. Companies offer the trips nightly, though your experience will be heightened if there is no moon. In the afternoon, take a boat excursion from Fajardo to Isla Palomino.

Logistics: Take Route 3, which leads all the way to Fajardo, where Route 987 leads to Cabezas de San Juan.

Days 3 and 4: Culebra

Culebra has some of the most beautiful, powdery soft beaches you'll find in all of Puerto Rico. It's a small, quiet island, so you won't find much to do except relax. But then that's the draw. There are no big hotels or fancy restaurants, only small guesthouses and some villas. If this sounds like too much of a get-away-from-it-all experience for your tastes, then skip Culebra and spend more time on Vieques, which has more resorts and better restaurants, and plenty of eco-focused activities. If you want to visit both islands, you can fly between Culebra and Vieques, but note that there's no ferry link.

Logistics: Drop off your rental car in Fajardo (or in Ceiba if you're flying)—you'll want to rent a sturdier four-wheel-drive vehicle once you get to Culebra, and you can't take a rental car on the ferry anyway. Take a 90-minute ferry trip from Fajardo or 10-minute puddle-jumper flight to the island from Ceiba. We recommend taking the plane, as views are spectacular.

Days 5 and 6: Vieques

Close—both in terms of atmosphere and geography—to the U.S. Virgin Islands, Vieques has an entirely different feel from the rest of Puerto Rico. If you've never been to Vieques, we strongly recommend you spend at least one night there. The beaches are seemingly endless, the snorkeling is remarkable, and the **Puerto Mosquito Bioluminescent Bay** is one of nature's best shows. A great way to explore the island is on a bicycle tour arranged by a local operator.

ATLANTIC OCEAN

✪ San Juan

Reserva Natural
Las Cabezas
de San Juan

Río Grande

Luquillo

Fajardo

Culebra

EL YUNQUE · La Mina
Falls

Dewey

Humacao

Puerto Rico

Isabel Segunda

Vieques

Caribbean Sea

Logistics: You'll want to fly between Culebra and Vieques—there are scheduled direct flights between the islands. Otherwise you'll need to return to Fajardo and take a ferry to Vieques.

Day 7: San Juan

From Vieques, take a puddle-jumper flight back to San Juan (or to Ceiba's airport to pick up your rental car). If you want to spend a day in Old San Juan, take a flight into Aeropuerto Fernando L. Ribas Dominicci; it's a short taxi ride from the airport's Isla Grande location to Old San Juan's colonial heart.

Logistics: If you are connecting to a flight back home, make sure your flight to San Juan is headed to Aeropuerto Internacional Luis Muñoz Marín. If it is going to San Juan's regional airport, Aeropuerto Fernando L. Ribas Dominicci, you'll have to take a taxi between the airports.

KIDS AND FAMILY

Puerto Rico is a family-friendly island, with no end of fun things for kids to see and do, including cave exploration, snorkeling with marine turtles, and going on nighttime excursions to bioluminescent lagoons. And many resort hotels arrange children's activities or have kids' clubs, freeing parents for romantic beach strolls and candlelit dinners.

Choosing a Place to Stay

Resort hotels make a point of catering to family needs. Most offer free rooms to children under 12 and can provide cribs. Here are a few questions to ask to gauge the level of family friendliness.

Are there discounted meals and activities? Do restaurants have kids' menus? Are there children's programs, and is there an age range? A children's pool?

El Conquistador, a Waldorf Astoria Resort, near Fajardo, has a long list of facilities for children, including the sensational Coqui Water Park. On the south coast, Copamarina Beach Resort & Spa has a children's pool and playground, plus kayaks, pedal boats, tennis, and heaps of other activities.

Condos and vacation rentals offer an inexpensive option, especially for larger families. They typically have multiple bedrooms and you can cook for yourselves. ESJ Towers, in Isla Verde, is right on the best beach in San Juan.

Things to Do

Vacationing in the Caribbean is all about the outdoors. Kids may even forget video games when they see the options: snorkeling, whale-watching, Boogie boarding, and cave exploring. And the list of great beaches is nearly endless. The wave action around Rincón can be too rough for youngsters, but Vieques and Culebra have the most fantastic, reef-protected sands good for snorkeling, and kids can go kayaking and fishing. Many beaches have riptides; always play it safe and heed posted warnings, such as red flags.

Parque Las Cavernas de Río Camuy. This huge cavern will leave kids wide-eyed. They'll have fun trying to discern imaginary figures in the surreal dripstone formations. Tiny *coquí* (frogs) hop around the cavern entrance, and children can spy for crabs and blind fish in the underground river. Bats flitting about overhead help keep kids enthralled. The tram ride to reach the caverns is icing on the cake.

Arecibo Lighthouse and Historical Park. Local families flock to this small theme park built around Los Morrillos lighthouse. It has a museum on seafaring, including pirates. In winter, kids can spy for whales from the lighthouse observation platform. The playground has a pirate cave and replica galleon, as well as a Taíno village.

Zoológico de Puerto Rico. This is a splendid zoo in Mayagüez, on the west coast. The highlight is an African wildlife park, with elephants, giraffes, lions, and rhinos. There are also tigers, big apes, and camel rides.

Museo del Niño. While exploring Old San Juan, head to this small three-level museum in a colonial mansion opposite the cathedral. It's a great learning experience for younger children, with exhibits spanning from hurricanes to human biology, plus interactive displays including those in the NASA Space Place.

Connections Travel. Frank Fournier of Connections Travel, a member of the International Gay and Lesbian Travel Association, is a reliable local travel agent for the gay and lesbian community. ☎ 800/973–5550 ⊕ *www.connectionstravelpr.com.*

SAN JUAN

WELCOME TO SAN JUAN

TOP REASONS TO GO

★ **Take a stroll:** Wander the cobblestone streets of Old San Juan—the fortifications and governor's mansion are UNESCO World Heritage Sites.

★ **Climb a battlement:** Explore Castillo San Felipe del Morro, the 16th-century fortress that dominates the waterfront; rangers provide a fascinating insight.

★ **Shop:** Head to Condado's Avenida Ashford, where you'll find most of the city's designer boutiques, including that of Nono Maldonado, one of the island's homegrown design talents.

★ **Catch some rays:** Balneario de Carolina, at the eastern tip of Isla Verde, is San Juan's best beach. Take time to parasail.

★ **Dine on the strip:** Dine at Marmalade, just one of many stellar restaurants along the eastern end of Calle Fortaleza, a trendy strip that locals call "SoFo."

1 Old San Juan. Still enclosed by its original fortified city walls, this enclave of blue-cobblestone streets is superbly preserved, with more than 800 structures of historic importance. Many date back to the 16th century. Many of the city's best restaurants and bars are here, as well as boutiques offering wares from cigars to designer clothing. Laid out in an easy-to-navigate grid, Old San Juan has enough sights and shops to enthrall for days.

Atlantic Ocean

0   1 mi
0   1 km

GETTING ORIENTED

San Juan wraps around the Bahía de San Juan (San Juan Bay) on the island's northern, Atlantic coast. Old San Juan, the original colonial city, occupies an isle on the northeast side of the bay and is connected by bridges to Condado and, farther east, the districts of Ocean Park and Isla Verde (home of the international airport), which together make up San Juan's hip, touristy, 5-mile-long (8-km-long) coastal strip lined with gorgeous beaches. These districts have the lion's share of hotels, restaurants, entertainment, and sights to see. South of Condado and Ocean Park, Santurce—setting for the city's main art museums—melds into Hato Rey, the city's business and banking district. The greater city fans out from here into suburbs with little touristic appeal.

2 Greater San Juan. The sprawling modern metropolis opens out like a fan on three sides of Old San Juan. Condado and Isla Verde are superb venues for lazing on the beach by day and living it up by night at casinos and ritzy nightclubs—many associated with the upscale hotels that line the shorefront. Even teetotalers will enjoy an educational tour of the Bacardí rum factory, while culture vultures will delight in the Museo de Arte de Puerto Rico.

3 San Juan Environs. White- and golden-sand beaches unspool along the Atlantic shoreline on either side of the city. Several are developed as *balnearios* (public beaches), such as Carolina Luquillo, and Piñones; they're popular with *sanjuaneros* on weekends, as is El Yunque National Forest. El Yunque offers fantastic hiking and birding only a one-hour drive, yet a world away, from San Juan.

Updated by
Paulina Salach

If you associate Puerto Rico's capital with the colonial streets of Old San Juan, then you know only part of the picture. San Juan is a major metropolis, radiating out from the bay on the Atlantic Ocean that was discovered by Juan Ponce de León. More than a third of the island's nearly 4 million citizens proudly call themselves *sanjuaneros*. The city may be rooted in the past, but it has its eye on the future. Locals go about their business surrounded by colonial architecture and towering modern structures.

By 1508 the explorer Juan Ponce de León had established a colony in an area now known as Caparra, southeast of present-day San Juan. He later moved the settlement north to a more hospitable peninsular location. In 1521, after he became the first colonial governor, Ponce de León switched the name of the island—which was then called San Juan Bautista in honor of St. John the Baptist—with that of the settlement of Puerto Rico ("rich port").

Defended by the imposing Castillo San Felipe del Morro (El Morro) and Castillo San Cristóbal, Puerto Rico's administrative and population center remained firmly in Spain's hands until 1898, when it came under U.S. control after the Spanish-American War. Centuries of Spanish rule left an indelible imprint on the city, particularly in the walled area now known as Old San Juan. The area is filled with cobblestone streets and brightly painted, colonial-era structures, and its fortifications have been designated a UNESCO World Heritage Site.

Old San Juan is a monument to the past, but most of the rest of the city is planted firmly in the 21st century and draws migrants island-wide and from farther afield to jobs in its businesses and industries. The city captivates residents and visitors alike with its vibrant lifestyle as well as its balmy beaches, pulsing nightclubs, globe-spanning restaurants, and world-class museums. Once you set foot in this city, you may never want to leave.

IF YOU LIKE

ARCHITECTURE

San Juan has been under construction for nearly 500 years, which shows in the city's wide range of architectural styles. The Old City's Spanish colonial row houses—brick with plaster fronts painted in pastel blues, oranges, and yellows—line narrow streets and alleys paved with *adoquines* (blue-gray stones originally used as ballast in Spanish ships). Several churches, including the Catedral de San Juan Bautista, were built in the ornate Spanish Gothic style of the 16th century. The massive, white marble El Capitolio, home of Puerto Rico's legislature, was completed in 1929. And firmly rooted in the 21st century are the gleaming high-rise resorts along the beaches in Condado and Isla Verde and the glistening steel-and-glass towers in the business and financial district of Hato Rey.

MUSIC

Music is a source of Puerto Rican pride, and is an inescapable part of nearly every festival, holiday, party, and even political protest. The brash Latin sound is best characterized by the music-dance form salsa, which shares not only its name with the word "sauce" but also its zesty, hot flavor. A fusion of West African percussion, jazz (especially swing and big band), and other Latin beats (mambo, merengue, flamenco, cha-cha, rumba), salsa music is sexy and primal. Dancers are expected to let go of all inhibitions. Most nightspots, including restaurants, offer live music several nights a week, especially Fridays and Saturdays.

NIGHTLIFE

As befits a metropolitan capital city, San Juan has a wide variety of restaurants and bars for people with all sorts of palates and party habits. Old San Juan, Condado, and the up-and-coming arts district of Santurce are big nighttime destinations. Many of the newer establishments have set their tables on terraces, the beach, indoor patios, or streetside to take advantage of the late-night atmosphere. Clubs and bars stay open into the wee hours of morning, closing only when the last patron leaves.

SAN JUAN PLANNER

WHEN TO GO

During the high season, mid-December through mid-April, hotels tend to be packed, though rarely full, and rates are a bit higher than in the off-season. Fall and spring are less expensive. The weather's still fantastic, and the tourist crush is less intense. However, a winter visit may allow you to participate in many of San Juan's annual events, particularly the lengthy and lively Christmas season celebrations, which extend through mid-January. The San Sebastián Street Festival, held in Old San Juan every January, consists of several nights of live music, food festivals, and *cabezudos* (parades). The Heineken JazzFest, each spring, is the Caribbean's showcase for local and international talent.

San Juan's weather is moderate and tropical year-round, with an average temperature of about 82°F (26°C). And although it's true that hurricane season accounts for much of the summer and fall, San Juan's still an attractive destination during those months—hotels charge their lowest rates, restaurant reservations are easier to come by, and fewer tourists roam the streets.

GETTING HERE

AIR TRAVEL

Airports Aeropuerto Internacional Luis Muñoz Marín (*SJU*). Puerto Rico's main aiport serves as the gateway to the Caribbean, with flights from AirTran, American Airlines, Delta, JetBlue, Southwest, Spirit Air, United, and US Airways. ⊠ *Carolina* ☎ *787/289–7240* ⊕ *www.aeropuertosju.com.*

International carriers include Air Canada from Toronto, Air France from Paris, British Airways from London, Iberia and Air Europa from Madrid, and Condor from Germany. Air Flamenco and Vieques Air Link offer daily flights from SJU and Isla Grande Airport (SIG) in San Juan to Vieques and Culebra. Cape Air flies between SJU and Vieques.

Aeropuerto Fernando L. Ribas Dominicci (*SIG*). Sometimes known as Isla Grande, the Aeropuerto Fernando L. Ribas Dominicci is in Miramar, near the Convention Center. It handles most short hops to Vieques and other nearby islands. ⊠ *Calle Lindbergh* ☎ *787/729–8751* ⊕ *http:// prpa.pr.gov/aeropuertos.*

Airline Contacts *For airline contact information, see Air Travel in "Travel Smart."*

Transfers Before you leave for Puerto Rico, check with your hotel about transfers; many larger hotels provide transport from the airport, free or for a fee, to their guests. Otherwise, your best bets are *taxis turísticos* (tourist taxis). Uniformed officials at the airport can help you make arrangements. They will give you a slip with your exact fare written on it to hand to the driver. Rates are based on your destination. A *taxi turístico* to Isla Verde costs $10. It's $15 to Condado and $19 to Old San Juan and the cruise-ship piers. There's a $1 charge for each bag handled by the driver.

The Baldorioty de Castro Expressway (Route 26) runs from the airport into the city. Exits are clearly marked along the way, though you should check with your hotel to determine which one is best for you to take. Plan on 25–30 minutes for the drive from the airport all the way west to Old San Juan.

FERRY TRAVEL

Autoridad de Transporte Marítimo. Part of the Department of Transportation, the Maritime Transport Authority runs passenger and cargo ferries from Fajardo to Culebra and Vieques. ⊠ *Carr De Maternillo, Fajardo* ☎ *787/494–0934* ⊕ *www.dtop.gov.pr.*

Service is from the ferry terminal in Fajardo, about a 90-minute drive from San Juan. There are a limited number of seats on the ferries, so get to the terminal in plenty of time. One-way tickets are $2 for Vieques and $2.25 for Culebra. *For schedule information, see Ferry Travel in "Travel Smart."*

GETTING AROUND
BUS AND TROLLEY TRAVEL

AMA (*Autoridad Metropolitana de Autobuses*). City buses thread through San Juan, running in exclusive lanes on major thoroughfares and stopping at signs marked "Parada." Destinations are indicated above the windshield. AMA bus B-21 runs through Condado all the way to Plaza Las Américas in Hato Rey. Bus A-5 runs from San Juan through Santurce and the beach area of Isla Verde. Fares are 75¢ and are paid in exact change upon entering the bus. Most buses are air-conditioned and have wheelchair lifts and lock-downs. ☎ *800/981–0097*.

The Municipio de San Juan operates free trolleys throughout Old San Juan. Trolleys run along three routes beginning at Pier 4, on Calle Gilberto Concepción de Gracia and running to the two forts plus Plaza de Armas.

CAR TRAVEL

Although car rentals are inexpensive (as little as $15 a day if booked in advance), we don't recommend that you rent a car if you're staying only in San Juan (at most you might want to rent a car for a day to explore more of the island). Parking is difficult—particularly in Old San Juan—and many hotels charge hefty daily rates; also, traffic can be very heavy. With relatively reasonable taxi rates, it simply doesn't pay to rent a car unless you are leaving the city.

The main highways into San Juan are Route 26 from the east (it becomes the Baldorioty de Castro Expressway after passing the airport), Route 22 (José de Diego Expressway) from the west, and Route 52 (Luis A. Ferré Expressway) from the south.

Car Rental Contacts Avis ✉ *San Juan International Airport, Terminal Building, Carolina* ☎ *787/253–5926* ⊕ *www.avis.com.* **Hertz** ☎ *800/654–3030* ⊕ *www.hertz.com.* **National** ☎ *888/222–9058* ⊕ *www.nationalcar.com.* **Thrifty** ☎ *800/847–4389* ⊕ *www.thrifty.com.*

Local Agencies Charlie Car Rental ☎ *787/728–2418* ⊕ *www.charliecars.com.* **Vias** ☎ *787/791–4120* ⊕ *www.viascarrental.com.*

TAXI TRAVEL

Taxis turísticos, which are painted white and have the *garita* (sentry box) logo, charge set rates based on zones; they run from the airport and the cruise-ship piers to Isla Verde, Condado, Ocean Park, and Old San Juan, with rates ranging from $10 to $20. Make sure to agree on a price before you get inside. City tours start at $36 per hour.

Although you can hail cabs on the street, virtually every San Juan hotel has taxis waiting outside to transport guests; if none are available, have one called. Radioed taxis might charge an extra $1 for the pickup.

Taxi Contacts Major Cab Company ☎ *787/723–2460.* **Metro Taxi** ☎ *787/725–2870* ⊕ *www.metrotaxipr.com.*

VISITOR INFORMATION

You'll find Puerto Rico Tourism Company information officers (identified by their caps and shirts with the tourism company patch) near the baggage-claim areas at Luis Muñoz Marín International Airport.

In Old San Juan the tourism headquarters is at the Old City jail, La Princesa; its main information bureau is opposite Pier 1 on Calle Tanca at Calle Gilberto Concepción de Gracia. Be sure to pick up a free copy of ¡*Qué Pasa!*, the official visitor guide. Information officers are posted around Old San Juan (near the cruise-ship piers and at the Catedral de San Juan Bautista) during the day.

La Oficina de Turismo del Municipio de San Juan, run by the city, has information bureaus in Old San Juan and in Condado.

Contacts Oficina de Turismo del Municipio de San Juan ⊠ *Calle Tetuán, corner Calle San Justo, Old San Juan* ☎ *787/480–2910* ⊠ *Alcaldía, 153 Calle San Francisco, Old San Juan* ☎ *787/480–2548* ⊠ *999 Av. Ashford, Condado* ☎ *787/644–7519.* **Puerto Rico Tourism Company** ⊠ *Ochoa Bldg., Calle Tanca and Calle Comercio, across from Pier 1, Old San Juan* ☎ *787/721–2400* ⊕ *www.seepuertorico.com* ⊠ *Luis Muñoz Marín International Airport, Carolina* ☎ *787/791–1014.*

EXPLORING

San Juan's metro area stretches for 12 miles (19 km) along Puerto Rico's north coast, and defining the city is rather like assembling a puzzle. Neighborhoods are irregular and sometimes overlap—locals disagree, for example, about where Condado ends and Ocean Park begins. The areas most visited by tourists run along the coast.

Farthest west is Old San Juan, the showplace of the island's rich history. On this peninsula you will find some of the city's finest museums and shops, as well as excellent dining and lodging options. To the east is Puerta de Tierra, a narrow strip of land sandwiched between the ocean and the bay. The area is home to a couple of famous hotels and two noteworthy parks, the Parque de Tercer Milenio and the Parque Muñoz Rivera, as well as Escambrón Beach. The rehabilitation project of the waterfront and cruise docks, Bahía Urbana, is bringing in new galleries, shops, and luxury housing developments. Beyond Puerta de Tierra is Condado, an upscale older neighborhood that is a mix of beautiful Spanish-style homes, larger apartment buildings, and resort hotels. Here you'll find designer fashions in the boutiques and on the people strolling down the main drag of Avenida Ashford. Ocean Park, to the east of Condado, is mostly residential, but the handful of inns and restaurants here are among the city's best. Don't miss Calle Loíza, parallel to McLeary Street; it's becoming the area's new gastronomic hub. Beyond Ocean Park is Isla Verde, a more commercial zone, and also where you'll find the biggest resorts on the best city beach.

You may want to explore a few other neighborhoods. South of Condado and Ocean Park lies Santurce, a business district with a growing artistic community, thanks to the Museo de Arte de Puerto Rico and the Museo de Arte Contemporáneo. La Placita de Santurce is home to two of San Juan's top restaurants, Santaella and José Enrique. Bordering Santurce and across the bay from Condado, the quieter, residential neighborhood of Miramar is also a great place for off-the-beaten-path dining. Hato Rey is a busy financial district, where you'll find the large

Plaza las Américas Mall. The mostly residential Río Piedras area is home to the Universidad de Puerto Rico.

OLD SAN JUAN

Old San Juan's 16th-century cobblestone streets, ornate Spanish town houses with wrought-iron balconies, ancient plazas, and eclectic museums are all repositories of the island's colorful history. Founded in 1521 by the Spanish explorer Juan Ponce de León, Old San Juan sits on an islet separated from the "new" parts of the city by a couple of miles and a couple of centuries. Ironically, its culture is youthful and vibrant, reflecting the sensibilities of stylish professionals, a bohemian art crowd, and university students who populate the streets. You'll find more streetfront cafés and innovative restaurants, more contemporary art galleries, more musicians playing in plazas, than anywhere else in San Juan.

Old San Juan slopes north, uphill, to Calle Norzagaray, which runs along the Atlantic shoreline and connects Castillo San Cristóbal to El Morro, the Old City's twin defensive bastions. On the north side of Calle Norzagaray you'll find a small neighborhood tucked beneath the city walls tight up against the ocean—this is La Perla, a rough area that you would be wise to avoid. The west end of the Old City overlooks San Juan Bay, and it's here that the rugged, towering walls of the original city are most evident. On Old San Juan's south side, along Calle Gilberto Concepción de Gracia, you'll find the commercial and cruise-ship piers that jut into San Juan Harbor.

GETTING AROUND

If you try to explore Old San Juan by car, you'll likely find yourself sitting in traffic jams for much of the day, especially on weekends when police change traffic patterns. Old San Juan is a walking city, with narrow, one-way streets, narrower alleys, little parking, and sights and shops packed together in an area hardly larger than one square mile. Some of the streets are steep and many are paved with cobblestones, so wear comfortable shoes as well as a hat and sunscreen—and drink plenty of water.

FERRY

The ferry between Old San Juan and Cataño is operated by the Autoridad de Transporte Marítimo. It costs a mere 50¢ one-way and runs daily every 30 minutes from 6 am until 10 pm. The ferry, which departs from Pier 2, is the one to take if you wish to visit the Bacardí rum factory.

Information Autoridad de Transporte Marítimo ☎ *787/497–7740* ⊕ *www. dtop.gov.pr/transporte_maritimo.*

PARKING

If you can't avoid taking a car into Old San Juan, park at La Puntilla, at the head of Paseo de la Princesa. It's an outdoor lot with the Old City's cheapest rates (you'll pay less than $5 for all-day parking). You could also try the Felisa Rincón de Gautier lot on Calle Gilberto Concepción de Gracia or the Frank Santaella lot between Paseo de Covadonga and

Calle Gilberto Concepción de Gracia. Parking starts at around $1 or so for the first hour. Many lots open early and close late; some are even open 24 hours a day, like the Felisa Rincón parking garage, known as "Doña Fela" to locals.

TROLLEYS

Free trolleys swing through Old San Juan all day, every day—departing from the main bus terminal area across from Pier 4 and taking three routes through the Old City. One route heads north to Calle Norzagaray, then west to El Morro, dropping you off at the long footpath leading to the fort. Then it retraces its route past Castillo San Cristóbal, west to Plaza de Armas, east on Fortaleza, west on Recinto Sur, and then back along Calle Gilberto Concepción de Gracia (also called Calle la Marina) to the piers. A second route takes you east to the Punta de Tierra district, then via Castillo San Cristóbal to El Morro, then via Calle Norzagaray and Plaza Colón and back to the piers. The third route follows a figure-8 route from Pier 4 north on Tanca, then west along San Francisco and east on Fortaleza, returning via Plaza Colón. The trolleys make regular stops (at 24 signs marked "Parada") on their routes. When you're finished touring, taxis can be found in several spots: in front of Pier 2, near the Catedral de San Juan Bautista, on the Plaza de Armas, or in Plaza de Colón. A map of trolley routes is available from the Puerto Rico Tourism Company information offices.

SAFETY

Old San Juan is generally safe, but keep in mind that pickpockets visit the same places as tourists. Keep money and credit cards out of back pockets, and avoid carrying open handbags. Avoid the Perla district and, if walking, stick to well-policed areas and well-lit streets by night. Women should take licensed taxis at night.

TIMING

Old San Juan is a small neighborhood, approximately seven city blocks north to south and eight east to west. In strictly geographical terms, it's easily traversed in a day. But to truly appreciate the numerous plazas, museums, boutiques, galleries, and cafés requires two or three days. *For a great half-day itinerary, see "Walking Old San Juan."*

GUIDED TOURS

In Old San Juan free trolleys can take you around, and the tourist board can provide you with a copy of ¡*Qué Pasa!* and an Old San Juan map, which contains a self-guided walking tour.

Legends of Puerto Rico. Legends of Puerto Rico has private and public walking tours of Old San Juan (including food and rum tastings), hop-on-hop-off bus tours and special holiday trips that let you experience a local Thanksgiving or Christmas. ☎ *787/605–9060* ⊕ *www. legendsofpr.com.*

Segway Tours of Puerto Rico. Segway Tours of Puerto Rico offers group tours of the city's historic district, using Segways for fun and easy transport. ⊠ *Pier 2, Old San Juan* ☎ *787/598–9455* ✏ *info@segwaytourspr. com* ⊕ *www.segwaytourspr.com.*

Festive street musicians are frequently seen and heard throughout Old San Juan.

Spoon Food Tours. Go off the beaten path with Spoon Food Tours, the island's most diverse culinary tour company. From walking and driving food tours to their newest drinking tour, the company offers travelers a unique opportunity to experience the gastronomy, culture, and history of Puerto Rico. Immerse yourself in the culture and sip and savor your way through San Juan with your passionate epicurean guide. ⊠ *Old San Juan* ☎ *787/249–4488* ⊕ *www.SpoonFoodTours.com.*

Flavors of San Juan. The friendly, well-informed guides of Flavors of San Juan can take you on walking tours of Old San Juan, combining visits to restaurants that are off the beaten path with a cultural and historical introduction to the city. ⊠ *Calle Recinto Sur, Old San Juan* ☎ *787/964–2447* ⊕ *www.sanjuanfoodtours.com.*

TOP ATTRACTIONS

Casa Blanca. The original structure on this site was a wooden house built in 1521 as a home for Ponce de León; he died in Cuba without ever having lived here. His descendants occupied the house's sturdier replacement, a lovely colonial mansion with tile floors and beamed ceilings, for more than 250 years. It was the home of the U.S. Army commander in Puerto Rico from the end of the Spanish-American War in 1898 to 1966. Several rooms decorated with colonial-era furnishings are open to the public. A guide will show you around, and then you can explore on your own. Don't miss the stairway descending from one of the bedrooms. (Despite local lore, this leads to a small room and not to a tunnel to nearby El Morro.) The lush garden, complete with watchtower, is a quiet place to unwind. ⊠ *1 Calle San Sebastián, Old San Juan* ☎ *787/725–1454* ⊕ *www.icp.gobierno.pr* 🎫 *Free* ☉ *Wed.–Sun. 8:30–4.*

Catedral de San Juan Bautista. The Catholic shrine of Puerto Rico had humble beginnings in the early 1520s as a thatch-roofed, wooden structure. After a hurricane destroyed the church, it was rebuilt in 1540, when it was given a graceful circular staircase and vaulted Gothic ceilings. Most of the work on the present cathedral, however, was done in the 19th century. The remains of Ponce de León are behind a marble tomb in the wall near the transept, on the north side. The trompe l'oeil work on the inside of the dome is breathtaking. Unfortunately, many of the other frescoes suffer from water damage. ⊠ *151 Calle Cristo, Old San Juan* ☎ *787/722–0861* 🎫 *$1 donation suggested* ☉ *Mon.–Sat. 9–5, Sun. 9–1.*

FAMILY **Castillo San Cristóbal.** This huge stone fortress, built between 1634 and
Fodor'sChoice 1790, guarded the city from land attacks from the east. The largest
★ Spanish fortification in the New World, San Cristóbal was known in the 17th and 18th centuries as the Gibraltar of the West Indies. Five freestanding structures divided by dry moats are connected by tunnels. You're free to explore the gun turrets (with cannon in situ), officers' quarters, re-created 18th-century barracks, and gloomy passageways. Along with El Morro, San Cristóbal is a National Historic Site administered by the U.S. Park Service; it's a World Heritage Site as well. Rangers conduct tours in Spanish and English. ⊠ *Calle Norzagaray at Av. Muñoz Rivera, Old San Juan* ☎ *787/729–6777* ⊕ *www.nps.gov/saju* 🎫 *$3; $5 includes admission to El Morro* ☉ *Daily 9–6.*

FAMILY **Castillo San Felipe del Morro** (*El Morro*). At the northwestern tip of
Fodor'sChoice the Old City is El Morro ("the promontory"), a fortress built by the
★ Spaniards between 1539 and 1786. Rising 140 feet above the sea, the massive six-level fortress was built to protect the harbor entrance. It is a labyrinth of cannon batteries, ramps, barracks, turrets, towers, and tunnels. Built to protect the port, El Morro has a commanding view of the harbor. You're free to wander throughout. The cannon emplacement walls and the dank secret passageways are a wonder of engineering. The fort's small but enlightening museum displays ancient Spanish guns and other armaments, military uniforms, and blueprints for Spanish forts in the Americas, although Castillo San Cristóbal has more extensive and impressive exhibits. There's also a gift shop. The fort is a National Historic Site administered by the U.S. Park Service; it's a World Heritage Site as well. Various tours and a video are available in English. ⊠ *Calle del Morro, Old San Juan* ☎ *787/729–6960* ⊕ *www.nps.gov/saju* 🎫 *$3; $5 includes admission to Castillo San Cristóbal* ☉ *Daily 9–6.*

Paseo de la Princesa. Built in the mid-nineteenth century to honor the Spanish princess of Asturias, this street has a broad pedestrian walkway and is spruced up with flowers, trees, benches, and street lamps. Unfurling westward from Plaza del Inmigrante along the base of the fortified city walls, it leads to the Fuente Raíces, a striking fountain depicting the various ethnic groups of Puerto Rico. Take a seat and watch the boats zip across the water. Beyond the fountain is the beginning of Paseo del

Morro, a well-paved shoreline path that hugs Old San Juan's walls and leads past the city gate at Calle San Juan and continues to the tip of the headland, beneath El Morro. ⊠ *Paseo de la Princesa, Old San Juan.*

WORTH NOTING

Alcaldía. San Juan's city hall was built between 1602 and 1789. In 1841, extensive alterations were made so that it would resemble the city hall in Madrid, with arcades, towers, balconies, and an inner courtyard. Renovations have refreshed the facade of the building and some interior rooms, but the architecture remains true to its colonial style. Only the patios are open to public viewings. A municipal tourist information center and an art gallery with rotating exhibits are in the lobby. ⊠ *153 Calle San Francisco, Plaza de Armas, Old San Juan* ☎ *787/480–2548* ☞ *Free* ☉ *Weekdays 8–4.*

Capilla del Cristo. According to legend, in 1753 a young horseman named Baltazar Montañez got carried away during festivities in honor of San Juan Bautista (St. John the Baptist), raced down Calle Cristo, and plunged over its steep precipice. Historical records maintain the man died, but legend contends that he lived. (Another version of the story has it that the horse miraculously stopped before plunging over the cliff.) Regardless, this chapel was built partly to prevent further calamities. Inside is a small silver altar dedicated to the Christ of Miracles. Above the altar hangs a religious painting by Puerto Rico's famous painter, José Campeche. You can peer in through the wrought-iron gates, which are usually closed. ⊠ *Calle Cristo, at the end, Old San Juan* ☞ *Free.*

FAMILY **Casa de Ramón Power y Giralt.** The restored home of 18th-century naval hero Don Ramón Power y Giralt is now the headquarters of the Conservation Trust of Puerto Rico. On-site are several displays highlighting the physical, cultural, and historical importance of land and properties on the island under the trust's aegis. The goal of the trust is to increase the amount of protected lands in Puerto Rico, from the actual 8 percent, to 33 percent by the year 2033. Displays are in Spanish but there are note cards in English to the changing exhibitions. A gift shop sells toys, Puerto Rican candies, and eco-friendly souvenirs. ⊠ *155 Calle Tetuán, Old San Juan* ☎ *787/722–5882* ⊕ *paralanaturaleza.org* ☞ *Free* ☉ *Tues.–Fri. 9–5, Sat. 9–4:30.*

Cementerio Santa María Magdalena de Pazzis. One of Old San Juan's best-kept secrets, this remarkable cemetery provides a peaceful respite from the bustle of the city. Sandwiched between El Morro and the La Perla neighborhood, it offers a panoramic view of the Atlantic Ocean and an enviable resting place for the many notable figures fortunate enough to be buried here. Dating back to the early 1800s, the cemetery was originally administered by Carmelite nuns. Today you can stop by the ornate tombs (many of which are topped with graceful marble sculptures) to pay your respects to an illustrious group of Puerto Rican political figures, intellectuals, artists, and revolutionaries, including José Celso Barbosa, José Ferrer, Pedro Albizu Campos, Rafael Hernández, Ricardo Alegría, and others.

Hear your footsteps echo throughout Castillo San Felipe's vast network of tunnels, designed to amplify the sounds of approaching enemies.

⚠ Although a robust police presence has made this area bordering La Perla safer, it's still a good idea to avoid coming after hours or at night. ✉ *West End of Calle Norzagaray, Old San Juan* 🎫 *Free* ☉ *Mon.–Fri. 7–3, Sat.–Sun. 7–noon.*

Fundación Nacional Para la Cultura Popular. This nonprofit foundation serves many functions: museum, performance space, dance and music school, and archive dedicated to preserving the contributions Puerto Ricans have made to music, dance, television, theater, film, and other culture. In a 300-year-old building once used by the Spanish as a meterological lookout, you can visit a rotating exhibition, come in the evening to hear live Latin music, or take a *bomba* or *plena* dance class. A small store sells music by Puerto Ricans in every genre, from classical to salsa. Signed posters from El Gran Combo, Tito Puente, and Willie Colon—as well as Ricky Martin's platinum record—line the walls. Check the website or call ahead for the performance schedule. ✉ *56 Calle Fortaleza, Old San Juan* ☎ *787/724–7165* ⊕ *www.prpop.org* 🎫 *Free* ☉ *Weekdays 10–5:30.*

Iglesia de San José. With its vaulted ceilings, this little church is a splendid example of 16th-century Spanish Gothic architecture. It was built under the supervision of Dominican friars in 1532, making it the second-oldest church in the Western Hemisphere. The body of Ponce de León, the Spanish explorer who came to the New World seeking the Fountain of Youth, was buried here for almost three centuries before being moved to the Catedral de San Juan Bautista in 1909. At this writing, much-needed renovations are under way, so check the website or call for the latest limited visiting schedule. ⊠ *Calle San Sebastián, Plaza de San José, Old San Juan* ☎ *787/727–7373* ⊕ *www.iglesiasanjosepr.org.*

La Fortaleza. Sitting atop the fortified city walls overlooking the harbor, La Fortaleza was built between 1533 and 1540 as a fortress, but it proved to be insufficient, mainly because it was built inside the bay. It was attacked numerous times and was occupied twice, by the British in 1598 and the Dutch in 1625. When El Morro and the city's other fortifications were finished, the Fortaleza became the governor's palace. Numerous changes have been made to the original primitive structure over the past four centuries, resulting in the current eclectic yet eye-pleasing collection of marble and mahogany, medieval towers, and stained-glass galleries. It is still the official residence of the island's governor, and is the Western Hemisphere's oldest executive mansion in continual use. Guided tours of the gardens and the building's exterior are conducted several times a day in English and Spanish. Call ahead, as the schedule changes daily. Proper attire is required: no sleeveless shirts or very short shorts. The tours begin near the main gate in a yellow building called the Real Audiencia, housing the Oficina Estatal de Preservación Histórica. ⊠ *Western end of Calle Fortaleza, Old San Juan* ☎ *787/721–7000* ⊕ *www.fortaleza.gobierno.pr* ▣ *Free* ⊙ *Weekdays 9–4:30.*

Museo de las Américas. On the second floor of the imposing former military barracks, Cuartel de Ballajá, this museum houses four permanent exhibits: Popular Arts, African Heritage, the Indian in America, and Conquest and Colonization. You'll also find a number of temporary exhibitions of works by regional artists. A wide range of handicrafts is available in the gift shop. ⊠ *Calle Norzagaray and Calle del Morro, Old San Juan* ☎ *787/724–5052* ⊕ *www.museolasamericas.org* ▣ *$3* ⊙ *Tues.–Sat. 9–noon, 1–4; Sun. noon–5.*

Museo de San Juan. A bustling marketplace in 1857, this handsome building now houses the small San Juan Museum. You'll find rotating exhibits of Puerto Rican art, plus tableaux and audiovisual shows that present the island's history. Concerts and other cultural events take place in the huge interior courtyard. Stop by on Saturday mornings to check out the small but lively farmer's market. ⊠ *150 Calle Norzagaray, at Calle MacArthur, Old San Juan* ☎ *787/480–3530, 787/480–3547* ▣ *Free* ⊙ *Tues.–Sun. 9–noon; 1–4.*

FAMILY **Museo del Niño.** This three-floor, hands-on "museum" is pure fun for kids. There are games to play, clothes for dress-up, a mock plaza with market, and even a barbershop where children can play (no real scissors here). There's also an immense food-groups pyramid, where children can climb to place magnets representing different foods. Older children will appreciate the top-floor garden where bugs and plants are on display, and the little ones can pretend to go shopping or to work at a construction site. For toddlers, there's a playground. Note that when the museum reaches capacity, it stops selling tickets. ⊠ *150 Calle Cristo, between Caleta Las Monjas and Caleta de San Juan, Old San Juan* ☎ *787/722–3791* ⊕ *www.museodelninopr.org* ▣ *$5, $7 children* ⊙ *Tues.–Thurs. 10–3:30, Fri. 10–5, weekends noon–5:30.*

Exploring
Old San Juan

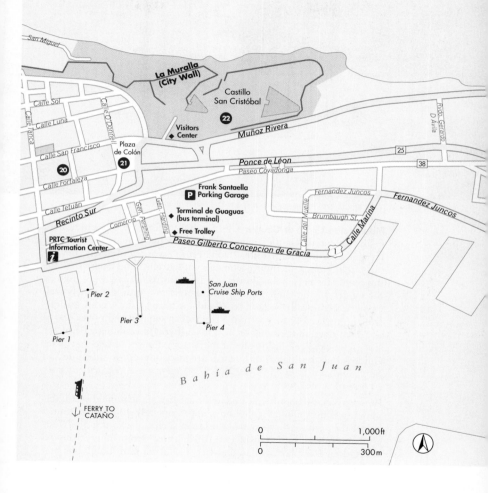

O c e a n

San Miguel

**La Muralla
(City Wall)**

Castillo
San Cristóbal

22

Calle Sol

Calle Luna

Calle O'Donnel

Calle Tanca

Visitors
◆ Center

Muñoz Rivera

Rvdo. Gerardo
D Ávila

Calle San Francisco

Plaza
de Colón

20 **21**

Ponce de Léon

25

Paseo Covadonga

38

Calle Fortaleza

Calle Tetuán

Frank Santaella
🅿 Parking Garage

Fernandez Juncos

Fernandez Juncos

Calle del Muelle

Recinto Sur

Gen. Flagring

Gen. Pershing

Comercio

◆ Terminal de Guaguas
(bus terminal)

◆ Free Trolley

Brumbaugh St.

Calle Marina

**PRTC Tourist
Information Center**

🛈

Paseo Gilberto Concepcion de Gracia

1

Pier 2

San Juan
• Cruise Ship Ports

Pier 3

Pier 4

Pier 1

B a h í a   d e   S a n   J u a n

FERRY TO
CATAÑO

0   1,000ft

0   300m

La Muralla, the city wall, towers over the harborside walkway that winds around the Old City.

Museo Felisa Rincón de Gautier. This tiny but fascinating museum honors Felisa Rincón de Gautier, who served as San Juan's mayor from 1946 to 1968. Throughout her life, "Doña Felisa" worked tirelessly on various public causes, including women's voting rights and health care for the poor. Her preschools, known as *Escuelas Maternas*, were used as the model for the United States' Head Start program. Extremely well connected politically both on the island and abroad, she was an egalitarian figure who rose to power at a time when women and politics were not mentioned in the same breath. Even if you have no interest in her story, you can peek inside one of the historic houses of Old San Juan. Guided tours in English or Spanish are available. ⊠ *51 Caleta de San Juan, Old San Juan* ☎ *787/723–1897* ⊕ *www.museofelisarincon.com* ✉ *Free* ☉ *Weekdays 9–4.*

Museo la Casa del Libro. Dedicated to the artistry of the printed word, this museum counts among its holdings approximately 400 books printed before the 15th century—one of the larger such collections in the Western Hemisphere. It also owns two royal decrees from King Ferdinand and Queen Isabella that date back to 1493, the year Columbus first reached Puerto Rico. Because the museum is in a temporary location while long-term restorations to the permanent building are under way, only a small portion of the 6,000-piece collection is on display: you can see a page from the Gutenberg Bible and a 12th-century lunar-cycle calendar, which is impressive and worth a quick look. The gift shop has a terrific collection of posters that draws customers from all over the world. ⊠ *199 Callejón de la Capilla, Old San Juan* ☎ *787/723–0354*

GREAT ITINERARIES

IF YOU HAVE 1 DAY

Many people find themselves with a single day—or even less—to explore San Juan. There should be no question about your destination—head to Old San Juan. Spend the entire day rambling around the cobblestone streets and ducking into the many shops, being sure to save plenty of time for exploring the turrets, towers, and dungeons of **Castillo San Felipe del Morro**, the original fortress on a rocky promontory at the Old City's northwestern tip *(see also the "Walking Old San Juan" feature).*

IF YOU HAVE 3 DAYS

It's only fitting that you spend the first day enjoying a walking tour of Old San Juan. What to see? **Castillo San Felipe del Morro** is at the top of the list. You might want to explore the equally enthralling **Castillo San Cristóbal,** which has underground tunnels and hidden passages, plus cannons and a more impressive museum than at San Felipe del Morro. The city's original fortress, the **Fortaleza,** wasn't much protection from marauding pirates, but it does a great job at sheltering the governor and can be toured. And **Casa Blanca,** a home built for Juan Ponce de León, is a wonderful place to explore how the Spanish lived in colonial days, though at this writing it was undergoing a lengthy renovation. Day 2 should be for lounging on a *playa* (beach). Choose from the city's finest at Condado, Ocean Park, or Isla Verde, and park yourself in a rented chair with a good book, a cold drink, and plenty of sunscreen. In the evening, make sure you enjoy the warm weather by dining alfresco. On your third day, hop the ferry across the bay to Cataño for a tour of the **Casa Bacardí Visitor Center.** Return in time for some shopping in the high-end shops and delightful arts-and-crafts galleries along Calle Cristo, then dinner in one of the trendy eateries on Calle Fortaleza.

IF YOU HAVE 5 DAYS

Follow the itinerary above for your first three days in San Juan. On Day 4, head for the Santurce district. You can immerse yourself in island art at the **Museo de Arte de Puerto Rico** and, nearby, the **Museo de Arte Contemporáneo de Puerto Rico.** Afterward, wander through the produce stalls at the Plaza del Mercado in Santurce, with a fresh papaya or soursop shake in hand, and have your palm read. Be sure to note the giant bronze sculptures of avocados by artist Annex Burgos. If hunger strikes, head to José Enrique, a favorite among locals. On the morning of Day 5, hit the beach once more; then head to Avenida Ashford in Condado for an afternoon of shopping in its ritzy boutiques.

⊕ *www.lacasadellibro.org* ⌦ *Free, but donation appreciated* ⊙ *Tues.–Sat. 11–5.*

NEED A BREAK?

Ben & Jerry's. On your hike up hilly Calle Cristo, stop at Ben & Jerry's at the corner of Calle Sol. Savor Vermont ice cream under a palm tree or enjoy fresh fruit smoothies next to a Green Mountain cow. ⊠ *61 Calle Cristo, Old San Juan* ☏ *787/977–6882* ⊕ *www.benandjerryspr.com.*

FAMILY **Parque de las Palomas.** The small, shaded park bordering Old San Juan's Capilla del Cristo has a large stone wall with pigeonholes cut into it. Hundreds of *palomas* (pigeons) roost here, and the park is full of cooing local children chasing the well-fed birds. Stop to enjoy the wide views over Paseo de la Princesa and the San Juan Bay. ⊠ *End of Calle Cristo, Old San Juan.*

Plaza de Armas. The Old City's original main square was once used as military drilling grounds. Bordered by Calles San Francisco, Rafael Cordero, San José, and Cruz, it has a fountain with 19th-century statues representing the four seasons as well as a bandstand, a small café and kiosk that sells local snacks and fruit frappés. The Alcaldía commands the north side. This is one of the most popular meeting places in Old San Juan, so you're likely to encounter lots of bustle: artists sketching caricatures, pedestrians waiting in line at food carts, and hundreds of pigeons waiting for handouts. ⊠ *Calle San José, Old San Juan.*

NEED A BREAK? **Café 4 Estaciones.** At Café 4 Estaciones, tables and chairs sit under a canvas canopy surrounded by potted plants. This tiny kiosk-café is the perfect spot to put down your shopping bags and rest your tired feet. Grab a *café con leche* (coffee with hot milk), an espresso, or cold drink, and watch the children chase the pigeons. It's open until 1 am. ⊠ *Plaza de Armas, Old San Juan.*

Plaza de Colón. The tallest statue of Christopher Columbus in the Americas stands atop a soaring column and fountain in this bustling Old San Juan square, kitty-corner to Castillo San Cristóbal. What was once called St. James Square was renamed in 1893 to honor the 400th anniversary of Columbus's arrival in Puerto Rico. Bronze plaques on the statue's base relate various episodes in the life of the explorer. Local artisans often line the plaza, so it's a good place to stop for souvenirs. Cool off with a fresh fruit frappé or smoothie at the newly opened kiosk. ⊠ *Old San Juan.*

Plazuela de la Rogativa. According to legend, the British, while laying siege to the city in 1797, mistook the flaming torches of a *rogativa*—religious procession—for Spanish reinforcements and beat a hasty retreat. In this little plaza, a monument of a bishop and three women commemorates the legend. The striking contemporary statue was created in 1971 by the artist Lindsay Daen to mark the Old City's 450th anniversary. The fine view of La Fortaleza and the harbor is a bonus. ⊠ *Caleta de las Monjas, Old San Juan.*

Puerta de San Juan. Dating back to 1520, this was one of the five original entrances to the city and is the only one still in its original state. The massive gate, painted a brilliant shade of red, gave access from the port and welcomed diplomats into the city. It resembles a tunnel because it passes through La Muralla, the 20-foot-thick city walls. ⊠ *Paseo de la Princesa, Old San Juan.*

Continued on page 54

WALKING OLD SAN JUAN

Old San Juan is Puerto Rico's quintessential colonial neighborhood. Narrow streets and plazas are still enclosed by thick fortress walls, and bougainvillea bowers spill over exquisite facades. A walk along streets paved with slate-blue cobblestones leads past colonial mansions, ancient churches, and intriguing museums and galleries. Vivacious restaurants and bars that teem with life young and old are always nearby, making it easy to refuel and reinvigorate anytime during your stroll.

by Christopher P. Baker

left, strolling down Calle del Cristo; top right, a view from El Morro; bottom right, dancers in front of Castillo San Cristóbal

A STROLL THROUGH OLD SAN JUAN

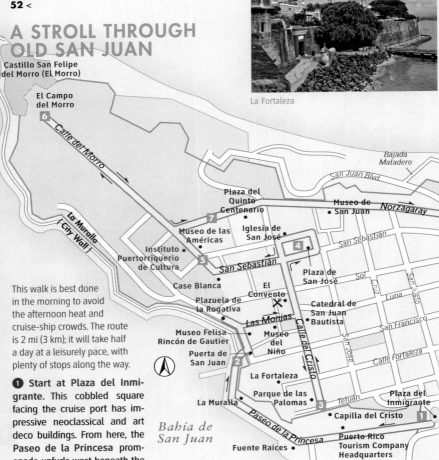

Castillo San Felipe del Morro (El Morro)

El Campo del Morro

6

Calle del Morro

La Muralla [City Wall]

La Fortaleza

Bajada Matadero

San Juan Blvd

Plaza del Quinto Centenario

Museo de San Juan

Norzagaray

7

Museo de las Américas

Iglesia de San José

San Sebastián

Instituto Puertorriqueño de Cultura

5

San Sebastián

4

Plaza de San José

Sol

San Justo

Cruz

Luna

Case Blanca

Plazuela de la Rogativa

El Convento

Catedral de San Juan Bautista

San Francisco

Museo Felisa Rincón de Gautier

Las Monjas

Museo del Niño

Calle del Cristo

San José

Calle Fortaleza

Puerta de San Juan

2

La Fortaleza

Parque de las Palomas

Plaza del Inmigrante

La Muralla

3

Tetuán

Capilla del Cristo

1

Paseo de la Princesa

Bahía de San Juan

Fuente Raíces

Puerto Rico Tourism Company Headquarters

This walk is best done in the morning to avoid the afternoon heat and cruise-ship crowds. The route is 2 mi (3 km); it will take half a day at a leisurely pace, with plenty of stops along the way.

❶ **Start at Plaza del Inmigrante.** This cobbled square facing the cruise port has impressive neoclassical and art deco buildings. From here, the **Paseo de la Princesa** promenade unfurls west beneath the ancient city wall, **La Muralla.** Artisans set up stalls under the palms on weekends. Midway along the brick-paved walkway, stop to admire the **Fuente**

Puerta de San Juan

Raíces monument and fountain: dolphins cavort at the feet of figures representing Puerto Rico's indigenous, Spanish, and African peoples.

❷ **Pass through the Puerta de San Juan.** This fortified entrance in La Muralla was built in 1520 and still retains its massive wooden gates, creaky on their ancient hinges. Immediately beyond, turn left and ascend to **Plazuela de la Rogativa,** a tiny plaza where a contemporary statue recalls

the torch-lit procession that thwarted an English invasion in 1797. The harbor views are fantastic. Then, walk east one block to reach the **Catedral de San Juan Bautista,** the neoclassical 19th-century cathedral containing the mausoleum of Ponce de León.

❸ **Head south on Calle del Cristo.** Sloping gradually, this lovely street is lined with beautifully restored colonial mansions housing cafés, galleries, and boutiques. Passing Calle

Castillo San Cristóbal

Calle del Cristo

Catedral de San Juan Bautista

ATLANTIC OCEAN

San Miguel

0 — 1/8 mi
0 — 1/8 km

La Muralla (City Wall)

8 Castillo San Cristóbal

Sol
Luna
O'Donnell
Tanca

♦ Visitors Center

Muñoz Rivera
9 Plaza de Colón
✕ Ponce de León 25
Teatro Tapía

Castillo San Felipe del Morro

roam the small museum, turrets, labyrinthine tunnels, and six levels of ramparts soaring 140 feet above the ocean.

7 Retrace your steps and turn left on **Calle Norzagaray**. This street runs atop the Atlantic shoreline, offering sweeping ocean vistas. On your right you'll pass the **Plaza del Quinto Centenario**, pinned by an impressive statue: the *Tótem Telúrico*. Beyond, stroll past the Galería Nacional (Convento de los Dominicos) to reach the **Museo de San Juan**. Housed in a former market, it traces the city's history and displays works by Puerto Rico's master painters.

8 Continue east to Castillo San Cristóbal. Spanning 27 acres, this multitiered fortress was completed in 1771 with mighty bulwarks that protected the city from eastern attack by land. It features superb historical exhibits and reenactments by soldiers in period costumes.

9 Exit the castle, turn south and walk one block to Plaza de Colón, This leafy square is lined with excellent cafés and restaurants where you can rest your feet and enjoy a great meal.

Fortaleza, note **La Fortaleza**, the official residence of the Puerto Rican Governor at the end of the street. Calle del Cristo ends at **Capilla del Cristo**, a chapel adorned within by silver *milagros* (token requests).

4 Return via **Calle del Cristo** and continue to Plaza de San José. Catercorner to the cathedral you'll find **El Convento**, a former convent turned hotel, with an excellent tapas bar. At **Plaza de San José** visit the **Iglesia de San José**, a simple

church dating from 1532 that is one of the oldest churches in the Western Hemisphere.

5 Walk west on **Calle San Sebastián**. This narrow street with colonial mansions painted in vibrant pastels ends at the gleaming white **Casa Blanca**. The oldest continually occupied residence in the Americas was originally the home of Ponce de León. Today it's a delightful museum furnished with period pieces. The garden is a tranquil spot for contemplation.

6 Follow **Calle del Morro** north. One block from Casa Blanca you'll emerge upon a broad grassy headland—the Campo del Morro—popular with kite-flying families. It's skewered by an arrow-straight gravel path that aims at the imposing **Castillo San Felipe del Morro (El Morro)**, guarding the harbor entrance. Allow one-hour to

CLOSE UP

Peaceful Music

Cellist Pablo Casals was one of the 20th century's most influential musicians. Born in Catalonia in 1876, he studied in Spain and Belgium, settled for a time in Paris, then returned to Barcelona. Tours in Europe, the United States, and South America brought him artistic and financial success and opportunities to collaborate with other prominent musicians.

By the advent of the Spanish Civil War, he was an internationally famous musician, teacher, and conductor. He was also an outspoken supporter of a democratic Spain. Forced into exile by Franco's regime, Casals arrived in Puerto Rico, his mother's birthplace, in 1956. Here the then-81-year-old maestro continued to work and teach.

He established the Casals Festival of Classical Music, making the island a home for sublime orchestral and chamber works. During two weeks each June, the Puerto Rico Symphony Orchestra is joined by musicians from all over the world.

In Catalan, Casals's first name is Pau, which appropriately means "peace." He and his friend Albert Schweitzer appealed to the world powers to stop the arms race, and Casals made what many experts say is his greatest work—an oratorio titled *The Manger*—his personal message of peace. Casals died in Puerto Rico in 1973, but his many legacies live on.

—Karen English

GREATER SAN JUAN

Old San Juan may be Puerto Rico's jewel, but each of San Juan's other neighborhoods has a distinctive character with its own special attractions.

GETTING HERE AND AROUND

Locals traveling in San Juan often complain about *el tapón* (traffic jam or, more literally, "cork"). A 15-minute drive can easily turn into 45 minutes depending on the road conditions. In addition, drivers can be unpredictable, using the shoulder as a through lane or drifting unpredictably from lane to lane, so be alert. If you choose to rent a car, get a good map. San Juan's roads are well marked, but one-way streets pop up out of nowhere.

Just east of Old San Juan, Avenidas Muñoz Rivera, Ponce de León, and Fernández Juncos are the main thoroughfares that cross Puerta de Tierra, leading to the neighborhoods of Condado, Ocean Park, Miramar, Santurce, and Isla Verde. Puente Dos Hermanos, the "Bridge of the Two Brothers," connects Puerta de Tierra with Condado. Avenida Ashford, which splits off into Avenida Magdalena for a few blocks, travels through Condado to Ocean Park. Calle Loíza connects Ocean Park with Isla Verde. These streets can be choked with traffic, so if you are traveling more than a few blocks, consider taking the speedier Route 26.

TIMING

Depending on what mode of transportation you choose, you can see the Greater San Juan area sights in a day; if you linger in the museums, exploring might require two days. Buses are the least expensive

The statues of Plaza de Armas's 19th-century fountain represent the four seasons.

but most time-consuming way to travel. Unfortunately, the beautiful new rapid-transit system, Tren Urbano, does not yet service the main tourist areas; however, if you're traveling to Bayamón, Guaynabo, Río Piedras, or another, more residential suburb, it's an option. Taxis are more convenient, and you won't get lost—consider hiring a taxi by the hour and covering your selected sights in a couple of hours. Taxis charge around $36 per hour for city tours, but the rate can be negotiable for long stretches of time.

PUERTA DE TIERRA

Just east of the Old City, Puerta de Tierra is home to a few notable hotels, a nice public beach, and several parks.

WORTH NOTING

El Capitolio. The white-marble Capitol, a fine example of Italian Renaissance style, dates from 1929. The grand rotunda, which can be seen from all over San Juan, was completed in the late 1990s. Fronted by eight Corinthian columns, it's a very dignified home for the commonwealth's constitution. Although the Senate and the House of Representatives have offices in the more modern buildings on either side, the Capitol is where the legislators meet. Guided tours, which last about an hour and include visits to the rotunda and other parts of the building, are by appointment only. ⊠ *Av. Constitución, Puerta de Tierra* ☎ *787/724–2030* ✉ *Free* ⊙ *Weekdays 9:15–3:45.*

CONDADO

For multiple shopping and dining options all within walking distance, look to Condado. Home to many of the city's moneyed elite, it's the most vibrant pedestrian neighborhood outside of Old San Juan. Here

Plucky pontiff: the bronze bishop of Plazuela de la Rogativa is a monument to the religious procession that, according to legend, repelled British invasion.

you'll find old Spanish-style homes next to sleek, modern apartment buildings and designer shops. The main street, Avenida Ashford, is fun to walk along, but the quieter residential areas are also very attractive. Many hotels are beachfront, though the beach is not as big or alluring as those in Isla Verde.

MIRAMAR

Across the bay from Condado, is Miramar, a quiet, mostly residential neighborhood. Recently, many young professionals have been moving to the area, resulting in a new wave of great bars and restaurants. It's the home to the Convention District and the Puerto Rico Conservatory of Music.

OCEAN PARK

Ocean Park is a partially gated residential community with a laid-back feel. If you've dreamed of staying in a quiet guesthouse on a more secluded beach—away from the crowds—this might be the spot for you.

ISLA VERDE

If you came to work on your tan—and you came to do it on a big, beautiful Caribbean beach—then Isla Verde, home to the nicest beach in the metropolitan area, is your place. The main commercial strip is not especially attractive: it's filled with fast-food restaurants and other businesses. You'll also need a car or taxi to get anywhere. That said, the resort-style hotels (many of them beachfront) offer so many amenities and so many restaurants on-site, you may not want—or need—to leave very often.

A GOOD TOUR

East of Old San Juan on Avenida Ponce de León you'll find **El Capitolio**, Puerto Rico's magnificent capitol building. Take Avenida Ashford east, branching off onto Avenida Magdalena and then Calle Loíza. At the corner of Avenida Ponce de León is the **Museo de Arte Contemporáneo de Puerto Rico**, with a fine collection of contemporary Latin-American art. If you're hungry, stop for lunch at the nearby **Plaza del Mercado**. Afterward, head east on Avenida Ponce de León, then north on Avenida José de Diego to reach the **Museo de Arte de Puerto Rico**, a former hospital that has been transformed into the island's most ambitious art museum.

From the museum it's a straight ride south on Avenida Ponce de León (Route 25) to the Río Piedras district, where you'll find the Universidad de Puerto Rico and its **Museo de Historia, Antropología y Arte**. Less than 1 mile (1½ km) to the west, at the junction of Routes 1 and 847, is the 75-acre **Jardín Botánico**.

SANTURCE

Venture into Santurce to explore a mostly commercial district with a growing artistic community, thanks to the Museo de Arte de Puerto Rico and the Museo de Arte Contemporáneo. You'll also find a thriving nightlife scene there on weekends. Nearby, **Hato Rey** is a busy financial district, where you'll find the large Plaza las Américas Mall.

TOP ATTRACTIONS

Fodor's Choice ★ **Museo de Arte de Puerto Rico.** One of the biggest museums in the Caribbean, this beautiful neoclassical building was once the San Juan Municipal Hospital. The collection of Puerto Rican art starts with works from the colonial era, most of them commissioned for churches. Here you'll find works by José Campeche, the island's first great painter. His *Immaculate Conception*, finished in 1794, is a masterpiece. Also well represented is Francisco Oller y Cestero, who was the first to move beyond religious subjects to paint local scenes. Another gallery room is filled with works by artists inspired by Oller. The original building, built in the 1920s, proved to be too small to house the museum's collection: the newer east wing is dominated by a five-story-tall stained-glass window, the work of local artist Eric Tabales. Entrance is free on Wednesdays 2–8. There's much more to the museum, including a beautiful garden filled with a variety of native flora and a 400-seat theater that's worth seeing for its remarkable hand-crocheted lace curtain. ✉ *299 Av. José de Diego, Santurce* ☎ *787/977–6277* ⊕ *www.mapr.org* 🎫 *$6* ⊘ *Tues. and Thurs.–Sat. 10–5, Wed. 10–8, Sun. 11–6.*

Museo de Arte Contemporáneo de Puerto Rico. This Georgian-style structure, once a public school, displays a dynamic range of works by both established and up-and-coming Latin American artists. Many of the works on display have strong political messages, including pointed commentaries on Puerto Rico's status as a commonwealth. Only a small part of the more than 900 works in the permanent collection is on display at any time, but it might be anything from an exhibit of ceramics to a screening of videos. ✉ *1220 Av. Ponce de León, at Av. R.H.*

Todd, Santurce ☎ *787/977–4030* 📋 *$5* ⊘ *Tues.–Fri. 10–4, Sat. 11–5, Sun. 1–5.*

WORTH NOTING

Plaza del Mercado (*La Placita*). Though mostly overlooked by tourists, La Placita, as known by locals, is one of the most charming corners of San Juan. At its center is a market hall dating from 1910. Inside you'll find bushels of fruits and vegetables, many of which you probably haven't seen before such as *guanábana* and *caimito*. Many chefs from the top city restaurants come here to find their produce. If all this food makes you hungry, dozens of storefront restaurants and bars face the central square. These places, mostly serving seafood, are quiet during the week but bustling on the weekends, especially in the evening. The area also has many *botánicas,* small shops that sell herbs, candles, and religious items. There may even be an in-house card or palm reader ready to show you your future. The square is between the Museo de Arte de Puerto Rico and the Museo de Arte Contemporáneo de Puerto Rico, making it a good place to stop for lunch if you are museum hopping. ✉ *Calle Dos Hermanos at Calle Capital, Santurce.*

RÍO PIEDRAS

The mostly residential Río Piedras area is home to the Universidad de Puerto Rico and a few notable sights.

WORTH NOTING

Jardín Botánico (*Botanical Garden*). This 75-acre forest of more than 200 species of tropical and subtropical vegetation is the Universidad de Puerto Rico's main attraction. Gravel footpaths lead to a graceful lotus lagoon, a bamboo promenade, as well as orchid and palm gardens. Not all plants and trees are labeled, so the garden is more of a tranquil retreat than an opportunity to learn about the vegetation. Trail maps are available at the entrance gate, and groups of 10 or more can arrange guided tours ($25). ✉ *Intersection of Rtes. 1 and 847, at entrance to Barrio Venezuela, Río Piedras* ☎ *787/758–9957* ⊕ *www. upr.edu* 📋 *Free* ⊘ *Daily 6–6.*

Museo de Historia, Antropología y Arte. The Universidad de Puerto Rico's small Museum of History, Anthropology, and Art offers rotating exhibitions in three areas. Its archaeological and historical collection covers the Native American influence on the island and the Caribbean, the colonial era, and the history of slavery. There's also a small collection of Egyptian antiquities. Art holdings include a range of Puerto Rican popular, graphic, folk, and fine art; the museum's prize exhibit is the painting *El Velorio* (*The Wake*), by the 19th-century artist Francisco Oller. If you're looking to see something in particular, call before you go, as only a small portion of the collection is on display at a time. Guided tours in English are available; call ahead to make a reservation. ✉ *Universidad de Puerto Rico, Av. Ponce de León, Río Piedras* ☎ *787/763–3939* 📋 *Free* ⊘ *Mon.–Tues. and Thurs.–Fri. 9–4:30; Wed. 9–8:30; Sun. 11:30–4:30.*

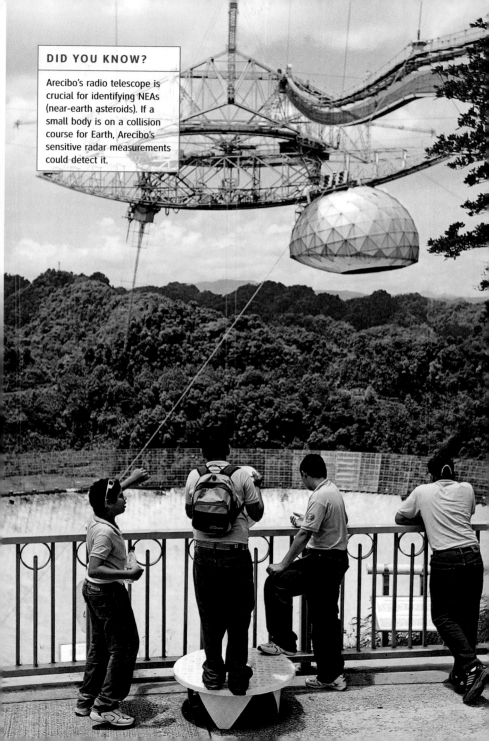

DID YOU KNOW?

Arecibo's radio telescope is crucial for identifying NEAs (near-earth asteroids). If a small body is on a collision course for Earth, Arecibo's sensitive radar measurements could detect it.

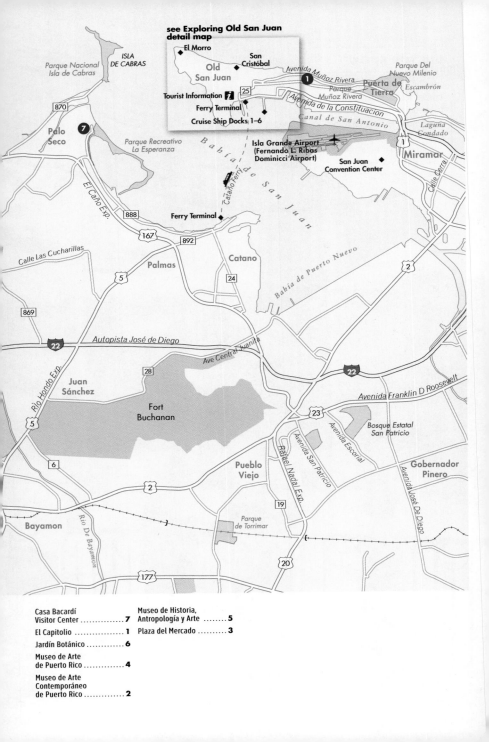

see **Exploring Old San Juan detail map**

El Morro

San Cristóbal

Old San Juan

Avenida Muñoz Rivera

Parque Del Nuevo Milenio

Puerta de Tierra

Escambrón

Tourist Information 🛈

Parque Muñoz Rivera

25

Avenida de la Constitución

Ferry Terminal

Cruise Ship Docks 1–6

Canal de San Antonio

Laguna Condado

Isla Grande Airport (Fernando L. Ribas Dominicci Airport)

San Juan Convention Center

Miramar

Calle Cerra

Parque Nacional Isla de Cabras

ISLA DE CABRAS

870

7

Palo Seco

Parque Recreativo La Esperanza

Bahía de San Juan

El Caño Exp.

888

Ferry Terminal

167

892

Cataño Ferry Line

Calle Las Cucharillas

Palmas

Cataño

Bahía de Puerto Nuevo

2

5

24

869

Autopista José de Diego

22

Ave Central Juanita

Río Hondo Exp.

28

Juan Sánchez

Fort Buchanan

22

Avenida Franklin D Roosevelt

5

23

Bosque Estatal San Patricio

6

Rafael Nadal Exp.

Avenida San Patricio

Avenida Escorial

Gobernador Pinero

Avenida José De Diego

2

Pueblo Viejo

19

Bayamon

Río De Bayamón

Parque de Torrimar

20

177

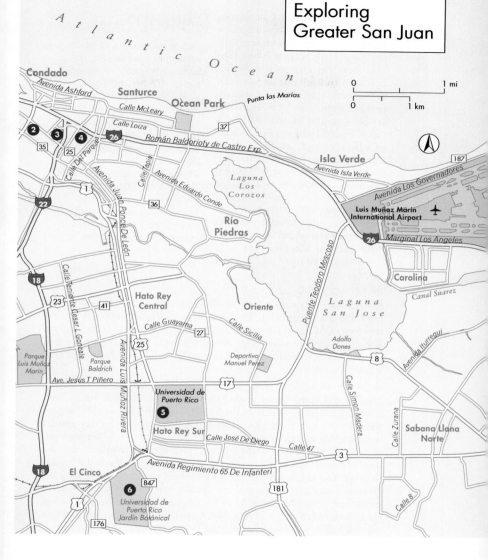

Exploring
Greater San Juan

SAN JUAN SUBURBS

The suburbs of Cataño, Bayamón, and Guaynabo, west and south of San Juan, are separate municipalities but in many ways indistinguishable from the city itself. Cataño, bordered by the Bahía de San Juan in the north, is an industrial suburb, perhaps most noted for its distillery belonging to Bacardí. Bayamón can be reached within 15 to 30 minutes from central San Juan; if you come by car, stop by the attractive central park, bordered by historic buildings. Guaynabo is a mix of residential and industrial areas and is worth visiting for its historical importance—Juan Ponce de León established the island's first settlement here in Caparra, and you can visit the ruins of the original fortification.

SAINTS ON PARADE

Each of Puerto Rico's 78 municipalities has a patron saint, and each one celebrates an annual festival near the saint's birthday, sometimes lasting a week or more. These festivals are a great opportunity to hear live music and buy local arts and crafts. San Juan celebrates its patron-saint feast in the *noche de San Juan* on June 23, when locals take to the beach. The event culminates at midnight, when crowds plunge into the Atlantic to flip over backward seven times, a cleansing ritual expected to bring good fortune.

GETTING HERE AND AROUND

Avenida Kennedy runs mostly north–south and leads to the suburbs of Bayamón and Guaynabo. The Casa Bacardí Visitor Center is an easy trip from Old San Juan—you simply take a ferry across the harbor. The other sites are a challenge to reach, as you must navigate some of the region's most traffic-clogged streets. Do yourself a favor and take a taxi or book a tour.

WORTH NOTING

Casa Bacardí Visitor Center. Exiled from Cuba, the Bacardí family built a small rum distillery here in the 1950s. Today it's the world's largest, with the capacity to produce 100,000 gallons of spirits a day and 21 million cases a year. You can hop on a little tram to take an approximately 45-minute tour of the visitor center, though you don't visit the distillery itself. Yes, you'll be offered two free samples. If you don't want to drive, you can reach the factory by taking the ferry from Pier 2 for 50¢ each way and then a *público* (public van service) from the ferry pier to the factory for about $2 or $3 per person. ⊠ *Bay View Industrial Park, Rte. 165, Km 2.6, at Rte. 888, Cataño* 🕾 *787/788–1500* ⊕ *www.casabacardi.org* 🎫 *Free* ⊙ *Mon.–Sat. 9–6, last tour at 4:15; Sun. 10–5, last tour at 3:45.*

SIDE TRIP FROM SAN JUAN

About an hour and fifteen minutes (depending on traffic, of course) west of San Juan, off Route 22, lies Arecibo, home of the world-famous Arecibo Observatory. If you're in the area visiting the nearby Río Camuy cave park or the Barceloneta outlets—or if you're just an astronomy

2

buff—it's worth a stop to see the massive radio telescope. Once you're out of the metropolitan area, the drive takes you through Puerto Rico's karst country, with its strangely beautiful limestone formations covered with vegetation.

Fodor'sChoice
★
FAMILY

Arecibo Observatory. Hidden among pine-covered hills, the Arecibo Observatory is home to the world's largest radar-radio telescope. Operated by the National Astronomy and Ionosphere Center of Cornell University, the 20-acre dish lies in a 563-foot-deep sinkhole in the karst landscape. If the 600-ton platform hovering eerily over the dish looks familiar, it may be because it was featured in the movie *Contact*. You can walk around the viewing platform and explore two levels of interactive exhibits on planetary systems, meteors, and weather phenomena in the visitor center. There's also a gift shop. Note that the trail leading up to the observatory is extremely steep. For those who have difficulty walking or have a medical condition, ask a staff member at the gate about a van that provides courtesy shuttle service to the observatory entrance. ⊠ *Rte. 625, Km 3.0, Arecibo* 🕿 *787/878–2612* ⊕ *www.naic.edu* 🖙 *$10* ⊙ *June, July, and mid-Dec.–mid-Jan., daily 9–4; Aug.–mid-Dec. and mid-Jan–May, Wed.–Sun 9–4.*

BEACHES

Just because you're staying in the city doesn't mean you'll have to forgo time on the *playa*. San Juan's beaches are among the island's best. With 365 different beaches in Puerto Rico, choosing where to spread out your towel might seem like a daunting task. The decision is easier now that seven have been designated with a Blue Flag. Chosen by the Foundation for Environmental Education, a nonprofit agency, Blue Flag beaches have to meet more than 30 criteria, focusing on water quality, the presence of a trained staff, and the availability of facilities such as water fountains and restrooms.

Two beaches on the east side of the island, Seven Seas in Fajardo and Luquillo Beach, made the cut. More surprisingly, two of the beaches are in San Juan: Balneario El Escambrón, in Puerta de Tierra, and Balneario de Carolina, in Isla Verde. A fifth is Punta Salinas in nearby Toa Baja. This means that five of Puerto Rico's finest beaches are within an hour's drive of the capital. The final two Blue Flag beaches are in the west and south: Boquerón in Cabo Rojo and Pelicano Beach in Ponce.

FAMILY

Balneario de Carolina. When people discuss a "beautiful Isla Verde beach," this is the one they're talking about. East of Isla Verde, this Blue Flag beach is so close to the airport that the leaves rustle when planes take off. Thanks to an offshore reef, the surf is not as strong as other nearby beaches, so it's especially good for children and families. There's plenty of room to spread out underneath the palm and almond trees. For meals there are picnic tables and barbecue grills. Although there's a charge for parking, there's not always someone there to take the money. **Amenities:** lifeguards; showers; toilets. **Best for:** swimming; walking. ⊠ *Ave. Los Gobernadores, Carolina* 🕿 *787/791–2410* 🖙 *$3 parking* ⊙ *Tues.–Sun. 8–5.*

FAMILY **Balneario El Escambrón.** In Puerta de Tierra, this government-run beach has a patch of honey-colored sand shaded by coconut palms. An off-shore reef means that the surf is generally gentle, so it's favored by families. Nearby restaurants make picnicking a breeze. **Amenities:** food and drink; lifeguards, showers; toilets. **Best for:** swimming; walking. ⊠ *Ave. Muñoz Rivera, Puerta de Tierra* 🚗 *Parking $5* ⊙ *Daily 8–5:30.*

FAMILY **Playa del Condado.** East of Old San Juan and west of Ocean Park, this long, wide beach is overshadowed by an unbroken string of hotels and apartment buildings. Beach bars, water-sports outfitters, and chair-rental places abound. You can access the beach from several roads off Avenida Ashford, including Calles Cervantes, Vendig, Condado, and Candina. The protected water at the small stretch of beach west of the Conrad San Juan Condado Plaza hotel is particularly calm and popular with families; surf elsewhere in Condado can be a bit strong. The stretch of sand near Calle Vendig (behind the Atlantic Beach Hotel) is especially popular with the gay community. If you're driving, on-street parking is your only option. **Best for:** partiers, people-watching. ⊠ *Ave. Ashford, Condado* ⊙ *Daily dawn–dusk.*

Playa de Ocean Park. The residential neighborhood east of Condado and west of Isla Verde is home to this 1-mile-long (1½-km-long) stretch of golden sand. The waters are often choppy but still swimmable—take care, however, as there are no lifeguards on duty. Windsurfers say the conditions here are nearly perfect. The tranquil beach is popular with young people, particularly on weekends, as well as gay men. Parking is a bit difficult, as many of the streets are gated and restricted to residents. **Best for:** partiers; windsurfing. ⊠ *Calle Santa Ana, Ocean Park* ⊙ *Daily dawn–dusk.*

WHERE TO EAT

In cosmopolitan San Juan European, Asian, Middle Eastern, and chic fusion eateries vie for your attention, with family-owned restaurants specializing in seafood or *comida criolla* (creole cooking, or local Puerto Rican food). U.S. chains such as McDonald's and Subway compete with chains like Pollo Tropical and El Mesón, which specialize in local cuisine. Many of the most innovative chefs here have restaurants in the city's large hotels, but don't be shy about venturing into stand-alone establishments—many concentrated in Condado and along Calles Fortaleza and San Sebastián in Old San Juan. Old San Juan is also home to a number of notable new restaurants and cafés, offering more artisanal-style cuisine—crop-to-cup coffee, rustic homemade pizzas, and creative vegetarian food—at affordable prices. There's a radiant pride in what the local land can provide, and these enthusiastic young restaurateurs are redefining what Puerto Rican food is, bite by tasty bite.

WHAT IT COSTS IN U.S. DOLLARS			
$	**$$**	**$$$**	**$$$$**
At Dinner	$8–$12	$13–$20	$21–$30	over $30

Prices are per person for a main course at dinner, or if dinner is not served at lunch.

Dress codes vary greatly, though a restaurant's price category is a good indicator of its formality. For less expensive places anything but beachwear is fine. Ritzier spots will expect collared shirts and long pants for men (jacket and tie requirements are rare) and chic attire for women. When in doubt, do as the Puerto Ricans often do and dress up.

For breakfast outside of your hotel, cafés or local bakeries (called panaderías) are your best bet. It's rare for such establishments to close between breakfast and lunch; it's slightly more common for restaurants to close between lunch and dinner. Although some places don't accept reservations, it's always a good idea to make them for dinner whenever possible. This is especially true during the busy season from November through April and on weekends at any time of the year.

OLD SAN JUAN

Use the coordinate (⊕ 1:A2) at the end of each listing to locate a site on the corresponding "Map 1: Where to Eat and Stay in Old San Juan."

$$$$
SEAFOOD

✕ **Aguaviva.** The name means "jellyfish," which explains why this ultra-modern place has dim blue lighting like a tranquil ocean, and lamps shaped like jellyfish floating overhead. Eating here is like submerging oneself into the sea. The extensive, ever-changing menu by Chef Hector Crespo features inventive ceviches, including the truffle tuna tartare with cucumber and green apple. For something more filling, try the lobster yuca gnocchi or the orzo paella, which is generously covered with an assortment of seafood. Chicken and chorizo with saffron beurre blanc are added to the dish making it oh so tasty and enough for two. You could also splurge on one of the *torres del mar,* or "towers of the sea." This gravity-defying dish comes hot or cold and includes oysters, mussels, shrimp—you name it. Don't pass up the Oysters Rockefeller; those alone are worth the trip. $ *Average main: $31 ⊠ 364 Calle Fortaleza, Old San Juan* ☎ *787/722–0665* ⊕ *www.oofrestaurants.com* ⊙ *No lunch* ⊕ *1:F4.*

$
BURGER

✕ **Bistro Burger.** After exploring El Morro, head to Bistro Burger on Calle San Sebastian for what locals consider the best burgers in town. Choose from the house burgers, all named after local artists, or build your own burger with homemade ingredients. The Daphne Elvira is a great choice made with chorizo and pork, Manchego cheese, red onion, and *acerola* (Caribbean cherry) ketchup on fresh foccacia bread. Don't leave without trying the *ropa vieja* egg rolls made with tender, stewed beef. The kitchen is open late on weekends, making Bistro Burger the perfect place to grab a bite after bar hopping on Calle San Sebastian. $ *Average main: $9 ⊠ 157 Calle San Sebastian,*

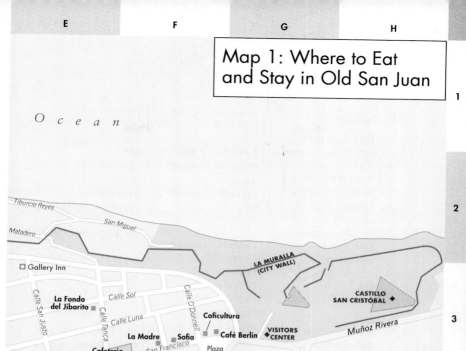

Map 1: Where to Eat and Stay in Old San Juan

Ocean

Tiburcio Reyes

San Miguel

Matadero

LA MURALLA
(CITY WALL)

Gallery Inn

Calle San Justo

Calle Tanca

Calle Sol

Calle Luna

Calle O'Donnell

CASTILLO
SAN CRISTÓBAL

La Fonda
del Jibarito

Caficultura

Muñoz Rivera

La Madre   Sofía   Café Berlin   VISITORS
CENTER

Cafetería
Mallorca

Calle San Francisco

Plaza
de Colón

Ponce de Léon

La Bombonera

Da House

Paseo Covadonga

Marmalade   Parrot Club

Casa Cortés
Chocobar

Hotel Milano   Calle Fortaleza   Aguaviva

Dragonfly

CasaBlanca
Hotel

Cuatro
Sombras

Toro Salao

Carli's Fine
Dining
& Piano

Calle Tetuán

Raíces   Recinto Sur

Brumbaugh St.

Calle del Muelle

FRANK SANTAELLA
PARKING GARAGE

TERMINAL DE GUAGUAS
(BUS TERMINAL)

FREE TROLLEY

Gen. Harding

Comercio   Pershing

Paseo Gilberto Concepcion de Gracia

SAN JUAN TOURIST
INFORMATION CENTER

Plaza

PRTC TOURIST
INFORMATION CENTER

Sheraton Old
San Juan Hotel & Casino

Pier 2

San Juan
Cruise Ship
Ports

Pier 3

Pier 1

Pier 4

Plazoleta
de San Juan

Bahía de San Juan

FERRY TO
CATAÑO

0   500ft

0   200m

BEST BETS FOR SAN JUAN DINING

Fodor's Choice ★

1919, $$$$, p. 75

Café Cuatro Sombras, $, p. 68

José Enrique, $$$, p. 81

Marmalade, $$$$, p. 72

Pikayo, $$$$, p. 79

Santaella, $$$, p. 81

St. Germain Bistro & Café, $, p. 73

Verde Mesa, $$$, p. 74

By Price

$

Bistro Burger, p. 65

Cafetería Mallorca, p. 69

Casa Cortés ChocoBar, p. 70

St. Germain Bistro & Café, p. 73

$$

Café Berlin, p. 68

El Patio de Sam, p. 70

Kasalta, p. 83

La Fonda del Jibarito, p. 71

$$$

Carli's Fine Dining & Piano, p. 69

Dragonfly, p. 70

El Picoteo, p. 70

La Cucina di Ivo, p. 71

Parrot Club, p. 73

Raíces, p. 73

Santaella, p. 81

Sofia Italian Kitchen, p. 73

Toro Salao, p. 74

Verde Mesa, p. 74

$$$$

1919, p. 75

Aguaviva, p. 65

Budatai, p. 78

Marmalade, p. 72

Pikayo, p. 79

By Experience

MOST ROMANTIC

Budatai, $$$$, p. 78

1919, $$$$, p. 75

BEST LOCAL FOOD

José Enrique, $$$, p. 81

Casita Miramar, $$, p. 82

La Jaquita Baya, $$, p. 83

Old San Juan ☎ 787/245-9062 ⊘ *Closed Mon. and Tues. No dinner Sun.* ✢ 1:D3.

$$ ✕ **Café Berlin.** A handful of tables spill onto a sidewalk deck lit with
INTERNATIONAL tiny lights at this bohemian and romantic restaurant overlooking Plaza
FAMILY Colón. There's something on the international menu for everyone, from
a tropical salmon dish with mango and mofongo to a New Orleans–
style muffaletta sandwich. There are also quite a few good vegan and
vegetarian dishes, including the meatless tacos with beans, cilantro, and
tomatoes, topped with feta cheese and served with a Caribbean rice that
includes sundried tomatoes and sweet plantains. Returning patrons get
a free *manjito* (a mango mojito) with an entrée order. Breakfast and
brunch on the first Sunday of every month are also popular; try the
banana raisin pancakes and the freshly baked breads. ⑤ *Average main:
$19* ✉ 407 Calle San Francisco, Old San Juan ☎ 787/722–5205 ⊕ *www.
cafeberlinpr.net* ✢ 1:F3.

$ ✕ **Café Cuatro Sombras.** If you want to try locally grown, single-origin,
CAFÉ shade-grown coffee, this micro-roastery and café is the place to do it.
Fodor's Choice Owners Pablo Muñoz and Mariana Suárez grow their beans in the
★ mountains of Yauco on a hacienda that has been in Muñoz family since
1846. The wood planks that line the banquette are from repurposed cof-
fee storage pallets, and the red accents that catch your eye throughout
the room recall perfectly ripe coffee beans. The name Cuatro Sombras,
or "four shades," refers to the four types of trees traditionally used
in Puerto Rico to provide shade for coffee plants. And although it's

the delicious, medium-bodied brew that steals the show, there's also a small but tasty menu of pastries and sandwiches. $ *Average main: $7* ⊠ *259 Calle Recinto Sur, Old San Juan* ☎ *787/724–9955* ⊕ *www. cuatrosombras.com* ⊗ *No dinner* ✢ *1:E4.*

$

CAFÉ

✗ **Café Don Ruiz.** Tucked away in the corner of the old Spanish military barracks, Café don Ruiz serves some of the finest coffee in town. The famil-run hacienda from Yauco is known for its handpicked coffee, grown over 3,000 feet above sea level. Our favorite is the medium dark roast, well balanced with essences of chocolate, caramel, and citrus. The shop also sells fruit frappés, sandwiches, and crepes. $ *Average main: $5* ⊠ *Cuartel de Ballaja, Calle Norzagaray corner Beneficencia, Old San Juan* ☎ *787/723–1462* ⊕ *www.cafedonruiz.com* ⊗ *Closed Mon.* ✢ *1:D3.*

$

CAFÉ

✗ **Cafetería Mallorca.** The specialty at this old-fashioned, 1950s-style diner is the *mallorca,* a sweet pastry that's buttered, grilled, and then sprinkled with powdered sugar. Wash one down with a cup of *café con leche.* For something more substantial, try the breakfast mallorca, which has ham and cheese; the menu also includes pancakes, egg dishes, sandwiches, and *comida criolla.* The waitstaff—all dressed in black uniforms—are friendly and efficient and most have worked there for years. It gets packed on weekends with locals, who consider it an institution. You pay at the counter on your way out. $ *Average main: $10* ⊠ *300 Calle San Francisco, Old San Juan* ☎ *787/724–4607* ⊗ *Closed after 5:30 pm* ✢ *1:F3.*

$$

CAFÉ

✗ **Caficultura.** One of the best cafés to open in San Juan in recent years, Caficultura prides itself both on its full coffee-bar menu and its delicious *cocina de mercado.* Many ingredients are sourced locally, and the menu changes by the season. For breakfast, which is served all day, try coconut milk French toast with pineapple jam and coconut shavings. Numerous vegetarian options are available, especially at lunch, when you'll also find many delicious gourmet sandwiches and heartier dishes on offer. The building is beautifully restored: distressed concrete walls meet an old, Spanish-style wood-beamed ceiling—hanging from it is a magnificent antique chandelier. The customers skew young and intellectual, with students, university professors, and museumgoing tourists all part of the mix. The youthful waitstaff is always friendly, but the downside is that no one seems in a rush to get the food to the table. $ *Average main: $15* ⊠ *401 Calle San Francisco, Old San Juan* ☎ *787/723–7731* ⊗ *No dinner* ✢ *1:F3.*

$$$

INTERNATIONAL

✗ **Carli's Fine Dining & Piano.** As you might guess from the name, the music is as much of a draw as the food at Carli's. The genial owner and host, Carli Muñoz, toured for a number of years with the Beach Boys (note the gold album on the wall) and plays nightly with his jazz trio, often accompanied by singers and musicians who happen to drop in. Inside the skyline-dominating Banco Popular building, this intimate supper-club bistro has elegant tables scattered around the room and a bar made of black Italian granite. Have a seat indoors or on the outdoor patio, and dine on such fusion specialties as New Zealand sautéed green mussels, U.S. filet mignon with wild mushroom sauce, or blackened ahi tuna with Cajun spices. $ *Average main: $25*

✉ *Plazoleta Rafael Carrión, Calle Recinto Sur and Calle San Justo, Old San Juan* ☎ *787/725–4927* ⊕ *www.carlisworld.com* ☯ *Closed Sun. No lunch* ✛ *1:E4.*

$
CONTEMPORARY

✕ **Casa Cortés ChocoBar.** The Cortés family has been making bean-to-bar chocolate for over 85 years and in 2013, they openend up Puerto Rico's first Choco Bar to share their passion with the world. The walls in this vivid, modern space are decorated with vintage ads from the 50s, original chocolate bar molds, a timeline of chocolate, and two flat screens that depict the family's chocolate-making process. From pastries to tapas, breakfast dishes to panini sandwiches, the chef successfully integrates chocolate into every bite without overpowering the dish. Try the ripe plantain *mofonguitos* filled with chocolate and bacon bits. The pan-fried jumbo shrimp with a chocolate lemon sauce are delicious! Locals from all over the San Juan metro area flock to ChocoBar for weekend brunch—arrive early to avoid a long wait. On Thursday, Saturday, and Sunday head upstairs to the gallery for a glimpse of the family's private art collection. ⑤ *Average main: $10* ✉ *210 Calle San Francisco, Old San Juan* ☎ *787/722–0499* ⊕ *www.casacortespr.com* ☯ *Closed Mon. No dinner* ✛ *1:E4.*

$$$
LATIN AMERICAN

✕ **Dragonfly.** Dark and sexy, this popular Latin-Asian restaurant, all done up in Chinese red, feels more like a fashionable after-hours lounge than a restaurant. The romantic ambience, created partly through tightly packed tables and low lighting, is a big draw. The small plates, meant to be shared, come in generous portions. Don't miss the Peking duck nachos and the pork and sweet plantain dumplings. Tuna sushi is turned on its head and served atop a deep-fried rice cake dressed with spicy mayo and seaweed salad. Make sure to try the inventive cocktails that nicely complement the food. Reservations aren't accepted, but we'll let you in on a secret to save yourself a frustrating wait: you can call ahead and get yourself put on the waiting list. ⑤ *Average main: $21* ✉ *364 Calle Fortaleza, Old San Juan* ☎ *787/977–3886* ⊕ *www.oofrestaurants.com* ⚱ *Reservations not accepted* ☯ *No lunch* ✛ *1:F4.*

$$
PUERTO RICAN

✕ **El Patio de Sam.** A great selection of more than 30 beers, including the locally brewed Medalla, makes this a popular "come as you are" spot, whether at the end of the workweek or after a long day of sightseeing. Just as appealing is the airy courtyard with a skylight that gives the place its name. The menu consists mostly of American and Puerto Rican fare. Save room for the homemade flan, which melts in your mouth. ⑤ *Average main: $16* ✉ *102 Calle San Sebastián, Old San Juan* ☎ *787/723–1149* ✛ *1:C3.*

$$$
SPANISH

✕ **El Picoteo.** You could make a meal of the small dishes that dominate the menu at this tapas restaurant on a mezzanine balcony at the Hotel El Convento, once a Carmelite convent. You won't go wrong ordering the grilled cuttlefish or the pistachio-crusted salmon with a Manchego-cheese sauce and passing them around the table. If you're not into sharing, there are several kinds of paella that arrive on huge plates. There's a long, lively bar inside; one dining area overlooks a pleasant courtyard, and the other looks out onto Calle Cristo. Even if you have dinner plans elsewhere, consider stopping here for a nightcap

Hotel El Convento's El Picoteo restaurant serves tasty tapas and generous paella.

or a midday pick-me-up. $ *Average main: $22* ✉ *Hotel El Convento, 100 Calle Cristo, Old San Juan* ☎ *787/723–9202* ⊕ *www.elconvento. com* ✛ *1:D3.*

$$$ ✕ **La Cucina di Ivo.** A pretty courtyard just steps from the cathedral has
ITALIAN been transformed into this traditional trattoria. The staff enters and leaves through leaded-glass doors on either side of the central courtyard that lead to the bar, the wine cellar, and intimate dining rooms. You'll want to dine alfresco, as ceiling fans keep everything cool. A fountain bubbles on one side of the courtyard, and rows of potted fig trees surround the wrought-iron café tables. The place is named for chef Ivo Bignami, and the kitchen turns out specialties of his native Milan. For a lighter meal, or a first course big enough to share with your date, order the light, fluffy gnocchi. Entrées include a wide range of pasta and risotto dishes, plus such mouthwatering temptations as filet mignon in truffle sauce. For dessert, try the classic and tasty tiramisu. $ *Average main: $24* ✉ *202 Calle Cristo, Old San Juan* ☎ *787/729–7070* ⊕ *www. lacucinadiivo.com* ☾ *Closed Sun.* ✛ *1:D4.*

$$ ✕ **La Fonda del Jibarito.** The menus are handwritten and the tables
PUERTO RICAN wobble, but *sanjuaneros* have favored this casual, no-frills, family-run restaurant—tucked away on a quiet cobbled street—for years. The *bistec encebollado*, goat fricassee, and shredded beef stew are among the specialties on the menu of typical Puerto Rican *comida criolla* dishes. The tiny back porch is filled with plants, and the dining room is filled with fanciful depictions of life on the street outside. Troubadors serenade patrons, which include plenty of cruise-ship passengers when ships are in dock. $ *Average main: $14* ✉ *280 Calle Sol, Old San Juan* ☎ *787/725–8375* ✛ *1:E3.*

Pineapples, plantains, and coconuts are among the bounty of locally grown produce found in markets and stands throughout the island.

$$ ✕ **La Madre.** La Madre is a hip Mexican restaurant, with a stylish young
MEXICAN   customer base to match. Yes, it covers the standards, including some
very tasty fish tacos, but you'll also find innovative, modern, interna-
tional interpretations of Mexican cuisine, like a Japanese-style mari-
nated skirt steak with mashed plantains and grilled corn, or pork ribs
marinated in beer and served with a chocolate-chili sauce. With well-
priced margaritas, you can afford to try several of the unusual flavors,
such as cucumber, soursop, Caribbean cherry, and tamarind. The sleek
dining room feels artsy and dreamlike, with classic cartoons and old
movies projected silently onto a wall. ⑤ *Average main: $18* ⊠ *351 Calle
San Francisco, Old San Juan* ☎ *787/647–5392* ✛ *1:F3.*

$$$$ ✕ **Marmalade.** Prepare to be impressed when you enter Old San Juan's
ECLECTIC   hippest—and finest—restaurant. Its U.S.-born owner-chef, Peter
Fodor's Choice   Schintler, apprenticed with Raymond Blanc and Gordon Ramsay;
★   here he's created a class act that's famous for its ultra-chic lounge
bar. The restaurant's sensual and minimalist orange-and-white decor
features high-back chairs and cushioned banquettes beneath recessed
halogen lights. The menu uses many sustainable and non-modified
ingredients prepared California-French fashion, resulting in complex
flavors and strong aromas. The yellowtail is served with lemongrass
and compressed watermelon while the pork cheeks are served with a
peach-poblano marmalade. For dessert, indulge in the Millionnaire's
ice cream, topped with honeycomb and shaved truffles. You can build
your own four- to six-course tasting menu, with or without pairings
from the *Wine Spectator* Award of Excellence wine list, or order à la
carte. In addition, the restaurant is accommodating to vegetarians,

vegans, and those with food allergies and/or dietary restrictions. Ⓢ *Average main: $32* ✉ *317 Calle Fortaleza, Old San Juan* ☎ *787/724–3969* ⊕ *www.marmaladepr.com* ⌖ *Reservations essential* ☾ *No lunch* ✛ *1:F4.*

$$$
LATIN AMERICAN
FAMILY

✕ **The Parrot Club.** Loud and lively, this place is intent on making sure everyone is having a good time. You're likely to strike up a conversation with the bartender as you enjoy the signature passion-fruit cocktail or with a couple at the next table in the covered courtyard. Something about the atmosphere—laid-back Caribbean decor, including murals of palm trees—makes connecting easy. The menu has contemporary variations of Latin classics. You might start with the *ropa vieja* (Caribbean-style stewed beef) nachos served with root vegetable chips followed by lime-infused grouper baked *en papillote* (in parchment) or roasted pork loin with sweet plantain and *arroz mamposteao*. There's also a full kid's menu available and live music, usually Thursday and Saturday nights. Ⓢ *Average main: $23* ✉ *363 Calle Fortaleza, Old San Juan* ☎ *787/725–7370* ⊕ *www.oofrestaraunts.com* ✛ *1:F3.*

$$$
PUERTO RICAN

✕ **Raíces.** You can't miss this lively restaurant thanks to the waitresses in all-white *campesina* (peasant) dresses. Themed as a country venue, with artsy re-creations of rustic life, the whole atmosphere feels a bit Disneyfied, but it doesn't stop the locals and tourists—who have seen it featured on various TV shows—from packing in for the *criolla* fare. The food is a tad overhyped, but the crowds willing to wait an hour or more for a table seem to disagree. The signature dishes are the giant deep-fried *Kan Kan* pork chop and mofongo with *churrasco* (marinated shirt steak). The garlic shrimp mofongo, served country-style in a *pilón* (pestle), is quite tasty. Drinks come in tin mugs, including fruity frappes. Ⓢ *Average main: $21* ✉ *315 Calle Recinto Sur, Old San Juan* ☎ *787/289–2121* ⊕ *www.restauranteraices.com* ⌖ *Reservations not accepted* ✛ *1:F4.*

$$$
ITALIAN

✕ **Sofia Italian Kitchen & Bar.** Everything in this red-walled and warmly atmospheric trattoria is the real deal, making it a delightful respite from busy Calle San Francisco. The calamari friti is a great starter, and standout entrees include the linguine alla pescatora with assorted seafood in a light pomodoro sauce and the filet mignon risotto. The plates of pasta are huge, so you might want to consider their still-generous half-order. Thin crust, Neapolitan-style pizzas are also available, and the braised osso buco with creamy polenta and baked tomatoes is a house specialty. Save room for—what else?—a tasty tiramisu or chocolate mousse. There's also a small but carefully edited wine list and a revamped cocktail menu. Ⓢ *Average main: $25* ✉ *355 Calle San Francisco, Old San Juan* ☎ *787/721–0396* ⊕ *www.ristorantesofia.com* ✛ *1:F3.*

$
INTERNATIONAL
Fodor's Choice
★

✕ **St. Germain Bistro & Café.** One of the city's hidden treasures, this charming French-inspired café-restaurant stands on a quiet cobbled street corner. The interior is just as inviting, with rustic white wooden tables and benches. St. Germain delivers exceptionally fresh, made-from-scratch food and friendly service. With an emphasis on seasonal, locally sourced ingredients, the menu leans slightly (but not entirely!) vegetarian and includes gourmet sandwiches, entrée salads, quiches, and pita pizzas. (Its lightness can be a welcome respite after you've been sampling the delicious but often-heavy *comida criolla*.) Start with an *agua fresca*, a mildly sweet fruit water that revives you quickly, even on the hottest of days. Then choose from options such as a refreshing grouper and shrimp ceviche, mushroom-and-Brie soup, or a spinach and mango salad with Dijon vinaigrette. Save room for the just-baked cakes that tempt you from glass stands on the counter. Sunday brunch is wildly popular, so come early, or stop by later in the evening for crepes and wine. ⑤ *Average main: $10* ✉ *156 Calle Sol, Old San Juan* ☎ *787/725–5830* ⊕ *www.stgermainpr.com* ⌦ *Reservations not accepted* ⊗ *Closed Mon.* ✛ *1:D3.*

$$$

SPANISH

✕ **Toro Salao.** The name means "Salty Bull," and there's something about this place that makes its moniker entirely appropriate. (And it's not just the bullfighting posters that decorate one of the two-story-high walls.) This popular Spanish-Puerto Rican tapas restaurant was opened by Emilio Figueroa, who helped turn the southern end of Calle Fortaleza into the city's top dining destination. There are plenty of small dishes to share, such as the pork in a sangria reduction; the tender seared octopus salad; and Spanish-style flatbread pizzas, called *cocas*. The dining room, with a bar lit up in lusty red, is pleasant enough, but the tables that spill onto the adjacent cobblestone square are even better, perfect for people-watching. Pair your tapas with a tropical white sangria, infused with brandy or our favorite, the refreshing rosemary mojito. Stop in on Saturday night for live Latin jazz. ⑤ *Average main: $25* ✉ *367 Calle Tetuán, Old San Juan* ☎ *787/722–3330* ⊕ *www.oofrestaurants.com* ⊗ *No lunch Jun.–Oct.* ✛ *1:F4.*

$$$

VEGETARIAN

Fodor's Choice

★

✕ **Verde Mesa.** With punched-tin ceilings, Mason-jar lighting fixtures, and eclectic decor inspired by Versailles' Petit Trianon, the focus at this vegetarian restaurant is on pleasing the senses. Much of the organic produce used in the regularly changing menu comes from the owners' farm and other local sources. The flavor combinations are anything but accidental. Start with a garlicky "hummus" of local pigeon peas. The signature Verde Mesa rice is a mixture of in-season vegetables and chickpeas that the owners say has turned many a skeptic into further exploring the culinary potential of vegetables. You'll also find quite a few expertly prepared tuna, salmon and scallop dishes, if you don't want to go all veggie. Your salmon might be cured with lavender and ginger and your scallop dish migh be served on a bed of parsnip mash, dressed with fig foam. Reservations are not accepted so arrive early; restaurant opens at 6 pm. ⑤ *Average main: $22* ✉ *107 Calle Tetuán, at Calle San José, Old San Juan* ☎ *787/390–4662* ⊕ *www.verdemesa. com* ⌦ *Reservations not accepted* ⊗ *Closed Sun. and Mon. No lunch* ✛ *1:D4.*

$

CAFÉ

✕ **Waffle-era Tea Room.** The only tearoom in Puerto Rico is hugely popular, and it recently relocated to a larger space where they now take reservations, making locals very happy. You can choose from nearly 30 loose teas, including white and fruity blends as well as black. The carefully crafted cocktail menu is a nice addition to the new space. But you'll probably be even more curious about the coffee setup, which looks like a mad-science experiment. It's a siphon fire-brewing system, a painstaking process popular in Japan. The menu consists of house-made sweet or savory waffles—or smaller "wafflitos," and a revamped tapas menu thats includes the signature ham-hugged dates. These savory delicacies are stuffed with Gorgonzola and cherry tomatoes, wrapped in fire-torched, brandy-infused prosciutto. You might also choose a "waffle-izza" with fresh tomato sauce and blowtorch-melted mozzarella. We're still thinking of the decadent crème brûlée wafflito. At the time of this writing, the plan is to keep open the original location at 103 Calle Tetuan. ⑤ *Average main: $9* ⌧ *252 Calle San José, Old San Juan* ☎ *787/721–9512* ⊕ *www.waffle-era.com* ⊘ *Closed Tues. and Wed. No dinner* ✛ *1:D4.*

PUERTA DE TIERRA

Use the coordinate (✛ 2:A1) at the end of each listing to locate a site on the corresponding "Map 2: Where to Eat and Stay in Greater San Juan."

$$$ ✕**Lemongrass.** Whether you sit inside the pagoda-style building or on
ASIAN the large outdoor terrace of this chic restaurant, you'll feel as if you've truly escaped to another world. Try their inventive sushi, such as the smoked salmon, Brie, and lingonberry roll. If you're not in the mood for fish, other options include spare ribs with tamarind sauce and fried yucca or lo-mein with crispy chicken cracklings. The ginger-orange and cardamon ice cream is a sweet finish. ⑤ *Average main: $27* ⌧ *Caribe Hilton, 1 San Gerónimo Grounds, Puerta de Tierra* ☎ *787/724–5888* ⊕ *www.lemongrasspr.com* ⊘ *No lunch* ✛ *2:B2.*

CONDADO

Use the coordinate (✛ 2:A1) at the end of each listing to locate a site on the corresponding "Map 2: Where to Eat and Stay in Greater San Juan."

$$$$ ✕**1919.** Michelin-starred Chef José Cuevas successfully operates this
ECLECTIC fine-dining restaurant in San Juan's most striking hotel, once home
Fodor's Choice to the Vanderbilt family. The main dining room is set on the Atlan-
★ tic Ocean, elegant and sophisticated, large yet intimate where tables are spread out to allow for privacy and comfort. Brazilian tiger wood tables, dark wooden floors, and three striking chandeliers with drooping pearl shells are remniscent of the Gatsby era. The Puerto-Rican born chef presents international cuisine with a strong focus on local ingredients. Choose from the prix-fixe menu or order a la carte. Standout dishes include eggplant confit in tomato water with local cucumber, clams *escabeche*, calabaza ravioli with sage brown butter, and the *chicharrones gremolata*. For pairings, choose from a 200+ wine selection or take advantage of the champagne table service. ⑤ *Average main: $36* ⌧ *The Vanderbilt Hotel, 1055 Av. Ashford, Condado* ☎ *787/724–1919* ⊕ *www.1919restaurant.com* ⊘ *Closed Sun. and Mon.; no lunch on Sat.* ✛ *2:C2.*

$$ ✕**Ali Baba.** Tucked discreetly off Ashford Avenue, Ali Baba turns out
MIDDLE EASTERN delicious, meticulously prepared Middle Eastern and Mediterranean food, thanks to its Turkish chef-owner. Given how unpretentious this small place is, the presentation is surprisingly elegant. Start with the

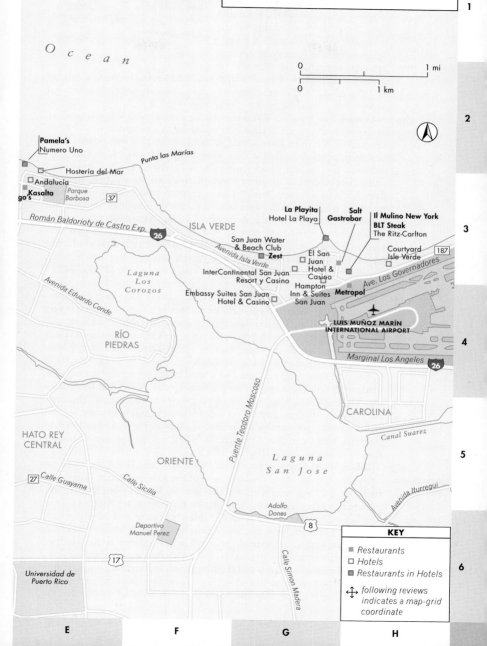

Map 2: Where to Eat and Stay in Greater San Juan

0   1 mi

0   1 km

Ocean

Pamela's
Numero Uno
Hostería del Mar
Andalucía
Kasalta
go's
Parque
Barbosa
37

Punta las Marías

Román Baldorioty de Castro Exp.
26

ISLA VERDE

Avenida Isla Verde

La Playita
Hotel La Playa

**Salt
Gastrobar**

**Il Mulino New York
BLT Steak**
The Ritz-Carlton

San Juan Water
& Beach Club
Zest

El San
Juan
Hotel &
Casino

**Courtyard
Isle Verde**
187

InterContinental San Juan
Resort y Casino

Hampton
Inn & Suites
San Juan

Embassy Suites San Juan
Hotel & Casino

Metropol

Ave. Los Governadores

**LUIS MUÑOZ MARÍN
INTERNATIONAL AIRPORT**

Avenida Eduardo Conde

Laguna
Los
Corozos

**RÍO
PIEDRAS**

Marginal Los Angeles
26

CAROLINA

Canal Suarez

**HATO REY
CENTRAL**

27 Calle Guayama

Calle Sicilia

ORIENTE

Puente Teodoro Moscoso

Laguna
San Jose

Avenida Iturregui

Deportivo
Manuel Perez

17

Adolfo
Dones

8

Calle Simon Madera

**Universidad de
Puerto Rico**

KEY

■ Restaurants
□ Hotels
■ Restaurants in Hotels

✛ following reviews
indicates a map-grid
coordinate

hummus, served with steaming homemade lavash, or the grilled cheese with fresh herbs and tomatoes. Entrées include an *iskender* kebab drizzled with browned goat butter, and moussaka, which is served warm, beneath a flame.

Sandwiches and vegetarian options are also available. Arrive early to avoid a long wait. $ *Average main: $15* ✉ *1214 Av. Ashford, Condado* ☎ *787/722–1176* ⊕ *www.alibabarestaurantpr.com* ⌀ *Reservations not accepted* ⊙ *Closed Mon. No dinner Sun.* ✛ *2:C2.*

$$$$ ✕ **Budatai.** You'll feel as if you're entering a secret club when you arrive
ASIAN at this stylish hot spot in Condado's poshest shopping district. The restaurant, on the third floor, is decked out in rich, dark colors, with Chinese lanterns that look as if they were designed by Salvador Dalí. The attentive service and the elegantly dressed crowd, however, never feel stuffy. The brainchild of one of Puerto Rico's best-known chefs, Roberto Treviño, it's a seamless mix of Latin-accented pan-Asian food, including duck fried rice with sweet plantains, pork dumplings, and halibut sashimi with coconut, yuzu, and toasted garlic. We couldn't get enough of the calamari, fried for a few seconds in hot oil and then quickly sautéed with sweet onions. The upstairs outdoor terrace is a good place to sip on their specialty cocktails, and there's brunch served on Sunday. $ *Average main: $34* ✉ *1056 Av. Ashford, Condado* ☎ *787/725–6919* ⊕ *www.budatai.com* ✛ *2:C2.*

$$ ✕ **di Parma.** This Italian trattoria in the Ventana al Mar Park only steps
PIZZA away from the ocean is a great choice for dining alfresco. Prices are very reasonable by Condado standards, and the service is above par. Start with the fresh tuna crostini with Brie or the signature tomato bruschetta. There are several pastas on the menu, but we opted for the stone oven pizzas. The traditional margherita is well executed, with fresh mozzarella di bufala and thin, crispy dough. For a local twist, try the Puertorriqueña, made with Bolognese sauce, ripe plantains, local cheese, and fresh cilantro. There is also a large variety of veggie pastas and pizzas. The small bar has a surprisingly large selection of whiskeys and bourbons, and the $28 wine list is unbeatable in the area. $ *Average main: $18* ✉ *1049 Av. Ashford, Ventana al Mar, Condado* ☎ *787/725–5202* ⊕ *www.diparmapr. com* ⊙ *No lunch Mon.–Thurs.* ✛ *2:C2.*

$$$ ✕ **O:liva.** Tucked away in the stylish O:live Boutique Hotel, the cuisine at
MEDITERRANEAN O:liva is a tribute to the coastal towns of the Mediterranean. The small, rustic chic dining area with wooden accents has an open kitchen and an array of artisan olive oils hanging on the wall. Chef Nicolas Gomez is a huge advocate of the farm-to-table movement and he utilizes the freshest local ingredients to complement his dishes. Whether it's French, Moroccan, Italian, or Spanish, you will be transported to the Mediterranean without leaving your table. Start with the roasted *korobuta* on a sweet Gorgonzola risotto and the foie gras with organic pumpkin marmalade. Then its up to you whether you want to visit Italy and sample the gnocchi with creamy pistachio pesto or head to France for the

duck breast. $⑤$ *Average main: $30* ✉ *O:live Boutique Hotel, 55 Calle Aguadilla, Condado* ☎ *787/705–9994* ⊕ *www.oliveboutiquehotel.com* ⊘ *Closed Sun. and Mon. No lunch.* ✛ *2:B2.*

$$$$
SEAFOOD
✕ **Perla.** Perla is an architectural wonder, and the most striking restaurant in San Juan. As soon as you step into the shell-shaped dining room, illuminated by artichoke lamps made from Murano glass, its seems as if you've entered a luxurious ocean liner. The kitchen is headed by Chef Lindell Smith, son of Dayn Smith, the restaurant's founder. After graduating from the Culinary Institute of America, Lindell worked under top chef José Andrés at Zaytinya in Washington, D.C. The cuisine at Perla is modern American, with a strong focus on seafood. The grilled prawns in a coconut-curry sauce are the perfect combination of sweet and spicy. Splurge on the baked lobster tail with lobster beurre blanc, grilled Swiss chard, and truffled mashed potatoes—a wonderful dish! Save room for dessert—the coconut cream cheese custard is the perfect way to end the evening. $⑤$ *Average main: $43* ✉ *1077 Av. Ashford, La Concha Hotel, Condado* ☎ *787/977–3285* ⊕ *http://perlarestaurant.com* ✍ *Reservations essential* ⊘ *No lunch.* ✛ *2:C2.*

$$$$
ECLECTIC
Fodor'sChoice
★
✕ **Pikayo.** Celebrity chef and Puerto Rico native Wilo Benet's flagship restaurant makes the most of its elegant surroundings at the Conrad San Juan Condado Plaza hotel. Works from local artists line the walls, and the atmosphere is formal but never hushed. The menu offers a twist on traditional Puerto Rican classics as well as more international flavors. Choose from the thoughtfully crafted tasting menu or order à la carte. There is a large selection of starters; particularly good are the pork belly sliders, the spicy tuna on crispy rice (known here as *pegao*), and the foie gras with ripe plantains and black truffle honey. For main courses, options include succulent petit duck magret with crimini mushrooms and a raspberry vinegar gastrique and North Atlantic swordfish in a pigeon pea *escabeche* with a ripe plantain emulsion. Don't be surprised if Benet himself stops by your table to make sure everything is just to your liking. $⑤$ *Average main: $37* ✉ *Conrad Condado Plaza, 999 Ashford Ave., Condado* ☎ *787/721–6194* ⊕ *www.wilobenet.com/pikayo* ⊘ *No lunch* ✛ *2:B2.*

$
CAFÉ
FAMILY
✕ **Pinky's.** High school students, tourists, and locals all pack in for some of the freshest wraps and sandwiches in town at this playful café, where the bustling servers wear cheeky "Eat Me!" T-shirts. You might not need another meal for the rest of the day if you manage to finish the Drunken Pilot, a breakfast dish that includes four eggs, spinach, tomato, onion, mushroom, and goat cheese. (Breakfast is available all day.) At lunch, try the popular Surfer, a hot, pressed sandwich with turkey, mozzarella, basil, tomato, and pesto mayo. Finally settling in to its new home in Condado after previous stints in Ocean Park and Santurce, Pinky's is also well-known for salads, *batidas* (fruit smoothies), and coffee. It's often nearly impossible to find a seat at lunchtime, but don't worry: order your food to go, and head to the beach to enjoy it alfresco. $⑤$ *Average main: $8* ✉ *1451 Av. Ashford, Suite 100B, Condado* ☎ *787/222–5222* ✍ *Reservations not accepted* ✛ *2:D3.*

$ ✕ **Via Appia.** Popular for decades with everyone from local politicians
ITALIAN   and families to sunburned tourists who just dragged themselves off the
FAMILY   beach, the bustling Via Appia is a no-frills restaurant that serves food
just as tasty as its higher-priced *paisanos*. They're particularly known
for their simple Italian dishes (we usually just stick with the pizza), but
during lunch, they dish up some delicious comida criolla, with specials
changing every day; try the *pollo guisado* (chicken stew) on Mondays.
The outdoor-seating area looks out on Condado's busy Ashford Avenue,
which makes for good people-watching. The wine bar next door has a
bit more ambience. ⑤ *Average main: $12* ✉ *1350 Av. Ashford, Condado*
☎ *787/725–8711* ✥ *2:C2.*

$$$ ✕ **Yerba Buena.** Tables on the terrace are hard to come by at this Cuban
CUBAN   restaurant, one of the busier spots in Condado. That's fine, because
the glassed-in dining room is even more comfortable and has exactly
the same view. Cuban classics such as *ropa vieja* ("old clothes"—meat
cooked so slowly that it becomes tender shreds) seamlessly comple-
ment local dishes served with imaginative presentation. The shrimp
has a coconut-and-ginger sauce; the halibut fillet, one of mango and
orange liqueur. The restaurant claims to use the "original" recipe for
its *mojito*, Cuba's tasty rum, lime, and mint drink. Live Latin music is
played on Monday, Friday, and Saturday nights. Don't miss the 17-piece
big band on Monday nights; get there early to grab a seat. ⑤ *Average
main: $25* ✉ *1350 Av. Ashford, Condado* ☎ *787/721–5700* ⊕ *www.
yerbabuenapr.com* ✥ *2:D2.*

SANTURCE

*Use the coordinate (✥ 2:A1) at the end of each listing to locate a site on
the corresponding "Map 2: Where to Eat and Stay in Greater San Juan."*

$$ ✕ **El Pescador.** If you want Spanish-style seafood dishes, head to El Pes-
SEAFOOD   cador at the Plaza del Mercado. Surrounding a fruit and vegetable
market that dates from 1910 are a few dozen restaurants that are the
real deal. Our favorite seafood restaurant is El Pescador, a narrow
storefront selling the freshest of seafood. If you come in the evening,
it might be cool enough to eat at one of the handful of tables on the
square. If not, settle for the green polka-dot tables in the dining room.
The *chillo entero frito* (fried whole red snapper) and *camarones al ajillo*
(shrimp with garlic) are tasty, but the standout is the *arroz con calamari*
(squid ink rice). This dramatic inky-black dish draws oohs and aahs
from surrounding customers when it arrives at your table. This is not a
late-night dinner place; they close at 7:30. ⑤ *Average main: $19* ✉ *178
Calle Dos Hermanos, Santurce* ☎ *787/721–0995* ✍ *Reservations not
accepted* ⊙ *Closed Mon.* ✥ *2:C3.*

$$$ ✕ **Gallo Negro.** Serving dishes that are difficult to find in San Juan,
MODERN   Gallo Negro operates in a small space reminiscent of a Brooklyn, New
AMERICAN   York, joint, with exposed brick walls and modern fixtures. Trained at
the French Culinary Institute, Chef María Mercedes expertly prepares
New American dishes, not tying herself to any particular cuisine.
The menu changes weekly but you will always find signatures such
as her Korean BBQ with daikon and kimchi or the duck breast in a

ginger and acerola glaze on a bed of mushroom risotto. Other days Vietnamese pho or Tonkotsu ramen are served. Besides great food, Gallo Negro is a whiskey bar with over 60 whiskeys in stock. Enjoy them neat or in a creative cocktail. Especially tasty is the Honey Old Fashioned made with honey peach syrup and Angostura. The area is not very welcoming at night so opt for a taxi, about a five-minute ride from Condado. Brunch is served on Sundays. ⑤ *Average main: $25* ✉ *1107 Av. Ponce de Leon, Santurce* 🖀 *787/554–5445* ⊘ *Closed Mon. No lunch.* ✛ *2:C2.*

$$$

PUERTO RICAN

Fodor's Choice

★

✕ José Enrique. Since 2007, Chef José Enrique's eponymous restaurant in La Placita de Santurce has been the preferred dining choice for locals. In 2013, the world started catching on when José was nominated for *Food & Wine* magazine's Best New Chefs. He is also the first Puerto Rican chef to receive the prestigious James Beard Award nomination, for a second consecutive year. At José Enrique, elevated Puerto Rican cuisine is served in a very casual setting that fits right in with the surroundings. The menu, brought to your table on an eraser board, changes all the time. The crab fitters are a staple as is the whole fried yellowtail snapper served over a root mash with avocado and papaya salsa. The restaurant's no reservation policy means that you will have to wait for your table. Put your name on the list and wander around La Placita, where you can sip on cheap drinks and mingle with the locals. ⑤ *Average main: $30* ✉ *176 Calle Duffaut, La Placita de Santurce, Santurce* 🖀 *787/725–3518* ⊕ *www.joseenriquepr. com* ⌦ *Reservations not accepted* ⊘ *Closed Sun. and Mon. No lunch Sat.* ✛ *2:C3.*

$$$

INTERNATIONAL

✕ Laurel Kitchen | Art Bar. After the popular Chayote closed, its chef-owner, Mario Pagán, moved shop to these elegant new digs in the Museo de Arte. As the host of cooking shows on Latin American television and a contestant on Food Network's *The Next Iron Chef*, Pagán is quite the showman; here he joyfully plays with familiar Puerto Rican ingredients and flavors, using haute-French techniques. His signature Chilean sea bass is served with an impossibly smooth yuca purée, over a port wine and foie gras reduction. Arugula salad with pancetta, papaya, goat cheese, and passion-fruit vinaigrette perfectly balances sour, salty, and sweet flavors. And crispy codfish *buñuelos* with cilantro-lime aioli recall the favorite Puerto Rican snack, *bacalaítos*. ⑤ *Average main: $30* ✉ *Museo de Arte de Puerto Rico, 299 Av. de Diego, Santurce* 🖀 *787/522–6444* ⊕ *www.laurelkitchenartbar.com* ⊘ *Closed Sun.–Mon. No lunch Sat.* ✛ *2:C3.*

$$$

PUERTO RICAN

Fodor's Choice

★

✕ Santaella. During his career, Chef José Santaella has trained with some of the best chefs in the world, including Ferrán Adriá, Eric Ripert, and Gary Danko. His apprenticeships and successful catering career paved the way for Santaella, his signature restaurant in Santurce's La Placita Marketplace. The neighborhood is anything but chic, but you'll see Santaella packed with well-dressed socialites, trendsetters, and the who's who of Puerto Rican society every night of the week. The decor is rustic yet elegant, with exposed walls, Edison light fixtures, an interior garden, and a sparkling bar. Chef Santaella fuses local and international ingredients to perfectly execute Puerto Rican nouvelle cuisine. The menu is dominated by tapas, which you can easily make into a meal. Our favorites include the ahi tuna skewers, goat cheese quesadilla, *morcilla* (blood sausage) fritters, and the foie gras terrine over fruit jam. The cocktail bar is one of the best on the island, so don't leave without trying one of the concoctions by Santaella's mixologists. We can't get enough of the Perfect Lady! ⑤ *Average main: $29* ⊠ *219 Calle Canals, La Placita de Santurce, Santurce* ☎ *787/725-1611* ⊕ *www.santaellapr.com* ☉ *Closed Sun. and Mon. No lunch Sat.* ✛ *2:C3*

MIRAMAR

$$$$ ✕ **Augusto's.** Under the direction of noted chef Ariel Rodríguez, this
EUROPEAN restaurant is one of the more celebrated in the San Juan area, popular with the city's elite. One of the few fine-dining restaurants left in San Juan, Augusto's serves well-executed international cuisine with strong, French influences. The osetra caviar with seared tuna is superb, and the venison carpaccio with shaved foie gras is outstanding. A prix fixe menu is also available with or without wine pairings. Begin with a classic cocktail like James Bond's Vesper Martini or chat with the sommelier, who will help you choose a bottle from the approximately 300 selections on the wine list. Local works of art decorate the walls of the formal, old-fashioned dining room, giving it a lively, modern touch. ⑤ *Average main: $32* ⊠ *Courtyard Marriott Miramar, 801 Av. Ponce de León, Miramar* ☎ *787/725–7700* ☉ *Closed Sun.–Mon. No lunch Sat.* ✛ *2:B2*.

$$$ ✕ **Bar Gitano.** Themed as a traditional Andalusian-style *tasca*, this
TAPAS extremely popular tapas bar is decorated with artwork created from Madrid bullfighting photographs. The marble bar and dark wood tables give an impression of casual elegance. The trendy crowd is always lively or borderline noisy, especially if there's a soccer match on. Celebrity chef Roberto Treviño serves a variety of tapas including blistered padrón peppers with salt and olive oil, dates wrapped with bacon and stuffed with Valdeón cheese, chargrilled octopus, *jamón Ibérico*, and *cocas* (Spanish flatbread pizzas). You'll also find paella and other main courses, if small plates aren't what you had in mind. Stop by for live flamenco on Thursday and Sunday nights. ⑤ *Average main: $25* ⊠ *1302 Av. Ashford, C-1, Condado* ☎ *787/294–5513* ⊕ *www.ootwrestaurants. com* ✛ *2:C2*.

$$ ✕ **Casita Miramar.** Nestled in the heart of Miramar, a predominantly
PUERTO RICAN residential neighborhood, Casita Miramar is a family-run restaurant known for its traditional comida criolla. It feels more like a home than a restaurant, which is what makes it such a great place to just sit back, relax, and enjoy your meal. Casita brings back Puerto Rican dishes that have long been forgotten by many restaurants, serving traditional favorites. The old photos of Miramar, vintage furniture, and colonial architecture will surely transport you back in time. The menu at Casita Miramar is written on a chalkboard and changes often, featuring local fruits, vegetables, and seasonal fish. ⑤ *Average main: $15* ⊠ *605 Av. Miramar, Miramar* ☎ *787/200–8227* ☉ *Closed Mon. and Tues.; no lunch Wed.—Fri.* ✛ *2:B2*

$$ ✗ **La Jaquita Baya.** La Jaquita, as it is known by locals, is one of the city's
PUERTO RICAN best farm-to-table restaurants. Chef Xavi Pacheco elevates commonly
home-cooked Puerto Rican dishes. At this casual eatery in Miramar
there's a small recreated farmers' market in the corner, which showcases
the chef's committment to sourcing directly from the producer. While
you browse the menu, a complimentary pigeon pea escabeche with
plantain chips will be brought out. The menu changes frequently but
staples like the fish tacitos, smoked pork, and homemade sausage are
fixed items. The house drink is the white or red *guarapeta*, a sangria
made with *guarapo* (sugar cane juice). ⑤ *Average main: $20* ✉ *801 Av.
Fernandez Juncos, corner of Calle Estado, Miramar* ☎ *787/993–5359*
⊘ *Closed Sun. No lunch Mon. and Sat.* ✥ *2:B2*

$$$ ✗ **Papillon Bistro.** For a break from Puerto Rican cuisine, head to Papil-
FRENCH lon Bistro in the Marriott Courtyard for traditional French cuisine pre-
pared by Chef Juan Camacho. As soon as you step into Papillon, you
forget that you are inside a hotel. The intimate atmosphere with antique
fixtures and wood elements is perfect for a romantic evening. The restaurant is open for breakfast, lunch, and dinner and serves brunch
on the weekends. The Confit Duck a L'Orange is excellently prepared
and the mussels with beer and roasted garlic are perfection! ⑤ *Average main: $22* ✉ *801 Ponce de Leon, Marriott Courtyard, Miramar*
☎ *787/919–0500* ✥ *2:B2*

OCEAN PARK

*Use the coordinate (✥ 2:A1) at the end of each listing to locate a site
on the corresponding "Map 2: Where to Eat and Stay in Greater San
Juan."*

$$ ✗ **Kasalta.** Those who think coffee can never be too strong should
CAFÉ make a beeline to Kasalta, which has an amazing pitch-black brew
that will knock your socks off. Make your selection from the display
cases full of luscious pastries, particularly the famous *quesito* (cream
cheese–filled puff pastry) and other tempting treats. Walk up to the
counter and order a sandwich, such as the Medianoche, made famous
after President Obama ordered one during his campaign on the island.
For dinner, dive into a fish dish, paella, or do like the locals and make
a meal out of the savory Spanish tapas. Occasionally the quality can
be uneven, and some staff members are curt with tourists. ⑤ *Aver-
age main: $16* ✉ *1966 Calle McLeary, Ocean Park* ☎ *787/727–7340*
⊕ *www.kasalta.com* ✥ *2:E3*

$$ ✗ **La Cueva del Mar.** For the freshest seafood and best value, head to La
SEAFOOD Cueva del Mar on Calle Loíza. This casual, marine-themed restaurant is
FAMILY a local favorite, often packed with an eclectic crowd. Families with kids,
beachgoers in flip flops, and businesspeople all flock to this restaurant,
reknowned for its fresh seafood. The grouper fish tacos, lightly fried and
topped with a spicy slaw, are a best seller—don't leave without trying
at least one. When in season, opt for the conch salad with *tostones* or
the conch *emapanadilla*, a local version of a turnover. For more substantial fare, order a Caribbean Spiny Lobster, a whole fried snapper
or the *arroz con mariscos*, La Cueva's version of a paella. Ask for the

homemade hot sauces, they pair wonderfully with the flavorful seafood dishes. Feel free to walk here for lunch but opt for a cab at night. Calle Loíza is still in its development phase and can be unwelcoming at night. Due to popular demand, La Cueva del Mar added a location in Old San Juan at the beginning of 2014. ⑤ *Average main: $13* ⊠ *1904 Calle Loíza, Ocean Park* ☎ *787/726–8700* ✛ *2:D3.*

$$
\text{PUERTO RICAN}
$$

$$ ✕ **Mango's at Ocean Park.** Mango's offers a fun, lively atmosphere perfect for a drink and bites after a day in the sun. The casual, 60s surfer-themed restaurant has a rustic, wooden deck and air-conditioned interior if you need to cool off from the Caribbean heat. The menu, diverse and quite tasty, is best described as Puerto Rican fusion. Highlights include the tuna *poke* with avocado and mango, crispy sweet-and-sour calamari, and the Thai paella in a coconut-curry sauce. The place becomes packed at night, perfect if you're looking for a hangout spot in Ocean Park. Stop by on Tuesday night for two-for-one appetizers and drinks and Wednesday for sushi night. Happy hour is well priced, live music is played most nights, and a great brunch is served on weekends. ⑤ *Average main: $16* ⊠ *152 Calle McLeary, Ocean Park* ☎ *787/998–8111* ⊕ *www.mangosoceanpark.com* ⊘ *Closed Mon.* ✛ *2:D3*

$$ ✕ **Nonna.** Great restaurants have recently been popping up in Ocean Park, on or near Calle Loíza. This new gastronomic hub is now home to Nonna, a cozy Italian restaurant that wonderfully executes traditional Italian dishes, paying tribute to the Italian *nonna* (grandmother). The pasta is made from scratch, as is the mozzarella *di bufala*. Start with the homemade mozzarella topped with candied tomatoes and hazelnuts, a creative and excellent take on a caprese salad. For pastas, our choice is the ravioli *di anatra*, filled with braised duck and pear in a porto wine reduction, topped with truffle butter. There is a nice selection of specialty pizzas made with Caputo flour from Naples. There are so many tempting choices on the menu that it might be hard to make a decision, but don't overlook the main dishes; especially delicious is the porkbelly. ⑤ *Average main: $19* ⊠ *103 Calle San Jorge, Ocean Park* ☎ *787/998–6555* ⊕ *www.nonnapr.com* ✛ *2:D3.*

ITALIAN

$$$ ✕ **Pamela's.** If you've always dreamed of fine dining for two right on the beach, only steps from where crashing waves meet the shore, head to this local favorite in Ocean Park. If you prefer air conditioning, an elegant glassed-in solarium awaits, complete with black cobblestone floors and slow-turning ceiling fans. The menu is a contemporary, creative mix of Caribbean spices and other tropical ingredients. To start, try the corn fritters with a spicy cilantro aioli. The restaurant prides itself on its fresh seafood, so move on to the rainbow trout, stuffed with crab and coconut and steamed in a banana leaf, or choose the seared salmon served with an *acerola* (Caribbean cherry) chimichurri. ⑤ *Average main: $30* ⊠ *Numero Uno Guest House, 1 Calle Santa Ana, Ocean Park* ☎ *787/726–5010* ⊕ *www.numero1guesthouse.com* ✛ *2:E2.*

CARIBBEAN

ISLA VERDE

Use the coordinate (✛ 2:A1) at the end of each listing to locate a site on the corresponding "Map 2: Where to Eat and Stay in Greater San Juan."

$$$$ ✕ **BLT Steak.** The sprawling dining room in this branch of Chef Laurent
STEAKHOUSE Tourondel's mini-chain invites you to relax: it's stylish and comfortable, with long leather banquettes, warm lighting, and glossy wood tables. Instead of bread, it's BLT's signature warm popovers that arrive at the table. Their version of that usually ho-hum menu standby, tuna tartare, is delicious—super-fresh fish topped with crispy shallots and served over avocado with a soy-lime sauce. As you might expect for a steakhouse located in a Ritz Carlton, the prices are not for the faint of heart. Splurge and go for the strip sirloin, weighing in at 22 ounces, or the Japanese Kobe steak, priced per ounce. Not in a carnivorous mood? Try jumbo shrimp in a cilantro and lemon confit. For dessert, there's a densely rich crepe soufflé bathed in passion-fruit sauce. $ *Average main: $50* ⊠ *The Ritz-Carlton, San Juan, 6991 Av. de los Gobernadores, Isla Verde* ☎ *787/253–1700* ⊕ *www.ritzcarlton.com/sanjuan* ⊗ *No lunch* ✛ *2:H3.*

$$$$ ✕ **Il Mulino New York.** You'll want for nothing at the San Juan outpost
ITALIAN of the Manhattan restaurant, where a team of tuxedoed waiters effortlessly coordinates your entire meal experience. The dark-wood-paneled walls and heavy velvet drapes are an odd juxtaposition with the tropical climate, but everything about this place is elegant and tasteful. Garlic bread, fried zucchini, and other antipasti arrive moments after you sit down, though you'll want to pace yourself and leave room for the mammoth entrées to come. Standouts include stuffed whole branzino (deboned tableside), linguini with seafood sauce, and veal grilled with sage and garlic. There's no fusion or haute cuisine here, just solid Italian dishes, painstakingly executed. All this perfection comes at a price, though a shot of homemade grappa might help ease the sticker shock. $ *Average main: $38* ⊠ *The Ritz-Carlton, San Juan, 6991 Av. de los Gobernadores, Isla Verde* ☎ *787/791–8632* ⊕ *www.ilmulino. com/puerto-rico* ⚐ *Reservations essential* ⊗ *No lunch* ✛ *2:H3.*

$$ ✕ **La Playita.** In a small hotel in Isla Verde the laid-back, beachy La Play-
ECLECTIC ita is famous for its burgers and mofongo with various fillings. Their menu also features a local catch of the day and more creative dishes like mahimahi in a mango-chipotle sauce. All the seating is outdoors; you can choose the deck and look out for manatees and sea turtles, or relax in a covered section near the bar, where you can try their signature passion-fruit mojitos, or their staple, the *Coco Loco*, a piña colada served inside a fresh cocount. The crowd is a fun mix of locals and tourists who have wandered over from nearby hotels to enjoy the breathtaking views. The service can be slow and the hotel needs a bit of a face-lift. $ *Average main: $20* ⊠ *Hotel La Playa, 6 Calle Amapola, Isla Verde* ☎ *787/791–1115* ⊕ *www.hotellaplaya.com* ✛ *2:G3.*

$$ ✕ **Metropol.** Across the street from a string of major hotels, this casual
CARIBBEAN restaurant doesn't look like much from the outside, but inside it's decorated in warm, tropical colors, and local art hangs on the wall. (You

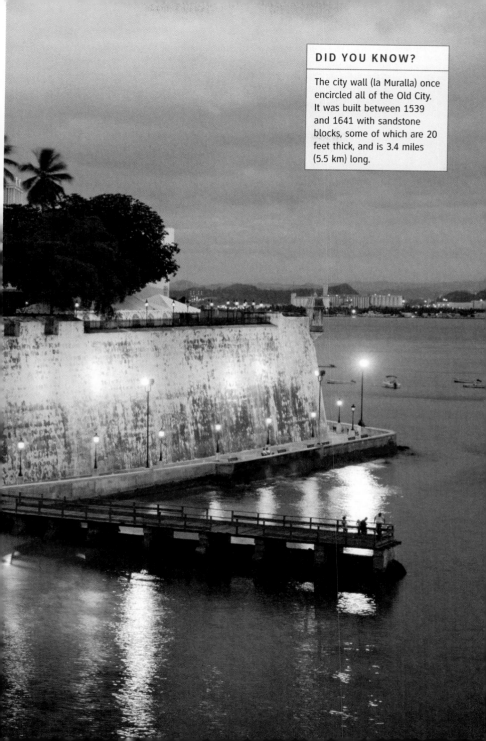

DID YOU KNOW?

The city wall (la Muralla) once encircled all of the Old City. It was built between 1539 and 1641 with sandstone blocks, some of which are 20 feet thick, and is 3.4 miles (5.5 km) long.

can shop from your table if you find a painting you like.) The kitchen turns out delicious versions of Cuban and Puerto Rican favorites at reasonable prices. Tasty options include Cornish game hen stuffed with *congri*, a mixture of black beans and rice; perfectly seasoned and tender beef churrasco; and fried chickpeas with ham and chorizo. The crowd is a pleasant mix of tourists and locals, families and groups of friends enjoying a relaxed evening out. The restaurant has several branches around the island, most in the metro area. ⑤ *Average main: $15* ✉ *Ave. Isla Verde, Anexo Club Gallistico, Isla Verde* ☎ *787/791–5585* ⊕ *www. metropolrestaurant.com* ✛ *2:H3.*

$$
ECLECTIC

✕ **Salt GastroBar.** When looking for a dining option in Isla Verde, look no further than Salt GastroBar. This surprising new addition to the neighborhood, located in an unconventional spot (inside the Howard Johnson Hotel) serves an impressive menu. Many dishes are elegantly presented on a Himalayan Salt Block Platter such as the Puerto Rican Mixta Bites and the Seafood Platter. The lobster mac and cheese with fontina, parmesan, and gruyere is rich and plentiful. Gastro brunch is served on Sunday. ⑤ *Average main: $17* ✉ *Howard Johnson Hotel, 4820 Ave. Isla Verde, Isla Verde* ☎ *787/919–7575* ⊕ *www.saltgastrobar. com* ⊘ *No lunch.* ✛ *2:G3*

$$$
PUERTO RICAN

✕ **Zest.** The lounge atmosphere, accented with white fixtures and blue lighting makes dining at Zest an unforgettable underwater experince. Chef Raúl Correo combines international haute cuisine with local ingredients to create his version of New Puerto Rican Cuisine. He is best known for his love of molecular gastronomy and his signature popcorn soup made with truffle butter and rosemary essence. Also tasty are the blue cheese and grilled pear dumplings with port wine reduction. Whether you are in Old San Juan or Condado, Zest is worth the trip. ⑤ *Average main: $25* ✉ *San Juan Water Beach Club Hotel, 2 Calle Tartak, Isla Verde* ☎ *787/728–3666* ⊘ *No lunch.* ✛ *2:G3*

WHERE TO STAY

San Juan prides itself on its plentiful clean, comfortable accommodations, and hoteliers, by and large, aim to please. All rooms are now no-smoking. Big hotels and resorts, several with casinos, and a few smaller establishments line the sandy strands along Condado and Isla Verde. If you want to do little but relax on the beach, enjoy ample resort amenities, and partake in lively nightlife, either is a good option. Between these two neighborhoods, the Ocean Park area has homey inns, as do the districts of Miramar and Santurce, although the latter two areas aren't directly on the beach. Independent travelers, artistic types, and anyone who wants to stay a little bit off the beaten tourist track might prefer these areas. Old San Juan has fewer lodging options, one of which has a casino, but most of the city's best boutique hotels are here. If you're a history or architecture buff or looking for a unique romantic experience, definitely stay in one of these colonial inns; many of the structures date back several hundred years, and will make you feel as if you've been transported to another era, even though most have flat-screen televisions and Wi-Fi. (Also consider the Old City if you're in town for a cruise, since the ports are within walking distance.) Keep in mind, though, that these buildings are old, and Puerto Rico has a tropical climate, so minor inconveniences like room mustiness or ongoing repairs might be possible.

> **PARADORES**
>
> The small, government-sponsored inns called *paradores* are primarily *en la isla* (out on the island) rather than in San Juan.

Staying in a self-catering apartment or condo has advantages over a resort, especially for families. You can cook when and what you want, and you can enjoy considerable autonomy. Several companies represent such properties in San Juan. When booking, be sure to ask about maid service, swimming pools, and any other amenities that are important to you.

PRICES

The city's rooms aren't inexpensive: for a high-end beach-resort room, expect to pay at least $200 to $300 for a double in high season—roughly mid-November through mid-April. For smaller inns and hotels, doubles start at $100 to $150. As a rule, if your room is less than $50 in high season, then the quality of the hotel might be questionable. Although most hotels operate on the European plan (EP, no meals included), some establishments do include breakfast or offer other meal plans.

WHAT IT COSTS IN U.S. DOLLARS				
	$	$$	$$$	$$$$
For Two People	$80–$150	$151–$250	$251–$350	over $350

Prices are the lowest cost of a standard double room in high season.

For expanded hotel reviews and current deals, visit Fodors.com.

APARTMENT RENTALS

Caleta 64 Apartments. Four nicely furnished boutique apartments that are just steps from the cathedral and Calle Cristo are available from Caleta 64. ⊠ *64 Caleta de San Juan, Old San Juan* ☎ *787/667–4926* ⊕ *www.caleta64.com.*

San Juan Vacations. Many properties in Condado and Isla Verde can be rented from this real estate company. ⊠ *Marbella del Caribe Oeste, Av. Isla Verde, S-5, Isla Verde* ☎ *787/727–1591* ✉ *sanjuvac@gmail.com.*

OLD SAN JUAN

Use the coordinate (✚ 1:A2) at the end of each listing to locate a site on the corresponding "Map 1: Where to Eat and Stay in Old San Juan."

$

HOTEL

Fodor's Choice

★

CasaBlanca Hotel. Mere steps away from some of the best dining in town, this boutique hotel in the heart of SoFo adds Moroccan-theme panache to Old San Juan. **Pros:** exotic decor; close to restaurants and nightclubs; great value for the money. **Cons:** some rooms dark; noise from street; smallish rooms; no elevator. ⑤ *Rooms from: $139* ⊠ *316 Calle Fortaleza, Old San Juan* ☎ *787/725–3436* ⊕ *www.*

BEST BETS FOR SAN JUAN LODGING

hotelcasablancapr.com 🛏 *26 rooms, 4 suites* ❍ *Multiple meal plans* ✛ *1:F4.*

$
B&B/INN **Da House.** In the same building as the fabled Nuyorican Café, a music venue that many patrons simply refer to as Da House, this popular property is part art gallery part hotel. **Pros:** hip vibe in a historic setting; artsy types to mingle with; friendly staff; excellent value. **Cons:** noise from nearby bars; simple accommodations. $ *Rooms from: $100* ✉ *312 Calle San Francisco, Old San Juan* ☎ *787/977–1180* ⊕ *www. dahousehotelpr.com* 🛏 *27 rooms* ❍ *No meals* ✛ *1:F3.*

$$
B&B/INN **The Gallery Inn.** No two rooms in this 200-year-old mansion are alike, but all have four-poster beds, hand-woven tapestries, and quirky antiques in every nook and cranny. **Pros:** one-of-a-kind lodging; ocean views; wonderful classical music concerts. **Cons:** several narrow, winding staircases; an uphill walk from rest of Old San Juan; sometimes-raucous pet macaws and cockatoos. $ *Rooms from: $160* ✉ *204–206 Calle Norzagaray, Old San Juan* ☎ *787/722–1808* ⊕ *www.thegalleryinn.com* 🛏 *20 rooms, 5 suites* ❍ *Breakfast* ✛ *1:E3.*

The narrow streets and sloping hills of Old San Juan are fantastic for walking. Driving? Not so much.

$$$
HOTEL
Fodor'sChoice
★

🏨 **Hotel El Convento.** There's no longer anything austere about this 350-year-old former convent. **Pros:** lovely building; atmosphere to spare; plenty of nearby dining options. **Cons:** near some noisy bars; small pool and small bathrooms. ⑤ *Rooms from: $285* ✉ *100 Calle Cristo, Old San Juan* ☎ *787/723–9020* ⊕ *www.elconvento.com* ↝ *52 rooms, 6 suites* ⦿ *No meals* ✛ *1:D3.*

$$
HOTEL

🏨 **Hotel Milano.** This affordable and conservative hotel is near the best and worst of Old San Juan. **Pros:** elevator on property; walk to shops and restaurants. **Cons:** overall outdated decor; on a busy street; noise from nearby bars. ⑤ *Rooms from: $165* ✉ *307 Calle Fortaleza, Old San Juan* ☎ *787/729–9050* ⊕ *www.hotelmilanopr.com* ↝ *30 rooms* ⦿ *No meals* ✛ *1:F4.*

$$
HOTEL

🏨 **Sheraton Old San Juan Hotel & Casino.** Rooms facing the water at this triangular-shaped hotel have spectacular views of the mammoth cruise ships that sail in and out of the nearby harbor. **Pros:** harbor views; near many dining options; good array of room types. **Cons:** chain-hotel feel to guest rooms; noise from casino overwhelms lobby and restaurants; uphill walk to the rest of Old San Juan. ⑤ *Rooms from: $229* ✉ *100 Calle Brumbaugh, Old San Juan* ☎ *787/721–5100, 866/376–7577* ⊕ *www.sheratonoldsanjuan.com* ↝ *200 rooms, 40 suites* ⦿ *No meals* ✛ *1:F4.*

$$
B&B/INN

🏨 **Villa Herencia Hotel.** The same owners as Da House transport guests back to the 19th century in this exquisitely restored former mansion that retains time-worn bare walls and original floral tile floors and beamed ceilings. **Pros:** delightful furnishings; great for art and architecture lovers; romantic to the max; close to shops and cafés of Old San Juan; rooftop terraces with baths. **Cons:** no in-room phone; no elevator. ⑤ *Rooms from: $180* ⊠ *23 Caleta de las Monjas, Old San Juan* ☎ *787/722–0989* ⊕ *www.villaherencia.com* ⌁ *6 rooms, 2 suites* �PO| *Breakfast* ⊕ *1:C4.*

PUERTA DE TIERRA

Use the coordinate (⊕ 2:A1) at the end of each listing to locate a site on the corresponding "Map 2: Where to Eat and Stay in Greater San Juan."

$$$
RESORT
FAMILY

▦ **Caribe Hilton San Juan.** Not many hotels can lay claim to their own fort, but Fortín San Gerónimo del Boquerón, which once guarded the entrance to San Juan Bay, is on the grounds of this sprawling resort, one of the largest in Puerto Rico. **Pros:** family-friendly atmosphere; private beach; lovely pool area. **Cons:** noisy lobby area; somewhat isolated, with few attractions or restaurants within walking distance. ⑤ *Rooms from: $329* ⊠ *1 San Gerónimo Grounds, Puerta de Tierra* ☎ *787/721–0303, 800/468–8585* ⊕ *www.caribehilton.com* ⌁ *816 rooms, 101 suites* ⏌O| *No meals* ⊕ *2:B2.*

CONDADO

Use the coordinate (⊕ 2:A1) at the end of each listing to locate a site on the corresponding "Map 2: Where to Eat and Stay in Greater San Juan."

$$
B&B/INN

▦ **Acacia Boutique Hotel.** This chic spot, a sister property to At Wind Chimes Inn, falls somewhere between a boutique hotel and a casual guesthouse. **Pros:** enormous hot tub with ocean views; good value for the neighborhood; guests can use At Wind Chimes Inn's facilities. **Cons:** several minutes' walk to most shops and restaurants; some outdated decorations in the rooms. ⑤ *Rooms from: $175* ⊠ *8 Calle Taft, Condado* ☎ *787/725–0068, 877/725–0668* ⊕ *www.acaciaseasideinn.com* ⌁ *20 rooms, 1 suite* ⏌O| *No meals* ⊕ *2:D2.*

$
B&B/INN

▦ **At Wind Chimes Inn.** Hidden behind a whitewashed wall covered with bougainvillea, this Spanish-style villa gives the impression of an exclusive retreat. **Pros:** charming architecture; on the edge of Condado; bar on-site (opens at 5 pm); includes use of facilities at Acacia Seaside Inn. **Cons:** on a busy street; old-fashioned rooms; only a few rooms have closets. ⑤ *Rooms from: $109* ⊠ *1750 Av. McLeary, Condado* ☎ *787/727–4153, 800/946–3244* ⊕ *www.atwindchimesinn.com* ⌁ *17 rooms, 5 suites, 1 apartment* ⏌O| *No meals* ⊕ *2:D2.*

$$$
RESORT

▦ **The Condado Plaza Hilton.** The island's only luxury hotel with both Atlantic and lagoon views is just five minutes from Old San Juan. **Pros:** excellent food at Pikayo; friendly staff; kid activity center, stunning views from some rooms; chic design. **Cons:** hallway noise; no bathtubs; small beach. ⑤ *Rooms from: $299* ⊠ *999 Av. Ashford, Condado* ☎ *787/721–1000* ⊕ *www.condadoplaza.com* ⌁ *509 rooms, 61 suites* ⏌O| *No meals* ⊕ *2:B2.*

$
HOTEL

▦ **Coral Princess.** The guest rooms in this art deco building—one of the few left in Condado—subtly reflect the boutique hotel's heritage with crisp lines, modern furnishings, and marble floors. **Pros:** good value; comfortable common areas; Wi-Fi in rooms; elevator on-site. **Cons:** not directly on the beach; small pool. ⑤ *Rooms from: $129* ⊠ *1159*

Ave. Magdalena, Condado ☎ *787/977–7700* ⊕ *www.coralpr.com* ⤳ *25 rooms* †○‖ *Breakfast* ✛ *2:C2.*

$$ HOTEL 🏨 **Doubletree by Hilton San Juan.** Slightly geared to business travelers the Doubletree offers an excellent value for anyone who doesn't need to be in central Condado or on the beach. **Pros:** excellent value for the neighborhood; attractive rooms; good on-site dining options. **Cons:** a bit of a walk to the beach and the main drag in Condado. ⑤ *Rooms from: $249* ✉ *105 Av. de Diego, Condado* ☎ *787/721–1200* ⊕ *www. sanjuandoubletree.com* ⤳ *184 rooms* †○‖ *No meals* ✛ *2:D3.*

$ HOTEL 🏨 **Hotel Miramar.** Catering mostly to cruise-ship passengers, this hotel sits in the middle of Miramar, an up-and-coming neighborhood located halfway between Condado and Old San Juan. **Pros:** short drive to Old San Juan and Condado; walking distance to excellent restaurants; rooftop terrace. **Cons:** simple rooms; not the most interesting neighborhood. ⑤ *Rooms from: $149* ✉ *606 Av. Ponce de León, Miramar* ☎ *787/977–1000* ⊕ *www.miramarhotelpr.com* ⤳ *50 rooms* †○‖ *Some meals* ✛ *2:B2.*

$$$ RESORT Fodor's Choice ★ 🏨 **La Concha—A Renaissance Resort.** Every detail at La Concha feels tropical and sexy, from the undulating ceiling in the sprawling lobby to Perla, the signature shell-shaped restaurant and an architectural marvel. **Pros:** stunning architecture; numerous on-site social activities; beautiful guestrooms. **Cons:** noisy bar/lobby, particularly when there's live music; beach can be narrow during high tide. ⑤ *Rooms from: $299* ✉ *1077 Av. Ashford, Condado* ☎ *787/721–7500* ⊕ *www.laconcharesort.com* ⤳ *257 rooms, 226 suites* †○‖ *No meals* ✛ *2:C2.*

$$ HOTEL 🏨 **O:live Boutique Hotel.** This lovely boutique hotel tucked away on a quiet street in Condado is reminiscent of a Mediterranean villa. **Pros:** beautiful décor; rooftop terrace; great in-house dining; close to shops and restaurants. **Cons:** small pool; see-through bathrooms not for everyone. ⑤ *Rooms from: $249* ✉ *55 Calle Aguadilla, Condado* ☎ *787/705–9994* ⊕ *www.oliveboutiquehotel.com* ⤳ *15 rooms* †○‖ *Breakfast* ✛ *2:B2.*

$$$ RESORT FAMILY 🏨 **San Juan Marriott Resort & Stellaris Casino.** The shape and color of a cardboard box, this lively, popular hotel doesn't add much to the skyline of Condado, but as soon as you step instead the impressive lobby—with its stunning coral sculpture carved from wood, chic spots for lounging, and welcoming bar—you'll feel you've arrived in the Caribbean. **Pros:** on one of the area's best beaches; near dozens of dining options; lots of amenities. **Cons:** uninspired architecture; lots of conventions. ⑤ *Rooms from: $300* ✉ *1309 Av. Ashford, Condado* ☎ *787/722–7000, 800/465–5005* ⊕ *www.marriottsanjuan.com* ⤳ *513 rooms, 12 suites* †○‖ *No meals* ✛ *2:C2.*

OCEAN PARK

Use the coordinate (✛ 2:A1) at the end of each listing to locate a site on the corresponding "Map 2: Where to Eat and Stay in Greater San Juan."

$
B&B/INN
⌦ **Andalucía.** In a Spanish-style house, this friendly little inn evokes its namesake region with such details as hand-painted tiles and ceramic pots filled with greenery. **Pros:** terrific value; helpful hosts; gorgeous courtyard. **Cons:** not right on the beach; some rooms are smaller than others. ⑤ *Rooms from: $99* ⌧ *2011 Calle McLeary, Ocean Park* ☎ *787/309–3373* ⊕ *www.andalucia-puertorico.com* ⥹ *11 rooms* ⑩ *No meals* ✛ *2:E3.*

$
B&B/INN
⌦ **Hostería del Mar.** Decorated in bright blues and whites, the stylish rooms at this beachfront inn have an Asian feel, with influences from Bali, Malaysia, and India. **Pros:** plasma-screen televisions; right on the beach; good on-site dining. **Cons:** long walk to other restaurants; no pool; Wi-Fi in lobby only. ⑤ *Rooms from: $139* ⌧ *1 Calle Tapia, Ocean Park* ☎ *787/727–3302* ⊕ *www.hosteriadelmarpr.com* ⥹ *23 rooms, 2 suites* ⑩ *No meals* ✛ *2:E2.*

$
HOTEL
Fodor's Choice
★
⌦ **Numero Uno Guest House.** It seems that first-time visitors to Numero Uno are destined to become repeat customers because it's quite common to hear guests trading stories about how often they've returned to this relaxing retreat. **Pros:** friendly atmosphere; great restaurant; right on the beach. **Cons:** a long walk to other restaurants; small pool. ⑤ *Rooms from: $150* ⌧ *1 Calle Santa Ana, Ocean Park* ☎ *787/726–5010, 866/726–5010* ⊕ *www.numero1guesthouse.com* ⥹ *11 rooms* ⑩ *Breakfast* ✛ *2:E2.*

ISLA VERDE

Use the coordinate (✛ 2:A1) at the end of each listing to locate a site on the corresponding "Map 2: Where to Eat and Stay in Greater San Juan."

$$
RESORT
⌦ **Courtyard by Marriott Isla Verde Beach Resort.** This 12-story resort tries to be all things to all people—and succeeds to a great degree. **Pros:** on a great beach; family-friendly environment; good value. **Cons:** you can hear airport noise from some rooms; noise from lobby. ⑤ *Rooms from: $235* ⌧ *7012 Av. Boca de Cangrejos, Isla Verde* ☎ *787/791–0404, 787/999–6300* ⊕ *www.sjcourtyard.com* ⥹ *260 rooms, 33 suites* ⑩ *No meals* ✛ *2:H3.*

$$$$
RESORT
FAMILY
Fodor's Choice
★
⌦ **El San Juan Resort & Casino.** Much of the classical appeal remains at this don't-miss destination in Isla Verde: the intricately hand-carved mahogany walls and ceiling in the lobby date back to 1955. **Pros:** beautiful pool; great dining options in and near hotel; on a fantastic beach. **Cons:** noise in the lobby from bars and casino; self-parking lot is a long walk from the hotel entrance; small bathrooms. ⑤ *Rooms from: $450* ⌧ *6063 Av. Isla Verde, Isla Verde* ☎ *787/791–1000* ⊕ *www.elsanjuanhotel.com* ⥹ *386 rooms, 22 suites* ⑩ *No meals* ✛ *2:G3.*

$$$
HOTEL
⌦ **Embassy Suites San Juan Hotel & Casino.** The glass elevators that whisk you up to your room overlook the plant-filled atrium, which includes a pond and waterfall. **Pros:** family-friendly place; pretty pool; full cooked-to-order breakfast and cocktail reception included. **Cons:** not on beach; chain-hotel feel; highway noise in pool area; dated rooms. ⑤ *Rooms from: $269* ⌧ *8000 Calle Tartak, Isla Verde* ☎ *787/791–0505, 888/791–0505* ⊕ *www.embassysuitessanjuan.com* ⥹ *299 suites* ⑩ *Breakfast* ✛ *2:G4.*

$$ ⛱ **Hampton Inn & Suites San Juan.** If you don't mind a short walk to the
HOTEL   beach, you can get a room at this friendly hotel for much less than at
many of the competitors across the road. **Pros:** good value; helpful
staff; breakfast included; new fitness center. **Cons:** 5- to 10-minute
walk to the beach; chain-hotel feel; some highway noise in pool area.
⑤ *Rooms from: $189* ✉ *6530 Av. Isla Verde, Isla Verde* ☎ *787/791–
8777* ⊕ *www.hamptoninn.com* ⟿ *147 rooms, 54 suites* ℃ *Breakfast*
✛ *2:H3.*

$$ ⛱ **Hotel La Playa.** As its name suggests, this small, friendly hotel is right
HOTEL   on the beach. **Pros:** great value; helpful staff; excellent location; ocean-
front restaurant. **Cons:** few on-site amenities; need to drive to most
other attractions; next to an abandoned building; no pool. ⑤ *Rooms
from: $153* ✉ *6 Calle Amapola, Isla Verde* ☎ *787/791–1115* ⊕ *www.
hotellaplaya.com* ⟿ *15 rooms* ℃ *Breakfast* ✛ *2:G3.*

$$$ ⛱ **InterContinental San Juan Resort & Casino.** Somewhat dowdy on the
RESORT   outside and modern on the inside, the 16-story InterContinental's main
FAMILY   draws are its great on-site restaurants, pool, and spectacular beach-
front location. **Pros:** lovely pool; on one of the city's best beaches;
multiple dining options. **Cons:** unattractive facade; cramped lobby.
⑤ *Rooms from: $319* ✉ *5961 Av. Isla Verde, Isla Verde* ☎ *787/791–
6100, 800/443–2009* ⊕ *www.icsanjuanresort.com* ⟿ *376 rooms, 22
suites* ℃ *No meals* ✛ *2:G3.*

$$$$ ⛱ **The Ritz-Carlton, San Juan.** Elegant marble floors and fountains don't
RESORT   undermine the feeling that this is a true beach getaway. **Pros:** top-
FAMILY   notch service; excellent restaurant options; spruce guest rooms and
Fodor's Choice modern spa and fitness center. **Cons:** not much is within walking dis-
★   tance; expensive for San Juan lodging. ⑤ *Rooms from: $629* ✉ *6961
Av. de los Gobernadores, Isla Verde* ☎ *787/253–1700, 800/241–3333*
⊕ *www.ritzcarlton.com/sanjuan* ⟿ *416 rooms, 11 suites* ℃ *No meals*
✛ *2:H3.*

$$ ⛱ **San Juan Water & Beach Club.** Water is everywhere at this boutique
HOTEL   hotel, from the droplets that decorate the reception area to the deluge
that runs down the glass walls of the elevators. **Pros:** fun atmosphere;
interesting design; great nightlife option; on the beach. **Cons:** dark hall-
ways; small pool. ⑤ *Rooms from: $219* ✉ *2 Calle Tartak, Isla Verde*
☎ *787/728–3666, 888/265–6699* ⊕ *www.waterbeachclubhotel.com*
⟿ *76 rooms, 4 suites* ℃ *No meals* ✛ *2:G3.*

DORADO

$$$$ ⛱ **Dorado Beach, A Ritz-Carlton Reserve.** Following a recent $342 million
RESORT   renovation, this Ritz-Carlton Reserve ups the ante with a roster of posh
Fodor's Choice offerings, including a restaurant from Fodor's Tastemaker Chef José
★   Andrés, and an incredible setting along three miles of Puerto Rican
coastline. **Pros:** all rooms are beachfront; top-notch facilities; golf, tennis, and water activities; award-winning spa; gourmet dining. **Cons:** $95
resort fee added daily; a 45-minute drive from San Juan. ⑤ *Rooms from:
$1,399* ✉ *100 Dorado Beach Drive, Dorado* ☎ *787/626-1100* ⊕ *www.
ritzcarlton.com/en/Properties/DoradoBeach* ⟿ *100 rooms, 14 suites, 1
villa* ℃ *No meals* ✛ *2:A5.*

NIGHTLIFE AND THE ARTS

Several publications will tell you what's happening in San Juan. ¡*Qué Pasa!*, the official visitors' guide, has current listings of events in the city and out on the island. *Bienvenidos*, published by the Puerto Rico Hotel & Tourism Association, is also helpful.

There are also publications for Spanish-speaking visitors, including the weekend section of the Spanish-language newspaper *El Nuevo Día*; the paper also gives a weekly rundown of events on its website, *www. elnuevodia.com*. *Sal!* (⊕ *www.sal.pr*) includes brief restaurant reviews and articles about dining and nightlife. (It's also available as a free downloadable app for iPhone and iPad and can be used in either English or Spanish.)

NIGHTLIFE

From Thursday through Sunday it's as if there's a celebration going on nearly everywhere in San Juan. Be sure you dress to party, particularly on Friday and Saturday nights; Puerto Ricans have flair, and both men and women love getting dressed up to go out. Bars are usually casual, but if you have on jeans, sneakers, and a T-shirt, you may be refused entry at nightclubs and discos.

Well-dressed visitors and locals alike often mingle in the lobby bars of large hotels, many of which have bands in the evening. Some hotels also have clubs with shows and/or dancing; admission starts at $10. Casino rules have been relaxed, injecting life into what was once a conservative hotel gaming scene, but you still won't be allowed in if you're wearing a tank top or shorts. There are more games, as well as such gambling perks as free drinks and live music.

In Old San Juan, Calle San Sebastián is lined with bars and restaurants. Salsa music blaring from jukeboxes in cut-rate pool halls competes with mellow Latin jazz in top-flight nightspots. The young and the beautiful often socialize in Plaza San José. Mid-January sees the Fiestas de la Calle San Sebastián, one of the Caribbean's best street parties.

Young professionals as well as a slightly older bohemian crowd fill Santurce, San Juan's historical downtown area, until the wee hours. The revitalized Plaza del Mercado (Calle Dos Hermanos at Calle Capital) has structures—many painted in bright colors—dating from the 1930s or earlier. On weekend nights the area's streets are closed to vehicular traffic. You can wander from dive bars to trendy nightspots and sway to music that pours from countless open-air establishments and the marketplace's front plaza.

BARS

El Barril. If you stop by this neighborhood bar at, say, 9 or 10 pm, you may find yourself alone with the bartender. It doesn't get going until 11 pm at the earliest, but 1 am is probably better if you want a true taste of San Juan nightlife. It closes, oh, when the last person leaves. There's music most nights, whether live performances or DJs. Although not a sports bar per se, this sister property of Bar Gitano (*see Night Bites,*

Continued on page 101

Salsa

A Guide to Puerto Rico's Favorite Music and Dance

Salsa: its hip-shaking rhythms and sensual moves embody the spirit of the Caribbean and Latin America. The songs and the steps create a language all their own—one that's spoken by passionate dancers and musicians the world over. But it's the Puerto Ricans who are the most fluent. Welcome to the home of salsa! Are you ready to dance?

As the first notes of the song sound, dancers come alive, eager to take their place on the floor with a partner whose skill matches their own. These are the most daring salsa devotees who are found in every corner of the island, dancers who won't quit moving until the music stops. Even as a bystander, it's impossible to stand still.

Salsa isn't a passive rhythm: it's animated, hot, and sensual, a metaphor for the Caribbean itself. In general, the themes of the songs mirror the moves of the dance, with choruses alluding to love, both forbidden and open. In the music and the movement, there's occasional improvisation among those who know the genre. Hips shake to the clave, which marks the basic rhythm, and shoulders shake from one side to the other, fanning the air. It's a democratic form, where experimentation is encouraged . . . you just have to be willing to get out there.

by Julie Schwietert Collazo

SALSA HISTORY

The late timbale master Tito Puente

Though salsa has its roots outside Puerto Rico, the island is directly responsible for the rhythm known by this name. As a musical form, the components of salsa can be traced back to Europe and Africa. During the colonial period, Spanish conquistadores arriving from the West Indies brought island rhythms along with them. They also brought the complex, multi-rhythmic riffs of Arabic music, an artifact of the Muslim conquest of the Iberian Peninsula that had become embedded in the music of Spain and Portugal. In Puerto Rico, all of these musical strands came together to create a new rhythm known as bomba.

The emergence of salsa was deeply influenced by musical forms from nearby Cuba and other parts of the Caribbean, as well as musical experimentation by diaspora Puerto Ricans living in New York. Among the most important of these mainland musicians was percussionist and band leader Tito Puente.

The history of salsa is the history of the new world. In salsa, there's evidence of rhythms from past ages, as well as the musical history of our own time. Salsa isn't a "pure" musical form, but represents—like Puerto Rico itself—a mixture of rhythmic elements, adapted by the inhabitants of the new world.

DID YOU KNOW?

■ The first use of the word "salsa" related to music was in 1937 by Cuban composer Igancio Pineiro in his popular song, "Echale Salsita." It continues to be a frequently recorded song today by artists in and outside Cuba.

■ The song "Oye Como Va" was originally composed by Tito Puente in 1963 and later recorded by Carlos Santana, who made it a number-one hit.

■ The contribution of salsa to jazz music dates from 1940, when Dizzie Gillespie and Stan Kenton incorporated salsa in their tunes, giving birth to "Latin jazz."

■ More than 30 countries celebrate salsa with annual festivals, among them, Poland, Israel, France, Serbia, and Japan.

SALSA SPEAK

ABRAZO: The *abrazo* is the positioning of the partners' hands and arms. The woman's left hand rests lightly on her partner's shoulder, while his right hand is placed on the small of her back to guide her. The abrazo establishes the space each partner maintains during turns.

Abrazo

VUELTAS: *Vueltas*, turns, are an important component of salsa. There are numerous styles, and they can occur in both directions, but all are determined and initiated by the male partner. Turns are spontaneous; their complexity depends upon the skill and experience of the dancers.

Vueltas

SOLOS: Solos—a favorite move of experienced dancers—are moments when the partners separate to move independently though still in response to each other. These are often synchronized with the solos of percussion musicians. Solos are also used as a means of rest after a series of complex turns before the pair comes together again for even more intricate turns.

Solos

SALSA STYLE

Two elements define salsa fashion: comfort and sensuality. Men and women both draw from the best of their wardrobes, with men often dressed in guayabera shirts, linen pants, and two-toned dance shoes. Suede shoes permit optimal movement for men and add a touch of elegance. Women typically wear dresses—often knee length or shorter—and open-toed, medium-heeled dance shoes with ankle support. For both men and women, freedom of movement and maximum ventilation are important elements of a salsa wardrobe.

The dance is an opportunity to show off your elegance and your sensuality, but your clothing should also honor the significance of the event and venue. Many dance organizers impose dress policies, prohibiting running shoes, sleeveless shirts, and overly informal or provocative clothing. Dress to impress.

Salsa dance shoes

NEXT STEPS

If you're ready to take to the dance floor, here are some of the best places to learn—and then show off—your moves.

LESSONS

The Academia de Baile Julie Mayoral. On the Plaza de las Delicias in Ponce, Mayoral's second floor studio is steaming hot, and her young, enthusiastic instructors will have you doing proper vueltas in no time. For a bit more than $5 for an hour lesson, Mayoral probably offers the best deal in Puerto Rico. Mayoral also has studios in Coamo and Yauco. Call her Ponce studio (☎787/843–2830) for information about lessons at any of the three studios.

In San Juan, dancer Paulette Beauchamp offers salsa classes for children and adults on Tuesday. Her studio, **DanzActiva** (☎787/775–9438 ⊕www.danzactiva.com), is in the historic Cuartel de Ballaja building in Old San Juan.

HOTELS

Locals and tourists alike take to the dance floor at the **San Juan Marriott Resort** and **Stellaris Casino** on weekends, when homegrown musicians provide a soundtrack for the salsa experience. Entry is free, but you'll need to purchase drinks if you decide to rest at one of the tables circling the dance floor.

CLUBS

Old San Juan's **Nuyorican Café** looks like a dive—and it is—but it's the heart of Puerto Rico's salsa scene. Though the café also hosts jazz and rock groups as well as poetry readings and experimental theatre, its reputation for world-class salsa has expanded far beyond the island. Call ahead for the current schedule (☎787/977–1276).

FESTIVALS

As the home of salsa, Puerto Rico hosts an annual **International Salsa Congress.** It's held in San Juan each July, though the site changes each year. The congress attracts thousands of aficionados from the island and from surprisingly far-flung places, including Japan, Korea, and Norway.

(left) A couple prepares for competition at the International Salsa Congress held in San Juan. (right) Young dancers performing at the International Salsa Congress.

below) is a good spot to catch an important game, whether Champions League soccer or American football. The new mixology menu has great cocktails and there's the signature passion fruit–spiked white sangria. Tasty burgers are available if hunger strikes but you can also order from the tapas menu next door. ⊠ *1302 Av. Ashford, Condado* ☎ *787/725–6919* ⊙ *Closed Sun.–Tues.*

El Batey. This legendary dive bar won't win any prizes for decor, but even still, it has an irresistibly artsy and welcoming vibe. Add your own message to the graffiti-covered walls (they have a B.Y.O.S., or Bring Your Own Sharpie policy), or hang your business card alongside the hundreds that cover the lighting fixtures. The jukebox has the best selection of oldies in town and locals crowd the back room for a game of pool. In the late afternoon, you might find owner David Jones, sitting at the bar who opened up the bar in the 1960s. ⊠ *101 Calle Cristo, Old San Juan* ☎ *No phone.*

Eternal Lounge. Decorated in the same modern style as the rest of the Condado Plaza Hilton, this sleek lounge turns into a club on weekends with a DJ spinning on Friday, Saturday, and Sunday nights. During the week, it's a nice spot for an evening cocktail. ⊠ *The Condado Plaza Hilton, 999 Av. Ashford, Condado* ☎ *787/565–7703* ⊕ *www.eternalpr.com.*

Fodor's Choice ★ **La Factoría.** La Factoría, the former Hijos de Borinquen, is hands-down the best mixology bar in San Juan. There's no sign on the door, so look for the terra cotta building on the corner of San Sebastián and San José. Artisanal cocktails are crafted with the highest quality ingredients. Many bitters are homemade as is the ginger beer, which is used in their popular Get Lucky Mule. You can order one of the specialty cocktails listed on the chalkboard (the Spiced Old Fashioned is fantastic) or chat with one of the bartenders who will create the perfect drink based on your preferences. Whether they're sweet, spicy, bitter, or something completely out of the box, these drinks will blow your mind. Behind the bar, there is a secret wooden door that leads to VINO Wine Bar, which has a great speakeasy feel. Tasty tapas are available and can be enjoyed in the adjacent room. The bars stay open until the sun comes up and there is a DJ most nights. ⊠ *148 Calle San Sebastián, Old San Juan* ☎ *787/594–5698.*

The Mezzanine at St. Germain. On top of St. Germain Bistro & Café, and in the former headquarters of the Nationalist Party, The Mezzanine is a contemporary take on the 1920s speakeasy. The chic space is conducive for sipping old-fashioneds or our favorite, the Peridot, made with gin and muddled basil and orange—very refreshing after walking the hills of Old San Juan. Tapas are served all day. Choose from the Brie and prosciutto *montaditos* with wild mushroom oil, the sweet and tangy meatballs, or the Greek-style ceviche. The Mezzanine also hosts one of the best happy hours in town, Tuesday through Friday from 4 to 8. Enjoy select tapas and cocktails for half off. You can't beat that in San Juan! Their boozy brunch is very popular on weekends. ⊠ *156 Calle Sol, 2nd Floor, Old San Juan* ☎ *787/724–4657* ⊕ *www.themezzaninepr.com* ⊙ *Closed Mon.*

CLOSE UP

The Piña Colada Wars

This mixture of pineapple juice, coconut cream, and liberal amounts of rum, always garnished with a wedge of pineapple and a maraschino cherry, was invented by Ramón Marrero at the Caribe Hilton in 1954, or by Ramón Portas Mingot at the Barranchina Bar in 1963, depending on who you believe. Was it Marrero, a young bartender who is said to have spent three months on a concoction that would appeal to patrons at the Beachcomber's Bar? (His secret? Using only fresh pineapple juice.) Or was it Mingot, an elderly bartender who was satisfying the whims of patrons at the bar in Old San Juan? (He said his were so frothy because he froze the pineapple juice and coconut cream mixture instead of simply adding crushed ice.)

The two venues have fought over bragging rights for decades. The Caribe Hilton issues press release after press release reminding people that the drink was born in its seaside bar. (If what its public relations department says is true, the drink celebrated its 50th anniversary in 2004.) The Barranchina Bar put up a plaque that tells passersby that it is the true birthplace of the beverage. The Caribe Hilton seems to have the edge. Coco López, the company that makes the coconut cream most often used in the drink, honored Marrero in 1978. In gratitude for his contributions to the "bartending arts," they presented him with a color television set. But the origin of the piña colada—which means "strained pineapple"—remains as unclear as the cocktail itself. You may have to sample several before you make up your own mind.

—Mark Sullivan

Mist. On the roof of the San Juan Water & Beach Club Hotel, this sexy spot offers some of the best ocean views anywhere in Isla Verde. On the weekends there's a DJ, and locals pack in to relax at the bar or on the leather beds reserved for bottle service. If you get hungry, order from the eclectic Socializers menu. Try the serrano ham flatbread with fig marmalade and goat cheese or the pork belly *banh mi.* ⊠ *San Juan Water & Beach Club, 2 Calle Tartak, Isla Verde* ☎ *787/725–4664* ⊕ *www. waterbeachclubhotel.com.*

Old Harbor Brewery. Serious beer-lovers know to head to this authentic microbrewery and restaurant close to the harborfront. More clubby than pubby, it packs in locals as well as tourists who come to taste the five delicious German-style beers, brewed in European-style open fermentation tanks. Order the five-beer sampler before making a selection for a pint-glass or liter stein. Live music, ranging from pop to jazz, is played on Thursday, Friday, and Saturday evenings. ⊠ *202 Calle Tizol, at Calle Recinto Sur, Old San Juan* ☎ *787/721–2100* ⊕ *www. oldharborbrewery.com.*

CASINOS

By law, all casinos are in hotels, and the government keeps a close eye on them. They're allowed to operate 24 hours a day, but individual casinos set their own hours. In addition to slot machines, typical games include blackjack, roulette, craps, Caribbean stud poker (a five-card stud game), and *pai gow* poker (a combination of American poker and the ancient Chinese game of *pai gow*, which employs cards and dice). That said, an easing of gaming regulations has set a more relaxed tone and made such perks as free drinks and live music more common. The range of available games has also greatly expanded. The minimum age is 18. Dress for the larger casinos in San Juan tends to be on the formal side, and the atmosphere is refined. Tank tops or shorts are usually not acceptable attire.

REGGAETÓN

If you go out to San Juan's popular dance clubs you're likely to hear this hip-hop–influenced mix of Jamaican reggae and dance-hall styles along with some Latin rhythms. The music has a strong electronic drum-machine beat, and the lyrics are in Spanish. Many believe that the music got its start in Puerto Rico, but its popularity has spread much farther.

The Casino at The Ritz-Carlton, San Juan. With its golden columns, turquoise and bronze walls, and muted lighting, the Ritz casino, the largest in San Juan, stays refined by day or night. There's lots of activity, yet everything is hushed. ⊠ *6991 Av. de los Gobernadores, Isla Verde* ☎ *787/253–1700* ⊕ *www.ritzcarlton.com/sanjuan.*

The El San Juan Casino. Neither the clangs of the slots nor the sounds of the salsa band disrupt the semblance of Old World. The polish continues in the adjacent lobby, with its huge chandeliers and mahogany paneling. ⊠ *6063 Av. Isla Verde, Isla Verde* ☎ *787/791–1000.*

InterContinental San Juan Resort & Casino. A blue neon light envelops you as you enter this casino, which draws locals and visitors with its elegant decor. Live music is usually available on Saturday nights. ⊠ *5961 Av. Isla Verde, Isla Verde* ☎ *787/791–6100* ⊕ *www.icsanjuanresort.com.*

San Juan Marriott Resort & Stellaris Casino. The crowd is casual and the decor tropical and bubbly at this spacious gaming room. Right outside, there's a huge bar, where Latin musicians perform Wednesday through Sunday, and an adjacent café. ⊠ *1309 Av. Ashford, Condado* ☎ *787/722–7000.*

Sheraton Old San Juan Hotel & Casino. It's impossible to ignore this ground-floor casino, the only place to gamble in Old San Juan. You can see the gaming room from the hotel's main stairway, the balcony above, and the lobby. Light bounces off the Bahía de San Juan and pours through its many windows; passengers bound off their cruise ships and pour through its many glass doors. ⊠ *100 Calle Brumbaugh, Old San Juan* ☎ *787/721–5100* ⊕ *www.sheratonoldsanjuan.com.*

DANCE CLUBS

Brava. A long line of young people can be spotted at the door of this chic club at the El San Juan Resort. The two-level club, each with its own DJ and dance floor, is one of the best places for dancing. Dress to impress at this 21+ club. ⊠ *El San Juan Resort & Casino, 6063 Av. Isla Verde, Isla Verde* ☎ *787/791-2781* ⊕ *www.bravapr.com* ☺ *Thurs.–Sat. 10pm–5am.*

GAY AND LESBIAN BARS AND CLUBS

With its sophisticated nightlife, San Juan has become a popular destination for gay and lesbian tourists. Condado, perhaps the heart of gay San Juan, is a favorite destination for happy hour. It hosts an annual gay pride march each June, full of music and dancing, that rivals those in similar cities around the world. Santurce, just south of Condado, has several bars and clubs that cater to men and women of all ages. Most are located on or near Avenida Ponce de León. Stay alert, as parts of this neighborhood can be dangerous at night; consider taking a taxi to your destination rather than walking after dark.

Atlantic Beach. The oceanfront deck bar of this hotel is famed in the gay community for its weekday happy hours from 5–10 pm. But the pulsating tropical music, exotic drinks, and ever-pleasant ocean breeze would make it a hit in any case. ✉ *Atlantic Beach Hotel, 1 Calle Vendig, Condado* ☎ *787/721–6900* ⊕ *www.atlanticbeachhotel.com.*

LATIN MUSIC

Nuyorican Café. There's something interesting happening at this hipper-than-hip, no-frills, wood-paneled performance space nearly every night, be it an early evening play, poetry reading, or talent show or, later on, a band playing Latin jazz, Cuban *son*, Puerto Rican salsa, or rock. On Wednesday nights, watch the owner play the conga drums with the house salsa band, Comborican. During breaks between performances the youthful, creative crowd chats in an alley outside the front door. There is usually a $5 cover charge. ✉ *312 Calle San Fransico, entrance on Callejón de la Capilla, Old San Juan* ☎ *787/977–1276* ⊕ *www.nuyoricancafepr.com* ☾ *Closed Mon. and Tues.*

NIGHT BITES

San Juan is a cosmopolitan city by Caribbean standards, welcoming to all kinds of visitors, with plenty of late-night places. The establishments listed here are generally open until at least midnight during the week and 2 am on weekends. But many are open much later. Old San Juan's Brickhaus, for example, proudly proclaims that its kitchen doesn't close until 3 am.

Bar Gitano. One of the few late-night dining options in Condado, Bar Gitano keeps the tasty tapas and sangria flowing until around midnight during the week, later on weekends. Mingle with the well-dressed locals and see what makes Puerto Rico such an exotic destination. ✉ *1309 Av. Ashford, C-1, Old San Juan* ☎ *787/294–5513* ⊕ *www.ootwrestaurants.com.*

La Taberna Lúpulo. If you love beer, don't leave Puerto Rico Rico without visiting La Taberna Lúpulo. At the island's largest craft beer bar you'll find 50 beers on tap and over 150 bottles of the finest European and American brews. This casual, hipster bar is open late and a great option for night bites. The menu changes weekly, with specials ranging from Vietnamese pho, Moroccan stew, curried chicken noodle, and Sloppy Sliders. Sunday "Hangover Brunch" is very popular among locals. They make some of the best Bloody Marys town. ✉ *151 Calle San Sebastian, Old San Juan* ☎ *787/721–3772.*

Pirilo. Day and night, locals flock to Pirilo to indulge in some of the finest pizza to be had in San Juan. The restaurant now boasts a second floor with substantial seating, high-vaulted ceilings, and a bar focused on brews. Owner Eduardo Rubio makes everything from scratch, most notably the pizza crust, which uses a 300-year-old starter as its base. You can have anything from a classic margherita pie to one based on the local *tripleta* sandwich. Given the nightly crowds, it's clear that others are in on the secret. It's always packed and there might be a wait, but everyone is having such a good time, you won't mind, especially with more than 50 craft brews available. ⊠ *201 Calle Fortaleza, Old San Juan* ☎ *787/721–3322.*

Señor Frog's. Latin America's answer to the Hard Rock Cafe, Señor Frog's attracts both hard-partying tourists and the cruise-ship crowd—no surprise, as it's located directly in front of the dock. (Look for the giant inflatable frog.) The just-okay menu is a nod to Mexico, with south-of-the-border favorites like nachos and quesadillas. When it comes to drinks, expect quantity over quality; their signature is the Yard, a tall plastic cup filled with your favorite adult beverage. There's often live music, a ladies' night, or other special events. ⊠ *Paseo Gilberto Concepción de Gracia, corner of Brumbaugh, Old San Juan* ☎ *787/977–4142* ⊕ *www.senorfrogs.com.*

THE ARTS

San Juan is arguably one of the most important cultural centers of the Caribbean, both for its homegrown culture and the healthy influx of visiting artists that the local population supports. The city hosts the Puerto Rico Symphony Orchestra, the world-renowned Pablo Casals classical-music festival in winter, and an annual series of opera concerts. Many hit plays in New York and other large markets get produced locally, and there are often three or four other local theatrical productions taking place on any given weekend, many of them downright adventurous.

PERFORMING ARTS

MAJOR EVENTS

The Casals Festival. The Casals Festival has been bringing some of the most important figures in classical music to San Juan ever since Pablo Casals, the famous cellist, conductor, and composer, started the festival in 1957. Casals went on to direct it until his death in 1973. It has continued to serve as a vibrant stage for top-notch classical performers since then. Most of the shows are held at the Centro de Bellas Artes Luis A. Ferré, but performances are also at the University of Puerto Rico and other venues. The festival takes place from mid-February through mid-March. Tickets are available at the box office of the Centro de Bellas Artes Luis A Ferré and through ⊕ *ticketpop.com* ⊠ *Luis A. Ferré Performing Arts Center, 22 Ponce de León Ave., Box office, Santurce* ☎ *787/918–1106* ⊕ *www.festcasalspr.gobierno.pr.*

Puerto Rico Heineken Jazzfest. San Juan is a great place to hear jazz, particularly Latin jazz, and the annual Puerto Rico Heineken Jazzfest, which takes place in March at the Tito Puente Amphitheater, is one of the best opportunities for it. Each year's festival is dedicated to a particular musician. Honorees have included Chick Corea, Mongo Santamaria, and Dizzy Gillespie. ⊠ *Av. Franklin Roosevelt* ☎ *866/994–0001, 787/294–0001* ⊕ *www.prheinekenjazz.com.*

TICKETS

Two major outlets sell tickets for events throughout Puerto Rico.

Ticket Center. With ticket counters available in many of the malls on the island, Ticket Center is a convenient way to score seats to most large-scale events. ☎ *787/792–5000* ⊕ *www.tcpr.com.*

Ticketpop. Here is a fast and easy method to purchase tickets online for major concerts, sporting events, and other shows. ☎ *866/994–0001, 787/294–0001* ⊕ *www.ticketpop.com.*

PERFORMANCE VENUES

Centro de Bellas Artes Luis A. Ferré (*Luis A. Ferré Center for the Performing Arts*). With four different theaters, the largest of which holds up to 1,900 people, this is the largest venue of its kind in the Caribbean. There's something going on nearly every night, from pop or jazz concerts to plays, operas, and ballets. It's also the home of the Puerto Rico Symphony Orchestra. ⊠ *22 Av. Ponce de León, Santurce* ☎ *787/724–4747, 787/620–4444* ⊕ *www.cba.gobierno.pr.*

Coliseo de Puerto Rico José Miguel Agrelot. Seating up to 18,000 people, this relatively new arena, affectionately known as "El Choliseo," is the top venue for international musical events on the island. Previous perfomers have included Ozzy Osbourne, Paul McCartney, Shakira, Beyoncé, and, of course, hometown favorite, Ricky Martin. ⊠ *50 Calle Arterial B, Hato Rey* ☎ *787/777–0800* ⊕ *www.coliseodepuertorico.com.*

Coliseo Roberto Clemente. Named after hall-of-fame baseball player Roberto Clemente, the arena has become an important island venue for concerts and fairs in addition to its status as a sports facility. Rap, reggae, salsa, jazz, and pop musicians all play this venue, which holds 8,000 people. ⊠ *500 Av. Roosevelt, across from Plaza las Américas, Hato Rey* ☎ *787/781–2586.*

Fundación Nacional Para la Cultura Popular. This multifaceted foundation hosts a variety of events, including Latin music and dance performances and classes. Check out the schedule online or call ahead to see what's on. ⊠ *56 Calle Fortaleza, Old San Juan* ☎ *787/724–7165* ⊕ *www.PRpop.org.*

Teatro Tapia. Named for Puerto Rican playwright Alejandro Tapia y Rivera, Teatro Tapia is the oldest theater in Puerto Rico and hosts traveling and locally produced theatrical and musical productions. Matinee performances with family entertainment are also held here, especially around the holidays. Stop by the box office to find out what's showing. ⊠ *Plaza Colón, Calle Fortaleza, Old San Juan* ☎ *787/480–5004* ⊕ *www.teatropr.com.*

GROUPS

Orquesta Sinfónica de Puerto Rico (*Puerto Rico Symphony Orchestra*). Under the direction of conductor Maximiano Valdés, the 80 members of this prominent orchestra perform a full 52-week season that includes classical-music concerts, operas, ballets, and popular-music

San Juan shopping options include Plaza las Américas, the largest mall in the Caribbean.

performances. The orchestra plays most shows at Centro de Bellas Artes Luis A. Ferré, but it also gives outdoor concerts at museums and university campuses around the island, and it has an educational outreach program in island schools. Pablo Casals, the impetus for this group, helped create it in 1956. ☎ 787/918–1108 ⊕ *www.sinfonicapr.gobierno.pr*.

SHOPS AND SPAS

In Old San Juan, Calle Fortaleza and Calle San Francisco have everything from T-shirt emporiums to jewelry stores to shops that specialize in made-to-order Panama hats. Running perpendicular to those streets is Calle Cristo, lined with factory-outlet stores, including Coach, Dooney & Burke, Guess, and Tommy Hilfiger. On weekends, artisans sell their wares at stalls around Paseo de la Princesa.

With many stores selling luxury items and designer fashions, the shopping spirit in Condado is reminiscent of that in Miami. Avenida Ashford is considered the heart of San Juan's fashion district. High-end chain stores such as Louis Vuitton, Ferragamo, and Gucci are huddled together in what was formerly a derelict shopping strip. They are betting that the newly renovated luxury hotel La Concha will attract people ready to plunk down their platinum credit cards. A little farther west along Avenida Ashford are the one-of-a-kind clothing retailers that make this neighborhood worth a visit.

Just as in most other American cities, however, the real shopping occurs in the mall, and the upscale mall here, Plaza Las Américas—the largest in the Caribbean—is not to be missed. Known to locals simply as

"Plaza," it's often host to artisan crafts fairs, art exhibitions, antiques shows, live Latin music, and pageants, depending on the time of year. Thanks to Puerto Rico's vibrant art scene, numerous galleries and studios are opening, and many are doing so in Santurce, Puerta de Tierra, and other neighborhoods outside the Old City walls. If you prefer shopping in air-conditioned comfort, there are plenty of malls in and just outside San Juan.

MARKETS AND MALLS

Plaza Las Américas. For a complete shopping experience, head to the massive Plaza Las Américas, which has more than 300 retailers, including the world's largest JCPenney store, Build-A-Bear Workshop, Carolina Herrera, ZARA, Gap, Sears, Macy's, Sephora, Coach, Forever 21, L'Occitane, and Armani Exchange, as well as multiple restaurants and movie theaters. ⊠ *525 Av. Franklin Delano Roosevelt, Hato Rey* ☎ *787/767–1525* ⊕ *www.plazalasamericas.com.*

OUTLETS

Old San Juan has turned into an open-air duty-free shop for people pouring off the cruise ships. Because they have only a few hours in port, they often pass by more interesting shops and head directly for the factory outlets on and around Calle Cristo. The prices aren't particularly good, but nobody seems to mind.

Belz Factory Outlet World. Belz Factory Outlet World has more than 135 factory outlet stores, including BCBG, Nautica, Nike, Guess, Gap, and Polo Ralph Lauren. It's in Canóvanas, about 20 minutes east of San Juan. ⊠ *18400 Rte. 3, Km 18.4* ☎ *787/256–7040* ⊕ *www. theoutlet66mall.com.*

Coach. Stylish, upscale handbags for men and women can be purchased at Coach for a discounted price. ⊠ *158 Calle Cristo, Old San Juan* ☎ *787/722–6830.*

Puerto Rico Premium Outlets. About an hour west of San Juan in quiet Barceloneta, Puerto Rico Premium Outlets has around 90 stores, including Banana Republic, Michael Kors, Perry Ellis, Carter's, and Ann Taylor, as well as a movie theater. If you get hungry, the best spot for lunch is the local branch of the tasty Cuban–Puerto Rican restaurant Metropol, which is right across from the outlets. ⊠ *1 Premium Outlets Boulevard, Barceloneta* ☎ *787/846–5300* ⊕ *www.premiumoutlets.com.*

Ralph Lauren. Ralph Lauren's shop in front of the piers has some of the best deals around. Stop here toward the end of your trip, as there are plenty of items (e.g., pea coats and scarves) that you won't be wearing until you get home. ⊠ *105 Paseo Gilberto Concepcion de Gracia, Harbor Plaza Building, Old San Juan* ☎ *787/724–1020.*

Tommy Hilfiger. There's signature Tommy gear for men and women at the Tommy Hilfiger in Old San Juan, and their staff is very friendly. ⊠ *206 Calle Cristo, Old San Juan* ☎ *787/729–2230.*

SPECIALTY SHOPS

ART

Galería Botello. The very influential Galería Botello displays the works of the late Angel Botello, who was hailed as the "Caribbean Gauguin" as far back as 1943. His work, which often uses the bright colors of the tropics, usually depicts island scenes. His paintings hang in the Museo de Arte de Puerto Rico. There are works on display here by other prominent local artists as well. ⊠ *208 Calle Cristo, Old San Juan* ☎ *787/723–9987* ⊕ *www.botello.com* ◷ *Closed Sun.*

Galería Viota. Galería Viota offers regularly changing works by contemporary Puerto Rican and Latin American artists. ⊠ *793 Av. San Patricio, Guaynabo* ☎ *787/782–1752* ⊕ *www.viotagallery.com.*

CIGARS

Cigar House. The Cigar House has an eclectic selection of local and imported cigars from Nicaragua, Honduras, and the Dominican Republic. At the lounge and bar, you can enjoy your purchase with a glass of your favorite spirit. ⊠ *257 Calle Fortaleza, Old San Juan* ☎ *787/723–5223* ⊕ *www.thecigarhousepr.com.*

CLOTHING

MEN'S CLOTHING

El Galpón. At El Galpón, knowledgeable owners Betsy and Gustavo will fit you with a Panama hat, from $65 to $900. You'll also learn that a genuine Panama hat is made in Ecuador. They also carry a large selection of Puerto Rican *santos,* hand-carved wooden saints. ⊠ *154 Calle Cristo, Old San Juan* ☎ *787/725–3945* ⊕ *www.elgalpon.net.*

Monsieur. The quality clothing at Monsieur is very sleek and stylish—everything for the well-dressed man. ⊠ *1126 Av. Ashford, Condado* ☎ *787/722–0918* ⊕ *www.monsieurpuertorico.com.*

Olé. Aficionados of the famous Panama hat, made from delicately hand-woven straw, should stop at Olé. The shop sells top-of-the-line hats for as much as $1,000 as well as more affordable hats that can be custom-fit. Take a few moments to browse the other goods for sale like the decade-old santos, hand-carved wood figurines of saints, and used books. ⊠ *105 Calle Fortaleza, Old San Juan* ☎ *787/724–2445.*

Otto. In his shop, Otto Bauzá stocks international lines of casual and formal wear for younger men. ⊠ *69 Av. Condado, Condado* ☎ *787/722–4609* ◷ *Closed Sun. and Mon.*

MEN'S AND WOMEN'S CLOTHING

Abitto. Hipper than most other Condado boutiques, Abitto carries designer fashion for men and women including John Galliano, Alexander McQueen, YSL, Versace, Roberto Cavalli, and others. ⊠ *1124 Av. Ashford, Condado* ☎ *787/724–0303* ◷ *Closed Sun.*

David Antonio. Prolific designer David Antonio runs a shop that's small but full of surprises. His joyful creations range from updated versions of the men's classic guayabera to fluid chiffon and silk tunics and dresses for women. ⊠ *69 Ave. Condado, Condado* ☎ *787/725–0600* ⊕ *www.davidantoniopr.com.*

Nono Maldonado. Nono Maldonado is well known for his high-end, elegant clothes for men and women, particularly those done in linen. He should know a thing or two about style—he worked for many years as the fashion editor of *Esquire* and presents a periodic couture collection. This second-floor store also serves as the designer's studio. ✉ *1112 Av. Ashford, 2nd floor, Condado* ☎ *787/721–0456* ⊕ *www. nonomaldonado.com* ⊗ *Closed Sun.*

WOMEN'S CLOTHING

Ambar. Garments by Cambodian-French designer Romyda Keth, whose use of exotic colors and sensuous fabrics meshes perfectly with Puerto Rico's tropical environment, are in the spotlight at Ambar. The store carries only one of each design (of which only eight to ten exist worldwide), ensuring that you're the only one on the entire island who will ever be wearing a particular look. ✉ *69 Av. Condado, Condado* ☎ *787/203–7049* ⊗ *Closed Sun.*

Cappalli. Noted local designer Lisa Cappalli sells her feminine, sensuous designs in this elegant boutique, which specializes in ready-to-wear and custom fashions including a small collection of whimsical, lacy wedding gowns. ✉ *206 Calle O'Donnell, Old San Juan* ☎ *787/289–6565* ⊕ *www.lisacappalli.net.*

Concalma. Designer Matilsha Marxuach, who has an eye toward sustainable fashion, has her hip line of fair-trade handbags, messenger bags, bathing suits, vintage clothing, and other items made by local designers. ✉ *207 Calle San Francisco, Old San Juan* ☎ *787/421–4212* ⊕ *www.concalmalinea.com.*

Harry Robles. Puerto Rican couture designer, Harry Robles, specializes in elegant evening and bridal gowns. ✉ *1752 Calle Loíza, Ocean Park* ☎ *787/727–3885* ⊕ *www.harryrobles.com.*

Marella. This boutique sells trendy women's apparel from labels that include Parker, Diane von Furstenberg, Yumi Kim, Karina Grimaldi, Ramona LaRue, and Alexis. ✉ *1300 Av. Ashford, Condado* ☎ *787/722–0010* ⊗ *Closed Sun.*

Mia. Mia is the place for youthful, sophisticated outfits that look as if they belong in an art gallery—either on display or on one of the artists. ✉ *1112 Av. Ashford, Condado* ☎ *787/721–5808.*

Nativa. The window displays at Nativa are almost as daring as the clothes it sells. The shop caters to trendy, young ladies looking for party dresses, jumpers, accessories, shoes, and more. ✉ *55 Calle Cervantes, Condado* ☎ *787/724–1396* ⊕ *www.nativaboutique.net* ⊗ *Closed Sun.*

Piña Colada Club. A great place to scout out casual resort wear, cover-ups, swimwear, and tropical-inspired jewelry, Piña Colada Club carries its own clothing line, as well as that of Karina Grimaldi, Indah, Maaji, and others. ✉ *1102 Av. Magdalena, Condado* ☎ *787/998–1980.*

Pure Soul. Sylma Cabrera sells chic resort wear made of natural fabrics by local artists and under her own label, Pure Soul. You'll also find stunning hand-made jewelry with semi-precious stones like quartz and lapis lazuli. ✉ *258 Calle San Justo, corner Tetuán, Old San Juan* ☎ *787/723–2800* ⊕ *www.puresoulboutique.com.*

Design Lions

Puerto Rico's young fashion designers have opened many a boutique and atelier in metropolitan San Juan during the last few years. Their styles may differ, but these young lions all share an island heritage—complete with a tradition of true craftsmanship—and a level of sophistication acquired after studying and traveling abroad. The result is a fascinating assortment of original, exclusive, high-quality designs.

With all the warmth and sun, it goes without saying that Puerto Rico's designers are most inspired when it comes to creations for the spring and summer seasons. Lacy, flowing creations and lightweight, if not sheer, fabrics dominate designs for women. For men the trend is toward updated linen classics in tropical whites and creams. Whatever you find will be one of a kind, with stylish—if not playful or downright sexy—lines. Some of these designers have their own shops in San Juan.

Which designers should you check out? Lisa Cappalli, a graduate of New York City's Parsons School of Design, favors lace, as lace making is a tradition in her family. David Antonio uses upbeat colors—bold reds and vibrant oranges—in his updated classics. Harry Robles is a bit more established than his peers; he specializes in gowns for women, and his draping designs are often dramatic and always elegant. Each of these young designers has a shop in San Juan.

To see their collections, consider visiting during San Juan Fashion Week, which takes place each year in March and September. The events are full of shows and cocktail parties, all organized by the Puerto Rico Fashion Designers Group under the leadership of island-fashion icons Nono Maldonado and Mirtha Rubio.

—Isabel Abislaimán

Suola. As you might expect at a shop named after the Italian word for "sole," the boot-shaped country is the origin of most of the mile-high heels here, which include designs by Alexander McQueen, Christian Louboutin, YSL, and Sergio Rossi. ⊠ *1060 Av. Ashford, Condado* ☎ *787/723–6653* ✆ *Closed Sun.*

The Velvet Room. Local fashion designer Natalia Collazo runs this hip boutique in Condado. You'll find one-of-a-kind clothing and jewelry pieces in her trendy showroom. At the time of this writing, Natalia is developing her own label. ⊠ *151 Ave. de Diego, Condado* ☎ *787/545–2855.*

FURNITURE AND ANTIQUES

El Alcázar. For nearly three decades, Robert and Sharon Bartos have been selling antiques and objet d'art from all over the world, with much of it from Europe. ⊠ *103 Calle San José, Old San Juan* ☎ *787/723–1229* ⊕ *www.elalcazar.com* ✆ *Mon.–Sat. 12–6, Sun. 2–6.*

GIFTS

Butterfly People. Exotic *mariposas* cover the walls of Butterfly People. Clear plastic cases hold common species as well as many rarer specimens. The butterflies come from certified farms and are gathered only once they "have completed their short life spans," as the store puts it. ⊠ *257 Calle de la Cruz, Old San Juan* ☎ *787/723–2432* ⊕ *www. butterflypeople.com* ☽ *Closed Fri.*

Spicy Caribbee. Kitchen items, cookbooks, jams, spices, and sauces from around the Caribbean are on offer at Spicy Caribbee. ⊠ *154 Calle Cristo, Old San Juan* ☎ *888/725–7259* ⊕ *www.spicycaribbee.com.*

HANDICRAFTS

Arte & Máscaras. Arte & Máscaras specializes in traditional Puerto Rican festival masks, known as *vejigantes,* and their walls are covered with masks from all over the island. The store carries a unique selection of masks by Juan Alindato, one of Puerto Rico's most famous *vejigante* artists. ⊠ *268 Calle San Francisco, Old San Juan* ☎ *787/453–9856.*

Eclectika. At this boutique, you'll find a variety of items, mostly from Indonesia. From bedspreads to beaded and wooden jewelry, furnishings to hand fans, you could easily loose track of time as you browse through the shop for unqiue gift ideas. Everything is reasonably priced and you might just end up keeping everything you bought for yourself! ⊠ *204 Calle O'Donnell, Plaza Colón, Old San Juan* ☎ *787/721–7236.*

Haitian Gallery. The shop carries Haitian masks, statues, paintings, and wooden works of art. The second floor houses a large slection of paintings from the Caribbean. ⊠ *367 Calle Fortaleza, Old San Juan* ☎ *787/725–0986* ⊕ *www.haitiangallerypr.com.*

Magia. The clever shop Magia carries what appear to be traditional crafts, but look more closely. Each work, most of which are done by artist-owner Manolo Díaz, is quite unique. A little wooden shrine, for example, might be sheltering an image of Marilyn Monroe. You can also find vintage costume jewelry and Puerto Rican *santos.* ⊠ *99 Calle Cristo, Old San Juan* ☎ *787/368–6164* ☽ *Closed Sun.*

Mi Pequeño San Juan. You might manage to find the hotel where you're staying reproduced in plaster at this shop, which specializes in tiny ceramic versions of San Juan doorways. The works, all created by hand right in the shop, make a wonderful souvenir. You can also pick up fine art prints. ⊠ *152 Calle Fortaleza, Old San Juan* ☎ *787/721–5040* ⊕ *www.mipequenosanjuan.com.*

Mundo Taíno. Near Plaza de Armas Square, Mundo Taíno sells high-quality folk art from around the island. ⊠ *151 San José, Old San Juan* ☎ *787/724–2005.*

Puerto Rican Arts & Crafts. For one-of-a-kind *santos,* art, ceramics, and festival masks, head for Puerto Rican Arts & Crafts. All artwork is made by local artists. ⊠ *204 Calle Fortaleza, Old San Juan* ☎ *787/725–5596* ⊕ *www.puertoricanart-crafts.com.*

JEWELRY

Bared & Sons. If you're in the market for a Rolex, Cartier, Bvlgari, or Brietling watch, visit Bared. The store also carries a large selection of fine jewelry. Look for the massive clock face on the corner. ⊠ *206 San Justo, Old San Juan* ☎ *787/724–4811.*

Catalá Joyeros. A family-run business since the 1930s, Catalá Joyeros is known for its large selection of pearls, precious stones, and jewelry design. ✉ *Plaza de Armas, 152 Rafael Cordero, Old San Juan* ☎ *787/722–3231* ⊕ *www.catalajoyeros.com* ☾ *Closed Sun.*

Club Jibarito. Club Jibarito has a fantastic collection of high-end watches by Audemars Piguet, Chopard, H.Stern, Harry Winston, Panerai, and other designers. ✉ *202 Calle Cristo, Old San Juan* ☎ *787/724–7797* ⊕ *www.clubjibarito.com.*

N. Barquet Joyero. One of the bigger jewelry stores in Old San Juan, N. Barquet Joyero carries pieces in 18K gold and is the exclusive vendor of Italian designer, Nanis. Their *coquí el original* brand, depicting the local tree frog, has become a popular souvenier. If you are looking for unique and high-end jewels, ask to browse the private back room. ✉ *201 Calle Fortaleza, Old San Juan* ☎ *787/721–3366* ⊕ *www.nbarquet.com.*

Portofino. Portofino has an especially good selection of watches. ✉ *250 Calle San Francisco, Old San Juan* ☎ *787/723–5113.*

Reinhold Jewelers. Reinhold Jewelers sells designs by Stephen Dweck, David Yurman, Tiffany & Co., and others. ✉ *Plaza Las Américas, 525 Av. Franklin Delano Roosevelt, Hato Rey* ☎ *787/754–0528* ⊕ *www.reinholdjewelers.com* ✉ *El San Juan Resort & Casino, 6063 Av. Isla Verde, Isla Verde* ☎ *787/791–2521.*

SPAS

Olas Spa at the Caribe Hilton. This full-service spa offers a range of luxurious treatments, including the popular four-hand massage, hydrotherapy, facials, and other body treatments. An Aveda salon is also on-site. ✉ *Caribe Hilton, Los Rosales Street, Gerónimo Grounds, Puerta de Tierra* ☎ *787/977–5500, 877/888–6527* ⊕ *www.olasspa.com.*

The Ritz-Carlton Spa, San Juan. Popular treatments at this posh spa include stone therapy, the balancing lomilomi massage, based on a Hawaiian ritual mimicking waves, and the Ritz-Carlton's signature facial. You can also schedule a private yoga class, weight training session, and salsa lessons. ✉ *6961 Av. de los Gobernadores, Isla Verde* ☎ *787/253–4131* ⊕ *www.ritzcarlton.com.*

Zen Spa. This family-run spa focuses on wellness, with staff trained in Western, Chinese, and Ayurvedic techniques, but all kinds of treatments are available. One facial uses silk fibers to firm and tone skin. You can also get a green tea clay wrap or a lymphatic drainage massage. An attached shop sells Kiehl's and Eminence Organics products, as well the house line, Zendera. ✉ *1054 Av. Ashford, Condado* ☎ *787/722–8433, 866/936–7720* ⊕ *www.zen-spa.com.*

SPORTS AND THE OUTDOORS

Many of San Juan's most enjoyable outdoor activities take place in and around the water. With miles of beach stretching across Isla Verde, Ocean Park, and Condado, there's a full range of water sports, including sailing, kayaking, windsurfing, paddleboarding, kiteboarding, Jet Skiing, deep-sea fishing, scuba diving, and snorkeling.

San Juan's well-equipped *balnearios* (public beaches) are among the best on the island.

Land-based activities include biking, tennis, and walking or jogging at local parks. With a bit of effort—meaning a short drive out of the city—you'll discover a world of championship golf courses and rain-forest trails perfect for hiking. Baseball is big in Puerto Rico, and the players are world-class; many are recruited from local teams to play in the U.S. major leagues. The season runs from October through February. Games are played in venues around the island.

BASEBALL

Does the name Roberto Clemente ring a bell? The late, great star of the Pittsburgh Pirates, who died in a 1972 plane crash delivering supplies to Nicaraguan earthquake victims, was born near San Juan and got his start in the Puerto Rican pro leagues. Many other Puerto Rican stars have played in the U.S. major leagues, including the brothers Roberto Alomar and Sandy Alomar Jr. and their father, Sandy Alomar. Three players have been inducted into the National Baseball Hall of Fame: Clemente, Roberto Alomar, and Orlando Cepeda.

BIKING

Most streets don't have bike lanes, and auto traffic makes bike travel somewhat risky; further, all the fumes can be hard to take. That said, recreational bikers are increasingly donning their safety gear and wheel-ing through the streets, albeit with great care.

Your best bet is to look into a bike tour offered by an outfitter. One popular 45-minute trip travels from Old San Juan's cobblestone streets to Condado. It passes El Capitolio and runs through either Parque del Tercer Milenio (oceanside) or Parque Luis Muñoz Rivera, taking you past the Caribe Hilton Hotel and over Puente Dos Hermanos (Dos Hermanos Bridge) onto Avenida Ashford. The truly ambitious can continue east to Ocean Park, Isla Verde, and right on out of town to the eastern community of Piñones and its beachside bike path.

Rent the Bicycle. For about $27 a day, this friendly operation offers bicycle rental with free delivery to all major San Juan hotels. They also offer guided tours of Old San Juan and greater San Juan beaches and parks. The bilingual guides are authorized by the National Park Service to give tours of the forts. ⊠ *Capitolio Plaza, 100 Calle del Muelle, Suite 205, Old San Juan* ☎ *787/661–2728* ⊕ *www.rentthebicycle.net.*

DIVING AND SNORKELING

The waters off San Juan aren't the best places to scuba dive, but several outfitters conduct short excursions to where tropical fish, coral, and sea horses are visible at depths of 30 to 60 feet. Escorted half-day dives start around $70 for one or two tanks, including all equipment; in general, double those prices for night dives. Packages that include lunch and other extras start at $100; others that include accommodations are also available.

Snorkeling excursions, which include transportation, equipment rental, and sometimes lunch, start at $55–$60. Equipment rents at beaches for about $10. Avoid unsupervised areas, as rough waters and strong undertows make some places dangerous.

Ocean Sports. Ocean Sports offers certified scuba courses; snorkeling excursions; specialty courses in nitrox diving; diving trips; airtank fill-ups; and equipment repairs, sales, and rentals. ⊠ *3086 Av. Isla Verde, Isla Verde* ☎ *787/723–8513* ⊕ *www.osdivers.com.*

FISHING

Puerto Rico's waters are home to large game fish such as snook, wahoo, dorado, tuna, and barracuda; as many as 30 world records for catches have been set off the island's shores. Prices for fishing expeditions vary, but they tend to include all your bait and tackle, as well as refreshments, and start at $600 (for a boat with as many as six people) for a half-day trip to around $1,000 for a full day, or around $200 per person for a full day on a split charter.

GOLF

Puerto Rico is the birthplace of golf legend and raconteur Chi Chi Rodriguez—and he had to hone his craft somewhere. The island has more than a dozen courses, including some of championship caliber. Several make good day trips from San Juan. Be sure to call ahead for details on reserving tee times; hours vary, and several hotel courses allow only guests to play or give preference to them. Greens fees start at $25 and go as high as $190.

Three golf clubs are within fairly easy striking distance of San Juan. The four 18-hole golf courses at the **Dorado Beach Resort** are just west of San Juan.

Dorado Beach Resort Golf. If you want Caribbean luxury and great golf with four flavors, go no further than the Dorado Beach Resort, an

> **A GOLF GREAT**
>
> Juan "Chi Chi" Rodriguez, who was born in Río Piedras, was the first Puerto Rican golfer to be inducted into the World Golf Hall of Fame.

iconic name for golf with a storied tradition in Puerto Rico with four 18-hole regulation courses. The famous East and the West Courses (closed for renovations at this writing) were designed by Robert Trent Jones, Sr. and are located in a secluded seaside sanctuary along two miles of northeasterly shore within the former Rockefeller estate. Two "Plantation Courses" the Sugarcane (more challenging) and the Pineapple (easier) complete the 72-hole offering. ⊠ *5000 Plantation Dr., Dorado* ☎ *787/262–1010* ⊕ *www.doradobeach clubs.com* ⊠ *East/West Courses, $255; Plantation Courses, $154.* ⚑. *East Course: 18 holes, 7000 yards, par 72; West Course: 18 holes, 6975 yards, par 72; Sugarcane: 18 holes, 7119 yards, par 72 ; Pineapple: 18 holes 7030 yards, par 72.*

There are more options to the east of the city. **Palmas del Mar Country Club** has two good golf courses. *For more information see "Golf" under "Humacao" in Chapter 3, El Yunque and the Northeast.* The spectacular **Río Mar Beach Resort & Spa** has a clubhouse with a pro shop and two restaurants set between two 18-hole courses. *For more information, see "Golf" under "Río Grande" in Chapter 3, El Yunque and the Northeast.*

HIKING

El Yunque is the only tropical rain forest within the U.S. National Forest System. The park is officially known as the Bosque Nacional del Caribe (Caribbean National Forest) and is a great day trip from San Juan, about an hour's drive east. *(For more information, see Chapter 3.)*

HORSE RACING

Hípodromo Camarero. Try your luck with the exactas and quinielas at Hípodromo Camarero, a large thoroughbred racetrack about 20 minutes east of San Juan. On race days the dining rooms open at 12:30 pm. Post time is at 2:30 pm every day except Tuesday and Thursday. There's an air-conditioned clubhouse and restaurant, as well as a bar where people occasionally dance to live rumba music. Parking and admission to the grandstand and clubhouse are free. ⊠ *Rte. 3, Km 15.3, Canóvanas* ☎ *787/641–6060* ⊕ *www.hipodromo-camarero.com.*

KAYAKING

The Laguna del Condado is popular for kayaking, especially on weekends. You can simply paddle around it or head out under the Puente Dos Hermanos to the San Gerónimo fort right behind the Caribe Hilton and across from the Conrad San Juan Condado Plaza. Kayaks rent for $25–$35 an hour.

2

SURFING

See also "Surfing Puerto Rico" feature in Chapter 6. Although the west-coast beaches around Isabela and Rincón are considered *the* places to surf in Puerto Rico, San Juan was actually the place where the sport got its start on the island. In 1958 legendary surfers Gary Hoyt and José Rodríguez Reyes began surfing at the beach in front of Bus Stop 2½, facing El Capitolio. Although this spot is known for its big waves, the conditions must be nearly perfect to surf here. Today many surfers head to Puerta de Tierra and a spot known as La Ocho (in front of Bus Stop 8). Another, called the Pressure Point, is behind the Caribe Hilton Hotel.

In Condado you can surf La Punta, a reef break behind the Presbyterian Hospital, with either surfboards or Boogie boards. In Isla Verde, white water on the horizon means that the waves are good at Pine Grove, the beach break near the Ritz-Carlton. East of the city, in Piñones, the Caballo has deep-to-shallow-water shelf waves that require a big-wave board known as a "gun." The surf culture frowns upon aficionados who divulge the best spots to outsiders. If you're lucky, though, maybe you'll make a few friends who'll let you in on where to find the best waves.

Tres Palmas Surf Shop. At Ocean Park beach, famous surfer Carlos Cabrero, proprietor of Tres Palmas Surf Shop, rents boards, repairs equipment, and sells all sorts of hip beach and surfing gear. ⊠ *1911 Av. McLeary, Ocean Park* ☎ *787/728–3377* ⊕ *www.trespalmaspr.com* ✉ *$25 for Boogie boards, $30 for short boards, $35 for foam boards, and $40 for long boards.*

TENNIS

If you'd like to use the tennis courts at a property where you aren't a guest, call in advance for information about reservations and fees.

Club Tennis de Isla Verde. The four lighted courts of the Club Tennis de Isla Verde are open for nonmember use at $20 per hour for up to four people, daily from 8 am to 10 pm. Reservations are required. ⊠ *Calles Ema and Delta Rodríguez, Isla Verde Park, Isla Verde* ☎ *787/727–6490, 787/642–3208.*

WINDSURFING AND PADDLEBOARDING

The waves can be strong and the surf choppy, but the constant wind makes for good sailing, windsurfing, or paddleboarding, particularly in Ocean Park and Punta Las Marías (between Ocean Park and Isla Verde). In general, you can rent a Windsurfer for about $75 an hour, including a lesson.

Velauno. You'll get the best paddleboarding and windsurfing advice and equipment from Jaime Torres at Velauno, a sort of clearinghouse for information on water sport events throughout the island. The store also sells surfboards and kites and offers repair services and classes. ⊠ *2430 Calle Loíza, Punta Las Marías* ☎ *787/728–8716* ⊕ *www.velauno.com.*

Velauno Paddleboarding. Across the street from the Condado Plaza Hilton on the Condado Lagoon, Velauno offers stand-up paddleboard tours and rentals. One-hour paddleboard rentals are $20, single kayaks $20 and doubles $25. All rentals include a free lesson. ⊠ *860-898 Av. Ashford, Condado Lagoon, Condado* ☎ *787/470-9099* ⊕ *www.velauno.com.*

YOGA

It's Yoga Puerto Rico. Husband-and-wife team David Kyle and Elizabeth Sallaberry found the hot, humid climate of Puerto Rico perfect for practicing and teaching ashtanga vinyasa yoga, one of the more vigorous forms of yoga. Their friendly studio, which has a large local following, offers classes ranging from beginner to advanced (most are held in English) as well as workshops from internationally renowned instructors. Be prepared to sweat, as the studio is intentionally not air-conditioned, though there are ceiling fans. The rate is around $17 for a drop-in class, which includes mat rental. ⊠ *1950 Av. McLeary, Ocean Park* ☎ *787/677–7585* ⊕ *www.itsyogapuertorico.com.*

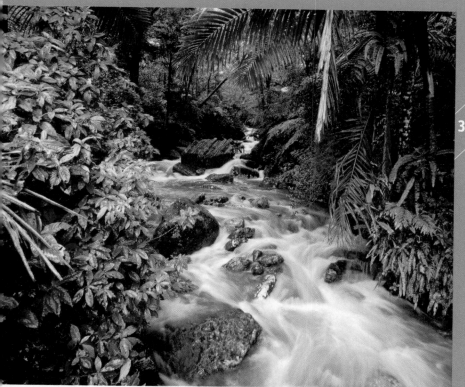

EL YUNQUE AND THE NORTHEAST

WELCOME TO EL YUNQUE AND THE NORTHEAST

TOP REASONS TO GO

★ **Take a hike:** Take in the spectacular waterfalls of El Yunque, the only rain forest within the U.S. National Forest system.

★ **Take a dip:** Relax at Luquillo Beach, one of the prettiest beaches in Puerto Rico and a family favorite.

★ **Take a seat:** Hang with locals at one of the dozens of outdoor seafood kiosks on the highway before you get to the Luquillo Beach. There are at least 60 to choose from.

★ **Hit the links:** Tee off on the tree-lined fairways of the area's many excellent golf courses, especially those at the St. Regis Bahia Beach and Palmas del Mar resorts.

1 The Northeastern Coast. Head southeast and inland of San Juan to escape the city crowds and discover Río Grande's natural green land and its long strips of pristine beach. Its closest neighbor is the region's magnificent natural wonder, El Yunque, a park you can explore in the air-conditioned comfort of a car in a few hours or hike for days and still not see all the greenery, waterfalls, and views. Nearby, Balneario de Luquillo (Luquillo Beach), Reserva Natural Las Cabezas de San Juan, and Fajardo are all worth exploring.

3

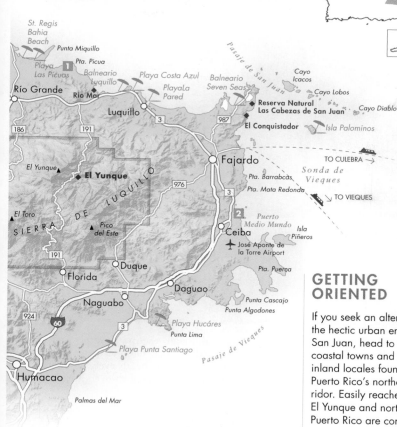

St. Regis
Bahia
Beach
Punta Miquillo
Pta. Picua
Playa
Las Picuas
Balneario
Luquillo
Playa Costa Azul
Balneario
Seven Seas
Cayo
Icacos
Cayo Lobos
Río Grande
Rio Mar
Playa La
Pared
Reserva Natural
Las Cabezas de San Juan
Cayo Diablo
Luquillo
3
987
El Conquistador
Isla Palominos
186
191
Fajardo
TO CULEBRA →
El Yunque
El Yunque
976
Pta. Barrabás
Sonda de
Vieques
3
Pta. Mata Redonda
TO VIEQUES
El Toro
Pico
del Este
Puerto
Medio Mundo
Isla
Piñeros
SIERRA
DE
LUQUILLO
191
Duque
Ceiba
José Aponte de
la Torre Airport
Florida
Pta. Puerca
Naguabo
Daguao
Punta Cascajo
Punta Algodones
924
60
3
Playa Hucáres
Punta Lima
Playa Punta Santiago
Pasaje de Vieques
Humacao
Palmas del Mar

Pasaje de San Juan

GETTING ORIENTED

If you seek an alternative to the hectic urban environs of San Juan, head to the pristine coastal towns and charming inland locales found along Puerto Rico's northeast corridor. Easily reached by car, El Yunque and northeast Puerto Rico are convenient enough for a quick day trip but beg exploration of at least two days. Kayak the lagoon in Piñones, take a surf lesson in Luquillo, sunbathe at Seven Seas Beach in Fajardo, horseback ride in the foothills of El Yunque— the list of exciting and/ or relaxing activities in this region goes on and on.

2 The Eastern Coast. Puerto Rico's eastern coast is home to some of the island's most popular attractions. Be sure to check out the beautiful beaches and crystal-clear snorkeling conditions of Fajardo before heading south to Naguabo. Naguabo is said to be the birthplace of the *pastelillo de chapín*, a popular dish that consists of trunkfish wrapped inside a deep-fried flour dough. Farther south and west, travelers will discover Humacao, home of the island's exceptional Palmas del Mar.

EL YUNQUE NATIONAL FOREST

El Yunque is the only tropical rain forest in the U.S. National Forest system, spanning 28,000 acres, reaching an elevation of more than 3,500 feet, and receiving an estimated average of 200–240 inches of rain each year.

The forest's 13 hiking trails are extremely well maintained; many of them are easy to navigate and less than one mile (1.6 km) long. If you prefer to see the sights from a car, as many people do, simply follow Route 191 as it winds into the mountains and stop at several observation points along the way.

(above) El Toro Mountain rises more than 3,500 ft (1,070 m), and on a clear day the view from the peak extends to the Atlantic Ocean.

WHEN TO GO

It's about 73°F year-round, so weather isn't much of a factor for seasonal planning. For easy parking and fewer crowds, be sure to arrive early in the day, although the park rarely gets crowded, by U.S. national park standards. Expect rain nearly every day, but keep eyes peeled post-showers for the best bird-watching.

PARK HIGHLIGHTS

Flora and Fauna. Each year more than half a million visitors from all over the world come to El Yunque to experience the rain forest's ecological treasures. Rivers and streams provide habitats for freshwater snails, shrimp, and crabs, while approximately 66 species of migratory birds either winter in or pass through El Yunque. Sonorous *coquí* frogs (tree frogs endemic to Puerto Rico), 14 different lizard species, and more than 1,200

3

insect species—ranging from ants to beetles to flies—all inhabit the forest.

Four major forest types, roughly stratified by elevation, are home to thousands of native plants including 150 fern species, 240 tree species (88 of these are endemic or rare and 23 are exclusively found in this forest). Two of the island's highest peaks rise out of the forest: El Toro and El Yunque, both at more than 3,500 feet (1,070 m).

El Yunque doesn't have bigger wildlife species like monkeys, large cats, and poisonous snakes, but there are hundreds of small creatures that find ecological niches. Many of these species exist nowhere else on the planet, such as the endangered Puerto Rican green parrot, Puerto Rican boa, and Puerto Rican Sharp-Shinned Hawk. If you're interested in bird-watching, pack your binoculars, because Puerto Rican Todies, Puerto Rican Lizard Cuckoos, five species of hummingbirds, flycatchers, and warblers are commonly spotted.

El Portal Visitor Center. Carve out some time to stop at the cathedral-like El Portal Visitor Center (✉ *$4, Free for children under 15 and senior citizens*). Enter via an elevated walkway that transports visitors across the forest canopy, 60 feet above the ground. Signs identify and explain the birds, animals, and other treasures seen among the treetops. Below the walkway, find a ground-level

nature trail with stunning views of the lower forest and coastal plain. Inside the center interactive exhibits explain El Yunque National Forest's history, topography, flora, and fauna. Watch the 15-minute film that introduces the rain forest, providing a greater understanding of its ecology, environment, and history. The facility also has a well-stocked bookstore and gift shop filled with useful tools for exploring the park, like trail maps. (Note: this is the only gift shop in El Yunque that takes credit cards, so plan accordingly.) On a sticky day the air-conditioning, clean restrooms, and benches overlooking the forest make for a pleasant post-hike respite.

Cascada La Coca. The first spectacular sight you're likely to see in El Yunque is Cascada La Coca (La Coca Falls), which plunges 85 feet down a flat sheet of solid rock. The waterfall is inches from the road, so it's visible from your car. The gate to the park, which opens at 7:30 am and closes at 6 pm, is just before the falls. ✉ *Rte. 191, Km 8.1.*

BEST WAYS TO EXPLORE

Hiking. The 13 official trails throughout El Yunque are quite civilized—paved, well-marked, and easy for both beginners and children. The trails on the north side of El Yunque, the park's main tourist hub, are ideal for folks with minimal or no hiking experience. There are several short trails (about ½ mile) that are completely paved. On the south side, expect fewer people and moderate to challenging hikes. These trails are not as well maintained as the marked trails found lower in the forest. Regardless of where you go, you'll be immersed in the sounds, smells, and scenic landscape of the park. Avid outdoor adventurers can hike between the north and south sides of El Yunque.

Driving A leisurely drive-through may not be as immersive as a hike, but you'll still encounter beautiful waterfalls, hibiscus, banana and orchid plants, lizards, and the occasional vista over the forest and out to the Atlantic Ocean. The main and most direct route to El Yunque, Route 3, is a multilane highway dotted with places to stop for cold drinks and typical Puerto Rican snacks. Obey the speed limit, as rental cars are frequently pulled over. From the highway, hop onto Route 191, the only road through the preserve. When hurricanes and mudslides haven't caused portions of the road to be closed, you can drive straight from the entrance to Km. 13, the base of Pico El Yunque. A stop at El Portal Visitor Center will teach you everything you need to know about your majestic surroundings. Make another quick stop to climb the winding stairs of Yokahú Tower for breathtaking views of the rain forest and the island. On your way back, stop at El Bosque Encantado, a food *kiosko* with *empanadas*, cold coconut drinks, and cliff's-edge views (on Route 191, Km 7.2). Take note that drivers don't always recognize common road courtesies, such as slow cars to the right, stop signs, and signals.

Ziplining. This adrenaline-fueled, half-day activity enables visitors to take a tree-to-tree canopy tour via a network of platforms, cables, and pulleys.

Step off a platform more than 80 feet in the sky and fly through the air as you take in bird's-eye views of the northern limit of El Yunque National Forest and El Yunque and Este peaks. For more information, contact **Yunke Zipline Adventure** (⊕ *yzapr.com* ☎ *787/242–3368*) or **Rain Forest Zip Line Corp** (⊕ *rainforestzipline.com* ☎ *787/370–1010*).

STAY THE NIGHT

If you're thinking about a second day at El Yunque, book a room near the rain forest instead of schlepping back to San Juan. (There is no lodging available within the reserve.) The St. Regis Bahia Beach Resort and Gran Meliá Puerto Rico are both within a 10-minute drive in Río Grande, but the two cottages at Sue's Place in Barrios Sabana, above the town of Luquillo, cannot be beat (⊕ *www.rainforestrental.com*). For a taste of local flavor, visitors leaving the El Yunque area may want to consider stopping off at the *friquitines* (seafood kiosks) that line Route 3 west of the beach turnoff. Frequented by locals and visitors alike, the kiosks are open all day and serve everything from cold drinks to stuffed lobsters, plates of fried fish (head and tail attached) and fritters (usually codfish or corn) to bagels and lox or Spanish-style tapas.

BEST ONE-DAY ITINERARY

Start at the **El Portal Rain Forest Center.** Drive about 2½ miles (2.4 km) to **La Coca Falls**—one of the best photo ops in the park. View it from your car or climb up slippery rocks to the base of the falls. Then drive about half a mile to **Torre Yokahú** (Yokahú Observation Tower), a lookout with vistas of 1,000-year-old trees, exotic flowers, and birds in flight. The tower has restrooms. Continue just beyond the halfway point to the **Area Pasadías Palma de Sierra.** Rangers here have information on closures, trail conditions, and daily activities. The center and the next two parking lots, Caimitillo and Palo Colorado, have trailheads to both **El Yunque summit** (about a half-day adventure) and **La Mina Falls.** Casual

hikers should follow the moderate **Big Tree Trail** to reach the falls—about a half-hour hike. Bring a swimsuit for the falls and water shoes or sandals to navigate the slippery rocks. More advanced hikers can follow **La Mina Falls Trail.** It's only .7 miles (1.1 km) long, but climbs to 2,132 feet. Plan 30–45 minutes each way. A little more than a mile up the road is one more trail, **Baño de Oro.**

Did You Know? El Yunque has had many names. President Theodore Roosevelt named it Luquillo Forest Reserve in 1903, and President Franklin Roosevelt changed its name to the Caribbean National Forest. In 2007 the area officially became El Yunque National Forest.

Updated by
Julie Schwietert
Collazo

Tree frogs, rare parrots, and wild horses only start the list of northeastern Puerto Rico's offerings. The backdrops for encounters with an array of flora and fauna include the 28,000-acre El Yunque tropical rain forest, the seven ecosystems in the Reserva Natural Las Cabezas de San Juan, and Laguna Grande, where tiny sea creatures appear to light up the waters.

As the ocean bends around the northeastern coast, it laps onto beaches of soft sand and palm trees, crashes against high bluffs, and almost magically creates an amazing roster of ecosystems. Beautiful beaches at Luquillo are complemented by more rugged southeastern shores. Inland, green hills roll down toward plains that once held expanses of coconut trees, such as those still surrounding the town of Piñones, or sugarcane, as evidenced by a few surviving plantations near Naguabo and Humacao.

The natural beauty and varied terrain continue in the area's other towns as well: Río Grande, which once attracted immigrants from Austria, Spain, and Italy, and Naguabo, which overlooks what were once immense cane fields and Cayo Santiago, where the only residents are monkeys.

You can golf, ride horses, hike marked trails, and plunge into water sports throughout the region. In many places along the coast, green hills cascade down to the ocean. On the edge of the Atlantic, Fajardo serves as a jumping-off point for diving, fishing, and catamaran excursions. Luquillo is the site of a family beach so well equipped that there are even facilities enabling wheelchair users to enter the sea.

EL YUNQUE AND THE NORTHEAST PLANNER

WHEN TO GO

In general, the island's northeast coast—preferred by those seeking abandoned beaches and nature reserves rather than casinos and urban glitz—tends to be less in demand than San Juan. The exceptions are at Easter and Christmas, when Luquillo and Fajardo become crowded with local sun worshippers, merrymakers, and campers. Island festivals also draw crowds, but planning a trip around one of them will give you a true sense of the region's culture. Be sure to make reservations well in advance if you're visiting during high season, which runs from December 15 through April 15.

GETTING HERE AND AROUND

AIR TRAVEL

Air Flamenco, Cape Air, and Vieques Air Link offer several daily flights between San Juan, Vieques, and Culebra. Trips to any of these destinations are between 10 and 20 minutes; the cost ranges from $60 one-way to $180 round-trip.

Information Air Flamenco ☎ *787/724–1818* ⊕ *www.airflamenco.net.* **Cape Air** ☎ *800/CAPE–AIR (227–3247)* ⊕ *www.capeair.com.*

Vieques Air Link ☎ *787/741–8331, 888/901–9247* ⊕ *www.viequesair link.com.*

CAR TRAVEL

Unless you are planning to hop directly onto a ferry to Vieques or Culebra, you should consider renting a car in eastern Puerto Rico. Even the destination resorts are fairly isolated, and you may appreciate the mobility if you want to get out and have a meal away from the resort or explore El Yunque or some of the great beaches. Rates start at about $40 a day, but it may be possible to rent directly from your lodging, so ask about packages.

From San Juan the east coast is accessible via Route 3, or Route 187 if you want to visit Piñones and Loíza. At Fajardo the road intersects with Route 53, which continues down the coast. Route 3 also continues along the coast, providing a more scenic, if slower, trip.

TAXI TRAVEL

You can flag cabs down on the street, but it's faster and safer to have your hotel call one for you. Cabs are usually metered; make sure it's clear whether a flat rate or a meter will determine the fare. Instead of renting a car, consider taking a taxi to Fajardo. The cost from the San Juan area should be about $80 for up to five people.

Humacao Taxi ☎ *787/852–6880.*

ABOUT THE RESTAURANTS

Some restaurants carry the tourist board's *meson gastronómico* designation. Such establishments specialize in typical island food. The eastern region has both formal restaurants, where reservations are necessary, and casual beachside eateries, where you can walk in unannounced in beach attire and have a fine meal of fresh fish. Bills generally don't include service charges, so a 15% tip is customary and expected. Most restaurants are open for dinner from late afternoon until about10 pm.

ABOUT THE HOTELS

The east coast has a wide variety of lodgings, from small inns and guesthouses in the mountains to large, lavish resorts along the coast. Government-approved *paradores* are also available. Often translated as "country inns," *paradores* offer affordable Puerto Rican hospitality and the cozy comforts of home outside the San Juan metro area. These small, privately owned properties are usually quite picturesque and found throughout the island's interior and more remote coastal towns. If you wish to get away from it all with a neatly packaged trip, eastern Puerto Rico has some of the island's top resorts: the St. Regis Bahia Beach Resort and El Conquistador, a Waldorf Astoria Resort. You'll also find extensive facilities and services at large, self-contained complexes like the Wyndham Río Mar and the Gran Meliá, making the list of regional offerings more than complete.

HOTEL AND RESTAURANT PRICES

Prices in our restaurant reviews are the average cost of a main course at dinner or, if dinner is not served, at lunch; taxes and service charges are generally included. Prices in the hotel reviews are the lowest cost of a standard double room in high season, excluding taxes, service charges, and meal plans (except at all-inclusives). Prices for rentals are the lowest per-night cost for a one-bedroom unit in high season.

For expanded lodging reviews and current deals, visit Fodors.com.

WHAT IT COSTS				
	$	$$	$$$	$$$$
Restaurants	$8–$12	$13–$20	$21–$30	over $30
Hotels	$80–$150	$151–$250	$251–$350	over $350

PACKING FOR EL YUNQUE

When you come to El Yunque, bring binoculars, a camera (preferably with a good zoom function), bottled water, and sunscreen; wear a hat or visor, good walking shoes, and comfortable clothes. Although daytime temperatures rise as high as 80°F (27°C), wear long pants, because some plants can cause skin irritations. There are no poisonous snakes in the forest (or on the island as a whole), but bugs can be ferocious, so a strong repellent is a must. And remember: this is a rain forest, so bring a poncho and be prepared for frequent showers.

SAFETY

Although crime isn't as high in the island's eastern areas as it is in San Juan, use prudence. Avoid bringing valuables with you to the beach; if you must do so, be sure not to leave them in view in your car. It's best to keep your car locked while driving, and steer clear of out-of-the-way beaches after sunset.

VISITOR INFORMATION

Cities usually offer information offices connected to the city hall, and most are open only during business hours on weekdays.

IF YOU LIKE

GREAT FOOD

In the east you'll find fine fare of all types. On the traditional side, look for the deep-fried snacks (often stuffed with meat or fish) known as *frituras*, as well as numerous dishes laced with coconut. Plantains are the star ingredient in the hearty *mofongo*, a seafood-stuffed dish, and also appear as *tostones* (fried plantain chips). Fresh fish is commonly prepared with tomatoes, onions, and garlic, or some combination of the three. These days the island's chefs are experimenting with flavor and texture, putting modern spins on classic dishes. Throughout the island, you'll find a blend of old and new cooking styles and techniques that will suit all palates.

GOLF

There's something to be said for facing a rolling, palm-tree-lined fairway with the distant ocean at your back. And then there are the ducks, iguanas, and pelicans that congregate in mangroves near some holes. That's what golf in eastern Puerto Rico is all about. The Arthur Hills–designed course at El Conquistador is one of the island's best. The Flamboyán course, a Rees Jones creation at Palmas del Mar Country Club, consistently gets raves, as do the courses at Westin Río Mar. The newest fairway is at St. Regis Bahia Beach Resort, where Robert Trent Jones Jr. oversaw construction of an eco-friendly green that overlooks the meeting place of the Espíritu Santo River and the Atlantic Ocean.

Contacts Fajardo Tourism Office ✉ 6 Calle Dr. Lopez, Fajardo ☎ 787/863–4013 ⊕ www.fajardopr.org.

Naguabo Tourism Office ✉ Playa Hucares Malecon, Naguabo ☎ 787/874–5904. **Río Grande Office of Tourism and Culture** ✉ Calle San José, Plaza de Recreo, Río Grande ☎ 787/887–2370 ⊕ www.riograndepr.org.

THE NORTHEASTERN COAST

Just east of San Juan, at the community of Piñones, urban chaos is replaced with the peace of winding, palm-lined roads that are interrupted at intervals by barefoot eateries and dramatic ocean views. Farther southeast and inland is Río Grande. Its namesake river rises within El Yunque, the short name for El Yunque National Forest, a sprawling blanket of green covering a mountainous region south of Río Grande. Back on the coast, Luquillo Beach has snack kiosks, dressing rooms, showers, and facilities that enable wheelchair users to play in the ocean.

Southeast of Luquillo sits the Reserva Natural Las Cabezas de San Juan, with its restored lighthouse and variety of ecosystems. Anchoring the island's east coast is Fajardo, a lively port city with a large marina and ferry service to the outer islands, as well as a string of offshore cays. Catamarans based here sail to and from great snorkeling spots, yachts stop by to refuel or stock up on supplies, and local fishing craft chug in and out as part of a day's work. ■TIP→ **Leave yourself plenty of time for driving to El Yunque or any of the resorts in the northeast. Route 3, the main route east, is notorious for bumper-to-bumper traffic.**

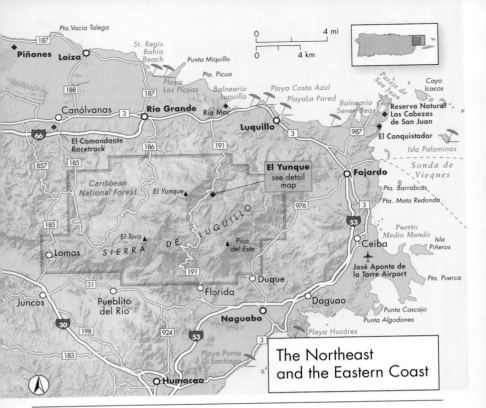

PIÑONES

10 miles (16 km) east of San Juan.

Funky Piñones is little more than a collection of open-air seaside eateries. Sand floors, barefoot patrons, and tantalizing seafood—traditionally washed down with icy beer—have made it popular with locals, especially on weekend evenings. Chilled *agua de coco* is served right from the coconut. During the day you can rent a bike and follow the marked seaside trail that meanders for 7 miles (11 km) through the mangrove forest and along the northern coastline. It takes about two hours to bike from one end and back, but allow some time to stop and take pictures, grab something to eat, and explore the scenic beach areas.

The area has grown as a nightlife destination, too, as fancier establishments, some with live music, have opened up. As midafternoon turns into evening and people begin to leave the beach for refreshments, the air is thick with smoke from grilled fish, beef and chicken kebabs (called *pinchos* here), and the kettles of oil used to fry codfish and crab fritters. When the giant orange Caribbean sun starts to fall behind the San Juan skyline, salsa and merengue—not to mention reggae and Latin pop—start to blare out from the jukeboxes and sound systems of the dozens of ramshackle establishments dotting Route 187, the sector's main road. Traffic on the two-lane road into and out of the area is daunting on

3

GREAT ITINERARIES

IF YOU HAVE 1 DAY

If you have only a day, or even less than a day, to visit eastern Puerto Rico, you should make a beeline to **El Yunque**. Route 3 is the quickest way. This rain forest has hiking trails of various lengths leading to secluded waterfalls and mountaintop towers with spectacular views. It's wonderful to explore even if you never get out of your car. If you are staying overnight, your best bet is nearby **Río Grande**.

IF YOU HAVE 3 DAYS

If you have a bit more time, you can see much more of the region. To avoid the unrelenting string of strip malls along Route 3, take Route 187, which winds along the coast. Stop for lunch at one of the seafood kiosks that line the beach at **Piñones**. Spend the night in or near **Río Grande**, a town that makes a good base for exploring the region. On your second day, get up early to beat the crowds to **El Yunque**. Make

sure to bring binoculars and watch for the rare Puerto Rican green parrot. On Day 3 you should head to **Luquillo**, which has one of the prettiest beaches on the island. Make sure to stop for lunch in one of the food kiosks on Route 3 just before you reach the town.

IF YOU HAVE 5 DAYS

If you have five days, follow the three-day itinerary above. On Day 4 head east along Route 3 to the coastal city of **Fajardo**, which has plenty of accommodations in every price range. Make sure you have called ahead to reserve a spot on a tour of Reserva Natural Las Cabezas de San Juan. If there's no moon, sign up for a nighttime excursion to the reserve's bioluminescent bay. On Day 5, take a snorkeling trip to some of the nearby coral reefs. Many people who travel to Fajardo take advantage of the ferry service or quick flights to the smaller islands of Vieques or Culebra.

Friday and Saturday nights, when many of these open-air bars host merengue combos, Brazilian-jazz trios, or reggae bands.

GETTING HERE AND AROUND

The approach to Piñones from San Juan is simple. Take Route 26 east or Route 37 east, follow signs for the Balneario de Carolina, then go straight on Route 187 and cross Punta Cangrejos. Door to door, the trip should take about 15 minutes. You can also get a taxi to Piñones or take the bus for about 75¢ (via C45), but the latter can take more than an hour. To avoid getting stranded, prearrange a pickup time for your taxi driver to return. Another option is to make Soleil Beach Club your destination. Yes, it's one of the priciest beachfront restaurants in Piñones, but it offers a complimentary shuttle for pickup and drop-off, which helps avoid the risks of drinking and driving.

Taxis AA American Taxi, Inc. ☎ *787/982–3466.* **Astro Taxi** ☎ *787/727–8888.*

EXPLORING

Paseo Piñones. One of the most pleasant ways to pass the time is walking along the Paseo Piñones. This 6½-mile (10½-km) boardwalk passes through sand dunes and crosses lagoons and mangrove forests. All the while, a line of coconut palms shades you from the sun. You'll share the path with bikers, joggers, and in-line skaters. Food kiosks abound. ⊠ *Route 187.*

BEACHES

Playa de Piñones. You'll find Playa de Piñones right in front of the cluster of food kiosks built by the government for resident cooks. A large barrier reef blocks the strong currents and serves as the foundation for the large bathing pools in front of a sandy beach. ⊠ *Route 187, Km 8.*

WHERE TO EAT

$$
SEAFOOD

✕ **Soleil Beach Club.** A bit more refined than some of its neighbors, this restaurant actually sits on a wooden platform positioned *above* the sand. Even nicer is the upstairs deck that lets you gaze at the ocean instead of the parking lot. The grilled USDA steak served with chimichurri is as good as it gets, and the fresh halibut fillet with beurre blanc and cassava mofongo is equally tasty. Save room for *postres* (dessert)—the coconut ice cream is worth every calorie. There are a couple of bars, and bands playing Latin music set the scene on weekend nights. Call ahead and you can arrange free transportation to and from your hotel—a very good deal. ⑤ *Average main: $19* ⊠ *Rte. 187, Km 4.6* ☎ *787/253–1033* ⊕ *www.soleilbeachclub.com.*

NIGHTLIFE

Nearly all the restaurants and cafés in Piñones have bands on weekends, most playing roof-shaking jazz and island rhythms, and locals go as much for the drinks and live entertainment as for the food. A largely Dominican clientele frequents many of these beachfront dance halls, and you're likely to see some smoking merengue dancing. Couples also twirl to salsa, bounce to *bomba*, or move to the grittier beats of local reggaeton. You'll easily find several open-air establishments drawing weekend crowds for their steamy dance floors inside and smoking barbecue pits outside.

Soleil Beach Club. Soleil Beach Club has bars upstairs as well as down, so you never have to go far to order a drink. This bar, the most upscale in Piñones can get packed on weekends, so go early to claim prime drinking real estate. ⊠ *Rte. 187, Km 4.5* ☎ *787/253–1033.*

SHOPPING

Artesanías Castor Ayala. Just east of Piñones is the town of Loíza, where you'll find Artesanías Castor Ayala, the place to get your authentic coconut *vejigante* masks, dubbed "Mona Lisas" because of their elongated smiles. Craftsman Raúl Ayala Carrasquillo has been making these pieces for more than 40 years, following in the footsteps of his late father. Collectors prize these wild masks, most with tentacle-like horns. His

---

CHIMICHURRI

When you get a steak in Puerto Rico, it usually is served with a little glass jar of a green herb-filled sauce, served with a small, plastic spoon. This is *chimichurri*, the traditional accompaniment to grilled steak. The sauce, made from finely chopped cilantro or parsley, garlic, lemon, and oil, can be sprinkled liberally or sparingly over the meat to give it a slight kick. You will rarely find steak sauce in Puerto Rico, except at an American chain, though you can frequently get ketchup if *chimichurri* isn't to your liking.

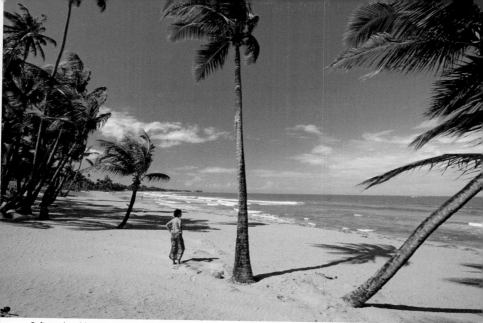
Soft sand and leaning palm trees are hallmarks of Luquillo beaches.

one-room shop, in a shack that was painted yellow many years ago, is on the road between Loíza and Río Grande. ⊠ *Rte. 187, Km 6.6, Loíza* ☎ *787/876–1130.*

Estúdio de Arte Samuel Lind. At Estúdio de Arte Samuel Lind, located on a short, dusty lane across the street from the Artesanías Castor Ayala, artist Samuel Lind sculpts, paints, and silk-screens images that are quintessentially Loízano. Lind's work is displayed in the two floors of his latticework studio. Of special note are his colorful folk-art posters that are inspired by everyday Puerto Rican life. ⊠ *Rte. 187, Km 6.6, Loíza* ☎ *787/876–1494* ⊕ *www.samuellind.com.*

SPORTS AND THE OUTDOORS

Piñones is bordered by a 10-mile (16-km) strip of beaches along the coast, which winds to a bluff called Vacía Talega, a once infamous lovers' lane with a wonderful view of an unspoiled coast lined with dense palm groves and towering sea grapes. The area has some fine surf, and several spots have become favorites of local and visiting surfers. You'll also find good fishing, snorkeling, and scuba opportunities. Away from the coast is Torrecilla Baja, one of the largest mangrove swamps on the island.

BICYCLING

The area's big outdoor attraction is a bike path that follows the swaying coconut palms on a quiet, breezy stretch, sometimes crossing over the main roadway but mostly running parallel to it. Along most of its 7 miles (11 km) it's a wooden boardwalk for bicycles.

COPI (Cultural and Ecotouristic Center of Piñones). Bike rentals are available to explore the Piñones Bicycle Trail in the Piñones State Forest and

Nature Reserve. Rentals, including helmets for children and adults; bicycles, baby seats, and double-bikes require a donation of $5. Be sure to check your equipment before you set out; some bikes are in better condition than others. COPI also rents double kayaks for a $15 donation; these can be taken out on the nearby Torrecilla Lagoon. ⊠ *Rte. 187, Km 4.2* ☎ *787/253–9707* ⊕ *www.copipr.com* ⊙ *9–5.*

DIVING AND FISHING TRIPS

Locals go fishing and crabbing right off the coast, and it's likely the crab fritters you eat in any beachfront shack are local as well.

Cangrejos Yacht Club. Charter-operated boating, deep-sea fishing, and scuba-diving trips are run out of the marina right below the bridge from Isla Verde. Call the yacht club to be referred to a captain who is appropriate for your trip. ⊠ *Rte. 187, Km 3.8* ☎ *787/791–1015* ⊕ *www. cangrejosyachtclub.com.*

Puerto Rico Angling. At Puerto Rico Angling, José Campos and his son run full- and half-day deep-sea fishing trips for up to six people for catch like tuna, wahoo, and dorado. They also offer fishing trips through the area's lagoon system. All charters practice tag and release. ☎ *787/724–2079* ⊕ *www.puertoricofishing.com.*

RÍO GRANDE

21 miles (35 km) southeast of San Juan.

This urban cluster of about 54,000 residents proudly calls itself "The City of El Yunque," as it's the closest community to the rain forest and most of the reserve falls within its district borders. Two images of the rare green parrot, which makes its home in El Yunque, are found on the city's coat of arms; another parrot peeks out at you from the town's flag.

Río Espíritu Santo, which runs through Río Grande, begins in El Yunque's highest elevations. It was once used to transport lumber, sugar, and coffee from plantations, and immigrants flocked to the region to take advantage of the employment opportunities.

GETTING HERE

Only 30 minutes from San Juan, Río Grande is easy to get to. From San Juan, take Road 26 toward Carolina until you reach Road 3. Then take Road 3 toward Fajardo for approximately 20 minutes until you see signs for Río Grande.

Museo del Cartel José Hernández. The Museo del Cartel José Hernández is devoted to posters and the artists who design them. The collection dates from the 1950s and consists of more than 200 pieces by 35 artists, including many eye-popping posters created for island festivals and art exhibits. ⊠ *37 Calle Pimentel, El Centro* ☎ *787/887–2370* 🎫 *Free* ⊙ *Mon.–Fri. 8–4.*

WHERE TO EAT

$$
PUERTO RICAN

✕ **Antojitos Puertorriqueñes.** "*Buen provecho,*" says owner Jorge Martinez as you sit down to an authentic meal at this no-frills spot serving Puerto Rican favorites. Whether you're stopping for breakfast en route to the rain forest, catching the unbeatable $5.50 lunch special—which changes daily and offers choices like fried pork with plantains, grouper in creole sauce, and roasted chicken with beans and rice—or relaxing with a cocktail before dinner, the joint delivers. The premises are equally straightforward—a covered patio with plastic tables and chairs and overhead fans, as well as a soundtrack provided by indigenous coquí frogs. $ *Average main: $13* ⊠ *160 Río Mar Blvd.* ☎ *787/888–7378.*

$$$$
CARIBBEAN
Fodor'sChoice
★

✕ **Fern Restaurant.** On the second floor of the St. Regis Bahia Beach's main Plantation House building, this stylish restaurant's indoor/outdoor space is a mix of textures and colors—banquettes with red pillow accents, mesh lamps, metallic-cork wall coverings, recycled kumbok wood tables with tangled brass legs—that create a lush environment for Jean-Georges Vongerichten's Caribbean Latin–inspired menu. An $82 tasting menu is available for those interested in sampling the chef's featured dishes, which include a delectable black-pepper octopus laced with indigenous *aji dulce* (sweet chili) for appetizer, and grouper with black beans and marinated beef-tenderloin entrées. Service is impeccable, and the extensive wine list will delight oenophiles. Save room for dessert, where local fruits figure prominently in delicious concoctions like coconut panna cotta. $ *Average main: $35* ⊠ *St. Regis Bahia Beach Resort, Route 187, Km 4.2* ☎ *787/809–8100* ⊕ *www.fernrestaurant.com* ⌔ *Reservations essential.*

$$$$
ITALIAN

✕ **Palio.** Northern Italian dishes, such as fettucine with lobster, shrimp, mussels, and scallops, veal Marsala, and filet of beef with a caramelized shallot Barolo reduction, are the star attractions at this top-notch restaurant where the staff is attentive and amiable. Specialty coffees are served in mugs engulfed in blue flames, a showstopper that has people at neighboring tables applauding. The dining room, with its black-and-white checkerboard floor and dark-wood paneling, is elegant and refined, and before sunset, you can catch a glimpse of the sea through the dramatic floor-to-ceiling windows. $ *Average main: $35* ⊠ *Río Mar Beach Resort & Spa, a Wyndham Grand Resort, 6000 Río Mar Blvd.* ☎ *787/888–6000* ⊕ *www.wyndhamriomar.com* ⌔ *Reservations essential* ⊘ *No lunch.*

$$$
SEAFOOD

✕ **Richie's Café.** Perched on a mountaintop, this restaurant—a convenient option for Wyndham Río Mar guests who don't want to dine on-property but are willing to pay resort prices—has a pair of open-air dining rooms with views to Vieques on a clear day. The atmosphere is festive; there's often a game playing on one of the big screens or a local band jamming on the weekend. Seafood is the specialty here—try the fried plantains filled with shrimp, conch, octopus, or lobster for an

---

IT'S DA BOMB(A)

The *bomba*—a musical and dance style for which the northeastern coast is famous—can be traced to the Kongo people of West Africa. Sometimes wearing a flouncy white dress, the woman of a dancing couple moves in a relatively fixed pattern of steps while her partner improvises to the drumbeat. A lead singer and a choir perform a call-and-response song—recounting a local story or event—while percussionists play maracas, *fuás* (wooden sticks that are smacked against a hard surface), *buleadores* (low-timbre, barrel-shape drums), and *subidores* (higher-pitch drums).

3

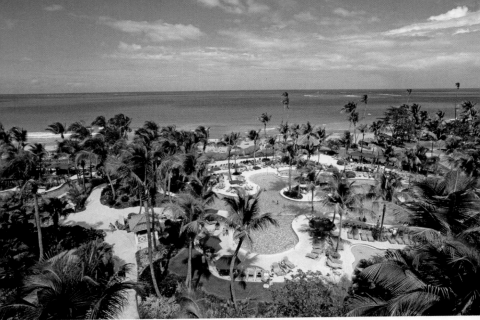

Water recreation options abound in the enormous pools of the Wyndham Río Mar Beach Resort.

appetizer, and then move on to the whole red snapper or pineapple rice with shrimp, which is served on the pineapple itself. Bring some insect repellent at night, as some readers have mentioned problems with mosquitoes. $ *Average main: $25* ⊠ *Route 968, Km 2.0* ☎ *787/887–1435, 787/909-8532* ⊕ *www.richiescafepr.com.*

WHERE TO STAY

$$$
RESORT

🍽 **Gran Meliá Puerto Rico.** This massive resort, on an enviable stretch of pristine coastline, has an open-air lobby with elegant floral displays that resemble a Japanese garden, and the swimming pool's columns call to mind ancient Greece. **Pros:** beautiful setting; lovely pool area; short walk to the beach. **Cons:** parking spots are scarce; facade is blank and uninviting. $ *Rooms from: $305* ⊠ *200 Coco Beach Boulevard, Coco Beach* ☎ *787/809–1770, 877/476–3542* ⊕ *www.gran-melia-puerto-rico.com* ⤳ *544 suites, 6 villas* ⦿ *Multiple meal plans.*

$$$
RESORT
FAMILY

🍽 **Río Mar Beach Resort & Spa, a Wyndham Grand Resort.** Guests come to this sprawling 500-acre resort to enjoy a host of outdoor activities, including championship golf and tennis, as well as hiking excursions in the nearby rain forest. **Pros:** expansive beachfront; good restaurants in hotel; plenty of outdoor activities. **Cons:** dark and depressing parking garage; sometimes there are long lines at the check-in desk. $ *Rooms from: $305* ⊠ *6000 Río Mar Blvd.* ☎ *787/888–6000* ⊕ *www.wyndhamriomar.com* ⤳ *600 rooms, 72 suites* ⦿ *No meals.*

$$$$
RESORT
Fodor's Choice
★

🍽 **St. Regis Bahia Beach Resort.** Between El Yunque National Forest and the Río Espíritu Santo, this luxurious, environmentally aware property has raised the bar for lodgings in Puerto Rico. **Pros:** privacy; impeccable service; luxurious amenities. **Cons:** isolated location; slim off-property restaurant selection; very, very expensive. $ *Rooms from: $800* ⊠ *Rte.*

187, Km 4.2 ☎ *787/809–8000* ⊕ *www.stregisbahiabeach.com* ⇨ *104 rooms, 35 suites* ❙◎❙ *No meals.*

NIGHTLIFE

Río Mar Beach Resort & Spa, a Wyndham Grand Resort. Pick a game—Caribbean stud poker, blackjack, slot machines—and then head to the Las Vegas–style casino at the Río Mar Beach Resort & Spa. If all that betting makes you thirsty, step into the Players Bar, which is connected to the gaming room. ⊠ *Río Mar Beach Resort & Spa, 6000 Río Mar Blvd.* ☎ *787/888–6000.*

SPORTS AND THE OUTDOORS

Activities in the Río Grande region are mostly oriented around the area's resorts, Wyndham Río Mar Beach Resort & Spa, and Gran Meliá Puerto Rico, as well as St. Regis Bahia Beach Resort.

GOLF

Fodor'sChoice ★ **St. Regis Bahia Beach Resort Golf Course.** Designed by Robert Trent Jones, Jr., this tranquil 18-hole course meanders alongside the island's Río Espíritu Santo and overlooks the Atlantic Ocean. Environmentally respectful, this challenging course traipses past scenic lakes, deep-rooted mangroves, and spectacular residences to blend into the area's rain forest surroundings, while ocean breezes add a degree of difficulty to lush, rolling fairways. Greens fees vary seasonally; rates and times are available on request. ⊠ *Rte. 187, Km 4.2* ☎ *787/957–1510.*

Trump International Golf Course. The Trump International Golf Club features two 18-hole courses designed by PGA Professional Tom Kite, and is bordered by 1,000 acres of coastline and outstanding views of El Yunque. ⊠ *100 Clubhouse Dr., Coco Beach* ☎ *787/657–2000* ⊕ *www. trumpgolfclubpuertorico.com* ⊠ *$145–165, twilight rate; $165–185 for the 18-hole Championship Course.*

The Wyndham Grand Río Mar Beach Resort & Spa. The Río Mar Country Club portion of the Resort features two of the region's more luxurious golf courses. The Ocean Course, designed by Tom and George Fazio dates back to 1975 and has slightly wider fairways than its sister course. Iguanas can usually be spotted sunning themselves near its fourth hole, but contrary to its name has only one isolated ocean hole, the par-three 16th. The newer River Course, designed by Greg Norman, has challenging fairways that skirt the Mameyes River. Either way, when you're finished your round you can enjoy the spacious modern clubhouse with a pro shop, and two restaurants, so you can grab a sit-down lunch or a quick beverage and a bite. If you're not a resort guest, be sure to reserve tee times at least 24 hours in advance. Fees include discounts for resort guests and twilight times with club and shoe rentals available. ⊠ *6000 Río Mar Blvd.* ☎ *787/888–6000* ⊕ *www.wyndhamriomar.com* ⊠ *Up to $200* ⚲ *36 holes: Ocean Course: 18 holes, 6782 yards, par 72; River Course, 18 holes, 6945 yards, par 72.*

HORSEBACK RIDING

Carabalí Rainforest Park. A family-run operation, this hacienda is a good place to jump in the saddle and ride one of Puerto Rico's Paso Fino horses. Hour-long rides take you around the 600-acre ranch, while two-hour treks take you to a river where you and your horse can take a dip. If you prefer something more high tech, rent a four-wheeler for an excursion through the foothills of El Yunque. ⊠ *Rte. 3, Km 31.6, Luquillo* ☎ *787/889–5820* ⊕ *www.carabalirainforestpark.com.*

TENNIS

Peter Burwash International Tennis Center. The facilities at International Tennis Center are the best in the area. Besides the 13 courts with spectacular views, there are lessons for everyone from novices to old pros. ⊠ *Río Mar Beach Resort & Spa, a Wyndham Grand Resort, 6000 Río Mar Blvd.* ☎ *787/888–7066* ⊕ *www.wyndhamriomar.com/recreation/tennis.html* ✆ *Court rentals start at $25/hour; hour private lessons begin at $45.*

WATER SPORTS

Dragonfly Adventures. You can rent sea kayaks ($25/hour for single-person kayaks, $35 and $45 for two- and three-person models, respectively) and arrange off-site scuba-diving excursions or full- and half-day snorkeling packages through on-site operator Dragonfly Adventures. Large catamaran snorkeling trips leave from the resort for the calm, crystal-blue seas, beautiful coral reefs, and deserted islands off the coast of northeastern Puerto Rico. Rates begin at $115 per person, including a buffet lunch, limited open bar, and snacks. A Dragonfly Adventures tour desk is also available on-site at the Gran Meliá, also in Río Grande. ⊠ *Río Mar Beach Resort & Spa, a Wyndham Grand Resort, 6000 Río Mar Blvd.* ☎ *787/888–6000* ⊕ *www.wyndhamriomar.com.*

SHOPPING

Treehouse Studio. The picturesque Treehouse Studio, not far from the rain forest, sells vibrant watercolors by Monica Linville, who also gives workshops. Call for an appointment and directions. ⊠ *Unmarked road off Rte. 3* ☎ *787/436–3153* ⊕ *www.monicalinville.com.*

EL YUNQUE

7 miles (11 km) southeast of Río Grande; 26 miles (43 km) southeast of San Juan.

For more information on El Yunque, see the special feature at the beginning of this chapter.

Fodor'sChoice
★ The more than 100 billion gallons of precipitation that El Yunque receives annually spawn rushing streams and cascades, outsize impatiens and ferns, and 240 tree species. In the evening, millions of inch-long coquís (tree frogs) begin their calls. El Yunque is also home to the cotorra, Puerto Rico's endangered green parrot, as well as 67 other types of birds.

GETTING HERE AND AROUND

You can take a taxi from San Juan to El Yunque (metered rates outside San Juan run about $36 per hour), but to get the most out of the rain forest it's best to rent a car, even if you have only a few hours to explore. From the greater San Juan area, take the Airport Expressway, Highway 26 (Baldorioty de Castro Avenue) and follow signs east to Carolina; once you are on the expressway, follow it to the end (approximately 14

Look closely at the small tree branches along El Yunque's nature trails and you may spot creatures such as the mountain garden lizard.

miles [22½ km]). At the final exit (Carolina), stay in the left-hand lane until you merge with Route 3. Continue on Route 3 approximately 13 miles (21 km) until you see the signs for Palmer–El Yunque. Turn right at the traffic signal and follow the road through the village of Palmer until you see the sign for Route 191. Turn left on Route 191 and follow it approximately 2 miles (3 km) until you see the El Yunque National Forest sign. The entrance to the El Portal Rain Forest Center is on your right just after you enter the forest.

TOUR OPERATORS

Many companies in San Juan offer excursions to El Yunque. A National Forest Service ranger leads one-hour English and Spanish tours from the **Palo Colorado Information Center** along the Caimitillo and Baño de Oro trails (🕑 *11 am–1 pm* 🎫 *$5, seniors and kids 5–12, $3*). Tours are first-come, first-served.

Acampa Nature Adventure Tours. Book a half-day excursion with Acampa Nature Adventure Tours and choose from a moderate hike at lower elevations of the forest to more challenging treks to the El Yunque peak at 3,500 feet. Rates start at $79, with a six-person minimum, and include round-trip transportation to/from your hotel, park fees, and lunch. ✉ *1221 Piñero Ave., San Juan* 📞 *787/706–0695* 🌐 *www.acampapr.com* 🕑 *Mon.–Thurs.*

Eco Action Tours. Eco Action Tours will pick you up at your hotel and take you to the rain forest, where small groups will hike, swim in the falls, and learn about the flora and fauna. Half-day rates are reasonable, starting at $58 (not including entry free). Full day tours are $68

El Yunque Trail

Los Picachos Trail

El Yunque Summit (Lookout Tower)

Los Picachos Lookout

El Yunque Trail

EL YUNQUE RECREATION AREA

Cascada La Cola

Torre Yokahú

191

El Portal Rainforest Center

Area Pasadías Palma de Sierra

El Yunque Trail

Mt. Britton Trail

Big Tree Trail

Cascada La Mina

Caimitillo Picnic Area

Mount Britton Observation Tower

Centro de Información Palo Colorado

Mt. Britton Trail

Roads closed here. Hiking only beyond this point

Trade Winds Trail

191

0   1/2 mile

0   3/4 km

El Yunque (Caribbean National Forest)

and can be combined with a stop at Luquillo Beach. ☎ *787/791–7509* 🌐 *www.ecoactiontours.com.*

ESSENTIALS

Admission Fees. There is no entrance fee for the El Yunque National Forest itself. There's an optional admission fee for the El Portal Rainforest Center ($4 adults, free for children under 15 and senior citizens).

Admission Hours. The road into El Yunque opens daily at 7:30 am and closes at 6 pm. Ranger stations are open 9–5, as is the Welcome Center.

Emergencies. If you witness an accident or an unlawful act or felony, or if you see something happening that looks wrong or suspicious, please contact the Law Enforcement and Investigation Patrol, José Ayala, at 787/888–5675 (office), 787/888–1880 (VHF radio paging), or 787/549–0075 (cellular).

Restrooms. There are picnic areas with sheltered tables and bathrooms as well as several basic eateries along the road through the rain forest.

EXPLORING

FAMILY **El Portal Rainforest Center.** Before you begin exploring El Yunque, check out the interactive displays—explaining rain forests in general and El Yunque in particular—at El Portal Rainforest Center, the information center near the northern entrance. The beautifully designed facility is where you can pick up a map of the park and talk to rangers about which trails are open. You can stock up on water, snacks, and souvenirs at the small gift shop—the only one in the park that accepts credit cards. ⊠ *Rte. 191, Km 4, off Rte. 3, Río Grande* ☎ *787/888–1880* ⊕ *www. fs.fed.us/r8/caribbean* ⊠ *$4, free for kids under 15* ☾ *Daily 9–4:30.*

WHERE TO EAT

$ ✕ **La Muralla.** The rangers at El Yunque swear by this place, a cement-
CARIBBEAN block building painted yellow and green just past Cascada La Coca. You won't find a cheaper meal anywhere in Puerto Rico, that's for sure. *Pasteles* (a local tamale-like snack) with rice and beans are served year-round for $6, and *arroz y habichuelas con pollo* (rice and beans with chicken) is a steal at less than $5. After a long hike, be sure to order one of the fruit shakes to quench your thirst, and take in the unusual artwork in the open-air dining room. Get here early, as the place closes at 5 pm. $ *Average main: $4* ⊠ *Rte. 191, Km 7.4, El Yunque, Río Grande* ▭ *No credit cards* ☾ *Closed Thurs.*

$ ✕ **Yuquiyú Delights.** Named for the Taino god of goodness, this open-
CARIBBEAN air dining room will be a sight for sore eyes if you've been hiking all day in the rain forest. The covered terrace is scattered with a few tiled tables, which are further shielded by umbrellas. The chalkboard out front usually lists a few specials like burgers and quesadillas filled with skirt steak. Off the kitchen, there's a little shop where you can stock up on water for the trail or snacks for the ride home. $ *Average main: $8* ⊠ *Rte. 191, Km 11.4, El Yunque, Río Grande* ☎ *787/396–0970* ⊕ *www.yuquiyudelightspr.com* ▭ *No credit cards* ☾ *Closed Tues. No dinner.*

SHOPPING

El Yunque Gift Shop. While in El Yunque, buy a recording of the tree frog's song, a video about the endangered green parrot, or a coffee-table book about the rain forest at the large El Yunque Gift Shop in El Portal Visitor Center. Tucked among the rain-forest gifts are other Puerto Rican items, including note cards, maps, soaps, jams, and coffee. ■TIP➔ **This is the only gift shop in El Yunque that accepts credit cards.** ⊠ *El Portal, Rte. 191, Km 4.3, Río Grande* ☎ *787/888–1880.*

Coquí International. Not far from the entrance to El Yunque are half a dozen souvenir shops selling identical T-shirts and rain forest tchotchkes. A cut above the rest is Coquí International. A trail with colorful coquís painted on the floor takes you past cubicles featuring local artists' original paintings, handwoven placemats, and one-of-a-kind items of clothing. Interesting jewelry, coconut mobiles shaped like fish, sharks, and insects, handmade soap, and wood carvings cram the space. You'll enjoy exploring this unique boutique where gentle music and incense set shoppers at ease. ⊠ *#54 Ave. Principal, El Yunque, Río Grande* ☎ *787/887–0770* ⊕ *www.coquistores.com.*

EL YUNQUE ECO-STAY

Casa Cubuy Ecolodge (⊕ www. casacubuy.com ☎ 787/874-4316) is a bit remote, located above Naguabo on the south side of the rain forest, but it's worth the trek. Guests of the tranquil B&B are treated to the sound of nearby waterfalls and are within walking distance of the Cubuy and Icacaos rivers and jungles of bamboo. Sunbathe on granite slabs and boulders or slip into a natural Jacuzzi. A short uphill trek from the house on a paved road takes you to the El Yunque National Forest recreational facility, where interpretive guides offer forest hikes. At night the serenading of the *coquís* lulls weary travelers to sleep. The emphasis here is on unplugging—rooms are television- and phone-free—and soaking up nature. Environmentally friendly features of this property include recycled water, solar panels to heat water, composted garbage to fertilize the fruit trees, eco-smart light bulbs, and erosion-prevention techniques for trails.

LUQUILLO

8 miles (13 km) northeast of Río Grande; 28 miles (45 km) east of San Juan.

Known as the Sun Capital of Puerto Rico, Luquillo has one of the island's best-equipped family beaches. It's also a community where fishing traditions are respected. On the east end of Balneario de Luquillo, past the guarded swimming area, fishermen launch small boats and drop nets in open stretches between coral reefs.

Like many other Puerto Rican towns, Luquillo has its signature festival, in this case the Festival de Platos Típicos (Festival of Typical Dishes), a late-November culinary event that revolves around one ingredient: coconut. During the festivities many of the community's 20,000 residents gather in the main square, Plaza de Recreo, to sample treats rich with coconut or coconut milk. There's also plenty of free entertainment, including folk shows, troubadour contests, and salsa bands.

GETTING HERE AND AROUND

Públicos run between San Juan and Fajardo and will let travelers off at Luquillo (about a 45-minute ride). Driving takes about the same amount of time. From San Juan, head out Route 3, get off at Route 193, and follow signs for Luquillo. If you want to explore the town (it's small but well worth the time), a car is helpful. Take note not to park in places where the curb is painted yellow—it's a parking violation.

BEACHES

FAMILY
Fodor's Choice
★

Luquillo Beach (*Balneario La Monserrate*). Just off Route 3, gentle Luquillo Beach is a magnet for families. Signs refer this beach as Balneario La Monserrate, but everyone simply calls it Luquillo Beach. It's one of Puerto Rico's distinguished Blue Flag beaches. Lined with colorful lifeguard stations and shaded by soaring palm trees, it's well equipped with food stands, picnic areas, and even cocktail kiosks. Lounge chairs and umbrellas are available to rent, as are kayaks and Jet Skis. Its most distinctive facility is the Mar Sin Barreras (Sea Without Barriers), a low-sloped ramp leading into the water that allows wheelchair users to take a dip. **Amenities:** food and drink; lifeguards, parking (fee); showers; toilets. **Best for:** partiers; swimming; walking. ⊠ *Off Rte. 3* ☎ *787/889–5871* ⊕ *www.parquesnacionalespr.com* 🎫 *$4 per car* ☽ *Wed.–Sun. 8:30–5.*

Playa Costa Azul. Waving palm trees and fishing boats add charm to the small Playa Costa Azul, although the ugly residential buildings along the water make an unattractive backdrop. The water here is good for swimming, and the crowds are thinner than elsewhere, but there are no facilities. **Amenities:** none. **Best for:** swimming. ⊠ *Off Rte. 193, near Rte. 3.*

Playa La Pared. Playa La Pared, literally "The Wall Beach," is a surfer haunt. Numerous local competitions are held here throughout the year, and several surfing shops are close by in case you need a wet suit or wax for your board. The waves here are medium-range. It's very close to Playa Luquillo/Balneario Monserrate, but has a separate entrance. There are no facilities. **Amenities:** none. **Best for:** partiers, surfing. ⊠ *Off Rte. 3.*

WHERE TO EAT

$$$
SEAFOOD
✕ **La Parrilla.** There are more than 50 *kioskos*, or food stands, along Highway 3 on the way to Luquillo Beach/Balneario Monserrate, most offering humble local fare, much of it fried. This full-service restaurant raises the bar for its culinary counterparts. Open every day, usually satisfying at least one rowdy tourist bus, the open-air spot delivers sizzling seafood in generous portions, from shrimp, salmon, and red snapper—deboned, stuffed with shrimp, and grilled to perfection—to plump lobsters. There are even a couple of steaks on the menu that are guaranteed to satisfy the biggest carnivores. Like all of its neighbors, this place faces the street, but there's a comfortable patio in the rear where you can kick back with an ice-cold beer or sangria and escape the traffic noise. ⑤ *Average main: $23* ⊠ *Luquillo Beach, Kiosk No. 2, Rte. 3* ☎ *787/889–0590* ⊕ *www.laparrillapr.com.*

$$
MEXICAN
✕ **Lolita's.** When it comes to Mexican food, this place is the real deal. For lunch, grab a few tacos, soft or crispy, for a mere $1.75 each. For dinner, try the *carne tampiqueña* (marinated skirt steak), *enchiladas suizas* (enchiladas in a mild green sauce), or *mole con pollo* (chicken in a spicy sauce laced with chocolate). There's a reason why devoted travelers have been returning for more than a decade. Generous portions are washed down with oversize margaritas. Or choose from a large selection of Mexican beers. The pleasant dining room, decorated with slightly kitschy paintings of simple village life, is on the second floor of a building just east of Luquillo. Very sparse parking can be tricky. ⑤ *Average main: $15* ⊠ *Rte. 3, Km 41.3* ☎ *787/889–5770, 787/889–0250.*

WHERE TO STAY

$
HOTEL
🛏 **The Yunque Mar Hotel & Parador.** This cute little hotel is just west of the popular Balneario Monserrate/Luquillo Beach, but the beach here is nearly as nice and almost always deserted. **Pros:** on a lovely beach; friendly owners; pool. **Cons:** building is on a crowded street; bland decor; no in-room safe; no elevator. ⑤ *Rooms from: $100* ⊠ *Calle*

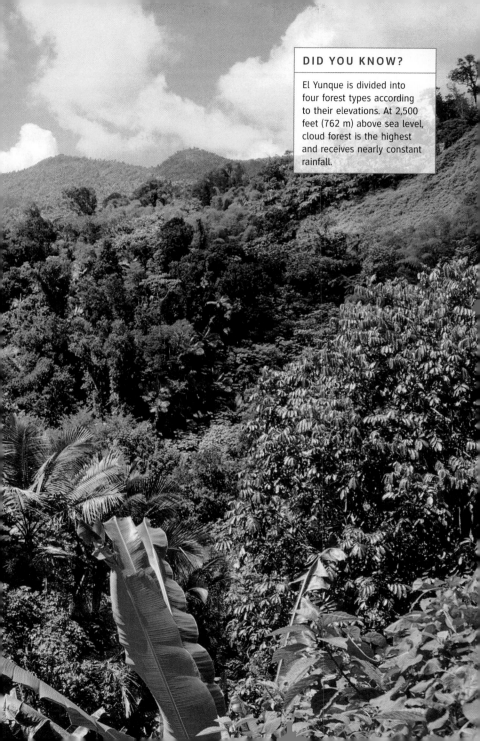

210 Parrots and Counting

The Taíno Indians called it the *iguaca*, Spanish speakers refer to it as the *cotorra*, and scientists know it as *Amazona vittata*. Whatever moniker it takes, the Puerto Rican green parrot—the only one native to the island—is one of the world's rarest birds. It nests primarily in the upper levels of El Yunque and in nearby Sierra de Luquillo. The bird is almost entirely green, though there are touches of blue on its wings, white rings around its eyes, and a red band just above its beak. It's only about 12 inches long, and its raucous squawk doesn't match its delicate appearance. The parrots mate for life. In February (the rain forest's driest season) they build nests within tree hollows and lay three to four eggs. Both parents feed the young.

When the Spanish arrived, the parrot population was an estimated one million on the main island, Vieques, and Culebra. But deforestation, hurricanes, and parasites have reduced the population (parrot hunting was common before being outlawed in 1940). By 1967 there were only 19 birds; a 1975 count totaled only 13.

But things are looking up, especially with the construction of breeding facilities in El Yunque and Bosque Río Abajo. At this writing, an estimated total of 500 green parrots were living in both the wild and captivity. Officials are optimistic that the numbers will continue to grow, and have had success with the breeding in captivity programs. If you're very observant (and very lucky), you just might spot one.

1 No. 6, Fortuna Playa ☎ *787/889–5555, 888/406-0992* ⊕ *www. hotelyunquemar.com* ⇱ *15 rooms, 2 suites* ⊙ *No meals.*

SPORTS AND THE OUTDOORS
SURFING
La Selva Surf Shop. Not far from Playa La Pared, La Selva Surf Shop has anything a surfer could need, including news about current conditions. Owned by surfer couple Bob and Sue, the shop sells sunglasses, sandals, bathing suits, and other beach necessities. Additionally, Bob can arrange for surfing lessons, and Sue rents out by the week a quaint two-bedroom guesthouse nestled above Luquillo in El Yunque's foothills. ⊠ *250 Calle Fernández Garcia Luquillo* ☎ *787/889–6205* ⊕ *www. rainforestrental.com.*

FAJARDO

7 miles (11 km) southeast of Luquillo; 34 miles (55 km) southeast of San Juan.

Fajardo, founded in 1772, has historical notoriety as a port where pirates stocked up on supplies. It later developed into a fishing community and an area where sugarcane flourished. Today it's a hub for yachts that use its marinas, divers who head to its good offshore sites, and day-trippers who travel by catamaran, ferry, or plane to the islands of Culebra and Vieques. With the most significant docking facilities on

DID YOU KNOW?

Much of El Yunque's forest canopy is dominated by the Puerto Rico royal palm, a relatively short tree (40 to 85 ft [12 to 18 m]) that thrives because it can withstand high, hurricane-force winds.

BEST LUQUILLO FOOD KIOSKS

Off Route 3, just before the exit for pristine Luquillo Beach, something of a culinary renaissance is occurring. Here you'll find 60-plus food shacks or *kioskos*, some with CIA-trained (Culinary Institute of America) chefs, offering everything from burgers to ceviche to stuffed lobster. Stop in for breakfast, lunch, dinner, or cocktails. These kioskos are turning out some of the island's best eats. Take your time surveying your options at establishments ranging from no-frills takeout counters to full-service restaurants. Once you've chosen, pull up a seat and get ready to feast.

Each kiosk is numbered. Here are a few of our favorites:

No. 2, La Parrilla. Head here for the original kiosko experience (*see also Where to Eat section*), and indulge in a lobster or steak as big as your head. ⊕ *www.laparrillapr.com.*

No. 12, El Jefe Burger Shack. Wrap your hands around stuffed burgers such as the green chili and jalapeño at El Jefe. Don't forget the smothered fries. ⊕ *www.eljefeburger.com.*

No. 38, Ceviche Hut. Their selection of fresh ceviches and classics like *pescado alo macho,* or fish in Peruvian seafood sauce, are solid choices.

the island's eastern side, Fajardo is a bustling city of 37,000—so bustling, in fact, that its unremarkable and somewhat battered downtown is often congested and difficult to navigate. Much of the tourist activity in Fajardo centers in the northern reaches of Las Croabas, near the gigantic El Conquistador Resort.

GETTING HERE AND AROUND

Getting around Fajardo is tricky without a car, especially if you plan on visiting several of the sights.

Car Rental **Enterprise.** Enterprise is the car rental provider servicing El Conquistador. ⊠ *El Conquistador, a Waldorf Astoria Resort, 1000 Av. El Conquistador* ☎ *787/801–3722* ⊕ *www.enterprise.com.* **Leaseway of Puerto Rico** ⊠ *Rte. 3, Km 44.4* ☎ *787/860–5000* ⊕ *www.leasewaypr.com.* **Thrifty Car Rental.** In central Fajardo's Marina Puerto Del Rey, Thrifty offers some of the island's most competitive rates. ⊠ *Route 3, Km 51.4, Marina Puerto Del Rey* ☎ *787/860–2030* ⊕ *www.thrifty.com.*

EXPLORING

TOP ATTRACTIONS

Reserva Natural Las Cabezas de San Juan. The 316-acre reserve on a headland north of Fajardo is owned by the nonprofit Conservation Trust of Puerto Rico. You ride in open-air trolleys and wander down boardwalks through seven ecosystems, including lagoons, mangrove swamps, and dry-forest areas. Green iguanas skitter across paths, and guides identify other endangered species. A half-hour hike down a wooden walkway brings you to the mangrove-lined **Laguna Grande,** where bioluminescent microorganisms glow at night. The restored **Fajardo Lighthouse** is the final stop on the tour; its Spanish-colonial tower has been in operation since 1882, making it Puerto Rico's second-oldest lighthouse.

The calm waters of Playa Luquillo are a draw for families and beachgoers looking for a relaxing ocean dip.

The first floor houses ecological displays; a winding staircase leads to an observation deck. The only way to see the reserve is on one of the many guided tours; reservations are required through the trust's comprehensive website. ⊠ *Rte. 987, Km 6* ☎ *787/722–5882 weekdays, 787/860–2562 weekends* ⊕ *www.paralanaturaleza.org* ✉ *$10.*

WORTH NOTING

Las Croabas. A few miles north of Fajardo is this fishing area, where seafood is sold in open-air restaurants along the ocean. A small park in the middle of town has a lovely waterfront walk, and it's easy to find outfitters for any kind of ocean adventure, from kayaking to sailing trips. ⊠ *Rte. 3, Km 51.2.*

Marina Puerto Chico. This lively marina off Route 987 is home to a cadre of glistening fishing boats, the offices of Mini-Boat Adventures, and one of the most popular restaurants on the east coast: El Varadero Seaside Grill (*see Where to Eat*). ⊠ *Rte. 987, Barrio Sardinera* ☎ *787/863–0834, 787/860–3721* ⊕ *www.marinapuertochico.com.*

Marina Puerto del Rey. Home to 1,100 boats, this is one of the Caribbean's largest marinas. This is the place to hook up with a scuba-diving group, arrange an excursion to Vieques's bioluminescent bay, or charter a fishing boat. The marina, located south of Fajardo, also has several restaurants and boating-supply stores. ⊠ *Rte. 3* ☎ *787/860–1000* ⊕ *www.puertodelrey.com.*

Villa Marina. The second-largest marina in Fajardo, it's home to charter-fishing boats as well as several catamaran operators who give day tours for swimming and snorkeling to the deserted islands right off

Puerto Rico's northeast coast. ⊠ *Rte. 987, Km 1.3, Playa Sardinera* ☎ *787/863–5131* ⊕ *www.villamarinapr.com.*

BEACHES

FAMILY   **Balneario Seven Seas.** One of Puerto Rico's prized Blue Flag beaches, Balneario Seven Seas may turn out to be the best surprise of your trip. This long stretch of powdery sand near the Reserva Natural Las Cabezas de San Juan has calm, clear waters that are perfect for swimming. There are plenty of picnic tables, as well as restaurants just outside the gates. **Amenities:** food and drink; parking (fee); showers; toilets. **Best for:** swimming. ⊠ *Rte. 195, Km. 4.8, Las Croabas* ☎ *787/863–8180* ⊕ *www.parquesnacionalespr.com* 🎫 *$4 parking* ☉ *Wed.–Sun. 8:30–5.*

WHERE TO EAT

$$$$ ╳ **Blossoms.** Hung with elaborate lanterns, this dining room is a fanci-
ASIAN   ful version of the Far East. The first thing you'll notice is the sound of meats and vegetables sizzling on the large teppanyaki tables. The chefs here know they're on stage and perform with a flourish. Despite the abundance of fresh fish, sushi bars are a rarity in this part of Puerto Rico, but the excellent one here has a seemingly endless array of sushi rolls to satisfy all cravings. Want traditional Chinese fare? Try the "Passion Love Boat" (lobster and shrimp) or "Full Steam Ahead" (steamed fish with scallions and black mushrooms). ⑤ *Average main: $35* ⊠ *El Conquistador Resort, Rte. 987, Km 3.4* ☎ *787/863–1000* ⊕ *www.elconresort.com* 🍽 *Reservations essential.*

$$$ ╳ **Calizo.** There's a string of seafood shacks in the village of Las Croabas,
SEAFOOD   all serving delicious fried fish. This open-air eatery, with tables covered by straw-topped umbrellas and anchored by a bustling square bar, takes things up a notch or two. Look for dishes like seafood salad in a spicy vinaigrette, mahimahi with scallops, a rich seafood paella, and chunks of lobster sautéed in cilantro butter. Wash it all down with a cold sangria. It's almost across from the Balneario Seven Seas, making it a great place to refuel after a day at the beach. The only drawback is that it's pricey. ⑤ *Average main: $29* ⊠ *Rte. 987, Las Croabas* ☎ *787/863–3664.*

$$ ╳ **El Varadero Seaside Grill.** At this no-frills seaside spot perched on the
SEAFOOD   docks of pretty Marina Puerto Chico, San Juan native Charlie Barrett has nailed the recipe for success. Simple yet cozy nautical touches serve as the backdrop for grilled fresh tuna, mahimahi, and snapper, as diners while away the hours watching the boats bob along the water. An extensive appetizer list rounds out the menu. At lunch be sure to order the two-fisted creole burger, a quintessentially Puerto Rican invention, topped with fried plantains and tangy creole sauce. Kids will love the mahimahi nuggets, and for those who like fire with their food, this friendly hangout makes five different kinds of hot sauce. ⑤ *Average main: $15* ⊠ *Marina Puerto Chico, Route 987* ☎ *787/860* ⊕ *www.elvaraderoseaside.com* ☉ *Closed Mon. and Tues.*

$$ ╳ **La Estación.** This laid-back spot has elevated Puerto Rican street food
PUERTO RICAN   to art form, thanks to two New Yorkers (one Puerto Rican) with res-
Fodor'sChoice   taurant pedigree who decided to leave the big city and open a new
★   spot dedicated to BBQ in an old gas station outside the El Conquistador Resort. Highlighting products obtained from local fishermen and

farmers, then smoking their own meats in an outdoor kitchen, Idalia Garcia and Kevin Roth's awesome joint is one of Puerto Rico's don't-miss culinary treats. Settle into one of the mismatched patio tables—be it made of teak, cedar, or concrete—order up a cocktail like the Passionate Don Q-osmo (a passion fruit cosmopolitan made with rum), and get ready to feast. Must-have plates include a side-splitting portion of meaty pork ribs marinated in *sofrito*, then dry-rubbed in BBQ sauce before smoking, a mixed seafood yuca mofongo (more moist than the plantain variety), a refreshing Puerto Rican green papaya salad with cashews, and some shrimp, shark, or pork *pinchos* (Puerto Rican kabobs). Don't skip dessert; the caramelized banana *pastelillo* with cinnamon, sugar, and vanilla ice cream is out of this world. ⑤ *Average main: $18* ⊠ *Route 987, Km 4, Las Croabas* ☎ *787/863–4481* ⊕ *www.laestacionpr.com* 𝄞 *Reservations essential* ⊘ *Closed Thurs.*

$$$
CARIBBEAN
✕ **Pasión por el Fogón.** At one of Fajardo's most beloved restaurants, Chef Myrta Pérez Toledo possesses a talent for taking traditional dishes and making them into something special. Succulent cuts of meat and fish are presented in unexpected ways—witness a perfectly cooked flank steak rolled into a cylinder standing on one end. But what makes this dish remarkable is the slightly sweet tamarind sauce that brings out the meat's earthy flavors. If you're a seafood lover, start with the lime-infused red-snapper ceviche, and then move on to the lobster medallions broiled in butter. For dessert, order the "Caribbean Sun," a version of an ice cream sundae that blends caramel, cinnamon, and chocolate toppings. ⑤ *Average main: $28* ⊠ *Rte. 987, Km 2.3, Barrio Sardinera* ☎ *787/863–3502* ⊕ *www.pasionporelfogon.net* 𝄞 *Reservations essential* ⊘ *No lunch weekdays.*

$$$$
SEAFOOD
✕ **Stingray Cafe.** Using the word *café* for this quiet restaurant inside the El Conquistador Resort at the bottom of the property's funicular is misleading. It's an elegant dining establishment with an impressive wine list heavy on New World and California reds. The menu features scallops with figs, a roasted pear salad, and a local pumpkin soup for appetizers, while thoughtful entrées like pan-seared cod with a lobster beurre blanc sauce paired with melt-in-your-mouth lobster risotto, and a medium-rare fillet of beef with roasted bacon and shallot sauce beg tasting. Though pricey, the waterfront setting offers a getaway from the hustle and bustle of the main property, and the staff and young chef aim to please the whims and palates of their diners. ⑤ *Average main: $35* ⊠ *El Conquistador Resort, 1000 Conquistador Avenue, Las Croabas* ☎ *787/863* ⊕ *www.elconresort.com* 𝄞 *Reservations essential.*

WHERE TO STAY

$
B&B/INN
▦ **Ceiba Country Inn.** About 5 miles (8 km) south of El Yunque in the town of Ceiba, colorful birds—the same ones from nearby El Yunque—flutter through Ceiba Country Inn's tropical foliage, and you can catch a glimpse of Culebra off the sunny patio. **Pros:** gorgeous setting; friendly owners; proximity to El Yunque; free Wi-Fi in public areas. **Cons:** far from tourist areas; several pets roam the property; no elevator. ⑤ *Rooms from: $95* ⊠ *Rte. 977, Km 1.2, Ceiba* ☎ *787/885–0471* ⊕ *www.ceibacountryinn.com* ⇆ *9 rooms* ⦿⊘ *Breakfast.*

$$$$
RESORT

⚅ **El Conquistador Resort.** Perched on a bluff overlooking the ocean, El Conquistador (The Conqueror) is a sprawling complex that has claimed the northern tip of the island and is one of Puerto Rico's most popular destination resorts. **Pros:** bright, spacious rooms; unbeatable views of nearby islands; good dining options; various meal plans available. **Cons:** must take a boat to reach the beach; long waits at the funicular taking guests between levels; self-parking is far from the hotel entrance; hidden fees like parking ($16/day) and kids club ($70/day). ⑤ *Rooms from: $400 ⊠ 1000 Av. El Conquistador* ☎ *787/863–1000, 888/543–1282* ⊕ *www.elconresort.com* ⤳ *750 rooms, 15 suites, 234 villas* ⑩ *Multiple meal plans.*

$
HOTEL
FAMILY

⚅ **Fajardo Inn.** The peach-colored buildings that make up this hilltop hotel offer lovely views of the islands poking out of the Atlantic Ocean. **Pros:** pretty grounds; family-friendly environment; good value. **Cons:** not on the beach; motel-like rooms. ⑤ *Rooms from: $150 ⊠ 52 Parcelas Beltran, Rte. 195, Beltran Sector* ☎ *787/860–6000, 888/860–6006* ⊕ *www.fajardoinn.com* ⤳ *125 rooms* ⑩ *No meals.*

NIGHTLIFE

Most of the evening action takes place in El Conquistador's lounges, but there are a few neighborhood bars where locals drink beer.

SPORTS AND THE OUTDOORS

DAY SAILS

Several reputable catamaran and yacht operators in Fajardo make excursions to the reefs and sparkling blue waters surrounding a handful of small islets just off the coast. Many of the trips include transportation to and from San Juan–area hotels. Whether or not you're staying in Fajardo, if you take a day trip on the water you'll see classic Caribbean scenes of coral reefs rife with sea life, breathtakingly clear water, and palm-fringed, deserted beaches. The day sails, with stops for snorkeling, include swimming breaks at deserted beaches and picnic lunches. Most of the craft are outfitted for comfort, with quality stereo systems, bathrooms, deck showers, and full-service bars. Many competent operators offer a nearly identical experience, so your selection will probably be based on price and which operators serve your San Juan hotel, or which operate out of the marina in Fajardo that you are visiting. Prices range from $55 to $95; price is affected by whether you join a trip in San Juan or in Fajardo and by what is included in the cost. Though they are quickly becoming standard features, ask if picnic lunches and a full-service bar are included.

East Island Excursions. At East Island Excursions catamarans ranging in size from 45 feet to 65 feet take you offshore for snorkeling. Two of the catamarans are powered, and this cuts down tremendously on travel time to outlying islands. Trips include stops at isolated beaches and a lunch buffet. East Island Excursions can accommodate those who wish to see the bioluminescent bay on Vieques and return to the mainland on the same evening. Transportation to Vieques is included, as is dinner at a local restaurant. All craft are outfitted with swimming decks, freshwater showers, and full-service bars. These vessels are some of the plushest for day sails in the area. ⊠ *Marina Puerto del Rey, Rte. 3, Km 51.4* ☎ *787/860–3434, 877/937–4386* ⊕ *www.eastwindcats.com.*

Erin Go Bragh. The *Erin Go Bragh III* is a 50-foot sailing yacht based in Fajardo that takes groups of six or fewer on tours of the glistening waters and nearby islands. Known for delicious barbecue picnic lunches, the outfitter also provides snorkel and fishing equipment. Overnight and longer charters are available for groups. Call for rates. ⊠ *Marina Puerto del Rey, Rte. 3, Km 51.4* ☎ *787/860–4401, 787/409–2511* ⊕ *www.egbc.net.*

Spread Eagle II. The *Spread Eagle II* is a 51-foot catamaran that heads out to isolated beaches on the islands off Fajardo. The trip includes an all-you-can-eat buffet, as well as unlimited piña coladas and tropical fruit punch. To top it off, you get a free snorkel to bring home. The boat is comfortable and well-equipped with a bathroom and freshwater deck shower so you can rinse off salt and sand. Sunset and moonlight cruises are also available. ⊠ *Dock J, Villa Marina Harbor, Rte. 987* ☎ *787/887–8821, 888/523–4511* ⊕ *www.snorkelpr.com.*

DIVING

La Casa del Mar Dive Center. La Casa del Mar Dive Center focuses its scuba and snorkeling activity on the islets of Palomino, Lobos, and Diablo in Fajardo, but also offers trips to Vieques and Culebra, as well as charters to Vieques' wondrous Puerto Mosquito bioluminescent bay. Full-day St. Thomas, U.S. Virgin Islands, dives are also available for $160, as are PADI certification courses. ⊠ *El Conquistador Resort, 1000 Av. El Conquistador* ☎ *787/863–1000, 787/860–3483* ✐ *www. scubapuertorico.net* ⌧ *Two-tank morning dive $99–$125, depending on equipment needs; single-tank afternoon dive $69–$94; snorkeling $60 per person.*

Sea Ventures Dive Center. At Sea Ventures Pro Dive Center you can get your diving certification, arrange dive trips to 20 offshore sites, and organize boating and sailing excursions. ⊠ *Marina Puerto del Rey, Rte. 3, Km 51.4* ☎ *787/863–3483, 800/739–3483* ⊕ *www.divepuerto rico.com.*

FISHING

787 Fishing Puerto Rico. Sail off on one of Captain Marcos Hanke's 22- or 26-foot sport fishing boats for deep-sea, light-tackle, or fly-fishing excursions. Inland, tarpon, snook, bonefish, and kingfish can be caught year-round, while game fish like marlin, sailfish, wahoo, tuna, and mahimahi await just offshore. Half-day (four hours) charters begin at $350, full-day charters (eight hours) on the 26-foot boat price at $950. Sunset fishing charters are also available. ⊠ *Marina Puerto Chico, Slips 4 and 6* ☎ *787/646–2585, 787/FISHING* ⊕ *www.787fishing.com.*

GOLF

Arthur Hills Golf Course at El Conquistador Resort & Waldorf Astoria Spa. Named for its designer, the 18-hole course at El Conquistador Resort is famous for its mountainous terrain that features elevation changes of more than 200 feet—rare in the Caribbean. From the highest spot, on the 15th hole, you have great views of the surrounding mountains and rain forest. The trade winds make every shot challenging—if the gorgeous views, strategic bunkering, and many water hazards haven't already distracted you. You are also likely to spot the harmless and generally timid iguanas that populate the area. ⊠ *1000 Av. El Conquistador* ☎ *787/863–6784* ⊕ *www.elconresort.com* ⊒ *Up to $185* ⚐ *18 holes, 6746 yards, par 72.*

KAYAKING

Several tour operators, including some based in San Juan, offer nighttime kayaking tours in the bioluminescent bay at the Reserva Natural Las Cabezas de San Juan, just north of Fajardo.

Kayaking Puerto Rico. This adventure outfitter has an excursion for all types of water (and kayak) lovers. They offer a host of day and night trips such as kayaking the glowing waters of Fajardo's bioluminescent lagoon, paddling along Culebra's reefs, snorkeling with local turtles, and piloting an eco-friendly, inflatable speedboat across crystal clear waters. Rates begin at $48 depending on activity; group rates and specials can be found online. ☎ *787/435–1665, 787/245–4545* ⊕ *www. kayakingpuertorico.com.*

THE EASTERN COAST

From Fajardo, a good way to explore the southeast is to travel along the old coastal road, Route 3, as it weaves on and off the shoreline and passes through small towns. The route takes a while to travel but offers terrific beach and mountain scenery.

NAGUABO

11 miles (18 km) southwest of Fajardo.

In this fast-growing municipality's downtown, pastel buildings give the main plaza the look of a child's nursery: a golden-yellow church on one side faces a butter-yellow city hall, and a pink-and-blue amphitheater anchors one corner. It's a good spot for people-watching until the heat drives you to the beach.

Offshore, Cayo Santiago—also known as Monkey Island—is the site of some of the world's most important rhesus-monkey research. A small colony of monkeys was introduced to the island in the late 1930s, and since then scientists have been studying their habits and health, especially as they pertain to the study of diabetes and arthritis. You can't land at Cayo Santiago, but Captain Frank Lopez sails a small tour boat—*La Paseadora*—around it.

GETTING HERE AND AROUND

To reach Naguabo, it takes about an hour driving from San Juan. It's just south of Fajardo off Route 53, along Route 31. From Route 31, turn down Calle Garzot to reach the town square. Although públicos run to and from Naguabo, public transportation within Naguabo is extremely limited, so a rental car is your best transportation option.

BEACHES

Playa Húcares. Playa Húcares is *the* place to be. Though the strip is a little rundown, an authentic vibe permeates the casual outdoor eateries and funky little shops that vie with the water for your attention. Locals sell ice out of trucks, and the heavy base of reggaeton music beats from the windows of passing cars. Two Victorian-style houses anchor one end of the waterfront promenade; a dock with excursion boats anchors the other, and a red, green, and blue painted bridge connects both sides of the town. ⊠ *Off Rte. 3, south of Naguabo.*

WHERE TO EAT

$ ✕ **Chumar.** As at the other seafood shacks along Playa Húcares, you
SEAFOOD order at the counter and then grab a seat at one of the plastic tables lining the sidewalk. It's right on the ocean, so you are almost guaranteed fresh fish. Paper plates and plastic cutlery accompany the down-home seafood, and the sight of locals nursing beers and shooting the breeze is commonplace. Afterward, you can stroll along the waterfront walkway across the street. ⑤ *Average main: $10* ⊠ *Rte. 3, Km 66, Playa Húcares* ☎ *787/874–0107.*

WHERE TO STAY

$ ▦ **Casa Cubuy Ecolodge.** El Yunque's southern edge is the setting for this
B&B/INN eco-friendly hotel where the rooms are simple—no phones or TVs—but comfortable, with tile floors, rattan furniture, and windows that show off one of the island's best views. **Pros:** spectacular setting; close to some of the island's best hiking trails; doting staff. **Cons:** basic rooms; access roads are often affected by landslides; lower-level rooms are small. ⑤ *Rooms from: $110* ⊠ *Rte. 191, Km 22, Barrio Río Blanco* ☎ *787/874–6221* ⊕ *www.casacubuy.com* ⇗ *10 rooms* ⑪ *Breakfast.*

SPORTS AND THE OUTDOORS

La Paseadora. For nearly 20 years, Captain Frank Lopez has been sailing visitors from Naguabo's Malecon around Cayo Santiago aboard his boat, *La Paseadora.* Lopez, a charming, well-informed guide, gears the outings to the group, and over the course of three hours, you can motor around and watch the monkeys at Monkey Island—one of the world's oldest primate colonies. Plan to make some fishing and snorkeling stops in local waters using onboard gear. ⊠ *Playa Húcares dock, Rte. 3, Km 66.6* ☎ *787/850–7881, 787/316–0441.*

HUMACAO

9 miles (15 km) southwest of Naguabo; 34 miles (55 km) southeast of San Juan.

Travelers flock to the Humacao area for one reason: the sprawling resort community called Palmas del Mar and its two world-class golf courses, the Flamboyán and the Palm. Although it's not thought of as a tourist destination, Humacao does have a handful of interesting neo-colonial buildings along its traffic-clogged downtown streets. These are worth a peek if you're stuck here on a rainy day.

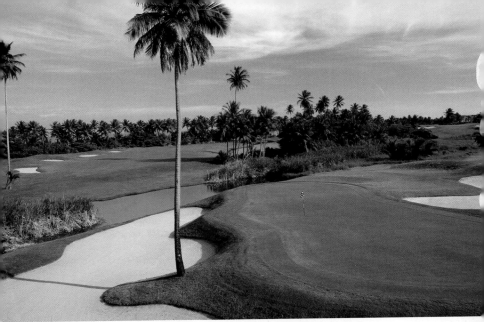
The Palmas del Mar Country Club features the Rees Jones–designed Flamboyán course.

GETTING HERE AND AROUND

Huamaco is served by two highways and one toll expressway. Route 30 serves as the main highway coming from points west (Caguas and Las Piedras), while Route 53 serves destinations to the north (Fajardo and Naguabo). Route 3, the main highway bordering the eastern coastline of the island from San Juan, passes through Humacao.

EXPLORING

WORTH NOTING

Museo Casa Roig. The former residence of sugar baron Antonio Roig Torruellas, Museo Casa Roig was built in 1919. Czech architect Antonio Nechodoma designed the facade, unusual for its wide eaves, mosaic work, and stained-glass windows with geometric patterns. This building, which bears more than a passing resemblance to those of Frank Lloyd Wright, was Puerto Rico's first 20th-century building to be included on the register of National Historic Places. The Roig family lived in the home until 1956; it was then abandoned before being turned over to the University of Puerto Rico in 1977. It's currently a museum and cultural center that houses historical photos, furniture, and rotating exhibits of works by contemporary island artists. ⊠ *66 Calle Antonio López* ☎ *787/852–8380* 🖃 *Free* ⊙ *Mon.–Fri. 10–4.*

Plaza de Humacao. Plaza de Humacao, downtown's broad square, is anchored by Catedral Dulce Nombre de Jesús (Sweet Name of Jesus Cathedral), which dates from 1869. It has a castlelike facade, and even when its grille door is locked, you can peek through to see the sleek altar, polished floors, and stained-glass windows dominated by blues. Across the plaza, four fountains splash under the shade of old trees.

People pass through feeding the pigeons, children race down the promenade, and retirees congregate on benches to chat. Look for the little monument with the globe on top; it's a tribute to city sons who died in wars. ⊠ *Av. Font Martel at Calle Ulises Martinez.*

Refugio de Vida Silvestre de Humacao. As you travel from Naguabo to Humacao, you'll pass stretches of beach and swaths of undeveloped land, including the swamps, lagoons, and forested areas of the Refugio de Vida Silvestre de Humacao. This nature reserve has an information office, restrooms, and campsites. ⊠ *Rte. 3, Km 74.3* ☎ *787/852–4440* 🖅 *Free* ⊙ *Weekdays 7:30–4:30.*

WHERE TO EAT

$
CAFÉ
✕ **Bistro Rico.** Most of Humacao's restaurants are within the bounds of the massive Palmas del Mar, and since you can't eat at Chez Daniel every night, Daniel Vasse opened this casual bistro next door to his original restaurant. The menu is mostly made up of sandwiches that are far from the ordinary. The sliced duck breast with caramelized red onions is simple but satisfying, as is the codfish with slices of hard-boiled eggs or the filet mignon with béarnaise sauce. The handful of entrées includes a smashing quiche Lorraine. The staff is friendly, and the simple decor is livened up with some slightly kitschy seaside murals. ⑤ *Average main: $12* ⊠ *Palmas del Mar, Anchor's Village Marina, Rte. 906, Km 86.4* ☎ *787/850–3838* ⊙ *Closed Sun.*

$$$$
FRENCH
Fodor'sChoice
★
✕ **Chez Daniel.** When the stars are out, it would be hard to find a more romantic setting than this waterfront eatery in the Anchor's Village Marina. Dozens of gleaming white boats are anchored so close that you could practically hit them with a baguette. The dining room has a chummy atmosphere, probably because many patrons seem to know each other. If you'd prefer alone time, ask for a table on one of the private terraces. Chef Daniel Vasse's French-country-style dishes are some of the best on the island. The exceptional Marseille-style bouillabaisse is full of fresh fish and bursts with the flavor of a white garlic sauce. Something less French, you say? Choose steak or fish simply prepared on the grill, and pair it with a bottle from the extensive wine cellar. Sunday brunch, with its seemingly endless seafood bar, draws people from all over the island, and runs $45 per person with drinks. ⑤ *Average main: $33* ⊠ *Palmas del Mar, Anchor's Village Marina, Rte. 906, Km 86.4* ☎ *787/850–3838* ⚓ *Reservations essential* ⊙ *Closed Tues.*

WHERE TO STAY

$
HOTEL
🏨 **Wyndham Garden at Palmas de Mar.** Amid acres and acres of condo developments and golf courses, Wyndham Garden is surprisingly modest in scale, given its opulent surroundings. **Pros:** access to all resort's amenities; beautiful pool area; outgoing staff; free Wi-Fi. **Cons:** uninspired architecture; small casino. ⑤ *Rooms from: $140* ⊠ *170 Candelero Dr.* ☎ *787/850–6000* ⊕ *www.wyndhamgardenatpalmasdelmar. com* 🛏 *84 rooms, 9 suites, 14 junior suites* 🍴 *No meals.*

NIGHTLIFE

Wyndham Garden at Palmas del Mar. The small casino at the Wyndham Garden at Palmas del Mar Resort offers everything from blackjack to slot machines. The action is liveliest on weekends. ⊠ *170 Candelero Dr.* ☏ *787/850–6000* ☉ *Daily 10 am–2 am.*

SPORTS AND THE OUTDOORS

FISHING

Karolette Sport Fishing. At Karolette Sport Fishing, you're in the capable hands of Captain Bill Burleson, who has fished these waters since 1966. He'll take you out for excursions in his bright yellow 46-foot Bertram powerboat. A half day of fishing along the continental shelf costs $750, while a full day (usually more than nine hours) of deep-water fishing costs $1,450. If nobody makes a catch, he'll cut the fee in half. ⊠ *Palmas del Mar, Anchor's Village Marina* ☏ *787/637–7992* ⊕ *www.puertoricodeepseafishing.com.*

Maragata Charters. Maragata Charters takes anglers out from Palmas del Mar on a 38-foot power catamaran. Snorkeling and combination trips to Monkey Island, Vieques, and Culebra are also offered. ⊠ *Palmas del Mar, Anchor's Village Marina, Slip No. 14* ☏ *787/850–7548 Marina, 787/637–1802 Cell* ⊕ *www.maragatacharters.com* ☑ *Four-hour tours start at $110 per person; eight-hour tours start at $215 per person.*

GOLF

Palmas del Mar Country Club. Palmas del Mar Country Club has two good golf courses: The Rees Jones–designed Flamboyán course was named for the nearly six-dozen flamboyant trees (also known as flame trees) that pepper its fairway. It begins its play through the villas, but improves on the back nine venturing into the forest and hills. It is considered one of the tougher courses in Puerto Rico. The older Gary Player–designed Palm course is a bit shorter in more of the resort style of play, with the 14th and 16th holes affording some wonderful Caribbean vistas. ⊠ *Palmas del Mar, Route 906* ☏ *787/656–3015* ⊕ *www.palmaspac.com* ☑ *From $100* ⛳ *36 holes. Flamboyan Course: 8 holes, 7117 yards, par 70; Palm Course: 18 holes, 6675 yards, par 71.*

VIEQUES AND CULEBRA

WELCOME TO VIEQUES AND CULEBRA

TOP REASONS TO GO

★ **Puerto Mosquito:** Kayak after dark on the astounding bioluminescent bay on Vieques.

★ **Playa Flamenco:** Catch some rays on this Culebra bay, consistently ranked as one of the world's best white-sand beaches.

★ **Refugio Nacional de Vida Silvestre de Culebra:** Bird-watch and hike in one of Puerto Rico's oldest nature refuges.

★ **El Resuelve:** Sample real Puerto Rican fare with the locals at this colorful roadside restaurant on Vieques.

★ **Playa Carlos Rosario:** Simply walk into the waters off this deserted Culebra beach to snorkel a fabulous coral reef.

1 **Vieques.** Two-thirds of this island is a wildlife refuge, and it's a fabulous destination for active travelers who like bicycling, kayaking, and fishing. It is fringed by gorgeous beaches, and a visit to the bioluminescent bay is an awesome experience visitors will never forget. Boutique hotels and trendy restaurants have recently begun to open, and the W Resort & Spa and Malecón House will appeal to urbane fashionistas.

GETTING ORIENTED

Vieques is 21 miles (33½ km) long and 4 miles (6½ km) wide, and has two small communities. Isabel Segunda, on the northern shore, is the main town, where the ferry docks. On the southern shore is the village of Esperanza, a string of low-cost bars, restaurants, and hotels along a waterfront promenade that is growing in size. Nearby is the world-famous bioluminescent bay, Puerto Mosquito. The bulk of the island consists of the Vieques National Wildlife Refuge. Within the park you'll find dozens of beaches with names such as Caracas, Pata Prieta, and Chiva, as well as many more that have no official names, and can be found off unpaved side roads. At 7 miles (11 km) long and 4 miles (6½ km) wide, Culebra is much smaller and less developed than Vieques. There's only one community, the tiny town of Dewey.

2 Culebra. The island is mostly unspoiled, a quality that brings many people back year after year. People come to Culebra to laze on Playa Flamenco, consistently rated one of the top 10 most beautiful beaches in the world, as well as many lesser-known but sensational expanses of sand. Snorkeling and diving on the cays surrounding Culebra are rated world-class.

Updated by
Julie Schwietert
Collazo

Although the islands of Vieques and Culebra—known as the "Spanish Virgins"—are only a few miles off the coast of Puerto Rico, they feel like another world. While the mainland rings with the adrenaline rush of Latin America, this pair of palm-fringed islands has the laid-back vibe of the Caribbean—not surprising, as St. Thomas and St. Croix are clearly visible from the eastern edges of Culebra.

Vieques and Culebra are alike in many ways. Neither has much traffic—in fact, you won't find a single traffic light on either island. High-rise hotels haven't cast a shadow on the beaches. And there are no casinos, fast-food chains, strip malls, or most other trappings of modern life. "Barefoot" is often part of the dress code at casual restaurants, and the hum you hear in your room more likely comes from a ceiling fan rather than an air conditioner. Things happen here *poco a poco*—slowly, at the islanders' easy pace.

Beautiful beaches abound on both islands. Many of the best stretches of sand on Vieques—Chiva, Caracas, and Green Beach, to name a few—are on land that was once part of a U.S. naval base. This means that development hasn't reared its ugly head. It also means there are few, if any, amenities, so bring plenty of water and a picnic lunch. Most accommodations provide guests with beach chairs, towels, and coolers for the day. Some will even pack guests lunches to take to the beach. The beaches on Culebra are just as unspoiled, as judged by the marine turtles that come ashore to lay eggs.

Wild horses roam Vieques, where two-thirds of the island is a wildlife refuge protecting coastal lagoons, mangrove wetlands, subtropical dry forest, and islands. Ecotourism is a key draw. Fishing in the turquoise flats just offshore is fantastic. And the island is tailor-made for exploring by bicycle and/or kayak. Off Culebra several cays delight birders with their colonies of boobies and other seabirds.

Some of the best snorkeling and diving in the Caribbean can be found in the waters surrounding Vieques and Culebra. You can sign up for a half-day or full-day excursion to nearby coral reefs, which teem with colorful fish. It's also possible to grab a mask and snorkel, and then simply wade out a few yards to see what you can see. Playa Esperanza, on the southern coast of Vieques, is a good place for beginners. More experienced snorkelers will prefer La Chiva (Blue Beach) or Green Beach.

VIEQUES AND CULEBRA PLANNER

WHEN TO GO

High season runs roughly from December 15 through April 15. Puerto Ricans flock here at Christmas and Easter, when Vieques and Culebra are packed with families enjoying the sun and sand. Be sure to make reservations well in advance if you're visiting during the holidays. The shoulder season, when prices are a bit lower, is a good option. Remember, however, that some restaurants and hotels are open only during high season. The only time you might want to avoid is late August through late October, when hurricanes can strike the area.

GETTING HERE AND AROUND

AIR TRAVEL

Air Flamenco. Air Flamenco flies daily from San Juan's Isla Grande Airport to Vieques and Culebra, and offers charters to both islands from San Juan International Airport (SJU). The airline also services Vieques with daily flights from the municipal airport in the town of Ceiba, which is about eight miles south of Fajardo. ☎ *787/724–1818* ⊕ *www. airflamenco.net.*

Cape Air. Cape Air offers daily flights year-round between San Juan International Airport (SJU) and Vieques. ☎ *800/CAPE–AIR 800–227–3247* ⊕ *www.capeair.com.*

Vieques Air Link. Vieques Air Link flies daily from San Juan's Isla Grande Airport and Ceiba's municipal airport to Vieques and Culebra. It also flies daily from San Juan International Airport (SJU) to Vieques. Charters are also available. ☎ *888/901–9247* ⊕ *www.viequesairlink.com.*

Vieques Air Link also flies from Ceiba (Fajardo). Flights from San Juan are 20 to 30 minutes, and one-way fares are between $65 and $125; flights from Ceiba are about 10 minutes, with one-way fares between $30 and $50. Small propeller planes that hold up to nine passengers are used.

Most international travelers fly from San Juan's Aeropuerto Internacional Luis Muñoz Marín (SJU) or nearby Aeropuerto Fernando L. Rivas Dominicci (SIG; more commonly known as Aeropuerto Isla Grande), which is cheaper. Vieques Air Link also flies from Ceiba's Aeropuerto José Aponte de la Torre (RVR) about 7 miles (12 km) south of Fajardo.

CAR TRAVEL

It's nearly impossible to see either island without renting a car. Scooters are another option, especially on Culebra, but not if you're headed to the beach. Road conditions and local driving habits are spotty. Both islands have local agencies, including several that specialize in SUVs.

Rates are between $40 and $95 a day. It's often cheaper to book a hotel-rental car package.

FERRY TRAVEL

Puerto Rico Ports Authority. The Puerto Rico Ports Authority runs passenger ferries from Fajardo to Culebra and Vieques. Service is from the ferry terminal in Fajardo, about 90 minutes' drive from San Juan. ☎ 787/494–0934 ⊕ *http://dtop.gov.pr/transporte_maritimo/index.asp* ⊲ *$2 per person from Fajardo to Vieques; $2.25 to Culebra. Children 3–11 and seniors 60–74 are $1. Passengers over 75 are free.*

Car ferries also link Fajardo to Vieques and Culebra, but rental agencies won't let you take their vehicles between the mainland and islands. A municipal parking lot next to the ferry costs $5–$7 a day. No ferries link Vieques and Culebra at present.

There's limited seating, so arrive about an hour ahead of the departure time. The Ports Authority (DTOP) claims to take phone reservations daily from 8 to 11 and 1 to 3, but it's difficult to get anyone to answer this number.

Fajardo Terminal. Schedules change often, and ferries are canceled frequently due to rough sea conditions. Call the Fajardo Terminal to confirm current schedules, and show up at least an hour before you intend to depart. ☎ 787/794–0934 ⊕ *www.dtop.gov.pr/transporte_maritimo/index.asp*.

ABOUT THE RESTAURANTS

Most of the restaurants on Vieques and Culebra are casual. Because even the most formal restaurants on the islands are on covered terraces or in open-air dining rooms, there's not a single establishment where you'll be frowned upon for wearing shorts. Pack a couple of nice shirts and you'll be set.

You'll find seafood at almost every eatery on Vieques and Culebra. The fish is as fresh as you'll find anywhere, since that red snapper was probably splashing around in the Caribbean that very morning. Here you can order your fish any number of ways. Many chefs are experimenting with European and Asian cooking techniques, so you may find your fish smoked or in a sushi roll.

Even if a restaurant focuses on a different type of food, you can be sure that mangos, papayas, and other tropical fruits will make an appearance. Bills often include a service charge; if it isn't included, a 15% tip is customary. Most restaurants are open for dinner from about 6 pm until about 10 pm.

ABOUT THE HOTELS

Vieques has a wide variety of lodgings, from surf shacks across from the beach to boutique hotels high up on secluded hillsides. There's something here for everyone. Looking for tropical splendor? Try Hacienda Tamarindo. Sexy sophistication? Head to W Resort & Spa. Interesting architecture? There's Hix Island House. An intimate inn where you'll meet fellow travelers? Head to Casa de Amistad or Trade Winds.

Culebra has fewer options. Dewey, the island's only town, has a handful of small inns that are easy on the wallet. Scattered around the island are a couple of more luxurious lodgings plus villa rentals. Nothing remotely resembles a chain hotel, and that's how the locals like it.

HOTEL AND RESTAURANT PRICES

Prices in our restaurant reviews are the average cost of a main course at dinner or, if dinner is not served, at lunch; taxes and service charges are generally included. Prices in the hotel reviews are the lowest cost of a standard double room in high season, excluding taxes, service charges, and meal plans (except at all-inclusives). Prices for rentals are the lowest per-night cost for a one-bedroom unit in high season.

For expanded lodging reviews and current deals, visit Fodors.com.

WHAT IT COSTS				
	$	**$$**	**$$$**	**$$$$**
Restaurants	$8–$12	$13–$20	$21–$30	over $30
Hotels	$80–$150	$151–$250	$251–$350	over $350

SAFETY

Drug-related violent crimes have recently increased on Vieques. Tourists are largely unaffected, but it pays to be on your guard. Avoid bringing valuables to the beach, and don't leave any personal items in your car. Rental agencies advise that you leave your car unlocked when parked at a beach so thieves won't break the windows to get inside. There's very little crime on Culebra.

WHAT TO PACK

Vieques has a pharmacy and a hospital, and Culebra's small hospital has a prescription-only pharmacy. Stock up on all supplies—such as allergy medications, contact-lens solution, or feminine supplies—before heading to the islands.

VISITOR INFORMATION

The islands' tourism offices are hit and miss when it comes to being open and offering helpful material.

Vieques Tourism Office. The Vieques Tourism Office is across the main square in Isabel Segunda. If you need portable information, ask them to print out a complete list of local businesses. ✉ *449 Calle Carlos Lebrón, Isabel Segunda, Vieques* ☎ *787/741–0800* ⊙ *Mon.–Sun. 8–4:30.*

Culebra Tourism Office. The Culebra Tourism Office is near the ferry dock in front of Banco Popular. The staffers will help you as best they can, even recommending restaurants that are off the beaten path. ✉ *250 Calle Pedro Marquez, Dewey, Culebra* ☎ *787/742–1033* ⊙ *Daily 8–4:30.*

VIEQUES

8 miles (13 km) southeast of Fajardo.

Looking for a place to play Robinson Crusoe? Then head to Vieques, where you can wander along almost any stretch of sand and never see another soul. You can while away the hours underneath coconut palms,

Vieques

Sonda de Vieques

Pasaje de Vieques

TO FAJARDO

Sidhia Hutchinson
Fine Art
Studio & Gallery

El Faro Punta Mulas

Isabel Segunda

Gringo Beach

Antonio R. Rodriguez Airport

Mosquito

ISLA DE VIEQUES

El Fortín Conde de Mirasol

Puerto Mosquito

Esperanza

Malecón

Vieques Conservation & Historical Trust

Vieques National Wildlife Refuge

Monte Pirata

Punta Arenas

Playa Plata (Green Beach)

Purple Beach

Cerro Matías Jalobre

Vieques National Wildlife Refuge

Ensenada Honda

Cayo Jalova

Bahia Salina del Sur

Playa Chiva (Blue Beach)

Playa Caracas

Puerto Ferro

Playa Sun Bay

Sun Bay

Playa Media Luna

Punta Salinas

Punta Este

Punta Este

Playa Plata

200 | 201 | 995 | 996 | 997

3 mi
3 km

Restaurants ▶

Bananas	7
Bilí	6
Carambola	4
Chez Shack	2
Conuco	1
Duffy's	5
El Quenepo	8
El Resuelve	9
Next Course	3

Hotels ▶

Bravo Beach Hotel	1
Casa de Amistad	2
Hacienda Tamarindo	6
Hector's	7
Hix Island House	4
La Finca Caribe	5
Malecon House	9
Seagate Hotel	10
Trade Winds	8
W Retreat & Spa	3

wade in the warm water, or get a mask and snorkel and explore coral reefs that ring the island.

For many years the island was known mostly for the conflict between angry islanders and aloof federal officials. Over the course of six decades the U.S. Navy used two-thirds of Vieques, mostly on the island's eastern side, as a bombing range, and the western tip as an ammunition dump. After an April 1999 bombing accident took the life of one resident, waves of protests brought the maneuvers to a standstill, and political pressure from the island's governor helped force the military to leave on May 1, 2003.

Ironically, the military presence helped keep the island pristine by keeping resort developers away. Today the military's former holdings have been turned into Vieques National Wildlife Refuge. The woodsy western end of the island is laced by trails that offer fabulous cycling around the base of Monte Pirata, the island's highest peak. More and more of the eastern part of the island is being opened every year, granting access to stupendous beaches shelving into calm turquoise waters. The park also protects Puerto Mosquito, a flask-shaped bay populated by microscopic organisms that glow when disturbed at night—a thrilling experience for kayakers *(see also Bioluminescent Bays feature in this chapter)*.

GETTING HERE AND AROUND

Isabel Segunda is the transportation hub of Vieques. The ferry drops off passengers at the town's dock, and propeller planes deposit passengers at Aeropuerto Antonio Rivera Rodríguez (VQS), which is a 10-minute cab ride from Isabel Segunda or a 15-minute taxi ride from Esperanza. Route 200 leads from the airport to Isabel Segunda, and Route 997 leads from Isabel Segunda to Esperanza. There's also a longer, more scenic route between the two towns: from Isabel Segunda, take Route 200 west to Route 201 south. After about 1 mile (1½ km), take Route 996 to Esperanza.

If you want to rent or gas up a car, you need to make a trip to Isabel Segunda. Try Vieques Car Rental or Maritza Car Rental

You can flag down taxis on the street, but it's faster and safer to have your hotel call one for you. Either way, agree on how much the trip will cost before you get inside the taxi, as many drivers are prone to rip off tourists with exorbitant fares. ■ TIP➔ **If you plan to rent a car on Vieques or Culebra, make sure you reserve it in advance, especially when visiting during high season. The rental agencies have a limited number of vehicles, and when they are gone you're out of luck.**

Airport Information Aeropuerto Antonio Rivera Rodríguez ⊠ *Route 200, Km 2.6, Vieques* ☎ *787/741–0515.*

Car Rental Avis ⊠ *Rte 200, Km 5, Vieques* ☎ *787/397–2533* ⊕ *www.avis.com.* **Vieques Car Rental** ⊠ *Route 200, Km 1, Monti Santo, Monti Santo, Vieques* ☎ *787/435–1323* ⊕ *www.viequescarrental.com.* **Maritza's Car Rental** ⊠ *Rte. 201, Vieques* ☎ *787/741–0078* ⊕ *www.maritzascarrental.com.*

Ferry Terminal Vieques Terminal ⊠ *Calle Morropo, Vieques* ☎ *787/494–0934* ⊕ *http://dtop.gov.pr/transporte_maritimo/index.asp.*

Taxis Lolo Felix Tours ⊠ *Vieques* ☎ *787/485–5447.*

GREAT ITINERARIES

IF YOU HAVE 1 DAY

If you are headed to one of the islands for an overnight excursion, your best bet is **Vieques**. Get here by plane, either from San Juan or Fajardo, to maximize your time on the island. Spend the day exploring the beaches, especially the half-moon-shaped **Sun Bay**. In the evening you can dine at one of the oceanfront restaurants in Esperanza, then head off for an excursion to **Puerto Mosquito**, a bay filled with glow-in-the-dark dinoflagellates. Spend the night in Esperanza or Isabel Segunda.

IF YOU HAVE 3 DAYS

If you have a few days, you can see most of Vieques. Start your first day in Isabel Segunda, where you can take a few snapshots of **El Faro Punta Mulas**, and then explore the hilltop **El Fortín Conde de Mirasol**. Head off for an afternoon by the ocean, perhaps at **Green Beach** or one of the delightfully deserted beaches on the northern part of the island. Enjoy happy hour at **Lazy Jack's**, a favorite hangout for expats, in Esperanza. In the cool of the evening, have dinner in one of the chic eateries nearby. On your second day, go for an early-morning mountain-bike ride in the western portion of **Vieques**

National Wildlife Refuge, a swath of wilderness that was once a naval base. Head for lunch at **El Resuelve**, or pack a picnic and head off to **Playa Media Luna** or another of the beautiful beaches along the southern coast. After dinner, make sure to book a tour of **Puerto Mosquito**. Spend your third day kayaking, snorkeling, and/or fishing. In the evening, head to W Retreat & Spa for a spa treatment, cocktails, and fine dining at **Sorcé**.

IF YOU HAVE 5 DAYS

If you have a few more days, you can see both Vieques and Culebra. *After following the itinerary above,* head to Culebra on your fourth day. (A 10-minute flight between the islands is the only way to travel between them.) Your destination should be Playa Flamenco, a long, curving beach of talcum-white sands and turquoise waters. The mountains beyond make a striking backdrop. Dine that evening at **Susie's** in the only town, diminutive Dewey. On your last day, try snorkeling in **Refugio Nacional de Vida Silvestre de Culebra**, the island's lovely nature preserve. One of the best places for a morning boat trip is **Isla Culebrita**, an islet dominated by a deserted lighthouse.

EXPLORING

Just because Vieques is sleepy doesn't mean there's nothing to do besides hit the beach. There are two communities—Isabel Segunda and Esperanza—where you can dine at a variety of excellent restaurants, stock up on supplies, or book a trip to the astonishing Puerto Mosquito, perhaps the world's most luminous bioluminescent bay.

ISABEL SEGUNDA

18 miles (29 km) southeast of Fajardo by ferry.

Isabel Segunda (or Isabel II, as it's often labeled on maps) has charms that are not immediately apparent. There's a lovely lighthouse on the

El Faro Punta Mulas, a lighthouse built in 1895, is now a small museum exhibiting Vieques historical items.

coast just east of the ferry dock, and on the hill above town you'll find the last fort the Spanish constructed in the New World. You can also find some of the best restaurants and a great bar here, as well as lodgings ranging from funky to fancy.

WORTH NOTING

El Faro Punta Mulas. El Faro Punta Mulas, a Spanish-built lighthouse above the ferry dock in Isabel Segunda, dates from 1895. It was built to guide vessels into the harbor, which is surrounded by a chain of dangerous reefs. Its red light is rumored to be seen from as far away as St. Croix and St. Thomas. In 1992, the elegant structure was carefully restored and transformed into a maritime museum that traced much of the island's history, including the visit by South American liberation leader Simón Bolívar. The tiny museum is open weekdays, but the lighthouse itself is worth a look on any day. ⊠ *At end of Rte. 200, Isabel Segunda, Vieques* ☎ *787/741–0060* ✉ *Free* ☾ *Weekdays 8–3.*

El Fortín Conde de Mirasol (*Count of Mirasol Fort*). On a hilltop overlooking Isabel Segunda is El Fortín Conde de Mirasol, the last military structure built by the Spanish in the New World. It was erected on Vieques's northern coast in 1840 at the order of Count Mirasol, then governor of Puerto Rico. Although it's tiny, it took more than a decade to complete, which meant Mirasol had to repeatedly ask for more money. (Queen Isabel, on being petitioned yet again, asked Mirasol whether the walls were made of gold.) The fort helped solidify Spanish control of the area, keeping British, French, Dutch, and Danish colonists away and dissuading pirates from attacking Isabel Segunda. After sitting empty for several decades, it was transformed into a museum in 1991. The museum has an impressive collection of artifacts from the Taíno Indians and other cultures that thrived on this and nearby islands before the arrival of the Spanish. It also has an impressive collection of small arms, plus exhibits on the island's years as a sugar plantation and its occupation by the U.S. Navy. On occasion, it presents temporary exhibitions of contemporary artists. ⊠ *Calle El Fuerte, Isabel Segunda, Vieques* ☎ *787/741–1717* 🖼 *$2* ⏱ *Wed.–Sun. 10–4.*

ESPERANZA

6 miles (10 km) south of Isabel Segunda.

The only time there's a traffic jam in Esperanza is when one of the wild horses frequently seen on the nearby beaches wanders into the road. This community, once a down-at-the-heels fishing village, now hosts a string of bars, restaurants, and small hotels on the waterfront drag. All of them overlook Playa Esperanza, a shallow stretch of sand made all the more picturesque by the presence of a tiny islet called Cayo Afuera.

WORTH NOTING

Malecón. In the evening, there's no better way to enjoy the sunset than a stroll along Esperanza's 200-yard-long Malecón, a waterfront walkway running the length of the beach. ⊠ *Esperanza, Vieques.*

FAMILY **Vieques Conservation & Historical Trust.** The Vieques Conservation & Historical Trust was established to help save Puerto Mosquito, one of the last remaining bioluminescent bays in the world. The small museum, located on the main drag in Esperanza, has interesting information about the bay, as well as the island's flora and fauna and history. A little pool lets kids get acquainted with starfish, sea urchins, and other denizens of the not-so-deep. There's also a tiny gift shop whose profits are funneled back into the foundation. Call ahead if you're coming at lunchtime, as the place is sometimes closed for an hour or more. ⊠ *138 Calle Flamboyán, Esperanza, Vieques* ☎ *787/741–8850* ⊕ *www.vcht. org* 🖼 *Suggested donation of $3* ⏱ *Mon.–Sun. 11–4.*

ELSEWHERE ON VIEQUES

Isabel Segunda and Esperanza are just a tiny portion of Vieques. Most of the island—more than two-thirds of it, in fact—was commandeered by the military until 2003. It's now a nature preserve that draws thousands of visitors each year.

TOP ATTRACTIONS

Fodor's Choice **Puerto Mosquito Bioluminescent Bay.** East of Esperanza, Puerto Mosquito ★ Bioluminescent Bay is one of the world's best spots to have a glow-in-the-dark experience with undersea dinoflagellates. Local tour operators offer kayak trips or excursions on nonpolluting boats to see the bay's microorganisms, which light up when the water around them is agitated. Look behind your boat, and you'll see a twinkling wake. Even the fish that swim through and jump from the water will bear an eerie glow. The high concentration of dinoflagellates sets the bay apart from the other spots around the world (including others in Puerto Rico) that are home to these micro-organisms. The bay is at its best when there's little or no moonlight; rainy nights are beautiful, too, because the raindrops splashing in the water produce ricochet sparkles that shimmer like diamonds. ⊠ *Reach via unpaved roads off Rte. 997, Vieques.*

Popular with local fisherman, the gentle waters of Esperanza Beach are ideal for small boats.

Vieques National Wildlife Refuge. A portion of the west and the entire eastern end of the island is administered by the U.S. Fish & Wildlife Service as the Vieques National Wildlife Refuge, comprising 18,000 acres—about 14,900 acres on the eastern end and 3,100 acres on the west—making it the biggest protected natural reserve in Puerto Rico. The 900-acre bombing range is permanently closed off, a consequence of its contamination by the ammunition shot over its 60-year existence. But most of the rest of eastern Vieques is pristine nature, astonishingly beautiful and well-forested, with a hilly center region overlooking powder-white sandy beaches and a coral-ringed coastline; it served mainly as a buffer zone between the military maneuvers and civilian population. The vast majority of this acreage remains off-limits to visitors as authorities carry out a search for unexploded munitions and contaminants. Nonetheless, many of the beaches on the northern and southern coasts are open to the public; in 2009 a new asphalt road opened up six southern beaches. ⊠ *Rte. 200, Km .04, Vieques* ☎ *787/741–2138* ⊕ *www.fws.gov.*

BEACHES

Vieques and Culebra are where you'll find Puerto Rico's most serene shores. Ideal for romantic strolls or family swims, the calm waters and long unspoiled stretches here are what you probably had in mind when you envisioned a Caribbean beach paradise.

Many of the beaches around Vieques were once named by the U.S. Navy, which assigned them random colors: Red Beach, Blue Beach, and Green Beach. Most beaches have since been renamed in Spanish by locals. Islanders know Sun Bay as Sombé. Those within the Vieques National Wildlife Refuge are open 6 am–sunset. Of Vieques's more than three-dozen beaches, Sun Bay east of Esperanza is easily the most popular. Although both islands' beaches are favored for their comparative isolation, crowds can gather on weekends at the most popular spots such as Culebra's spectacular Playa Flamenco. On weekdays, however, it's not uncommon for large swaths of shore on either island to be sparsely populated.

Balneario Sun Bay. Just east of Esperanza, this mile-long stretch of sand skirts a perfect crescent-shaped bay. Dotted with picnic tables, this beach gets packed on holidays and weekends. On weekdays, when the crowds are thin, you might see wild horses grazing among the palm trees. Parking is $3, but often there is no one at the gate to take your money. **Amenities:** food and drink; parking (fee); showers; toilets. **Best for:** snorkeling; swimming; walking. ⊠ *Rte. 997, Esperanza, Vieques* ☎ *787/741–8198* ⊕ *www.parquesnacionalespr.com* ☜ *$3 parking* ☽ *Wed.–Sun. 8:30–5.*

Green Beach. On the western edge of the island, at the end of a long unpaved road marred by potholes, this beach faces the Vieques Passage. Miles of coral reef just offshore attract snorkelers and divers, but caution is required due to strong currents. From the shore you can catch a glimpse of El Yunque on the mainland. **Amenities:** none. **Best for:** snorkeling; solitude ⊠ *At the western end of Rte. 994, off Rte. 200, Vieques.*

La Chiva (*Blue Beach*). Some consider this the most beautiful beach on Vieques. It has a handful of covered cabañas with individual parking spots so that guests can claim their own personal stretch of sand and survey an expansive, tranquil horizon. Beware of strong surf in some spots. **Amenities:** none. **Best for:** solitude; walking. ⊠ *Off Rte. 997, 2½ miles (4 km) east of Esperanza, Vieques.*

Fodor's Choice
★
Pata Prieta. Not so secret Secret Beach, as Pata Prieta is also known, is a heavenly cove for those seeking privacy. This tiny yet beautiful horseshoe-shaped stretch of sand, reached via a brambling dirt road, is calm and secluded. You can find yourself completely alone, or one of a few couples embracing in the crystal clear water. Relish the unadulterated bliss of this perfect spot, an Eden like no other. **Amenities:** none. **Best for:** snorkeling, swimming. ⊠ *Off Rte. 997, east of Playa Caracas, Vieques.*

Playa Caracas (*Red Beach*). Also known as Red Beach, Playa Caracas is one of the first stretches of sand you reach when you head east of Esperanza on Route 997. This beach is well-maintained and boasts covered cabañas for lounging away from the sun. Less rustic than some of the nearby beaches, this spot is sheltered from waves. **Amenities:** toilets. **Best for:** snorkeling; swimming; walking. ⊠ *Off Route 997, Vieques.*

Playa Esperanza. People staying in any of the inexpensive accommodations in Esperanza can simply walk across the road to this beach. There's good snorkeling by the derelict pier and across the bay around Cayo Afuera, an uninhabited islet. Manatees are occasionally spotted here, as well as barracudas and nurse sharks. If you're looking for swimming or sunbathing, keep moving; there are much better beaches

Continued on page 178

BIOLUMINESCENT BAYS
Plankton Pyrotechnics in Puerto Rico

San Juan

Lagunas Grande

Vieques

Bahía de Fosforescente

Puerto Mosquito

Puerto Rico's bioluminescent bays are beautiful. The slightest stirring of these waters, whether from the swish of a stick or droplets of rain, produces tiny bursts of teal-blue light. The darker the night, the better the bright; a moonless sky affords the most gorgeous marine moments in these wondrous bays.

by Francesca Drago

It's estimated that there are only 12 bio bays in the world, but it's difficult to determine exactly because the phenomenon occurs sporadically in warm seas. Puerto Rico has three. **Puerto Mosquito** in Vieques is the most spectacular bay. It won a Guinness World Record for most outstanding bioluminescent bay in the world. **Lagunas Grande** in Fajardo is not as bright, but convenient to see from San Juan. **Bahía de Fosforescente** in La Parquera's deserves an honorable mention even though water pollution, primarily from gas- and diesel-powered tourist boats, has darkened its luster.

Positively glowing! Puerto Rico's bio bays will literally have you beaming with joy.

4

IN FOCUS BIOLUMINESCENT BAYS

WHAT'S IN THE WATER?

The undersea shooting stars are produced by microscopic algae called dinoflagellates, or "dinos." They convert chemical energy into light energy and emit tiny flashes when the water is disturbed. Scientists have theorized that their sudden sparks are a defense mechanism—a way to startle and disorient a predator and perhaps attract a larger predator to eat the first one.

A bio bay's brightness is a measure of its health. Dinoflagellates use the energy from sunlight to photosynthesize. Their luminescence is influenced by circadian rhythms, meaning their brightness depends on the light-dark conditions over a 24-hour period. One full day of sunshine and no clouds will result in two nights of plankton brilliance—with the second night brighter than the first. A cloudy day may still produce a bright night, but the following night won't be as spectacular. Artificial and ambient light will disrupt the fragile cycles of these "living lanterns" and erase their natural bioluminescence. Preservation of bio-bay brightness depends on public awareness about the harmful effects of light pollution and thoughtful planning for future land development.

(top) "Glow angel:" a swimmer creates water wings in Puerto Mosquito Bay (bottom) The species of dinoflagellate Pyrodinium Bahamenese, found in Puerto Mosquito, is only 1/500 of an inch

NEW MOON

Bioluminescence is best experienced on a cloudy or moonless night. The darkest nights occur during the new moon phase, when its face is in shadow. Ask your tour guide what the moon phase will be and when it will rise, because a full moon may not actually appear in the sky until after your planned excursion.

New Moon Calendar, 2015/2016

- Jan 20/Jan 10
- Feb 18/Feb 8
- Mar 20/Mar 9
- Apr 18/Apr 7
- May 18/May 6
- Jun 16/Jun 5
- Jul 16/Jul 4
- Aug 14/Aug 2
- Sep 13/Sep 1
- Oct 13/Oct 1 & 30
- Nov 11/Nov 29
- Dec 11/Dec 29

PUERTO MOSQUITO: A BAY IN BALANCE

Vieques

Puerto Mosquito
Bay

Sun Bay

Playa
Media Luna

Caribbean Sea

Dinoflagellates occur sporadically in tropical waters around the world, but the highest concentration on earth can be found in Puerto Mosquito Bay in Vieques. Billions of dinos dwell here because their habitat is balanced by a number of ecological features and protections.

"Channel surf:" A kayaker paddles the channel leading to Puerto Mosquito Bay

❶ Puerto Mosquito Bay is a **designated wildlife preserve**. This special zoning prevents rampant development, pollution, and destruction of the surrounding forest, which acts as a natural barrier against strong winds and rain.

❷ Salt-tolerant **mangrove trees** are vital for healthy coastal ecosystems. Their pronged roots stabilize the silt-rich shoreline, helping to filter sediments and reduce erosion, while leaves and bark fall into the water, where they rot and provide food and nutrients essential to the dinos' diet (e.g., vitamin B12). Moreover, the mangroves absorb carbon dioxide and store carbon in their sediments, which makes them a vital resource for reducing greenhouse gasses in the atmosphere.

❸ The long, narrow **channel leading to the ocean** acts as a buffer that minimizes how much seawater flows into the bay daily and limits the amount of dinoflagellates (and nutrients) that are swept out with the tides. This enables the dinos to concentrate in the bay's shallow refuge.

❹ The **channel exit** at the windward end of the bay allows sufficient water exchange with the sea to keep it from overheating or stagnating. The water in Puerto Mosquito remains calm and warm, creating the ideal environment for dinoflagellates to thrive in.

EXPLORING THE BAYS

Kayaks are an environmentally friendly way to explore the bays.

Seeing your oars glow as they blade through the water is a magical experience. Go with an operator that uses glow sticks to illuminate the stern of each kayak (for minimal light interference) and reviews safety practices at the start. Never book a tour with an operator who is unlicensed or uses gas- or diesel-powered boats. Ask your hotel concierge for assistance. On Vieques all hotels listed in our Where to Stay section will help arrange tours of Puerto Mosquito Bay.

RECOMMENDED OUTFITTERS

IN VIEQUES
Island Adventures runs nightly bio bay tours and an educational tour aboard an open-air electric boat. (Prone to motion sickness? Be advised that a 45-minute cruise on a catamaran and 15-minute bus ride on a rough, unpaved road is part of this trip.) **Abe's Snorkeling & Bio Bay Tours** provides sturdy kayaks and knowledgeable guides for day and night trips to Puerto Mosquito.

IN FAJARDO
The two-hour night tour at **Las Cabezas Nature Reserve** *(see Exploring, Fajardo, chapter 3)* takes you on a winding boardwalk through mangroves to the water's edge. Strike the dark lagoon with a stick and marvel at the flashing wakes, or stir the water to "draw" with light.

For more information on recommended outfitters, see Boating & Kayaking in this chapter.

KNOW BEFORE YOU GLOW

■ Paddling through the long, dark mangrove channel to reach Mosquito Bay is exciting but also challenging. Kayaking can be strenuous and requires teamwork; book with small groups, if possible, because crowds with varying experience and endurance can lead to exasperation and delay.

■ People with little or no kayak experience, or with small children, may prefer a pontoon trip that provides an easy and safe way to swim in luminescent water.

■ Puerto Mosquito is aptly named. Wear a hat, water shoes, and nylon pants as protection from bites. A lightweight, waterproof windbreaker worn over a bathing suit is ideal.

■ Jellyfish are sometimes present but cannot be seen in the dark water. Look carefully.

■ Bring towels and a change of clothes for the ride home.

In the zone: the forest of Puerto Mosquito is protected land

After the sun sets, the undersea stars shine

Destruction of mangroves, dredging, land development, and overuse of the bays' waters endanger the bio bays. Light pollution is especially harmful, since artificial and ambient light suppress the luminescence of the dinoflagellates. The Vieques Conservation and Historical Trust (VCHT) held its first symposium in the fall of 2008, convening expert scientific and technical authorities to discuss conservation of the bio bays. The goal, said Trust marine expert Mark Martin, was to "involve everybody," including government and the public, and rally commitments and resources to ensure the continuous scientific monitoring of Puerto Mosquito. The VCHT wants to name Puerto Mosquito a UNESCO World Biosphere Reserve to preserve it for future generations.

Here's what you can do to help maintain the pristine condition of this precious natural resource:

■ Book with licensed operators who use kayaks or electric boats only.

■ Swimming is banned in all the bio bays but Puerto Mosquito. Shun those operators who ignore the law.

■ Dinoflagellates absorb basic chemicals directly from the water. Bug repellents containing DEET will kill them. Rinse off any remnants of suntan lotion, perfume, and deodorant before swimming.

■ Do not throw any objects in the water or litter in any way.

■ Support the conservation efforts of the VCHT.

nearby. **Amenities:** none. **Best for:** snorkeling, walking. ⊠ *Esperanza Malecón, Esperanza, Vieques.*

FAMILY   **Playa Media Luna.** Ideal for families because the water is calm and shallow, this is also a good spot to try snorkeling. There are no facilities. **Amenities:** none. **Best for:** families, snorkeling, swimming. ⊠ *Off Rte. 997, east of Playa Sun Bay, Vieques.*

WHERE TO EAT

$ ✕ **Bananas.** This longtime, open-air favorite with playful rainforest
CARIBBEAN   murals climbing the walls in a prime spot in Esperanza that ogles the Caribbean is geared toward gringos. If you're looking for authentic island food, this isn't your place. But they certainly serve up some good Puerto Rican fare. Claim a spot at one of the curvy red concrete tables or under an umbrella-shade out front and order the red-snapper sandwich (popular at lunchtime), or the jerk chicken. Salads are excellent, including the *caribeño* (fresh greens with curried chicken), but be sure to save room for the namesake dish—deep fried bananas with finger-lickin' hot honey sauce. When the sun goes down, Bananas is one of the hot spots on this side of the island. With breakfast items and smoothies on the menu, you can spend the night at the attached no-frills guesthouse and stay through dawn. ⑤ *Average main: $12* ⊠ *142 Calle Flamboyán, Esperanza, Vieques* ☎ *787/741–8700* ⊕ *www.bananasguesthouse.com.*

$$ ✕ **Bili.** Next door to Bananas, this airy and colorful Mediterranean-
CARIBBEAN   style tapas restaurant deserves better than the overflow from its more established neighbor. It has the same view, sleeker decor, and more authentic food, prepared by Eva Bolívar, former private chef to a Puerto Rican governor. For lunch, order a tasty sandwich such as dorado wrap with caramelized onions, plantains, and roasted peppers. For something heartier, try seafood paella—the house specialty. Stop by for a beer in the evening and you won't have to shout to be heard. ⑤ *Average main: $17* ⊠ *144 Calle Flamboyán, Esperanza, Vieques* ☎ *787/741–1382.*

$$$ ✕ **Carambola.** It's hard to imagine a more romantic setting than this din-
CARIBBEAN   ing room with unbeatable views of the ocean. Through the open doors are smaller tables scattered around the open-air terrace. The service is formal, and so are the meals. The former five- or seven-course set meals have been replaced by an à la carte menu featuring such main courses as lamb chops with a rosemary passion fruit goat cheese or the yuca mofongo with seafood. In low season, dining is sometimes restricted to the less elegant terrace. ⑤ *Average main: $25* ⊠ *Inn on the Blue Horizon, Rte. 996, Km 4.2, Esperanza, Vieques* ☎ *787/741–3318* ⊕ *www. innonthebluehorizon.com.*

$$ ✕ **Chez Shack.** Owned by one of the more eccentric personalities on the
ECLECTIC   island, the original Duffy (of Duffy's in Esperanza), this restaurant is not exactly a shack—but it's close. Whether it will be open or closed on any given night during high season is anyone's guess, as Duffy himself is in his 90's. If you're lucky enough to experience the joint, it's set in a delightfully ramshackle wooden building off the beaten track on Route 995, off Route 201—a road that winds through Vieques's tropical hills. The dining room is inches from the pavement, but it's unlikely a single

car will pass by while you're enjoying your meal. Chicken, beef, and seafood such as baked crab are prepared to tender perfection, but the menu changes according to whim. It's famous for its weekly barbecue night with a steel band (schedule changes from week to week); on other nights good jazz or island rhythms usually flow from the sound system. $ *Average main: $17* ⊠ *Rte. 995, Km 1.8, Vieques* ☎ 787/435–9789 ⌲ *Reservations essential.*

$$
PUERTO RICAN
Fodor's Choice
★

✕ **Conuco.** A mix of locals and gringos frequent Conuco, soft-spoken Puerto Rico native Rebecca Betancourt's homage to local food with an upscale twist. Barnlike open windows look out onto one of Isabel Segunda's main streets, and within, the airy room is simple but cozy, enhanced by bright yellow walls, seafoam chairs, white table tops, and ceiling fans. A back patio offers alfresco dining. Start with sangria rum punch, then move on to *any* of the menu's many selections; they're all that wonderful. Piping-hot arepas are piled high with pepper and octopus salad, while small *tostones rellenos* (fried plantains) are shaped into cups filled with a citrusy ceviche. *Sorullitos* (cheesy corn fritters) and *bacalaítos* (cod fritters) are reimagined with modern flair. The only thing trumping the flavors of a juicy *churrasco* (skirt steak) and overflowing seafood *mofongo* is the wow-factor of Betancourt's presentations. Elevating cooking to art form, this local spot is one that will have you dreaming about Vieques long after you've left the island. $ *Average main: $15* ⊠ *110 Luis Muñoz Rivera, Isabel Segunda, Vieques* ☎ 787/741–2500 ⊕ *www.restauranteconuco.com* ⊘ *Closed Sun. and Mon. No lunch.*

$
CARIBBEAN

✕ **Duffy's.** At some point during your time in Vieques, you should end up at Duffy's, the island's most popular hangout. Customers crowd around the bar here, which might make you think the food is secondary, and you wouldn't be entirely wrong. You'll find standard burger and fries, but the waterfront restaurant has a chalkboard listing scrawled specials like conch fritters, scallop ceviche, grilled rib eye, and pan-seared pork loin, all a step above your usual beach fare. The rest of the menu fills out with wraps, sandwiches, and fried finger food. So why do people ignore the dozen or so tables scattered around the open-air dining room in favor of sitting elbow-to-elbow at the bar? Turns out that owner Michael Duffy, son of the owner of Chez Shack, is a real character. Locals love chewing the fat with him, and you will, too. $ *Average main: $12* ⊠ *140 Calle Flamboyán, Esperanza, Vieques* ☎ 787/741–7600.

$$$
ECLECTIC
Fodor's Choice
★

✕ **El Quenepo.** Elegant yet unpretentious, El Quenepo brings fine dining and a touch of class to the Esperanza waterfront. Six stable doors on an inviting powder blue building open to expose ocean views. The menu, which changes yearly, features local herbs and fruits such as *quenepas* and breadfruit in the artfully prepared dishes that owners Scott and Kate Cole call "fun, funky island food." Scott is the chef, known for his seafood specials highlighting the daily catch; Kate is the consummate hostess. Start with the popular grilled Caesar salad followed by sensational *mofongo* stuffed with shrimp and lobster in sweet-and-spicy *criollo* sauce. Oenophiles will appreciate the large wine list, and the sangria is delicious. Lucky walk-ins can grab a seat at the more casual

CLOSE UP

Vieques Libre

For nearly six decades the U.S. Navy had a stranglehold on Vieques. It controlled the island's eastern half and western end and exerted enormous influence over the destiny of the civilian area in between. Though long protested, the bombing, shelling, and amphibious landings continued. When an off-target bomb killed a civilian on Navy land in April 1999, opposition began to transform the island's placid beaches into political hotbeds.

Protesters camping out on the bombing range kept it shut down from 1999 to 2000. Hundreds of Puerto Rican residents were arrested for trespassing on Navy land during war games. They were joined by celebrity protesters from the United States, including environmental lawyer Robert F. Kennedy Jr. (who gave his baby daughter the middle name Vieques), the wife of Reverend Jesse Jackson, and Reverend Al Sharpton, all of whom were arrested for trespassing on the bombing range. For much of 2000 and 2001 protests were so commonplace that there were semipermanent encampments of opponents. Songs such as "Paz Pa' Vieques" ("Peace for Vieques") began to surface, as did bumper stickers and T-shirts with protest slogans. Latin pop celebrities such as singer-songwriter Robie Draco Rosa (who wrote Ricky Martin's "Livin' la Vida Loca"), actor Edward James Olmos, singer Millie Correjter, protest singer

Zoraida Santiago, and other actors, painters, doctors, and lawyers added to the fanfare when they joined the activities.

President Bill Clinton finally agreed that residents could vote on whether to continue to host the Navy. A non-binding referendum held in 2001 found that 68% of the island's voters wanted the military to leave immediately. Although some members of Congress argued that the Navy should stay indefinitely—their cries grew louder after September 11, 2001, when even local protesters called for a moratorium on civil disobedience—the administration agreed to withdraw the troops. As a result of the protests, the Navy finally withdrew from its Atlantic Fleet training grounds in May 2002. In 2003 the naval base was officially closed. By the end of 2005 much of the former military base was transformed into the Vieques National Wildlife Refuge. Today there are concerns that the sustained bombing activity produced high levels of contamination that are linked to health issues such as higher cancer rates among residents. This is widely regarded as a long-term exposure issue that doesn't affect vacationers, but visitors who may be concerned about potential risks associated with travel to the area should check the Centers for Disease Control website (⊕ www.cdc.gov) for the latest information.

---

high bar tables, but for the true experience of this gem, make a reservation. [$] *Average main: $25* ⊠ *148 Calle Flamboyán, Esperanza, Vieques* ☎ *787/741–1215* ⌦ *Reservations essential* ⊘ *No lunch. Closed Mon.*

$ ✕ **El Resuelve.** When you hanker for hearty platters of real local fare with

PUERTO RICAN   real island-born locals, this is the place to be. Bustling at lunch and by night, this open-air *colmado* (grocery-restaurant) presses up against the main Isabel II–Esperanza road. It's barely more than a shack with a counter and shaded aluminum and plastic seating out back. Service is laid-back to the max, but it's worth the wait for *albondigas* (meatballs), crab empanadas, chicken with rice and beans, barbecue ribs, and—for the daring—boiled pigs' ears. Locals sometimes kick up their heels out back, where there's a pool table and slot machine. ⑤ *Average main: $7* ✉ *Route 997, Km 1, Isabel Segunda, Vieques* ☎ *787/741–1427* ▬ *No credit cards* ☽ *Closed Mon. and Tues.*

$$$
ECLECTIC
✕ **Next Course.** Warm colors like red, yellow, and orange fill the consistently packed dining rooms at Next Course. Billed as "cuisine inspired by travel," the space is laced with ethnic nuances like beaded Indian pillows and gold-leaf Buddhas. The menu is an amalgam of flavors from balsamic drizzled mozzarella to sesame-crusted yellowfin tuna with seaweed salad to baby back ribs. This seemingly incongruous assortment comes together beautifully in well-executed dishes by chef Buddy Stone, an Arizona-by-way-of St. John-transplant who spent two years creating the specials in the kitchen at beloved Duffy's. His fans followed him to Next Course, and judging by the vibe of this buzzing spot, it looks like he's in Vieques to stay. ⑤ *Average main: $25* ✉ *Route 201, Vieques* ☎ *787/741–1028* ⚓ *Reservations essential.*

WHERE TO STAY

PRIVATE VILLA RENTALS

One good way to visit Vieques is to rent one of the beautiful vacation homes that have been built in the hilly interior or along the coasts. These are concentrated in three major areas: Bravos de Boston, Esperanza, and Pilón. Several local real-estate agents deal in short-term rentals of at least a week. A popular rental is Bravos House, which has weekly summer rates as low as $900 and in-season rates of $1,500 per week (⊕ *www.viequeshouse.net*).

Rainbow Realty. A list of rental properties is available from this gay-friendly company. ✉ *278 Calle Flamboyán, Esperanza, Vieques* ☎ *787/741–4312* ⊕ *www.viequesrainbowrealty.com.*

$
HOTEL
⌕ **Bravo Beach Hotel.** Several blocks north of the ferry dock in Isabel Segunda, this completely renovated boutique hotel feels more suited to swank South Beach than laid-back Vieques. **Pros:** gorgeous building; beautiful pools; friendly management. **Cons:** out of the way location in residential neighborhood; can't swim on property's beach. ⑤ *Rooms from: $135* ✉ *1 North Shore Rd., Isabel Segunda, Vieques* ☎ *787/741–1128* ⊕ *www.bravobeachhotel.com* ⇌ *7 rooms, 2 suites, 1 villa* ⏍ *Breakfast.*

$
B&B/INN
⌕ **Casa de Amistad.** If you're looking for a budget-friendly property in the city center, this groovy little guesthouse not far from the ferry dock in Isabel Segunda is the place to be. **Pros:** gay-friendly; funky furnishings. **Cons:** drive to beaches; cheaper rooms lack en-suite bathrooms; no elevator. ⑤ *Rooms from: $80* ✉ *27 Calle Benito Castaño, Isabel Segunda, Vieques* ☎ *787/741–3758* ⊕ *www.casadeamistad.com* ⇌ *9 rooms* ⏍ *No meals.*

$$ 🏨 **Hacienda Tamarindo.** The 250 year-old tamarind tree rising more
HOTEL   than three stories through the center of the main building gives this
plantation-style house and former dance hall its name. **Pros:** beautiful
views; nicely designed rooms; excellent breakfasts. **Cons:** you have to
drive to beaches; small parking lot; no full-service restaurant; no eleva-
tor. ⑤ *Rooms from: $155* ⊠ *Rte. 997, Km 4.5, Esperanza, Vieques*
☎ *787/741–8525* ⊕ *www.haciendatamarindo.com* ↰ *16 rooms, 1 pent-
house suite* ❍| *Breakfast.*

$ 🏨 **Hector's By the Sea.** Reached by a steep and denuded dirt road, this tiny
HOTEL   property perches on a bluff overlooking a lovely beach. **Pros:** hot tub
under the stars; truly marvelous ocean vistas. **Cons:** no credit cards; iso-
lated location; meager facilities; maid service every 3–4 days. ⑤ *Rooms
from: $150* ⊠ *Rte. 996, Km 4.3, Esperanza, Vieques* ☎ *787/741–1178*
⊕ *www.hectorsbythesea.com* ↰ *3 studio-style rooms* ▭ *No credit cards*
❍| *No meals.*

$$ 🏨 **Hix Island House.** Constructed entirely of concrete and set in the mid-
HOTEL   dle of Vieques's tropical forest surroundings, Hix House echoes the
gray granite boulders strewn around Vieques, and the four buildings
do manage to blend seamlessly with the environment. **Pros:** acclaimed
architecture; secluded setting; friendly staff. **Cons:** the lack of windows
means bugs (especially pesky mosquitoes) get in; damp linens and clothing after tropical showers; no elevator. ⑤ *Rooms from: $175* ⊠ *Rte.
995, Km 1.5, Vieques* ☎ *787/741–2302* ⊕ *www.hixislandhouse.com*
↰ *19 rooms* ❍| *Breakfast.*

$ 🏨 **La Finca Caribe.** An edgy, off-beat inn run along the lines of a Berke-
B&B/INN   ley, California commune, this eco-friendly hillside getaway seemingly
miles from anywhere has an irresistible rustic appeal. **Pros:** communal
hibachi; social informality; nature-focused. **Cons:** far from island services; no air-conditioning, no Wi-Fi. ⑤ *Rooms from: $85* ⊠ *Rte. 995,
Km 1.2, Vieques* ☎ *787/741–0495* ⊕ *www.lafinca.com* ↰ *6 rooms, 2
cabins, 2 houses* ❍| *No meals.*

$$ 🏨 **Malecón House.** Posh boutique spots like this seaside escape in Espe-
B&B/INN   ranza are raising the bar on lodging in Vieques. **Pros:** affordable rates
for a waterfront property; tasty breakfasts; welcoming hosts. **Cons:** in-
town location isn't for those seeking seclusion. ⑤ *Rooms from: $175*
⊠ *105 Calle Flamboyán, Esperanza, Vieques* ☎ *787/741–0663* ⊕ *www.
maleconhouse.com* ↰ *13 rooms* ❍| *Breakfast.*

$ 🏨 **Seagate Hotel.** Energetic and effusive owner-manager Penny Miller
HOTEL   lavishes attention on guests at her spic-and-span hilltop hotel that over-
looks the island's picturesque, historic fort. **Pros:** friendly and helpful
owner-manager; handy for exploring town. **Cons:** small rooms; animal
presence; no restaurant. ⑤ *Rooms from: $95* ⊠ *Barrio Fuerte, Isabel
Segunda, Vieques* ☎ *787/741–4661* ⊕ *www.seagatehotel.com* ↰ *15
rooms* ❍| *Breakfast.*

$ 🏨 **Trade Winds.** The best of a string of inexpensive guesthouses along
B&B/INN   the main road in Esperanza, this place has an unbeatable location
across from the Malecón, or waterfront promenade. **Pros:** good
value; many nearby dining options. **Cons:** right on the noisy street;
no elevator. ⑤ *Rooms from: $80* ⊠ *107 Calle Flamboyán, Esperanza,*

Vieques ☎ *787/741–8666* ⊕ *www.tradewindsvieques.com* ⤵ *11 rooms* ⦿*Breakfast.*

$$$$
RESORT
Fodor'sChoice
★

🏨 **W Retreat & Spa.** Hovering over two gorgeous beaches, the über-hip W Retreat & Spa is the island's hot spot for urbane fashionistas, yet remarkably, it manages to simultaneously be family-friendly. **Pros:** sensational decor; full-service spa; free transfers to/from airport. **Cons:** high prices even in low season; $60 daily resort fee. ⑤ *Rooms from: $919* ✉ *Rte. 200, Km 3.2, Isabel Segunda, Vieques* ☎ *787/741–4100* ⊕ *www.wvieques.com* ⤵ *156 rooms, 20 suites* ⦿*No meals.*

NIGHTLIFE

Al's Mar Azul. Not far from the ferry terminal, Al's Mar Azul is the place to be come sunset. An open-air deck overlooks the ocean, and nautical decor lines the walls of this popular, spirited bar. Enjoy a game of darts or pool, lip-sync to a song off the jukebox or, on karaoke nights, whip the crowd into a frenzy with your best rendition of popular hits. ✉ *Calle Plinio Peterson, Isabel Segunda, Vieques* ☎ *787/741–3400.*

Bananas. Bananas is the place for burgers and beer—not necessarily in that order. There's occasional live music and dancing, and on Mondays, $1.50 bottles of Medalla, the local brew. ✉ *142 Calle Flamboyán, Esperanza, Vieques* ☎ *787/741–8700* ⊕ *www.bananasguesthouse.com.*

Duffy's. Hands-down, Duffy's is the most popular bar on the island, thanks to the jawboning of owner Michael Duffy, live music, daily specials, and a prime location on Esperanza's Malecón. ✉ *140 Calle Flamboyán, Esperanza, Vieques* ☎ *787/741–7600* ⊕ *www.duffysesperanza.com.*

La Nasa. La Nasa is the only establishment on the waterfront side of the street in Esperanza. This simple wooden shack, decorated with strings of Christmas lights the entire year, serves up cheap beer and rum drinks and draws island-born *Viequenses*, rather than expats. Locals congregate on plastic chairs out front to play cards or stare off into the placid Caribbean from an open-air back room. On weekends, the place explodes into a street party of salsa and merengue dancing. ✉ *Calle Flamboyán, Esperanza, Vieques.*

SHOPPING

Most residents do their shopping on the mainland, so there are very few shops on Vieques. You'll find mostly clothing stores that lean toward beach attire, as well as a few art galleries.

Funky Beehive. Boutiques selling trendy resort wear for men and women have been popping up in Vieques, and one of the best is Funky Beehive, an eclectic shop full of dresses, tunics, local jewelry, hats, beach bags, home accessories, and soaps. Prices range from $10–$100. ✉ *359 Antonio Mellado, Suite 2, Esperanza, Vieques* ☎ *787/741–3192* ⊙ *10–5 Mon.–Sat.*

Kim's Cabin. In business on Vieques since the late 80s, Kim's Cabin, named for the jovial owner's one-time lover, is a local institution. Sparse rooms painted powder blue showcase jewelry and island attire such as cotton sarongs, straw bags, and hats for women. Tunics and button-down short-sleeved shirts for men line the back room. ⊠ *136 Calle Flamboyán, Esperanza, Vieques* ☎ *787/741–3145* ⊕ *www. islavieques.com/kimscabin.html.*

Siddhia Hutchinson Fine Art Studio & Gallery. Since the late 80s this gallery has showcased pastel watercolor prints of Caribbean scenes, as well as limited-edition ceramic dinnerware. The gallery is a hip, sophisticated place for Caribbean artists to see and be seen, hosting openings of local artists, and it features a number of island artworks. ⊠ *Hotel Carmen, Calle Munoz Rivera, Isabel Segunda, Vieques* ☎ *787/741–1343* ⊕ *www. siddhiahutchinsongallery.com* ⊙ *Mon.–Sat. 10–4.*

Fodor's Choice
★

Sol Creation. The carefully cultivated collection at Sol Creation could easily be found in New York's Soho or L.A.'s Melrose Avenue. The boudoir setting of the pretty boutique opens onto three side rooms—treasure chests of playful, bohemian island duds made from crushed linen, silk, fine cotton, and gauze. Haphazardly strewn chunky leather belts and long, romantic necklaces add character to the neatly hanging garments, and owner Sol Beckedorff, a wonder at styling, is as lovely as her shop. The men's collection is equally lush. Prices range from $35–$250. Note that the owner also has a small, lovely shop with the same type of goods inside the lobby of the W Hotel. ⊠ *370 Calle Antonio Mellado, Esperanza, Vieques* ☎ *808/280–6223* ⊕ *www.solcreationboutique.com.*

SPORTS AND THE OUTDOORS

BIKING

Vieques Adventure Company. Garry Lowe at Vieques Adventure Company can set you up with mountain bikes and all the equipment you need starting at $25. They'll even bring the bikes to wherever you are staying. Customized tours of the island—which range from easy rides on country roads to muddy treks into the hills—are $150 for a half-day tour. ⊠ *Calle Robles, Esperanza, Vieques* ☎ *787/692–9162* ⊕ *www. viequesadventures.com.*

BOATING AND KAYAKING

Various outfitters offer trips to Puerto Mosquito, the island's celebrated bioluminescent bay. Most are trips in single-person kayaks, which can be a challenge if you lack experience or endurance. A better option for most people is a boat—an electric-powered model is best, as the gas-powered ones harm the environment.

Abe's Snorkeling and Bio-Bay Tours. Local boy Abe is one of Vieques's most animated characters, so it's no surprise that his kayaking tours to Puerto Mosquito are the most popular. Over the course of two hours, for $45 per person, guests kayak into the glowing bay for a once-in-a-lifetime experience. For an entire day on the water, Abe's All-in-One Tour involves kayaking through mangrove lagoons, snorkeling coral reefs, watching the sunset on a secluded beach, and visiting the bio-bay after dark. Lunch is provided; the tour costs $150 per person. ⊠ *Esperanza, Vieques* ☎ *787/741–2134* ⊕ *www.abessnorkeling.com.*

Island Adventures. If you don't want to ply the waters with a paddle, Island Adventures offers nightly excursions through the glowing

Vieques has a number of bays and protected coves that provide calm surf perfect for beginners.

waters of Puerto Mosquito aboard an electrically powered double-pontoon boat for $45 per person. ⊠ *Vieques* ☎ *787/741–0720* ⊕ *www. biobay.com.*

Marauder Sailing Charters. Marauder Sailing Charters operates the *Marauder*, a 34-foot sailing yacht anchored off Esperanza that can accommodate up to six passengers. It sails around the southern coast, allowing a close-up look at the pristine nature of the island. There's a midday stop at a secluded spot for swimming, snorkeling, and sunbathing, followed by a gourmet lunch with open bar. Half-day and full-day trips, sunset cruises, brunch cruises, and custom and private charters are available. All charters depart from Esperanza. ⊠ *Esperanza, Vieques* ☎ *787/435–4858* ⊕ *www.maraudersailingcharters.com.*

DIVING AND SNORKELING

Black Beard Sports. If you want to get your own snorkeling or diving equipment, head to this water-sports shop in downtown Isabel Segunda. The team arranges diving trips and PADI certification courses, as well as kayaking, biking, snorkeling, and hiking ecotours. A second location of Black Beard Sports can be found at the W Retreat & Spa. ⊠ *101 Calle Muñoz Rivera, Isabel Segunda, Vieques* ☎ *787/741–1892* ⊕ *www. blackbeardsports.com.*

FISHING

Vieques Adventure Company. Vieques Adventure Company will take you on kayak fly-fishing trips for bonefish and tarpon. "It's extreme fishing," says owner and trip leader Garry Lowe. "When you're in a kayak and have a 50-pound tarpon on the line, you're going to go for a ride!" Rates are from $350 per two people. ⊠ *Vieques* ☎ *787/692–9162* ⊕ *www.viequesadventures.com.*

Vieques Sport Fishing. Captain J. Ferguson has been a charter fisherman since 1989, and off Vieques's coast he navigates a 26-foot boat into waters laden with tuna, mahimahi, dorado, kingfish, and marlin. Four-hour deep-sea trips begin at $350. ⊠ *103 Calle Hucar, Vieques* ☎ *787/450–3744, 787/502–3839* ⊕ *www.viequessportfishing.com.*

CULEBRA

17 miles (28 km) east of Fajardo by ferry.

Culebra is known around the world for its curvaceous coastline. Playa Flamenco, the tiny island's most famous stretch of sand, is considered one of the top 10 best beaches in the world. If Playa Flamenco gets too crowded, as it often does around Easter or Christmas, many other neighboring beaches will be nearly deserted. And if you crave complete privacy, hire a motorboat to take you to one of the nearby islets such as Isla Culebrita or Cayo Luis Peña. It won't be difficult to find a little cove that you will have all to yourself.

Archaeological evidence shows that Taíno and Carib peoples lived on Culebra long before the arrival of the Spanish in the late 15th century. The Spanish didn't bother laying claim to it until 1886; its dearth of freshwater made it an unattractive location for a settlement. The U.S. Navy and Marine Corps, however, thought it was a very valuable piece of real estate. Although President Theodore Roosevelt created a wildlife refuge in 1909, the military used this island, as well as nearby Vieques, for target practice and amphibious assault training beginning in WWII. Despite their smaller numbers, the residents of Culebra managed to oust the military after staging sit-ins on the beach. The military left Culebra in 1975.

GETTING HERE AND AROUND

Aeropuerto Benjamin Rivera Noriega (CPX). Culebra's one-room facility has car and scooter rental counters. The airport is about three minutes from downtown Dewey. Route 250 leads east and south of the airport. Route 251 leads northeast to Playa Flamenco. ⊠ *Intersection of Rtes. 250 and 251, Culebra* ☎ *787/742–0022.*

Car Rental Carlos Jeep Rental. Renting a car or scooter is imperative to get around Culebra. Carlos is a good place to choose a Jeep, car, or golf cart. Daily rates from $40 (four-passenger golf cart)–$75. ⊠ *Aeropuerto Benjamin Rivera Noriega, Culebra* ☎ *787/742–3514* ⊕ *www.carlosjeeprental.com.*

Taxi Willy's Taxi. Willy's Taxi is a full-service operator offering taxi service, Jeep rental, and water taxi trips to Isla Culebrita. ⊠ *Culebra* ☎ *787/742–3537.*

EXPLORING

Almost everything about Culebra is diminutive. The island's only community, named in honor of U.S. Admiral George Dewey (island-born locals hate the association and prefer to call the town simply "el

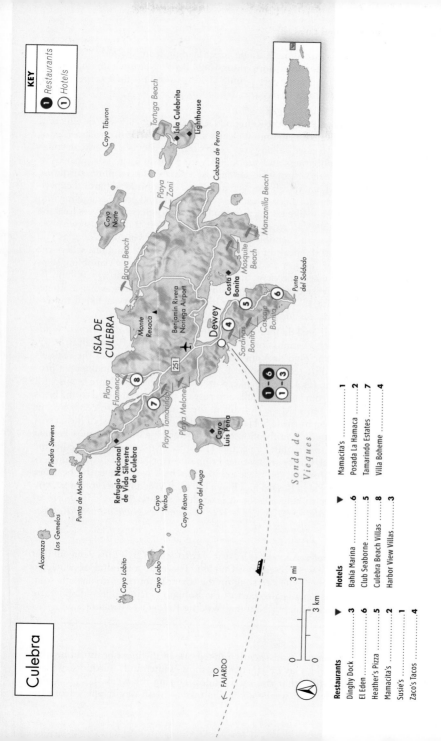

Culebra

Los Gemelos
Alcarraza

Cayo Lobito
Cayo Lobo

Piedra Stevens

Punta de Molinos

Cayo Yerba
Cayo Ratón

Cayo del Auga

Cayo Tiburón

Cayo Norte

Tortuga Beach

Isla Culebrita
Lighthouse

Playa Zoni

Cabeza de Perro

ISLA DE
CULEBRA

Brava Beach

Monte
Resaca

Playa
Flamenco

Benjamin Rivera
Noriega Airport

**Refugio Nacional
de Vida Silvestre
de Culebra**

7

8

251

Playa Tamarindo

Playa Melones

**Cayo
Luis Peña**

Manzanilla Beach

Mosquite
Beach

**Costa
Bonita**

4

5

6

Punta
del Soldado

Dewey

Sardinas
Bonita

Casa de
Bonita

1–6
1–3

Sonda de
Vieques

TO
FAJARDO

0   3 mi

0   3 km

pueblo"), is set along a single street leading from the ferry dock. You can explore the few shops along Calle Pedro Márquez in a half hour. The one-room airport is ½ mile (1 km) to the north. Except for one resort, few hotels have more than a dozen rooms.

TOP ATTRACTIONS

Fodor's Choice
★
Isla Culebrita. Part of the Refugio Nacional de Vida Silvestre de Culebra, uninhabited Isla Culebrita is clearly visible from the northeast corner of Culebra. An essential day-trip excursion, this islet is a favorite destination for sunbathers and snorkelers who want to escape the crowds at Playa Flamenco. Isolation set against a palate of crystalline, turquoise waters and dewy, lush greens makes for a one-of-a-kind natural experience. On the northern shore there are several tidal pools; snuggling into one of them is like taking a warm bath. Snorkelers and divers love the fact that they can reach the reef from the shore and carouse with sea turtles, rays, and schools of colorful fish. Bring your sneakers, as you can hike to the peak of the island in about 20–30 minutes, where the spectacular ruins of an old lighthouse await. Climb 54 crumbling steps to the top where the views of the surrounding Caribbean are sublime. Be warned; the structure is tumbledown so enter at your own risk. To get to Culebrita, take a dive boat or hire a water taxi service like Gammy's Water Tour. ⊠ *Culebra.*

Refugio Nacional de Vida Silvestre de Culebra (*Culebra National Wildlife Refuge*). Commissioned by President Theodore Roosevelt in 1909, Refugio Nacional de Vida Silvestre de Culebra is one of the nation's oldest wildlife refuges. Some 1,500 acres of the island make up a protected area. It's a lure for hikers and bird-watchers: Culebra teems with seabirds, from laughing gulls and roseate terns to red-billed tropic birds and sooty terns. Maps of trails in the refuge are hard to come by, but you can stop by the U.S. Fish & Wildlife Service office east of the airport to find out about trail conditions and determine whether you're headed to an area that requires a permit. The office also can tell you whether the leatherback turtles are nesting. From mid-April to mid-July, volunteers help monitor and tag these creatures, which nest on nearby beaches, especially Playa Resaca and Playa Brava. If you'd like to volunteer, you must agree to help out for at least three nights. ⊠ *Rte. 250, north of Dewey, Culebra* ☎ *787/742–0115* ⊕ *www.fws.gov/caribbean/Refuges* ⊠ *Free* ☉ *Daily dawn–dusk.*

WORTH NOTING

Cayo Luis Peña. A kayak is a great way to reach Cayo Luis Peña, an islet just off the western edge of Culebra. There are a handful of protected beaches where you can soak up the sun and not run into a single soul. Cayo Luis Peña is also part of the Refugio Nacional de Vida Silvestre de Culebra (Culebra National Wildlife Refuge). ⊠ *Culebra.*

BEACHES

FAMILY
Fodor's Choice
★
Playa Flamenco. Consistently ranked one of the most beautiful beaches in the world, Playa Flamenco has snow-white sands, turquoise waters, and lush hills that rise on all sides. During the week, it's pleasantly uncrowded; on weekends it fills up fast with day-trippers from the

mainland. With kiosks selling simple dishes and vendors for lounge-chair and umbrella rentals, it's easy to make a day of it. Don't miss the tanks on the northern end of the beach—a reminder that this area was once a military base. **Amenities:** food and drink; parking (free); showers; toilets. **Best for:** swimming; walking. ⊠ *Rte. 251, west of the airport, Culebra* ☎ *787/742–0700* ☼ *Daily dawn–dusk.*

Playa Melones. Just west of Dewey, this is a favorite spot for snorkelers. The reef that runs around the rocky point is easy to reach from shore. Locals swear this is the best place to watch sunsets. To get here, head uphill on the unmarked road behind the church. **Amenities:** none. **Best for:** snorkeling, swimming, sunset. ⊠ *Camino Vecinal, west of Dewey, Dewey, Culebra.*

Playa Zoni. On the island's northeastern end, this beach is long and narrow—perfect for afternoon strolls. From the shore you can catch a glimpse of Isla Culebrita, not to mention St. Thomas and St. Croix. Leatherback turtles nest here. **Amenities:** none. **Best for:** swimming, walking. ⊠ *At the end of Rte. 250, 7 miles (11 km) northeast of Dewey, Culebra.*

WHERE TO EAT

$$
SEAFOOD
✗ **Dinghy Dock.** Culebra's version of heavy traffic—the arrival and departure of the water taxi—takes place around the dock that gives this restaurant its name. The menu leans toward grilled meats, from hamburgers and wraps to sirloin steaks. Daily specials often highlight the restaurant's forte: creole-style seafood, including swordfish and yellowtail, as well as lobster. The adjacent open-air bar is usually packed with expats, and a cast of local characters. It can get noisy, and the service is anything but doting, so don't expect a quiet dinner for two. ⑤ *Average main: $18* ⊠ *Calle Fulladoza, Dewey, Culebra* ☎ *787/742–0233.*

$$$
ECLECTIC
✗ **El Eden.** Deli and grocery by day, full-service restaurant by night, the funky El Eden is a little bit of everything when it comes to eating and drinking on Culebra. Set inside a can't-miss trailer trimmed with year-round Christmas lights, what started out as a deli serving sandwiches on fresh baked bread morphed into a liquor store, and now churns out soups, local catch, *churrasco* (skirt steak) platters, pastas, and a signature saffron lobster risotto. Mismatched outdoor furniture, a nautical-themed bar, and friendly owners Richard and Luz only add to the warm feel of the place. Whether you're looking for quality ingredients for a dinner recipe, a bottle of wine, takeout for the beach, or a sit-down meal, El Eden is your spot. ⑤ *Average main: $23* ⊠ *836 Sardinas, Culebra* ☎ *787/742–0509* ⊕ *www.eledenculebra.com.*

$$
PIZZA
✗ **Heather's Pizza.** Pizza on the tiny Puerto Rican island of Culebra, you ask? Yep, and pretty good pizza at that. This cute little spot on Dewey's main drag has become something of hot spot since new owner Willie Vasquez came on the scene last year. Playful blue walls and orange tables front a full bar that stays open until the wee hours, while the oven bakes irresistible pizzas and pastas that keep diners coming back for more. The Pizza Boricua, topped with mozzarella, ground beef, sweet plantains, and cilantro, is a local favorite, and the spaghetti with meat

sauce, at $9, is a heaping plate of undeniable goodness. Chalkboard specials are featured daily and takeout is available. $⑤ Average main: $15 ✉ Calle Pedro Marquez 14, Dewey, Culebra ☎ 787/742–3175.

$
CARIBBEAN
✕ **Mamacita's.** Pull your dinghy up to the dock and watch the resident iguanas plod past at this simple open-air, tin-roofed restaurant on a rough-plank deck beside the Dewey Canal. Tarpon cruise past in the jade waters below, and the to and fro of boaters also keeps patrons amused. Doubling as Culebra's favorite local watering hole and gringo hangout, palm tree trunks litter the space, which is painted in a rainbow of pink, purple, and green. With a nightly changing menu, Mamacita's down-home dishes play a part in the appeal. The menu is heavy on burgers and sandwiches, but seafood dishes include an excellent mahimahi. $⑤ Average main: $12 ✉ 66 Calle Castelar, Dewey, Culebra ☎ 787/742–0322 ⊕ www.mamacitasguesthouse.com.

$$$
ECLECTIC
✕ **Susie's.** Susie's is truly the island's only upscale restaurant, yet it's casual and unpretentious. *Sanjuanera* owner-chef Susie Hebert learned her culinary skills at San Juan's swank Caribe Hilton and Ritz-Carlton hotels before settling on Culebra and opening her fine-dining restaurant, a soothing Zen space filled with banquettes, pillows, and couches. A lively bar opens onto patio dining off the canal. The Caesar salad here excels; follow with sautéed jumbo shrimp in ginger-lime and coconut vinaigrette, Szechuan-style sesame-crusted tuna, or mahimahi with beurre blanc and scallion-ginger sauce. Feeling carnivorous? The filet mignon with a simple truffle au jus is divine. $⑤ Average main: $21 ✉ Rte. 250, Dewey, Culebra ☎ 787/340–7058 ⊕ www.susiesculebra. com ⌖ Reservations essential ⊘ Closed Thurs.

$
MEXICAN
Fodor's Choice
★
✕ **Zaco's Tacos.** After spending years in the kitchen of the popular hangout Mamacita's, chef Zach Sizer decided to open his own joint, a no-frills taco spot delivering fresh, flavorful, affordable grub. Good thing he did; Zaco's Tacos is a runaway success. Arched ceilings are painted in bright primary colors, lending a warm, festive feel to the cozy space. An outdoor wood terrace in the back offers open-air dining and Sunday brunch, though most just prefer to order some delicious beer-battered fish, *carnitas* (pork), or seared tuna tacos at the bar. For the adventurous, pork belly, cow, and tongue tacos are on the menu, as well as heartier burritos. Refresh with a light hibiscus tea, or a more obvious indulgence—one of the many tequila-saturated margaritas. $⑤ Average main: $7 ✉ 21 Calle Pedro Marquez, Dewey, Culebra ☎ 787/742–0243 ⊕ www.zacostacos.com ⊘ Closed Thurs.

WHERE TO STAY

VILLA RENTALS

Lovely vacation homes are scattered around Culebra.

Culebra Island Realty. Culebra Island Realty has a few dozen vacation properties for rent, ranging from studios to three-bedroom houses. ✉ Calle Escudero, Dewey, Culebra ☎ 787/435–6752 ⊕ www. culebraislandrealty.com.

$
HOTEL
▦ **Bahía Marina.** If you're looking for space to spread out or bring the family, these one- and two-bedroom villas with sweeping views of the

nearby nature reserve or ocean are made for you. **Pros:** beautiful setting; good restaurant. **Cons:** feels like an apartment complex; outside town; no elevator. ⑤ *Rooms from: $139* ✉ *Calle Fulladoza, Km 1.5, Culebra* ☏ *787/742–0535* ⊕ *www.bahiamarina.net* 📞 *18 villas.*

$$
HOTEL
Fodor's Choice
★

🏠 **Club Seaborne.** The most sophisticated place to set down roots in Culebra, this cluster of slate-blue plantation-style cottages paints a pretty picture on a hilltop overlooking Fulladoza Bay. **Pros:** lovely cottages; lush gardens; rates include airport or ferry transfers. **Cons:** some steps to negotiate; no elevator; spotty Internet and cell phone reception. ⑤ *Rooms from: $249* ✉ *Rte. 252, northwest of town, Culebra* ☏ *787/742–3169* ⊕ *www.clubseabourne.com* 📞 *3 rooms, 8 villas, 1 cottage* ⑪ *Breakfast.*

$
RENTAL
FAMILY

🏠 **Culebra Beach Villas.** This is the only lodging on Playa Flamenco, or any beach in Culebra for that matter, and for that reason alone this place is worth your consideration. **Pros:** on the best beach in Puerto Rico; secluded. **Cons:** can get noisy with families; inconsistency in units; management not always available. ⑤ *Rooms from: $125* ✉ *Playa Flamenco, off Rte. 251, Playa Flamingo, Culebra* ☏ *787/409–2599* ⊕ *www.culebrabeach.com* 📞 *18 cabins* ⑪ *No meals.*

$
RENTAL

🏠 **Harbor View Villas.** Straddling a ridge that guarantees the breezes, this simple property is also a sure bet for winning views south over the harbor and north over the isle. **Pros:** spellbinding views; great restaurant. **Cons:** Robinson Crusoe–basic accommodations; a steep uphill climb from the entrance gate; unkempt grounds littered with junk. ⑤ *Rooms from: $125* ✉ *Off Calle Vecinal, Dewey, Culebra* ☏ *787/742–3855* ⊕ *www.culebrahotel.com* 📞 *2 villas, 2 suites* ⑪ *No meals.*

$
HOTEL

🏠 **Mamacita's.** The best rooms in Mamacita's venerable guesthouse have balconies overlooking the canal, but this is a decidedly no-frills establishment befitting budget-minded travelers. **Pros:** friendly staff; pickup point for water taxis. **Cons:** basic rooms; no elevator; on a narrow street. ⑤ *Rooms from: $89* ✉ *66 Calle Castelar, Dewey, Culebra* ☏ *787/742–0090* ⊕ *www.mamacitasguesthouse.com* 📞 *10 rooms, 1 suite* ⑪ *No meals.*

$
HOTEL

🏠 **Posada La Hamaca.** This small bright orange building, which shares Mamacita's mangrove-lined canal, has spic-and-span guest rooms—as simple as they come—with louvered windows and calming color schemes. **Pros:** walk to shops and restaurants; laid-back atmosphere; cheap rates. **Cons:** some rooms are small; constant clunking noises from adjacent bridge; no elevator; no parking. ⑤ *Rooms from: $90* ✉ *68 Calle Castelar, Dewey, Culebra* ☏ *787/742–3516* ⊕ *www.posada.com* 📞 *12 rooms* ⑪ *No meals.*

$$
RENTAL

🏠 **Tamarindo Estates.** On a 60-acre estate hidden away on the western coast of Culebra, this string of one- and two-bedroom beach-apartment cottages is on a long, sandy beach. **Pros:** peaceful location; pretty pool area. **Cons:** short walk to the beach; isolated far from dining options; no housekeeping service. ⑤ *Rooms from: $166* ✉ *Off Rte. 251, Culebra* ☏ *787/742–3343* ⊕ *www.tamarindoestates.com* 📞 *12 cottages* ⑪ *No meals.*

$$
B&B/INN

🏠 **Villa Boheme.** Colorful and breeze-swept, this Spanish-style guesthouse, painted baby blue and white, is centrally located next to popular

Surfer crossing is often the extent of traffic flow in the town of Dewey, Culebra.

Dinghy Dock. **Pros:** expansive view of the bay; walk to restaurants and shops. **Cons:** basic furnishings; no elevator; few on-site amenities. ⑤ *Rooms from: $115* ✉ *368 Calle Fulladoza, Dewey, Culebra* ☎ *787/742–3508* ⊕ *www.villaboheme.com* ⮌ *11 rooms* ⦿ *No meals.*

NIGHTLIFE

Blue Bar at The Spot. Blue walls evoke the feeling of the surrounding ocean at this former lunch spot turned late-night hangout and coffee bar. Favorite local bartender Gretchen Costa tends to cocktails here, serving specialty shots with unique Caribbean flair. The must-order drink is the "Drunken Seagull," a refreshing libation that certainly can sneak up on you after a couple of rounds. Shrug off the hangover with a shot of cappuccino or espresso. ✉ *14 Calle Pedro Marquez, Dewey, Culebra* ☎ *787/742–0203.*

Dinghy Dock. Dinghy Dock is the spot where the island's expat community begins piling into the bar around sunset. It can be a raucous scene, especially when there's a band. The party continues into the wee hours, even during the week. ✉ *Calle Fulladoza, Dewey, Culebra* ☎ *787/742–0233.*

El Batey. For a good local scene, head to El Batey, housed in a cement-block building halfway between the airport and the town of Dewey. Popular on the weekends, when locals dance to salsa music, El Batey serves great burgers to help you absorb the booze. ✉ *Calle Escudero, Dewey, Culebra* ☎ *787/742–3828.*

Mamacita's. The island's favorite gringo watering hole is always jumping, with a weekday happy hour from 4 to 6 pm and Saturday night's live music jam, featuring local conga band, Wiki Sound Machine. Don't miss the bar's signature drink, the frozen Bushwhacker—a delicious but deadly mix of rum, vodka, Bailey's, amaretto, Kahlua, and coconut. ⊠ *66 Calle Castelar, Culebra* ☎ *787/742–0090* ⊕ *www. mamacitasguesthouse.com.*

SHOPPING

Culebra is smaller than Vieques but has much better shopping. Dewey has several shops on its main drag that sell trendy jewelry, clothing, and a range of souvenirs from tacky to terrific.

Fango. Fango is the island's best place for gifts. Local artist Jorge Acevedo paints scenes of island life and Culebra's natural tableau of mangroves and seascapes. You could easily spend an hour browsing his one-of-a-kind works and original T-shirts, and if you happen to be around on a Saturday, follow him to Tinguito Restaurant, where he plays conga music. ⊠ *Altos del Restaurante Tinguito, Dewey, Culebra* ☎ *787/435–6654* ⊕ *www.artefango.com.*

Island Boutique. Island Boutique sells local apparel like sarongs, handmade jewelry, and original souvenirs such as windchimes. ⊠ *4 Calle Pedro Marquez, across the ferry depot, Dewey, Culebra* ☎ *787/742–0439.*

La Cava. La Cava stocks a little bit of everything. Forgot your snorkel? Left your bathing suit at home? Need a new pair of flip-flops, or a souvenir for your favorite cousin? La Cava is the perfect place to meet all those needs. ⊠ *138 Calle Escudero, Dewey, Culebra* ☎ *787/742–0566.*

SPORTS AND THE OUTDOORS

BIKING

Culebra Bike Shop. Because there's very little traffic, biking is a good way to explore the island. You can rent bikes for $15 a day at Culebra Bike Shop. The shop is next door to the Dinghy Dock and also rents kayaks and snorkel gear. ⊠ *Hotel Kokomo, Calle Pedro Marquez, Dewey, Culebra* ☎ *787/742–0589* ⊕ *culebrabikeshop.com.*

BOATING AND KAYAKING

Culebra Eco Tours. A fast-paced alternative to kayaking, Culebra's only Jet Ski outfitter offers a different way to cruise the island's crystal clear waters. Rates start at $160 per person. Pick-up at your hotel can be arranged. ⊠ *Culebra* ☎ *787/902–7928* ⊕ *www.culebraecotours.net.*

Gammy's Water Tours. One of the few licensed captains on the island, Culebra native Gammy Rohlsen is the man to hire for simple water-taxi service or for more comprehensive fishing or snorkeling adventures to Cayo Luis Peña or Isla Culebrita, St. Thomas, and Vieques. ⊠ *Calle 1, Culebra* ☎ *787/423–2469.*

Pez Vela Charters. Operating out of Bahia Marina, sail trips on Captain Bill Penfield's 33-foot catamaran are a true island experience. Most popular is the Picnic Sail, which includes a bit of everything Culebra is known for—a visit to nearby Culebrita and Cayo Norte, snorkeling, swimming—plus a hot lunch. Prices start at $125 per person and include all gear. Custom charters and private excursions can also be arranged. ✉ *Bahia Marina, Fulladoza Bay, Culebra* ☎ *787/215–3809* ⊕ *www.culebracatamaran.com.*

DIVING AND SNORKELING

Aquatic Adventures. Captain Taz Hamrick takes guests out on snorkeling and PADI-certified scuba trips, as well as charters to the surrounding keys. You can also book a sunset cruise on their 26-foot boat, the *Raz-Ma-Taz.* ✉ *372 Sector Fulladoza, Dewey, Culebra* ☎ *787/209–3494, 515/290–2310* ⊕ *www.diveculebra.com.*

Culebra Divers. Run by Monika and Walter Rieder, Culebra Divers is the island's premiere dive shop, catering to those new to scuba as well as those adept at underwater navigation. Travel to more than 50 local sites on one of the company's 25-foot cabin cruisers and hope to spot wildlife like spotted eagle rays, octopus, moray eels, and turtles. Spring for an underwater scooter, which propels you through the sea like James Bond. You can also rent a mask and snorkel to explore on your own. ✉ *4 Calle Pedro Marquez, Dewey, Culebra* ☎ *787/742–0803* ⊕ *www.culebradivers.com.*

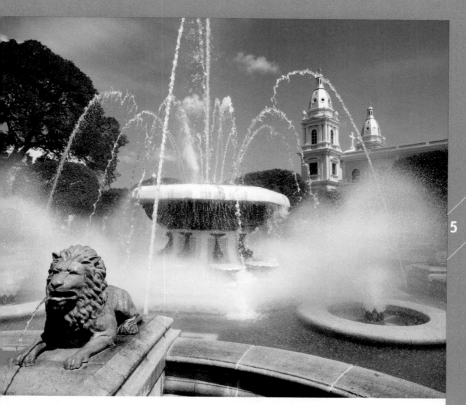

PONCE AND THE PORTA CARIBE

WELCOME TO PONCE AND THE PORTA CARIBE

MUSEO DE ARTE DE PONCE

TOP REASONS TO GO

★ **Parque de Bombas:** Marvel at a century-old firehouse whose red-and-black color scheme has inspired thousands of photographers.

★ **Bosque Estatal de Guánica:** Hike where the cactus may make you think you're in the American Southwest.

★ **Hacienda Buena Vista:** Sample a cup of the local brew at the historic, beautifully restored coffee plantation outside Ponce.

★ **San Germán:** Stroll cobblestone streets lined with architectural treasures; then dine on fine Puerto Rican cuisine high above the main plaza.

★ **Casa Cautiño:** Step back in time to a colonial-era residence in the community of Guayama.

0 — 10 mi
0 — 10 km

1 Ponce. Reminiscent of Old San Juan before cruise ships arrived, Ponce has a yesteryear charm and increasingly cosmopolitan vibe that delight many visitors. Take a trolley tour of the colonial past, explore some of the best museums on the island, and at night join residents for local ice cream at King's Cream on the beautiful Plaza de las Delicias.

2 The Southeastern Coast. Underexplored and untrammeled, the southeast is one of the least-visited parts of the island. Start with a seaside meal in Salinas, where the famous *mojo isleño* sauce was created; then hop into the hills to relax in the baños de Coamo, a thermal spring used for hundreds of years.

Villalba 143 155
139 149
Coto Laurel
Hacienda Juana Díaz
Buena Vista
Ponce 1
Potala
Pastillo 52
Santa
Isabel Pta.
Petrona
Caja de
Muertos

Coamo 14
Bañnos
de Coamo
Salinas 1
Bahía de
Rincón Coquí

Aibonito 52 181 Humacao
Cayey 53
184 182 3
SIERRA DE CAYEY
15 181
Patillas Yabucoa
Guayama Maunabo Pta.
Arroyo 3 Yeguas

C a r i b b e a n   S e a

5

GETTING ORIENTED

3 **The Southwestern Coast.** Discover the island's first and most inexpensive bioluminescent bay in La Parguera; the university town of San Germán, whose churches and colonial mansions date back as far as five centuries; and the fascinating dry forest at Guánica.

Ponce is the region's dynamic center, with a surrounding metropolitan area that includes a slew of vibrant attractions and sophisticated restaurants and hotels rivaled only by San Juan's. To the southeast the shoreline is rugged and the villages more rural and isolated. Small seaside inns and some of the island's best seafood can be found here. Slightly inland from the coast are the colonial town of Coamo and its thermal baths. In the southwest, dense dry forest, such as the Bosque Estatal de Guánica, and mangroves hide undiscovered bays, inlets, and quaint fishing villages. Here you will also find the beautiful historic city of San Germán, one of Puerto Rico's oldest settlements.

THE MASKS OF PUERTO RICO

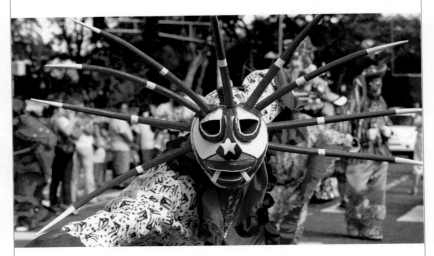

Puerto Rico's masks are one of the premier expressions of folk art on the island, a tradition that dates back to Spain in the early 17th century.

During the Fiestas de Santiago Apóstol (Saint James Festivals), brightly dressed *vejigantes* (pronounced veh-hee-GAN-tays) represented the Devil in a holy battle between good and evil. Their costumes consisted of long robes and grotesque masks, and they would wave cow bladders, or *vejigas*, on long sticks at anyone they passed. Parading as devils, their intention was to frighten sinners to compel them to return to church for Lent. Today balloons and plastic bottles have replaced the cow bladders, and the now more playful masks have become one of Puerto Rico's most distinguished forms of artistic expression. A week before Ash Wednesday *vejigantes* wearing long, colorful robes and brightly painted horned masks, turn the normally placid city of Ponce into a hotbed of rowdiness. The masked mischiefmakers prowl city streets, scaring and fascinating anyone in their path.

(above) Red, white, and boo! During festivals, vejigante masks frighten and delight spectators along parade routes.

ISLAND ART

The best hand-designed masks in Puerto Rico come from three parts of the island: Ponce, Loíza, and Hatillo. Mask making is a family tradition in these towns, and styles are passed down for generations. For a fine souvenir and a memorable experience, head to one of the local artisans' workshops. Small masks cost $20 or $30; larger ones by well-known makers may cost more than $1,000.

PONCE

Ponce's vejigante masks are made of papier-mâché and are most prominent during the February Carnaval. Many have African and Native American elements; it's even possible to detect influences from ancient Greece and Rome. All masks have at least two horns, but most have several protruding from the forehead, chin, and nose. Some antique masks have more than 100 horns. At the beginning of the 20th century, masks were usually painted red with yellow dots or vice versa, but today they come in every imaginable color and pattern.

Where to Go: One of the best-known mask-making families is the Caraballo family from Playa de Ponce near El Ancla restaurant *(see review in Where to Eat)*. To purchase a mask, show up at the door to their home, and if someone is there you'll be allowed to browse their workshop. You're most likely to have success in February leading up to Ponce's Carnaval. ✉ *24 San Tomas, Playa de Ponce* ☎ *No phone.*

LOÍZA

Founded by freed and escaped African slaves, Loíza is known as the island's Capital of Traditions for its bomba and plena music and dance, and traditional Taíno and African cuisine. Loíza's masks are created from coconut husks, and the individual shape of each determines the face and placement of the nose and lips.

The teeth are made of bamboo and the tongue is made of coconut shell.

Where to Go: For generations the Ayala family, whose workshop sits just east of town, has been the most renowned of Loíza's mask makers. Their masks appear during the Saint James Festival of Loíza each July. ✉ *Artesanias y Folclorica de la Familia Ayala, Barrio Mediana Alta, Rte. 187, Km 6.6* ☎ *787/886–1654.*

HATILLO

Hatillo was founded in 1823 by settlers from the Canary Islands. These *isleños,* in honor of King Herod's soldiers, the first Christian martyrs or Holy Innocents, would dress head to toe in costumes with a cape, hat, and mask made of fine metallic screening meant to resemble the face of a Spaniard. Today the masked performers run through surrounding neighborhoods, joined by children, singing and dancing. The annual mask festival, Día de las Máscaras, is held every December 28.

Where to Go: ✉ *Puerto Rico Flea Market, Rte. 2, Km 86, Bo. Carrizales* ☎ *No phone.*

5

Updated by
Julie Schwietert
Collazo

Not as popular as San Juan or Vieques, the south is a region full of underrated attractions, fine food, and a laid-back, authentic vibe that is hard to come by elsewhere. From lush tropical mountains to arid seacoast plains, Puerto Rico's southern region lets you sample the island from a local's perspective.

Though rich in history, the area also provides ample opportunities for golf, swimming, hiking, and cave exploration. Snaking roads between major highways reveal a glimpse of how rural Puerto Ricans enjoy life. Every mile or so you'll see a café or bar, which is the local social center. The only traffic jams you'll likely encounter will be caused by slow-moving farmers taking their goods to the local market.

At the center of everything is Ponce, the "Pearl of the South." Farmers attracted to the rich soil in the area, which was perfect for growing sugarcane, founded Ponce in 1692. Evidence found at the Tibes Indian ceremonial site, just north of the city, suggests that people have been living here since 400 BC. Many residents still carry the last names of the dozens of European pioneer families who settled here during the 19th century. The region's largest city, Ponce is home to some of the island's most interesting architecture, excellent restaurants, and one of its most important art museums. Nearby San Germán, the second-oldest city in Puerto Rico, is known for its two historic main squares, well preserved in a wide variety of architectural styles.

On the coast, Guayama and Patillas show off their splendors as little-known destinations for beachgoers. But the real party is at La Parguera, which attracts a young but noisy crowd. If you're willing to explore beyond the casinos, high-rises, and daily traffic congestion of the island's capital, the south is a wise escape from Puerto Rico's usual tourist fare. Don't be surprised by the help many of its residents will offer whether you ask for it or not. Southern *puertorriqueños* are known for their friendliness as well as their hospitality.

PONCE PLANNER

WHEN TO GO

The towns of Patillas, Guánica, and La Parguera are popular with Puerto Ricans during Easter and Christmas and during summer, when children are out of school, and Ponce's spirited pre-Lenten carnival, held the week before Ash Wednesday, draws many visitors. For the rest of the year, much of the south is quiet and receives only a fraction of the number of visitors as other parts of the island, though the weather is equally superb and most facilities remain open. It's not unusual for hotels to close for two weeks to a month during October and November, when tourism slows down. Hotels tend to lower rates from May through November, so check ahead for deals. Some *paradores*—small, government-sponsored inns—and hotels require a minimum two- or three-night stay on weekends.

GETTING HERE AND AROUND

AIR TRAVEL

The only international flights are on JetBlue, which flies from several U.S. cities.

Transfers: Taxis at the airport use meters; expect to pay about $6 to get to downtown Ponce. Some hotels have shuttles to and from the airport, but you must make arrangements in advance.

Airlines JetBlue ☎ *800/538–2583* ⊕ *www.jetblue.com.*

Airport Contacts Aeropuerto Mercedita ✉ *Rte. 506, off Rte. 52, Ponce* ☎ *787/842–6292.*

BUS TRAVEL

There's no easy network of buses linking the towns in southern Puerto Rico with San Juan or with each other. Some municipalities and private companies operate buses or *públicos* (usually large vans) that make many stops. Call ahead; although reservations aren't usually required, you'll need to check on schedules, which change frequently. The cost of a público from Ponce to San Juan is about $15–$20; agree on a price beforehand.

Bus Contacts Choferes Unidos de Ponce ✉ *Terminal de Carros Públicos, Calle Vives and Calle Méndez Vigo, Ponce Centro, Ponce* ☎ *787/764–0540.*

CAR TRAVEL

Getting around southern Puerto Rico without a car can be quite frustrating. You can rent cars at the Luis Muñoz Marín International Airport and other San Juan locations. There are also car-rental agencies in some of the larger cities along the south coast. Rates run about $35–$65 a day. A road map is essential in southern Puerto Rico. So is patience: allow extra time for twisting mountain roads and wrong turns. Many roads, especially in rural areas, aren't plainly marked.

TAXI TRAVEL

In Ponce you can hail taxis in tourist areas and outside hotels. In smaller towns it's best to call a taxi. You can also hire a car service (make arrangements through your hotel); often you can negotiate a lower rate than with a taxi.

ABOUT THE RESTAURANTS

Not all the culinary hot spots are in San Juan. In fact, people from the capital drive to Ponce or Guánica to see what's new on the horizon. Some of the more ambitious restaurants in this part of Puerto Rico are experimenting with Asian and Latin fusion cuisines, which means you might find pork with tamarind glaze or guava sauce, or snapper in a plantain crust. But what you'll mostly find is open-air eateries serving simple, filling fare. The southern coast is known for seafood, particularly Salinas and Ponce, both of which have a string of popular seaside restaurants. A 15%–20% tip is customary; most restaurants won't include it in the bill, but it's wise to check.

ABOUT THE HOTELS

Modest, family-oriented establishments near beaches or in small towns and the occasional restored colonial hacienda or mansion are the most typical accommodations. Southern Puerto Rico doesn't have the abundance of luxury hotels and resorts found to the north and east; however, Hilton Ponce Golf & Casino Resort and Copamarina Beach Resort are self-contained complexes with a dizzying array of services.

HOTEL AND RESTAURANT PRICES

Prices in our restaurant reviews are the average cost of a main course at dinner or, if dinner is not served, at lunch; taxes and service charges are generally included. Prices in the hotel reviews are the lowest cost of a standard double room in high season, excluding taxes, service charges, and meal plans (except at all-inclusives). Prices for rentals are the lowest per-night cost for a one-bedroom unit in high season.

For expanded lodging reviews and current deals, visit Fodors.com.

WHAT IT COSTS				
	$	$$	$$$	$$$$
Restaurants	$8–$12	$13–$20	$21–$30	over $30
Hotels	$80–$150	$151–$250	$251–$350	over $350

SAFETY

For the most part, the south is safe. You won't encounter big-city crime, but you should take a few simple precautions. Don't wear flashy jewelry outside tourist areas. Keep an eye on your belongings at the beach, and don't leave valuables locked in your car for all to see. Avoid out-of-the-way beach areas after dark.

TOUR OPTIONS

Alelí Tours and Encantos Ecotours in La Parguera offer ecological tours of the southwestern area, including two- or three-hour kayak trips that cost about $40. Aventuras Tierra Adentro and VIP Tours in Ponce offer city tours, horseback riding, and island-hopping adventures.

Contacts Alelí Tours ✉ *Rte. 304, Km 3.2, La Parguera* ☎ *787/390–6086* ⊕ *www.alelitours.com.* **Aventuras Puerto Rico** ☎ *787/380–8481* ⊕ *www.*

IF YOU LIKE

DIVING AND SNORKELING

Southern Puerto Rico is a divers' destination, which means unspoiled reefs and lots of fish. You can arrange for dive boats at Ponce's La Guancha, at Paradise Scuba in La Parguera, and at Copamarina Beach Resort in Guánica. Shore diving and snorkeling are best around islands or cays or along the southwestern coast.

HIKING

Vegetation in the region is dramatically different from that of the rest of the island. Near Guánica is the 9,900-acre Bosque Estatal de Guánica, a rare dry tropical forest. With more than 100 species of birds, it's known for its excellent bird-watching. There are good trails throughout the area, but printed guides and trail maps are hard to come by. Ask locals for directions to their favorite paths.

5

aventuraspuertorico.com. **Encantos Ecotours Southwest** ☎ 787/272–0005 ⊕ *www.ecotourspr.com.* **VIP Tours** ☎ 787/536-4683 ⊕ *www.viptourspr.com.*

VISITOR INFORMATION

In Ponce the municipal tourist office is open weekdays from 8 to 4:30, as is the small information desk in the Parque de Bombas. Smaller cities generally have a tourism office in the city hall, open weekdays from 8 to noon and 1 to 4.

Contacts Ponce Municipal Tourist Office ✉ *2nd fl. of Citibank, Plaza de las Delicias, Ponce Centro, Ponce* ☎ *787/841-8044* ⊕ *www.visitponce.com.* **Puerto Rico Tourism Company** ✉ *122 Calle Villa, Suite B, Ponce* ☎ *787/290-2911* ⊕ *www.seepuertorico.com.*

PONCE

21 miles (34 km) southwest of Coamo.

"Ponce is Ponce and the rest is parking" is the adage used by residents of Puerto Rico's second-largest city (population 166,000) to express their pride in being *ponceños*. The rivalry with the island's capital began in the 19th century, when European immigrants from England, France, and Spain settled here. Because the city's limits extend from the Caribbean to the foothills of the Cordillera Central, it's a lot hotter in climate than San Juan. Another contrast is the neoclassical architecture of the elegant homes and public buildings that surround the main square.

Many of the 19th-century buildings in Ponce Centro, the downtown area, have been renovated, and the Museo de Arte de Ponce—endowed by its late native son and former governor Luis A. Ferré—is considered one of the Caribbean's finest art museums. Just as famous is Ponce's pre-Lenten carnival. The colorful costumes and *vejigante* (mischief-maker) masks worn during the festivities are famous throughout the world *(see special feature in this chapter)*. The best dining in Ponce is just west of town. Seafood restaurants line the highway in an area known as Las Cucharas, named for the spoon-shaped bay you'll over-look as you dine.

GETTING HERE AND AROUND

The fastest route through the region is the Luis A. Ferré Expressway (Route 52), a toll road that runs from San Juan to Ponce, crossing the island's central mountain range. The trip from Condado or Old San Juan takes about two hours. Route 2, also a toll road, connects to San Germán, Mayagüez, and the western part of the island.

Ponce offers a free tour to its major attractions on its "chu chu" train and trolleys. They run daily from 9 to about 5, and leave from Plaza de las Delicias. Ask for the current schedule at the Parque de Bombas. On Sunday Guayama has a free trolley that runs to many sights. A trolley tour of San Germán is available by appointment. On weekends there are free horse-and-carriage rides around the plaza, or you could just walk. All downtown sights are within a few blocks of the main square.

Car rental is typical for most visitors to Ponce and makes exploring the surrounding region considerably easier. Most hotels have parking lots, while metered parking is easy to come by in the center.

Car Rental Avis ⊠ *Aeropuerto Mercedita, Rte. 506, off Rte. 52* ☎ *787/842–6154* ⊕ *www.avis.com.* **Budget** ⊠ *Aeropuerto Mercedita, Rte. 506, off Rte. 52* ☎ *787/848–0907* ⊕ *www.budget.com.* **Dollar** ⊠ *Calle Marginal Solar 4, Km 263.2* ☎ *787/843–6940* ⊕ *www.dollar.com.* **Enterprise** ⊠ *1023 Ave. La Ceiba, Ponce Centro* ☎ *787/812–3722.*

Taxi and Trolley Borinquen Taxi ☎ *787/843–6000.* **Ponce Trolley and Chu Chu Tren** ⊠ *Plaza de las Delicias, Ponce Centro* ☎ *787/284–3338.*

EXPLORING

Plaza de las Delicias (Plaza of Delights), with its trees, benches, and famous lion fountain, is a perfect people-watching square in which to spend an hour or two, especially on a Sunday afternoon. The old red-and-black firehouse is right on the plaza and has a fire-fighting museum on its second floor. Ponce is known for its museums, and has several dedicated to music, art, history, sports, and architecture. Ponceños are proud of their city, nicknamed the "Pearl of the South," and offer all visitors a warm welcome.

PONCE CENTRO

At the heart of Ponce Centro is Plaza de las Delicias, with trees, benches, and the famous lion fountain. Several interesting buildings are on this square and adjacent streets, making the area perfect for a leisurely morning or afternoon stroll.

TOP ATTRACTIONS

Museo de la Historia de Ponce. Housed in two adjoining neoclassical mansions, this museum includes 10 rooms with exhibits covering the city's residents, from Taíno Indians to Spanish settlers to the mix of the present. Hour-long guided tours in English and Spanish give an overview of the city's history. The descriptions are mostly in Spanish, but displays

Ponce Centro

of clothing from different eras are interesting to see. ✉ *53 Calle Isabel, at Calle Mayor* ☎ *787/844–7071* ☏ *Free* ☉ *Tues.–Sun. 8–4.*

FAMILY
Fodor's Choice
★
Parque de Bombas. After El Morro in Old San Juan, this distinctive red-and-black-striped building may be the second-most-photographed structure in Puerto Rico. Built in 1882 as a pavilion for an agricultural and industrial fair, it was converted the following year into a fire-house. Today it's a museum tracing the history—and glorious feats—of Ponce's fire brigade. Kids love the antique fire truck on the lower level. Short tours in English and Spanish are given on the half hour, and you can sign up for free trolley tours of the historic downtown here. Helpful tourism officials staff a small information desk inside the door. ✉ *Plaza de las Delicias* ☎ *787/284–3338* ⊕ *www.visitponce. com* ☏ *Free* ☉ *Daily 9–5.*

WORTH NOTING

Casa Armstrong-Poventud. Banker and industrialist Carlos Armstrong and his wife, Eulalia Pou, lived in this neoclassical house designed and built for them in 1901 by Manuel V. Domenech. The building recently underwent a top-to-bottom renovation, and now you can admire the ornate facade, which is chock-full of columns, statues, and intricate moldings. Original furnishings belonging to the family are on display.

GREAT ITINERARIES

IF YOU HAVE 1 DAY
Many residents of San Juan think nothing of a day trip to **Ponce**. If you head south on Route 52, you'll be there in less than two hours. There's plenty to do here, including a tour of the recently renovated Museo de Arte de Ponce. The best way to spend an hour or two is to stroll around the lovely Plaza de las Delicias. Make sure to dine in one of the area's outstanding restaurants.

IF YOU HAVE 3 DAYS
From San Juan, head south on Route 52 until you reach **Ponce**, the "Pearl of the South." Spend the afternoon strolling around the Plaza de las Delicias, poking into the beautiful Catedral de Nuestra Señora de Guadalupe and the striking Parque de Bombas. On the following day, visit some of the other attractions in and around the city, perhaps the Museo de Arte de Ponce, the Castillo Serrallés, or Hacienda Buena Vista.

Dedicate your final day to **Guánica**, where you'll find wonderful beaches and deserted cays; spend the night here before heading back to San Juan. If you are in the mood for hiking, there's the Bosque Estatal de Guánica.

IF YOU HAVE 5 DAYS
Make a leisurely trip south from San Juan on Route 52, spending a night in **Coamo**. These hot springs were thought by some to be Ponce de León's Fountain of Youth. Continue on your second day to **Ponce** for two days of exploring. Travel west along the coast and settle at a waterfront hotel in **Guánica**. In the evening you can take a boat trip to the bioluminescent bay in **La Parguera**. On your last day, explore the beautifully preserved colonial city of **San Germán**, making sure to see the lovely colonial-era chapel known as the Capilla de Porta Coeli.

⊠ *Calle Unión, across from Catedral de Nuestra Señora de Guadalupe* ☎ *787/290–1530* 📼 *Free* ⊘ *Wed.–Sun. 8–4:30.*

Catedral de Nuestra Señora de Guadalupe. This pale blue cathedral has always been one of the city's jewels, but it regained much of its luster after a complete renovation in 2007. Dedicated to the Virgin of Guadalupe, it is built on the site of a 1670 chapel destroyed by earthquakes. Part of the current structure, where Mass is still held, dates from 1835. After another earthquake in 1918, new steeples and a roof were put on and neoclassical embellishments were added to the facade. Inside, you'll see stained-glass windows and two alabaster altars. ⊠ *Plaza de las Delicias* ☎ *787/842–0134.*

Museo de la Música Puertorriqueña. At this museum you'll learn how Puerto Rican music has been influenced by African, Spanish, and Native American cultures. On display are dozens of instruments, such as the *tres* (a small string instrument resembling a banjo), as well as memorabilia of local composers and musicians. The small museum takes up several rooms in a neoclassical former residence, which alone is worth the trip. ⊠ *Calle Isabel and Calle Salud* ☎ *787/848–7016* 📼 *Free* ⊘ *Wed.–Sun. 8:30–4:30.*

Today it's a museum, but for more than 100 years Parque de Bombas served as Ponce's main firehouse.

NEED A BREAK?

King's Cream Helados. An institution for more than 40 years, King's Cream Helados, across from Plaza de las Delicias, is *the* place for ice cream in Ponce. It serves 12 varieties, from tamarind, peanut, and passion fruit to classics like chocolate and vanilla. A bench in the tiny storefront seats three, but most folks take their cups and cones across the street and stake out shady benches around the fountain. King's is open daily from 9 am to midnight. ✉ *9223 Calle Marina* 🕾 *787/843–8520.*

Teatro La Perla. This theater was restored in 1941 after an earthquake and fire damaged the original 1864 structure. The striking interior contains seats for 1,047 and has excellent acoustics. It's generally open for a quick peek on weekdays. ✉ *Calle Mayor and Calle Cristina* 🕾 *787/843–4322* 🎟 *Free* ⊙ *Weekdays 8–4:30.*

GREATER PONCE

The greater Ponce area has some of Puerto Rico's most notable cultural attractions, including one of the island's finest art museums and its most important archaeological site.

TOP ATTRACTIONS

Castillo Serrallés. This lovely Spanish-style villa—such a massive house that people in the town below referred to it as a castle—was built in the 1930s for Ponce's wealthiest family, the makers of Don Q rum. Guided tours give you a glimpse into the lifestyle of a sugar baron. The dining room is a highlight, with its original hand-carved furnishings. A permanent exhibit explains the area's sugarcane and rum industries. The extensive garden, with sculptured bushes and a shimmering reflection pool, is considered the best kept on the island. The large

A GOOD WALK: PONCE CENTRO

Start on the tree-lined Plaza de las Delicias. (You'll find parking nearby on Calle Marina, Calle Isabel, and Calle Reina.) Dominating it is the **Catedral Nuestra Señora de Guadalupe**, dating from 1835. Across the street is **Casa Armstrong-Poventud**, home of the Institute of Culture's Ponce branch. Leaving Armstrong-Poventud, cross back to the plaza, circle south by the Alcaldía, and continue to the plaza's east side to visit the red-and-black-striped fire station, **Parque de Bombas.**

From the intersection of Calles Marina and Cristina, take Calle Cristina a block east to one of the city's first restoration projects, **Teatro La Perla**, at the corner of Cristina and Mayor. One block north of the theater, at Calles Mayor and Isabel, is a former home that's now the **Museo de la Historia de Ponce**. A block east, at the corner of Calles Salud and Isabel, is the **Museo de la Música Puertorriqueña**. Four blocks west (you will go by Plaza de las Delicias again, and Calle Isabel will turn into Calle Reina) is the 1911 architectural masterpiece **Casa Wiechers-Villaronga.** For more early-20th-century architecture, continue west on Calle Reina, where you'll see examples of *casas criollas,* wooden homes with spacious front balconies that were popular in the Caribbean during the early 1900s.

TIMING

Although it's possible to see Ponce Centro in one morning or afternoon, it's best to devote a full day and evening. Explore the streets and museums during daylight, and then head for the plaza at night, when the lion fountain and street lamps are illuminated and townspeople stroll the plaza. With police officers on nearly every corner, this area is very safe to explore. ■TIP→ Several of the city's most popular museums—Casa Wiechers-Villaronga and the Museo de la Música Puertorriqueña—are not air-conditioned, so they close early when the weather is hot. If you want to see these sites, make sure to arrive before 11 am.

cross looming over the house is an observatory you can visit; from the top, you can see all the way to the Caribbean Sea. ⊠ *17 El Vigía, El Vigía* ☎ *787/259–1774* ⊕ *www.castilloserralles.org* 🎟 *$12.80, includes admission to Cruceta El Vigía, Japanese Garden, and Butterfly Garden* ⊗ *Thurs.–Sun. 9:30–5:30.*

FAMILY
Fodor's Choice
★

Hacienda Buena Vista. Built by Salvador de Vives in 1838, Buena Vista was one of the area's largest coffee plantations. It's a technological marvel—water from the nearby Río Canas was funneled into narrow brick channels that could be diverted to perform any number of tasks, including turning the waterwheel. (Seeing the two-story wheel slowly begin to turn is fascinating, especially for kids.) Nearby is the two-story manor house, filled with furniture that gives a sense of what it was like to live on a coffee plantation nearly 150 years ago. Make sure to take a look in the kitchen, dominated by a massive hearth. In 1987 the plantation was restored by the Puerto Rican Conservation Trust, which leads four tours a day (at least one in English). The tours are by reservation only, so make sure to call several days ahead. After seeing the plantation,

Greater Ponce

505
504
503
132
10
10
9
139
14
9
501
14

Río Portugués
Calle 7
Avenida Betances
Río Bucaná

see Ponce Centro detail map

Charles M. Terry Park
◆ Teatro La Perla
Plaza las Delicias

3 **4**
5
6
1

C. Victoria
Avenida Simón
132
10
2
163
585
10
2

Río Pastillo
Río Cañas
Mantaner Athletic Field
500

Avenida Las Américas
14 **14** **133** **578** **1**
1

Ponce By-Pass
2
Autopista Luis Ferré
Ave. Matecón
Río Portugués
52
10
C. Virtud
Ave. Hostos
C. Comercio
Avenida Matecón
Río Bucaná
Autopista Luis Ferré
Río Matilde

TO
↙ EL TUQUE

Caribbean Sea

Punta Peñoncillo
La Guancha **2**

0   1/2 mile
0   3/4 km

A GOOD TOUR: GREATER PONCE

The **Museo de Arte de Ponce** is on Avenida Las Américas, south of Plaza de las Delicias and not far from the Luis A. Ferré Expressway (Route 52). Anyone with a taste for art can happily while away many hours in its galleries. East of the museum you can pick up Route 14 south to the Caribbean and **La Guancha**, a boardwalk with food kiosks, a playground, and a child-friendly public beach. It's a good place to relax and let the younger generation work off energy. From here, if you retrace your path north past downtown you'll be heading to Calle Bertoly and El Vigía (Vigía Hill), where the **Cruceta El Vigía** towers over the city and the **Castillo Serrallés**, a former sugar baron's villa, is a popular attraction.

Farther north on Route 503 is the **Centro Ceremonial Indígena de Tibes,** which displays native artifacts dating back more than 1,500 years. You'll have to backtrack to reach Route 10, then head north to **Hacienda Buena Vista,** a former coffee plantation that's been restored by the Puerto Rican Conservation Trust. (Call ahead to arrange a tour. Reservations are required.)

You can drive to all these sights or hop on the free trolleys or "chu chu" trains that run from Plaza de las Delicias to the museum, La Guancha, and El Vigía. You'll need a car or a cab to reach the Centro Ceremonial Indígena de Tibes or Hacienda Buena Vista.

you can buy coffee beans and other souvenirs at the gift shop. Allow yourself an hour to travel the winding road from Ponce. ✉ *Rte. 123, Km 16.8, Sector Corral Viejo* ☎ *787/722–5882 weekdays, 787/284–7020 weekends* ⊕ *www.paralanaturaleza.org* 🖃 *$10* ⊙ *Wed.–Sun., tours at 8:30, 10:30, 1:30 and 3:30.*

FAMILY **La Guancha Promenade.** Encircling the cove of a working harbor, the seaside boardwalk features a small lookout tower and kiosks where vendors sell local food and drink. The adjacent park has a large children's area filled with playground equipment and, on weekends, live music. The nearby public beach has restrooms, changing areas, a medical post, and plenty of free parking. On Sunday night, this place gets packed with locals strolling the boardwalk. ✉ *End of Rte. 14, La Guancha* ☎ *787/844–3995.*

Fodor'sChoice **Museo de Arte de Ponce.** Designed by Edward Durrell Stone, who also
★ designed the original Museum of Modern Art in New York City and the Kennedy Center in Washington, D.C., Ponce's Art Museum is easily identified by the hexagonal galleries on the second story. The museum has one of the best art collections in Latin America, which is why residents of San Juan frequently make the trip down to Ponce. The 4,500-piece collection includes works by famous Puerto Rican artists such as Francisco Oller, represented by a lovely landscape called *Hacienda Aurora.* There are plenty of European works on display as well, including paintings by Peter Paul Rubens and Thomas Gainsborough. The highlight of the European collection is the pre-Raphaelite paintings, particularly the mesmerizing *Flaming June,* by Frederick Leighton,

The stately lobby of the Museo de Arte de Ponce

which has become the museum's unofficial symbol. You can take a break in the museum's three sculpture gardens, or relax in Restaurant Al Sur. Watch for special exhibits, such as a recent one examining the work of video artists. ⊠ *2325 Boulevard Luis A. Ferre Aguayo, Sector Santa María* ☏ *787/840–1510* ⊕ *www.museoarteponce.org* ✉ *$6* ⊙ *Wed.–Mon. 10–6.*

WORTH NOTING

Centro Ceremonial Indígena de Tibes (*Tibes Indian Ceremonial Center*). This archeological site, discovered after flooding from a tropical storm in 1975, is the most important on the island. The ancient ceremonial center dates from AD 300 to 700 and includes nine playing fields used for a ritual ball game that some think was similar to soccer. The fields are bordered by smooth stones, some of which are engraved with petroglyphs that researchers say might have ceremonial or astronomical significance. The most eye-catching part of the site is the *Plaza de Estrella*, or Plaza of the Star, where the stones are arranged in a pattern that resembles a rising sun. Experts say it might have been used to chart the seasons. A village with several thatched huts has been reconstructed in an original setting. Be sure to visit the small museum before taking a walking tour of the site. ⊠ *Rte. 503, Km 2.5, Barrio Tibes* ☏ *787/840–2255, 787/840–5685* ⊕ *www.ponce.inter.edu/tibes/tibes.html* ✉ *$3* ⊙ *Tues.–Sun. 8–4:30.*

Cruceta El Vigía. At the top of Cerro Vigía—a hill where the Spanish once watched for ships, including those of marauding pirates—is this colossal concrete cross built in 1801. You can climb the stairs or take a glass elevator to the top of the 100-foot cross for a panoramic view across the city. Purchase tickets at nearby Castillo Serrallés. ⊠ *17 El Vigia, across from Castillo Serrallés, El Vigía* ☎ *787/259–3816* ⊕ *www. castilloserralles.org* ⊠ *$12.80 includes admission to Castillo Serrallés and Butterfly Garden; $5.50 for admission just to cross and Japanese garden.* ⊙ *Thurs.–Sun. 9:30–5:30.*

OFF THE BEATEN PATH

Caja de Muertos. With a name that comes from its coffinlike shape, Caja de Muertos is a few miles off the coast and has the best beaches in the Ponce area. It is the second-best spot in southern Puerto Rico for snorkeling, after La Parguera. Due to the hawksbill turtles that nest between May and December, the island is protected by the Reserva Natural Caja de Muertos, but you can still swim, snorkel, and dive. A 30-minute hike across the island will take you to a small lighthouse that dates back to 1887. There are bathrooms and picnic tables for day use but not much else. Ask one of the many boatmen at La Guancha to take you out for about $30 round-trip. Scheduled boats costing $25 round-trip leave La Guancha Friday through Sunday at 8:30 am, returning around 3:30 pm. During summer, the boat trips depart daily. ⊠ *Boats leave from La Guancha, at the end of Rte. 14.*

BEACHES

Isla Caja de Muertos (*Coffin Island*). Named "Coffin Island" due to its shape, Isla Caja de Muertos is five miles off the coast and has the best beaches in the Ponce area. Stretching for two miles, it's one of the best snorkeling spots in southern Puerto Rico, second only to La Parguera. Due to the hawksbill turtles that nest between May and December, the island is protected by the Reserva Natural Caja de Muertos but you can still swim, snorkel, and dive here. A 30-minute hike across the island will take you to a small lighthouse that dates back to 1887. Scheduled boats leave La Guancha Friday through Sunday at 8:30 am and daily in high season. You'll need to pack in what you need (drinks and food) and pack out your garbage. **Amenities:** toilets. **Best for:** snorkeling; swimming; walking. ⊠ *Boats leave from La Guancha, at the end of Rte. 14.*

La Guancha. Ponce's public beach isn't anything to write home about, but the shallow water makes it nice for children. You'll find bathrooms, a playground, and a few kiosks selling fried food. There's some shade under thatched umbrellas, but bring sunscreen. **Amenities:** food and drink; parking; toilets. **Best for:** swimming. ⊠ *At the end of Rte. 14.*

WHERE TO EAT

$$

SEAFOOD

✕ **El Ancla.** Families favor this laid-back restaurant, whose dining room sits at the edge of the sea. The kitchen serves generous and affordable plates of fish, crab, and other fresh seafood with *tostones* (fried plantains), french fries, and garlic bread. Try the shrimp in garlic sauce, salmon fillet with capers, or the delectable mofongo stuffed with seafood. Finish your meal with one of the fantastic flans. The piña coladas—with or without rum—are exceptional. ⑤ *Average main:*

The reflection pool is just one highlight of a guided tour through the gardens and villa of Castillo Serrallés.

$20 ✉ *805 Av. Hostos Final, Ponce Playa* ☎ *787/840–2450* ⊕ *www. restauranteelancla.com.*

$$
ECLECTIC
✕ **Lola.** In the heart of downtown, this trendy bistro has an eclectic menu to match the décor. Grab a seat in a red velvet booth and start with the sampler of mahimahi nuggets, bruschetta, fried plantains, and egg rolls. The menu ranges from tuna steak to filet mignon to three-cheese risotto. Be sure to ask about the daily specials, which are always worth trying. This is a great place to admire work by local artists and sip on a Lola Martini (grapefruit, cranberry, champagne, lime, and rum). ⑤ *Average main: $18* ✉ *Ramada Inn, Calle Reina and Calle Union, Ponce Centro* ☎ *787/813–5033* ⊕ *www.lolacuisine.com.*

$$
SEAFOOD
✕ **Pito's Seafood.** Choose from the waterfront terrace or one of the enclosed dining rooms at this longtime favorite east of Ponce in Las Cucharas. No matter where you sit, you'll have a view of the ocean. The main attraction is the freshly caught seafood, ranging from lobster and crab to salmon and red snapper. For total indulgence, try the fresh oysters or shrimp wrapped in bacon—both specialties of the house. There's also a wide range of chicken and beef dishes. The plantain cups stuffed with chicken or seafood make an excellent starter. From the expansive wine cellar you can select more than 25 different wines by the glass. Listen to live music on Friday and Sunday night. ⑤ *Average main: $20* ✉ *Rte. 2, Km 218.5, Sector Las Cucharas* ☎ *787/841–4977* ⊕ *www.pitosseafoodpr.com.*

$$$
GREEK
✕ **Santorini.** The only Greek restaurant in Puerto Rico, this open-air establishment has successfully captured the cuisine and atmosphere of its namesake island. Statues of goddesses line the pathway leading to

a dual-level dining area, decorated with 1960s-era movie posters from Greece. Nearly ever dish is bathed in olive oil and vinegar, including the salads and sandwiches. You'll also find plenty of Caribbean food and Spanish tapas like conch fritters and stuffed lobster hamburgers. On Friday and Saturday, the bar is open late for drinks and dancing. Request a table on the lower deck, where water gently laps near your table. ⑤ *Average main: $25* ✉ *Rte. 2, Km 218, Sector Las Cucharas* ☎ *939/644–9021* ⊕ *www.santorini-olr.com* ☙ *Closed Mon. and Tues.*

WHERE TO STAY

$$
RESORT
FAMILY

⌕ **Hilton Ponce Golf & Casino Resort.** The south coast's biggest resort sits on a black-sand beach about 4 miles (6 km) south of downtown Ponce. **Pros:** good golf; large casino; game room and pool for kids. **Cons:** isolated location; must drive to off-property restaurants/attractions. ⑤ *Rooms from: $159* ✉ *1150 Av. Caribe, La Guancha* ☎ *787/259–7676, 800/445–8667* ⊕ *www.hiltoncaribbean.com* ⇆ *254 rooms, 9 suites* ⑩ *No meals.*

$
HOTEL
FAMILY

⌕ **Holiday Inn.** With all the modern comforts you'd expect from a Holiday Inn, this five-story hotel has a 24-hour casino, a huge pool, and a restaurant and bar where live music can be heard weekends. **Pros:** game room for kids; large pool area. **Cons:** far from the beach; foot traffic from casino and bar. ⑤ *Rooms from: $146* ✉ *3315 Ponce Bypass, west of downtown* ☎ *787/844–1200* ⊕ *www.holidayinn.com/ponce* ⇆ *110 rooms, 6 suites* ⑩ *No meals.*

$
HOTEL

⌕ **Hotel Bélgica.** Near the central square, this hotel dating from 1872 is both comfortable and economical, with worn yet clean rooms with hardwood floors, high ceilings, and wrought-iron beds. **Pros:** a taste of old Ponce; friendly staff; excellent rates. **Cons:** front-facing rooms are noisy; some rooms don't have windows; lots of steps and no elevator. ⑤ *Rooms from: $80* ✉ *122 Calle Villa, Ponce Centro* ☎ *787/844–3255* ⊕ *www.hotelbelgica.com* ⇆ *20 rooms* ⑩ *Breakfast.*

$
HOTEL

⌕ **Hotel Meliá.** In the heart of the city, this family-owned hotel has been a local landmark for over a century. **Pros:** great location on the main square; walking distance to downtown sites; good dining options near hotel. **Cons:** decor is somewhat outdated; front rooms can be noisy. ⑤ *Rooms from: $120* ✉ *75 Calle Cristina, Ponce Centro* ☎ *787/842–0260, 800/448–8355* ⊕ *www.hotelmeliapr.com* ⇆ *68 rooms, 6 suites* ⑩ *Breakfast.*

$
HOTEL
FAMILY

⌕ **Howard Johnson.** Two minutes from Mercedita Aeropuerto, this hotel is a good choice if you have an early morning flight. **Pros:** close to airport; pretty pool. **Cons:** no elevator; restaurant serves lunch only on weekends. ⑤ *Rooms from: $135* ✉ *103 Turpó Industrial Park, Airport* ☎ *787/841–1000* ⊕ *www.hojo.com* ⇆ *117 rooms, 3 suites* ⑩ *No meals.*

$
HOTEL

⌕ **Ramada Inn Ponce.** In a stunningly restored building that dates back to 1882, Ramada Inn sits right on the main square. **Pros:** excellent location; lively bar and restaurant. **Cons:** regular rooms lack charm; small pool gets foot traffic from attached restaurant. ⑤ *Rooms from: $119* ✉ *Calles Reina and Calle Unión, Ponce Centro* ☎ *787/813–5050* ⊕ *www.ramadaponce.com* ⇆ *70 rooms* ⑩ *No meals.*

NIGHTLIFE AND THE ARTS

NIGHTLIFE

BARS AND CLUBS

Kenepa's Cafe. On the main square, Kenepa's Cafe has live music and strong drinks. Locals crowd around the bar every night of the week. ⊠ *Edificio Café Plaza, 3 Calle Unión, Ponce Centro* ☎ *787/363–6674.*

CASINOS

The casinos in Ponce can't hold a candle to their counterparts in San Juan.

Hilton Ponce Golf & Casino Resort. Hilton Ponce Golf & Casino Resort has a rather cramped casino that's open 24 hours a day. ⊠ *1150 Av. Caribe, La Guancha* ☎ *787/259–7676* ⊕ *www.hiltoncaribbean.com/ponce.*

Holiday Inn Ponce. Holiday Inn Ponce has a small casino with 333 slot machines and 10 tables. The casino is open 24/7. ⊠ *3315 Ponce Bypass, El Tuque* ☎ *787/844–1200* ⊕ *www.holidayinn.com/ponce.*

THE ARTS

Teatro La Perla. Check for Spanish-language theater productions and concerts at the Teatro La Perla, a neoclassical masterpiece in the center of Ponce. ⊠ *Calle Mayor and Calle Cristina, Ponce Centro* ☎ *787/843–4322.*

SHOPPING

On holidays and during festivals, artisans sell wares from booths in Plaza de las Delicias. Souvenir and gift shops are plentiful in the area around the plaza, and Paseo Atocha, a pedestrian mall with shops geared to residents, runs north of it.

Mi Coquí. Mi Coquí has shelves filled with carnival masks, colorful hammocks, freshly ground coffee, and bottles and bottles of rum. ⊠ *9227 Calle Marina, Ponce Centro* ☎ *787/841–0216.*

Plaza del Caribe Mall. Plaza del Caribe Mall, just outside town, is one of the island's largest malls and has such stores as Sears, Puma, Foot Locker, and American Eagle Outfitters. ⊠ *Rte. 2, Km 224.9* ☎ *787/259–8989* ⊕ *www.plazadelcaribe.net.*

Ponce Mall. Ponce Mall, with more than 30 stores, is an older shopping center, with many local clothing and discount stores. It also has a large IKEA, TJ Maxx, and Designer Shoe Warehouse. ⊠ *Rte. 2, Km 225.8* ☎ *787/844–6170* ⊕ *www.poncemallpr.com.*

Utopia. Utopia sells carnival masks, carved figurines, and other crafts. ⊠ *78 Calle Isabel, Ponce Centro* ☎ *787/848–8742.*

TAKE A WALK

In downtown Ponce people embrace the Spanish tradition of the *paseo*, an evening stroll with family and friends around Plaza de las Delicias, which is spectacular at night when its old-fashioned street lamps glow and the fountain is lit. The boardwalk at La Guancha is also a lively scene with bands playing on weekends. You can buy a bag of sardines and feed seagulls and pelicans right out of your hand.

SPORTS AND THE OUTDOORS

DIVING AND SNORKELING

You'll see many varieties of coral, parrotfish, angelfish, and grouper in the reefs around the island of Caja de Muertos. Snorkeling around La Guancha and the beach area of the Ponce Hilton is also fairly good.

Island Venture. Rafi Vega's Island Venture offers two-tank dive excursions for $65, as well as snorkeling trips for $35. The company also takes day-trippers from La Guancha to Caja de Muertos—a 45-minute boat ride—for a day of relaxing on the beach. ☎ 787/842–8546 ⊕ *www. islandventurepr.com.*

GOLFING

Costa Caribe Golf & Country Club. The Costa Caribe Golf & Country Club, Ponce's only course, has 27 holes, a driving range, and pro shop adjoining the Ponce Hilton. To get here, take Route 12 to Avenida Caribe. ✉ *1150 Av. Caribe* ☎ *787/817–2650* ⊕ *www.costacaribe-resort. com* ⚑ *$69 per round, $45 twilight.*

THE SOUTHEASTERN COAST

As you cross the Cordillera Central the scenery becomes drier and more rugged. The Caribbean sparkles in the distance, and the plain between the sea and the mountains, once the heart of the sugarcane industry, is now the domain of cattle. Tucked into the foothills is Coamo, a popular hot-springs resort since the early 1900s. Closer to the coast is Guayama, with a tree-lined square surrounded by many historic buildings.

COAMO

21 miles (34 km) northeast of Ponce, 20 miles (33 km) southwest of Cayey, 13 miles (20 km) northwest of Salinas.

Founded by the Spanish in 1579, Coamo was the third city established in Puerto Rico. It dominated the south of the island until the mid-1880s, when political power shifted to Ponce. Coamo town, however, remained an important outpost; several decisive battles were fought here during the Spanish-American War in 1898.

The thermal springs outside Coamo are believed by some to be the Fountain of Youth for which Ponce de León was searching. In the mid-1800s, a fashionable resort was built nearby, and people have been coming to soak in the waters ever since. Coamo is also famous for the San Blas Half-Marathon, which brings competitors and spectators from around the world. The race, held in early February, covers 13 miles (18 km) of the city's hilly streets.

GETTING HERE AND AROUND

Coamo sits fairly close to the Luis A. Ferré Expressway (Route 52), the toll road that connects San Juan and Ponce; it is about 20 miles northeast of Ponce. You can take the turnoff onto Route 153, though there is also access from several points in the Cordillera. Públicos from Ponce connect with Coamo's town center.

EXPLORING
WORTH NOTING

Iglesia Católica San Blás. On Coamo's main square, the Iglesia Católica San Blás has a gorgeous neoclassical facade. Dating from 1563, the whitewashed building is one of the oldest churches on the island. ✉ *Calle Mario Braschetti* ☎ *787/825–1122* ☉ *Daily 6:30–noon.*

Museo Histórico de Coamo. Off the main square, the Museo Histórico de Coamo is appropriately housed in the former residence of one of the city's illustrious citizens, Clotilde Santiago, a wealthy farmer and merchant born in 1826. The museum is on the second floor of this sprawling, tangerine-colored building, which dates from 1863. Several rooms are decorated with colonial-style furnishings; photographs of the town and the Santiago family line the walls. ✉ *29 Calle José I. Quintón* ☎ *787/803–6716* 🎟 *Free* ☉ *Weekdays 8–4:30.*

Piscinas Aguas Termales. Outside Coamo you can take a dip at the famous Piscinas Aguas Termales, the thermal springs that are said to have curative powers. Day-trippers can bathe in the steamy modern pool for $3. There's also a changing room at the end of a path. ✉ *Rte. 546, Km 1.7* ☎ *787/825–6668* 🎟 *$3* ☉ *Daily 7–9.*

WHERE TO EAT

$$
PUERTO RICAN

✕ **La Ceiba.** The highway leading to Coamo is lined by dozens of fast-food restaurants. Luckily, there are a few family-owned eateries worth stopping for, one of the best of which is this open-air cantina. You'll find the usual mofongo with chicken or beef, as well as some other typical Puerto Rican dishes like fried pork or red snapper stuffed with seafood. The menu features a variety of fish as well as lobster, shrimp and octopus. If you are a fan of cheesecake, the chef makes eight different flavors (the pistachio is delicious). World-class margaritas are served at the bar. $ *Average main: $15* ✉ *Rte. 153, Km 12.8* ☎ *787/825–2299* ⊕ *www.restaurantelaceiba.com.*

SPORTS AND THE OUTDOORS
GOLF

Coamo Springs Golf Club and Resort. The Coamo Springs Golf Club and Resort is popular for its rugged beauty and affordable greens fees. It's the only 18-hole course with Bermuda grass on the island. When it's raining in the capital, *sanjuaneros* may drive down here for a day of play. The 6,647-yard course, designed by Ferdinand Garbin, is open daily from 7 to 7. ✉ *Rte. 546, Km 1* ☎ *787/825–1370* ⊕ *www.coamosprings.com* 🎟 *$40* ⛳ *18 holes, 6647 yards, par 72.*

SALINAS

27 miles (41 km) east of Ponce.

Most visitors are familiar with this town only because of seeing its name on an exit sign along Route 52. Islanders, however, know that the road from the expressway exit to Salinas leads to some of Puerto Rico's best seafood restaurants. Most of them are along the seafront in the Playa de Salinas area, reached by heading south on Route 701.

GETTING HERE AND AROUND

You can take either the Luis A. Ferré Expressway (Route 52), the toll road that connects San Juan and Ponce, or the more scenic Route 1 along the coast east from Ponce to reach Salinas.

WHERE TO EAT

$$$
SEAFOOD

✕ **El Balcón de Capitán.** This *meson gastronómico*, hidden among a string of oceanfront seafood restaurants south of the center in the Playa de Salinas area, is one of the most respected on Puerto Rico's southern coast. Sit in either the open-air patio or air-conditioned dining room and bar and sample specialties like *mofongo relleno de mariscos* (seafood-stuffed plantains) or the many preparations of mahimahi, red snapper, *arrayao*, octopus, lobster, or conch. The paella with seafood is a house specialty. ⑤ *Average main: $25* ⊠ *Rte. 701, Playa de Salinas* ☎ 787/824–6210.

$$
PUERTO RICAN

✕ **El Roble.** In operation since 1961, this restaurant is still considered one of the best in town. Don't be surprised to see flapping fish delivered straight off the boats and into the kitchen, where chefs prepare dishes like grouper fillet stuffed with seafood. The red snapper is delicious, and like all the fish on the menu it can be prepared fried, buttered, breaded, or with a vinaigrette. There's also a children's menu and a large selection of wines. Be prepared for the collection of fish mounted on the walls. ⑤ *Average main: $18* ⊠ *Rte.701, Playa de Salinas* ☎ 787/824–2377.

WHERE TO STAY

$
HOTEL
FAMILY

▩ **Manatee Eco Resort.** True to its name, this eco-friendly hotel has energy-efficient lighting, solar-heated water, and its own private well. **Pros:** eco-friendly property; easy wildlife viewing; kids under 13 stay free. **Cons:** some common areas smell of cigarette smoke; restaurant's hours of service are inconsistent. ⑤ *Rooms from: $79* ⊠ *296 Playita Final* ☎ 787/824–6688 ⊕ *www.manateeecoresort.com* ⌁ *26 rooms* ⏚ *Breakfast.*

$
HOTEL

▩ **Marina de Salinas.** Several different types of mangroves shade this hotel, and the spacious rooms are cheerfully decorated with tropical colors, wicker furniture, and paintings of fishing boats. **Pros:** off-the-beaten-path vibe; lovely mangrove trees; kayaks for rent. **Cons:** basic rooms; no elevator. ⑤ *Rooms from: $95* ⊠ *End of Rte. 701, Playa Ward* ☎ 787/824–3185, 787/752–8484 ⊕ *www.marinadesalinas.com* ⌁ *30 rooms; 2 suites* ⏚ *No meals.*

> **SALINAS HAS THE MOJO**
>
> When you stop in Salinas—and you should—be sure to try local seafood with *mojo isleño*, a popular sauce made from tomatoes, onions, and spices, which was created here.

GUAYAMA

18 miles (29 km) east of Salinas, 17 miles (28 km) southeast of Cayey, 31 miles (49 km) southeast of Barranquitas.

Guayama was founded in 1736, but the city was destroyed by fire in the early 1800s. It quickly recovered when the sugarcane industry grew by leaps and bounds, and the wealth that the surrounding plantations brought to town is evident in the number of striking neoclassical homes on the streets surrounding the main square. Some have been beautifully restored, whereas others are crumbling. One of the finest 19th-century homes, Casa Cautiño, is now a museum.

The nearby countryside is home to Paso Fino horses. Each March at the Marcelino Blondet Stadium you can watch these high-stepping show horses strut their stuff during the Feria Dulce Sueño, a fair named after one of the island's most famous Thoroughbreds. Folk music and crafts are part of the festivities.

GETTING HERE AND AROUND

From the north or west, take either Route 53 or the coastal Route 3 to reach Guayama. On Sunday Guayama has a free trolley that runs to many sights.

Information Guayama Trolley ⊠ *Alcaldía de Guayama, Calle Vicente Pales* ☎ *787/864-7765.*

EXPLORING

TOP ATTRACTIONS

Casa Cautiño. Built for sugar, cattle, and coffee baron Genaro Cautiño Vázquez and his wife, Genoveva Insúa, Casa Cautiño is an elegant neoclassical home dating from 1887. The painstakingly restored exterior features a balcony with ornate grillwork. You'll be swept back in time walking through the home's rooms, which are filled with the original Victorian-era furnishings. Don't miss the modern-for-its-time bathroom, complete with a standing shower. The museum is on the main square. ⊠ *1 Calle Palmer, at Calle Vicente Palé Matos* ☎ *787/864-9083* ⚑ *Free* ☉ *Tues.–Sat. 9–4:30, Sun. 10–4.*

NEED A BREAK?

Rex Cream. The fruit-flavored ice cream at Rex Cream is hard to pass up. Flavors vary, depending on what produce is in season, but often include coconut, lime, pineapple, tamarind, and *guanábana* (soursop). You can also get milk shakes—the mango is outstanding. ⊠ *24 Calle Derkes* ☎ *787/864-1608.*

WORTH NOTING

Centro de Bellas Artes. Just a few blocks from the main square, the Centro de Bellas Artes is housed in a beautifully restored neoclassical building. Paintings by local artists fill its 11 rooms. ⊠ *Calle McArthur and Rte. 3* ☎ *787/864-7765* ⚑ *Free* ☉ *Tues.–Sun. 9–4:30.*

Iglesia San Antonio de Padua. One of the prettiest churches on the southern coast, Iglesia San Antonio de Padua was begun in 1827 but not completed until 40 years later. Don't set your watch by the time on the clock; the hand-painted face is frozen at the time the church was "baptized." The bells in the tower were cast in gold and bronze in 1835. ⊠ *5 Calle Ashford.*

SPORTS AND THE OUTDOORS

GOLF

Aguirre Golf Club. Running through an old sugar plantation, the Aguirre Golf Club was built in 1925 for the executives of a local sugar mill. Open daily, the 9-hole course is short but tough. ⊠ *Rte. 705, Km 3, off Rte. 3, Aguirre* ☎ *787/853-4052.*

5

El Legado Golf Resort. The El Legado Golf Resort, designed by golf legend and native son Chi Chi Rodríguez, is a 7,213-yard, 18-hole course with 12 lakes. ⊠ *Rte. 713, off Rte. 53, Cimarrona* ☎ *787/866–8894* ⊕ *www. ellegadogolfclub.com* ⊙ *Closed Mon. except holidays.*

THE SOUTHWESTERN COAST

With sandy coves and palm-lined beaches tucked into the coastline's curves, southwestern Puerto Rico fulfills everyone's fantasy of a tropical paradise. The area is popular with local vacationers on weekends and holidays, but many beaches are nearly deserted on weekdays. Villages along the coast are picturesque places where oysters and fresh fish are sold at roadside stands.

GUÁNICA

24 miles (38 km) west of Ponce.

Juan Ponce de León first explored this area in 1508, when he was searching for the elusive Fountain of Youth. Nearly 400 years later U.S. troops landed first at Guánica during the Spanish-American War in 1898. The event is commemorated with an engraved marker on the city's *malecón,* or jetty. Sugarcane dominated the landscape through much of the 1900s, and the ruins of the old Guánica Central sugar mill, closed in 1980, loom over the town's western area, known as Ensenada. Today most of the action takes place at the beaches and in the forests outside Guánica.

GETTING HERE AND AROUND

From Ponce, Route 2 connects with Guánica via Route 116 and extends to San Germán and Mayagüez. The town hugs Guánica Bay and runs almost immediately into the neighboring village of Ensenada.

EXPLORING

Bosque Estatal de Guánica (*Guánica State Forest*). The 9,900-acre Bosque Estatal de Guánica, a United Nations Biosphere Reserve, is a great place for hiking expeditions. It's an outstanding example of a tropical dry coastal forest, with some 700 species of plants, ranging from the prickly-pear cactus to the gumbo limbo tree. It's also one of the best places on the island for bird-watching, since you can spot more than 100 species, including the pearly-eyed thrasher, the lizard cuckoo, and the nightjar.

One of the most popular hikes is the **Ballena Trail,** which begins at the ranger station on Route 334. This easy 1¼-mile (2-km) walk follows a partially paved road and takes you past a mahogany plantation to a dry plain covered with stunted cactus. A sign reading "Guayacán centenario" leads you to an extraordinary guayacán tree with a trunk that measures six feet across. The moderately difficult **Fuerte Trail** takes you on a 3½-mile (5½-km) hike to an old fort built by the Spanish Armada. It was destroyed during the Spanish-American War in 1898, but you can still see the ruins of the old observatory tower.

In addition to going in the main entrance on Route 334, you can enter on Route 333, which skirts the forest's southwestern quadrant. You can also try the less explored western section, off Route 325. ⊠ *Rte. 334* ☎ 787/821–5706 ✉ *Free* ⊗ *Daily 9–5.*

BEACHES

Balneario Caña Gorda. The gentle waters at this beach on Route 333 wash onto a wide swath of sand fringed with palm trees. This is one of the few beaches in Puerto Rico that is part of the Blue Flag Program, meaning that it meets high environmental standards. There is a designated area roped off for swimmers, and lifeguards remain on duty most afternoons. You'll also find picnic tables, restrooms, showers, and changing facilities. During high season there are beach-chair rentals, food vendors, and paid parking. **Amenities:** food and drink; lifeguards; parking (fee); toilets. **Best for:** snorkeling; swimming; walking. ⊠ *Rte. 333, Km 5.9, west of Copamarina Beach Resort.*

Gilligan's Island. Off the southwest coast, near Guánica, is Gilligan's Island, a palm-ringed cay skirted by gorgeous beaches. You'll find picnic tables and restrooms but few other signs of civilization on this tiny island, officially part of the Bosque Estatal de Guánica. Wooden boats line up at the small dock in the San Jacinto section of Guánica, off Route 333 just past the Copamarina Beach Resort. Boats depart every hour from 9 to 5. Round-trip passage is $8. The island is often crowded on weekends and around holidays, but during the week you can find a spot to yourself. Nearby **Isla de Ballena,** reached by the same ferry, is much less crowded. **Amenities:** toilets. **Best for:** swimming; solitude (midweek, low season) ⊠ *Off Rte. 333* ☎ 787/821–4941 ✉ *Free* ⊗ *Daily 9–5.*

Playa Jaboncillo. Rugged cliffs make a dramatic backdrop for this little cove off Route 333, but the water can be rough. The road down to the beach is extremely steep and rocky and shouldn't be attempted without a four-wheel-drive vehicle. **Amenities:** parking. **Best for:** swimming; solitude ⊠ *Rte. 333, west of Copamarina Beach Resort.*

Playa Santa. You can rent canoes, kayaks, and pedal boats at this beach at the end of Route 325 in the Ensenada district. This beach is popular with local teenagers and can get congested, but the mile-long shoreline is kept clean and preserved. **Amenities:** food and drink; parking; water sports. **Best for:** swimming; sunset; walking ⊠ *Rte. 325, west of Guánica, Ensenada.*

WHERE TO EAT

$$$ ✕ **Alexandra.** Puerto Ricans drive for miles to reach this restaurant in
CARIBBEAN the Copamarina Beach Resort. You won't find such creative cuisine anywhere else west of Ponce. The kitchen makes traditional dishes into something special; take the salmon fillet with a mango and lemon crust served with eggplant and pumpkin lasagna, for example, or the roasted chicken stuffed with prosciutto and Manchego cheese in a Marsala sauce. A standout is the lobster with roasted potatoes in butter and thyme. The elegant dining room looks out onto well-tended gardens; if you want to get closer to the flora, ask for a table outside on the terrace. The only disappointment may be noisy children, who tend to run

A Guide to Puerto Rico's Carved Saints

Hand-carved religious figures, or Santos, are an important part of Puerto Rico's cultural history.

Hand-carving wooden *santos* (saints) is one of Puerto Rico's oldest traditional art forms, and the practice has survived for centuries. But you wouldn't know it to walk into one of the local souvenir shops, which often line their shelves with imported pieces. Authentic santos carving thrives today—you just have to know where to find the artisans—and their handiwork.

HISTORY OF THE SANTOS

Influenced by its African, Spanish, and American roots, as well as its Caribbean neighbors and Latin American ties, Puerto Rico has achieved a unique artistic identity through its continual willingness to integrate many traditions. Its artists have worked hard to preserve their culture, and nowhere is their effort more evident than in their hand-carved santos figures.

The history of the *santos* is traced back to the arrival of Spanish missionaries in the late 15th and early 16th centuries. The missionaries spread God's word by telling stories animated and illustrated with carved santos. According to carver Miguel Díaz, missionaries left santos behind with prospective converts so they could pray at home. Churches were few and far between, but santos placed on home altars could help keep the spirit of God alive between missionaries' visits. Though missionaries no longer visit homes, and churches are more abundant, santos still enjoy a place of honor in many Puerto Ricans' homes and have become a popular art form, highly prized by collectors on the island and abroad.

ABOUT THE SAINTS

Santos are not entirely unique to Puerto Rico; just as Spanish missionaries brought them to the island, they also carried them to many other countries. Each country, though, personalized the santos to its own culture over the years. In Puerto Rico the most common figures are the Three Kings, Saint Barbara, Saint Francis, and The Powerful Hand (*La Mano Poderosa*—a member of the Holy Family tops each finger of a hand bearing the stigma). The santos are typically carved in cedar. Once carved, they are brushed with a coat of gesso and then painted. Santos can also be found in ceramic.

WHERE TO FIND THEM

Once you stop looking in souvenir shops, it just takes a little scouting to find santos, as well as the artisans who carve them.

The best place to find santos during business hours in Old San Juan is **Puerto Rican Arts & Crafts** (✉ *204 Calle Fortaleza, Old San Juan* ☎ *787/725–5596* ⊕ *www. puertoricanart-crafts.com*). The store, which ensures that its entire stock comes from the hands of artisans who live on the island, carries the santos of the late self-taught carver Domingo Orta and of Antonio Avilés Burgos, who was once recognized as artisan of the year and is the third generation of carvers in his family.

After hours, artisans can often be found working wood and selling their santos during craft fairs held along Old San Juan's Plaza Dársena, located between the cruise piers and Paseo de la Princesa. Friday and Saturday evenings are sure bets, as are Sunday afternoons.

The Powerful Hand santos

Puerto Rican Arts and Crafts Store

Miguel Diaz. If you're interested in visiting an artisan's workshop, carver Miguel Diaz hosts visitors in his studio in Carolina. ☎ *787/392–8857* ✉ *tallertabonuco@gmail.com* ⊕ *tallerta-bonuco@gmail.com.*

Aviles Family. The Aviles family maintains a museum of its generations of craft work. Visits are by appointment only. ✉ *Santurce, San Juan* ☎ *787/455–4217.*

PRICES

As with most art and handicrafts, prices depend on several factors, including the carver's history, the quality of craftsmanship, the setting where the pieces are sold, the amount of decoration or elaboration, and the size of the piece. The average size of a santo is 7 to 8 inches, though some are smaller and many carvers produce larger pieces for commissions and other special occasions.

In general, expect prices for santos to begin at $40 and to go up considerably. Some santos fetch as much as several hundred dollars.

Bargaining is not considered as permissible in Puerto Rico as it is in other Spanish-speaking countries. A carver's stated price is likely the lowest he or she is willing to go.

Southwestern Coast and the Porta Caribe

Fish the waters off La Parguera for blue marlin, tuna, or reef fish.

in and out of the pool area. ⑤ *Average main: $28* ⊠ *Copamarina Beach Resort, Rte. 333, Km 6.5* 🖀 *787/821–0505* ⊕ *www.copamarina.com* ⌲ *Reservations essential* ⊘ *No lunch.*

WHERE TO STAY

$$
RESORT
FAMILY
Fodor's Choice
★

🖫 **Copamarina Beach Resort & Spa.** Without a doubt the most beautiful resort on the southern coast, Copamarina is set on 16 palm-shaded acres facing the Caribbean Sea. **Pros:** tropical decor; plenty of activities; great dining options. **Cons:** somewhat distant from other attractions; noise from all the kids. ⑤ *Rooms from: $190* ⊠ *Rte. 333, Km 6.5* 🖀 *787/821–0505, 800/468–4553* ⊕ *www.copamarina.com* ⌁ *104 rooms, 2 villas* ⭐️ *Multiple meal plans.*

$
RENTAL
Fodor's Choice
★

🖫 **Mary Lee's by the Sea.** This meandering cluster of apartments sits upon quiet grounds full of brightly colored flowers. **Pros:** feels like a home away from home; warm and friendly owner; near pristine beaches and forests. **Cons:** weekly maid service unless requested daily; no nightlife and no pool. ⑤ *Rooms from: $110* ⊠ *Rte. 333, Km 6.7* 🖀 *787/821–3600* ⊕ *www.maryleesbythesea.com* ⌁ *10 apartments* ⭐️ *No meals.*

$
HOTEL

🖫 **Parador Guaníca 1929.** This colonial-style building is very pretty, with lovely arches adding more character than you usually find along the southern coast. **Pros:** historic setting; pretty pool area; basketball and volleyball courts. **Cons:** no beach; slightly off the beaten path. ⑤ *Rooms from: $113* ⊠ *Rte. 3116, Km. 2.5, Ensenada* 🖀 *877/784–6835* ⊕ *www.paradorguanica1929pr.com* ⌁ *27 rooms* ⭐️ *No meals.*

SPORTS AND THE OUTDOORS

DIVING AND SNORKELING

Dramatic walls created by the continental shelf provide great diving off the Guánica coast. Shallow gardens around Gilligan's Island and Cayo de Caña Gorda (off Balneario Caña Gorda) also attract snorkelers and divers.

Dive Copamarina. Dive Copamarina offers instruction and trips. ⊠ *Copamarina Beach Resort, Rte. 333, Km 6.5* ☎ *787/821–0505* ⊕ *www.copamarina.com.*

HORSEBACK RIDING

Gaby's World. In nearby Yauco, Gaby's World is a 204-acre horse ranch that conducts half-hour, one-hour, and two-hour rides through the hills surrounding Yauco. There are also pony rides and a playground for children. The on-site steak house serves Yauco's specialty, *chuletas can-can*, enormous pork chops. ⊠ *Rte. 127, Km 5.1, Yauco* ☎ *787/344–4218.*

LA PARGUERA

8 miles (13 km) west of Guánica, 15 miles (24 km) southwest of Yauco.

La Parguera is best known for its bioluminescent bay. Although it is not nearly as spectacular as the one in Vieques, it's still a beautiful sight on a moonless night. Boats, including some glass-bottom vessels, line up at the town dock and depart several times each evening for 45-minute trips across the bay. During the day you can explore the nearby mangrove forest.

The town bursts at the seams with vacationers from other parts of the island on long holiday weekends and all during the summer. The town's dock area feels a bit like Coney Island, and not in a good way. Vendors in makeshift stalls hawk cheap souvenirs, and ear-splitting salsa music pours out of open-air bars. There are signs warning people not to drink alcoholic beverages in the street, but these are cheerfully ignored.

If you're driving through the area between February and April, keep your eyes open for roadside vendors selling the area's famous pineapples, called *piñas cadezonas*. In late June there's the colorful Fiesta de San Pedro, honoring the patron saint of fishermen.

GETTING HERE AND AROUND

You can reach La Parguera from Guánica via Route 116, which turns into Route 318 when it heads to San Germán. Públicos depart from the turnoff at Route 304 and head to Lajas, where connections can be made to San Germán.

EXPLORING

WORTH NOTING

Bahía de Fosforescente (*Phosphorescent Bay*). On moonless nights, large and small boats line up along the dock to take visitors out to view the Bahía Fosforescente. Microscopic dinoflagellates glow when disturbed by movement, invading the waves with thousands of starlike points of light. The bay's glow has been diminished substantially by pollution—both light pollution from nearby communities and water pollution from toxic chemicals being dumped into the bay. (And,

Many of La Parguera's restaurants and shops overlook the bay.

yes, the smoke-belching boats that take tourists to the bay are doing damage, too.) If you've seen the bioluminescent bay in Vieques (*see the feature in Chapter 4*), give this one a pass. If not, you may find it mildly interesting. While it's not necessary to make a reservation— plenty of operators try to rustle up customers on the docks around sunset—Paradise Scuba runs the most reputable excursions in the area. Visit their dive shop for more information. ✉ *Rte 304, Km. 3.5* ⊕ *www.paradisescubasnorkelingpr.com.*

Bosque Estatal de Boquerón (*Boquerón State Forest*). The eastern section of the Bosque Estatal de Boquerón is made up of miles of mangrove forests that grow at the water's edge. Boats from the dock in La Parguera can take you on cruises through this important breeding ground for seabirds. You can also organize a kayak trip. ✉ *Boats leave from marina at La Parguera, off Rte. 304.*

BEACHES

Isla Mata de la Gata. For about $5 per person, boats will transport you to and from this small island just off the coast for a day of swimming and snorkeling. **Amenities:** changing rooms and grilling areas. **Best for:** snorkeling, swimming. ✉ *Boats leave from marina at La Parguera, off Rte. 304, La Parguera.*

Playita Rosada. The small beach doesn't compare to some of the longer beaches on the southwestern coast, but it's a convenient place for a quick swim. There's also a square dock built like a picture frame where locals gather to splash in the center of this natural swimming pool. **Amenities:** none. **Best for:** swimming. ✉ *At the end of Calle 7, La Parguera.*

WHERE TO EAT

$$
SEAFOOD

✕ **La Casita.** The so-called Little House isn't little at all—it's a sizable establishment that sits smack in the middle of the town's main road. Generous portions make this family-run restaurant one of the town's favorites. Try the *asopao*, a stew made with shrimp, lobster, or other types of seafood. The mofongo with octopus in garlic sauce is very flavorful. You can take a table in the rather bland ground-floor dining room or on the second-floor terrace, which has a view of the water. ⑤ *Average main: $20* ⊠ *Rte. 304, Km 3.3* ☎ *787/899–1681.*

WHERE TO STAY

$$
HOTEL

🔆 **Villa Parguera.** The rooms in this gingerbread-trimmed hotel are clustered around small courtyards filled with bright tropical flowers. **Pros:** family atmosphere; plenty of entertainment options; walking distance to the marina. **Cons:** bland rooms; pool area gets crowded; noise from nearby bars; no elevator. ⑤ *Rooms from: $155* ⊠ *Rte. 304, Km 3.3* ☎ *787/899–7777* ⊕ *www.villaparguera.net* ↝ *74 rooms* ⦿ *No meals.*

NIGHTLIFE AND THE ARTS

La Parguera's dock area heats up after sunset, when crowds come to take excursions to the Bahía Fosforescente.

Villa Parguera. The live floor show on Saturday night includes a buffet. The show changes frequently but includes live music, dancing, and comedy of the seltzer-in-your-pants variety. ⊠ *Villa Parguera, Rte. 304, Km 2.3* ☎ *787/899–7777, 787/899–3975.*

SHOPPING

Outdoor stands near the docks sell all kinds of souvenirs, from T-shirts to beaded necklaces.

SPORTS AND THE OUTDOORS

DIVING AND SNORKELING

Endangered leatherback turtles, eels, and an occasional manatee can be seen from many of the sites that attract divers and snorkelers from all parts. There are more than 50 shore-dive sites off La Parguera, including the famous Black Wall that starts out at 60 feet and then suddenly drops 200 into a vast canyon.

Paradise Scuba. Paradise Scuba offers classes and trips, including night-snorkeling excursions in phosphorescent waters. Divers will enjoy the 150-foot vertical drop at the Black Wall, considered one of the most spectacular dive sites in Puerto Rico. Their most popular package is the sunset snorkel tour, which includes snacks, drinks, and a trip to the phosphorescent bay. ⊠ *Hostal Casa Blanca, Rte. 304, Km 3.5* ☎ *787/899–7611* ⊕ *www.paradisescubasnorkelingpr.com.*

FISHING

Parguera Fishing Charters. You can spend a day or half-day fishing for blue marlin, tuna, or reef fish with Capt. Mickey Amador at Parguera Fishing Charters. Lunch is included in the price. ⊠ *Rte. 304, Km 3.8* ☎ *787/382–4698, 787/899–4698* ⊕ *www.puertoricofishingcharters.com.*

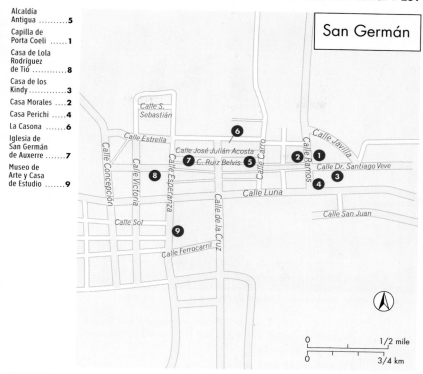

San Germán

SAN GERMÁN

6 miles (10 km) north of La Parguera, 104 miles (166 km) southwest of San Juan.

During its early years, San Germán was a city on the move. Although debate rages about the first settlement's exact founding date and location, the town is believed to have been established in 1510 near Guánica. Plagued by mosquitoes, the settlers moved north along the west coast, where they encountered French pirates and smugglers. In the 1570s they fled inland to the current location, but they were still harassed. Determined and creative, they dug tunnels and moved beneath the city (the tunnels are now part of the water system). Today San Germán has a population of 35,000, and its intellectual and political activity is anything but underground. It's very much a college town, and students and professors from the Inter-American University often fill the bars and cafés.

Around San Germán's two main squares—Plazuela Santo Domingo and Plaza Francisco Mariano Quiñones (named for an abolitionist)—are buildings in every conceivable style of architecture found on the island, including mission, Victorian, creole, and Spanish colonial. The city's tourist office offers a free, guided trolley tour. Most of the buildings are private homes; two of them—the Capilla de Porta Coeli and the

Iglesia de San Germán de Auxerre is a 17th-century church that's still in use today.

Museo de Arte y Casa de Estudio—are museums. Strip malls surround the historic center, and the town is hemmed to the south and west by busy seaside resorts.

GETTING HERE AND AROUND
San Germán sits just off Highway 2 between Ponce and Mayagüez on Route 122. Being a university town, it is a transportation hub with públicos departing to nearby villages such as Mayagüez and Lajas from the intersection of Calle Luna and Route 122. A trolley tour of San Germán is available by appointment.

San Germán Trolley ⌧ *Alcaldía de San Germán, 136 Calle Luna* ☎ *787/892–3500.*

TOP ATTRACTIONS

Capilla de Porta Coeli (*Heaven's Gate Chapel*). One of the oldest religious buildings in the Americas, this mission-style chapel overlooks the long, rectangular Plazuela de Santo Domingo. It's not a grand building, but its position at the top of a stone stairway gives it a noble air. Queen Isabel Segunda decreed that the Dominicans should build a church and monastery in San Germán, so a rudimentary building was built in 1609, replaced in 1692 by the structure that can still be seen today. (Sadly, most of the monastery was demolished in 1866, leaving only a vestige of its facade.) The chapel now functions as a museum of religious art, displaying painted wooden statuary by Latin American and Spanish artists. ⌧ *East end of Plazuela Santo Domingo* ☎ *787/892–5845* 🖾 *$3* ⊙ *Mon.–Fri. 9–12 and 1–4.*

La Casona. On the north side of Plaza Francisco Mariano Quiñones, this two-story home was built in 1871 for Tomás Agrait. (If you look

A GOOD TOUR: SAN GERMÁN

The best place to start is Plazuela Santo Domingo, the sun-baked park in the center of the historic district. At the eastern edge of the park is the **Capilla de Porta Coeli**, perched at the top of an imposing set of stairs. From the top you get a good view of the rest of the city. Several historic homes, none of them open to the public, are within a block of the Capilla de Porta Coeli. Across the street is the **Casa Morales**, striking for its Victorian-style gables. It would not look out of place in any New England hamlet. Half a block east on Calle Dr. Santiago Veve are two criollo-style houses, **Casa Kindy** and Casa Acosta y Forés. A block south of the Capilla de Porta Coeli is one of the most beautiful homes in San Germán, **Casa Ortiz Perichi**.

Head west through Plazuela Santo Domingo. The hulking yellow building you see at the northwest corner of the park is the rear of the **Alcaldía Antigua**. It faces the town's other park, the Plaza Francisco Mariano Quiñones. This park is more popular with locals, as the tree-shaded benches are a pleasant place to watch the world go by. On the park's northern edge is **La Casona**, one of the town's best-preserved criollo-style buildings. The most imposing structure on the park, however, is **Iglesia de San Germán de Auxerre**.

A block and a half west of the church is the **Casa de Lola Rodríguez de Tió**, on Calle Dr. Santiago Veve. It's one of the best examples of criollo-style architecture in the city. Backtrack to Calle Esperanza and head two blocks south to where you'll find the **Museo de Arte y Casa de Estudio**.

TIMING

San Germán's historic district is compact, so you can cover all the sights in about an hour. You'll want to budget a bit more time to stroll around the nearby streets. Be sure to wear comfortable shoes, as there will be a lot of walking uphill and downhill on cobbled streets.

closely, you can still see his initials in the wrought-iron decorations.) For many years it served as a center of cultural activities in San Germán. Today, it holds several shops. ⊠ *Calle José Julien Acosta and Calle Cruz.*

WORTH NOTING

Alcaldía Antigua (*Old Municipal Building*). At the eastern end of Plaza Francisco Mariano Quiñones, this Spanish-colonial-style building served as the town's city hall from 1844 to 1950. Once used as a prison, the building is now the headquarters for the police department. ⊠ *East end of Plaza Francisco Mariano Quiñones.*

Casa de Lola Rodríguez de Tió. Part of the San Germán Historic District, which is listed on the National Register of Historic Places, this house bears the name of poet and activist Lola Rodríguez de Tió. A plaque claims she lived in this creole-style house, though town officials believe it actually belonged to her sister. Rodríguez, whose mother was a descendant of Ponce de León, was deported several times by Spanish authorities for her revolutionary ideas. She lived in Venezuela and then in Cuba, where she died in 1924. The museum, which houses

Rodríguez's desk and papers, isn't open regular hours; call ahead to schedule a tour. ✉ *13 Calle Dr. Santiago Veve* ☎ *787/892–3500* 🔳 *Free* ⊙ *By appointment only.*

Casa de los Kindy. East of the Plazuela de Santo Domingo, this 19th-century home is known for its eclectic architecture, which mixes neoclassical and criollo elements. Note the elegant stained-glass over the front windows. It's now a private residence. ✉ *64 Calle Dr. Santiago Veve.*

Casa Morales. Facing Plazuela de Santo Domingo, this Victorian-style house was designed in 1913 by architect Pedro Vivoni for his brother, Tomás. The gleaming white structure has numerous towers and gables. The current owners have kept it in mint condition. It is not open to the public. ✉ *38 Calle Ramos.*

Casa Perichi (*Casa Ortiz Perichi*). You'll find an excellent example of Puerto Rican ornamental architecture in this elegant mansion, which sits a block south of Plazuela Santo Domingo. This gigantic white home, part of the San Germán Historic District, which is on the National Register of Historic Places, was built in 1920. Note the sensuous curves of the wraparound balcony and wood trim around the doors. It's not open to the public. ✉ *94 Calle Luna.*

Iglesia de San Germán de Auxerre. Dating from 1739, this neoclassical church has seen many additions over the years. For example, the impressive crystal chandelier imported from Barcelona was added in 1866. Be sure to take a look at the carved-wood ceiling in the nave. This church is still in use, so the only time you can get a look inside is during services. ✉ *West side of Plaza Francisco Mariano Quiñones* ☎ *787/892–1027* ⊙ *Mass Mon.–Sat. at 7 am and 7:30 pm and Sun. at 7, 8:30, 10 am, and 7:30 pm.*

Museo de Arte y Casa de Estudio. This early 20th-century home—built in the criollo style with some obvious neoclassical influences—has been turned into a museum. Displays include colonial furnishings, religious art, and artifacts of the indigenous peoples; there are also changing exhibits by local artists. ✉ *7 Calle Esperanza* ☎ *787/892–8870* 🔳 *Free* ⊙ *Wed.–Sun. 10–noon and 1–3.*

WHERE TO EAT

$ ✕ **Chaparritas.** On San Germán's main drag, this place certainly feels like
MEXICAN a traditional cantina. The Mexican food here is the real deal. Although you'll find some dishes that are more Tex than Mex, such as the cheesy nachos, the kitchen does best with more authentic tacos, burritos, and enchiladas. For something a bit unusual, try the shrimp fried in tequila. ⑤ *Average main: $12* ✉ *Calle Luna 171* ☎ *787/892–1078* ⊙ *Closed Sun.–Wed.*

$ ✕ **Tapas Café.** One of the biggest surprises in San Germán is this won-
SPANISH derful little restaurant facing Plaza Santo Domingo. The dining room looks like a Spanish courtyard, complete with blue stars swirling around the ceiling. Don't expect tiny portions just because the eatery serves tapas—several of the dishes, including the medallions of beef topped with a dab of blue cheese, could pass as full entrées anywhere. You'll find old favorites on the menu, including spicy sausage in red wine, but some new creations as well, such as the yam-and-codfish fritters.

$ Average main: $8 ⊠ 50 Calle Dr. Santiago Veve ☎ 787/264–0610 ⊘ Closed Mon.–Tues. No lunch Wed.–Thurs.

WHERE TO STAY

$

B&B/INN

⛯ **Villa del Rey.** On a quiet country road, Villa del Rey is set among banana and papaya trees, and this family-run inn couldn't be simpler, but it's clean and comfortable. **Pros:** decent pool and authentic ambience. **Cons:** could use an all around face-lift; rooms are slightly musty; no Internet; staff doesn't speak English. $ Rooms from: $90 ⊠ Rte. 361, Km 0.8, off Rte. 2 ☎ 787/642–2627, 787/642–2627 ⊕ www.villa delrey.net ⤳ 19 rooms, 2 suites ⚬ Breakfast.

RINCÓN AND THE
PORTA DEL SOL

WELCOME TO RINCÓN AND THE PORTA DEL SOL

TOP REASONS TO GO

★ **Visit El Combate:** Hike to the lighthouse at this peninsula, which juts out into the Caribbean Sea.

★ **Pamper yourself at the Horned Dorset Primavera:** Relax in your private plunge pool at perhaps the most romantic inn in the Caribbean.

★ **Please your palate at the "Golden Mile":** Sample fresh seafood at any of the dozens of oceanfront eateries in Joyuda.

★ **Catch a Wave at Playa Tres Palmas:** Challenge the waves here or at any of Rincón's world-famous surfing spots.

★ **Explore Desecheo Island or Mona Island:** Enjoy snorkeling, diving, or fishing around these spectacular islands.

1 Rincón. The first World Surfing Championships in 1968 put Rincón on the map, and its laid-back vibe and epic waves have kept it there. Paddle out to one of the town's 15 surf spots, or experience horseback riding on the beach and fishing in the crystal Caribbean waters. One of Rincón's greatest attractions is the diving and snorkeling at nearby Desecheo Island.

2 Mayagüez. Stroll the marble-paved square of Plaza Colón, where a statue of Christopher Columbus commemorates the site where he allegedly disembarked. Visit architectural gems such as Nuestra Señora de la Candelaria Cathedral, built in 1780, or experience an artistic performance at the Teatro Yagüez, which dates back to 1909. Savor the flavor of Mayagüez by sampling traditional *brazo gitano* ("gypsy arm") jelly rolls baked at the century-old Ricomini Bakery.

3 Cabo Rojo. Sample the island's freshest catch at Joyuda's Milla de Oro (Golden Mile), a string of more than 15 waterfront restaurants built on stilts. Slurp fresh oysters and clams from one of the many vendor carts lining the fishing town of Boquerón. Hike to the Cabo Rojo Lighthouse at Puerto Rico's southwestern tip.

4 The Northwestern Coast. The colorful fishing boats that line Playa Crashboat are a photographer's dream. Relax over a rum punch at an oceanfront bar while watching surfers get barreled at Jobos Beach. Explore the hidden waterfalls at Gozalandia, also known as El Charco de la Leche ("Puddle of Milk"), near San Sebastián.

0 — 4 mi
0 — 4 km

San Antonio ○   Isabela ○

Mora
○ 2

4 Playa Crashboat

Aguadilla ○   110   112

Bahía de Aguadilla   **C O R D I L L E R A**

Playa Domes   **Moca** ○   *J A I C O A*

Pta. Higüero   115   **Aguada** ○   110   111

Playa Tres Palmas

Rincón ○

← TO DESECHEO ISLAND

1 ○ **Córcega**

LA CADENA SAN FRANCISCO

Pta. Cadena   2   **Añasco** ○   109

108

Maní ○   *M O N T A Ñ A S   D E*

Estación Experimental de Agricultura Tropical ◆   *U R O Y A N*

2

Mayagüez ○   105   **Las Vegas** ○

Bahía de Mayagüez   *L A S   M E S A S*

Joyuda ○   2

Hormigueros ○   119

102   100

3   114   **San Germán** ○

Cabo Rojo ○   102

Pta. Caranero   *M O N T E   G R A N D E*

Pta. Guaniquilla   103   **Lajas** ○

Boquerón ○   101

Bahía de Boquerón   ◆ **Refugio de Vida Silvestre**

100

Bosque Estatal de Boquerón ◆   ○ **Pole Ojea**

← TO MONA ISLAND

Bahía Salinas   *Bahía Sucia*

El Combate   Cabo Rojo

GETTING ORIENTED

The speedy Highway 22 and the more meandering Highway 2 head west from San Juan and swing around the northwestern part of the island, skirting the beaches of the northern coast. A short 45 minutes from the capital you'll pass through the resort town of Dorado; after Arecibo, Highway 2 continues along the coast, where the ragged shoreline holds some of the island's best surfing beaches, and a steady contingent of surfers in Aguadilla and Rincón gives the area a laid-back atmosphere. Past Mayagüez, Highway 100 leads to an area known as Cabo Rojo, where you'll find seaside communities like Joyuda, Boquerón, and El Combate.

6

Updated by
Paulina Salach

The "Gateway to the Sun" is how tourism officials describe the island's western coast. Unlike the area around San Juan, the Porta del Sol is relatively undiscovered. Even around Rincón, which has the lion's share of the lodgings, the beaches are delightfully deserted. And in places like Aguadilla and Isabela, two sleepy towns on the northwestern corner of the island, it's easy to find a stretch of shoreline all to yourself.

Adventurers since the time of Christopher Columbus have been drawn to the jagged coastline of northwestern Puerto Rico. Columbus made his first stop here on his second voyage to the Americas in 1493. His exact landing point is the subject of ongoing dispute: both Aguadilla, on the northernmost tip of the coast, and Aguada, just south of Aguadilla, claim the historic landing, and both have monuments honoring the explorer.

Less than a century ago western Puerto Rico was still overwhelmingly rural. Some large fruit plantations dotted the coast, while farther inland coffee was grown on hillside *fincas* (farms). The slow pace of rural life began to change during the mid-20th century. New roads brought development to the once-isolated towns. They also brought international surfers, who were amazed to find some of the world's best waves in Rincón, Isabela, and Aguadilla. Now there are top-notch hotels, interesting natural areas to explore, and almost every kind of water sport imaginable.

RINCÓN AND THE PORTA DEL SOL PLANNER

WHEN TO GO
Winter weather is the best, and it's the height of the surfing season, so you'll need to book well in advance. Between December and March you might get a glimpse of the humpback whales that winter off the coast.

During the summer many family-oriented hotels fill up with *sanjuaneros* escaping the city for the weekend—some hotels require a two-night stay. Larger resorts normally drop their rates in summer by at least 10%. The weather gets hot, especially in August and September.

GETTING HERE AND AROUND

AIR TRAVEL

Aguadilla is a convenient gateway to western Puerto Rico, thanks to several daily international flights. United Airlines flies from Newark to Aguadilla, Spirit flies from Fort Lauderdale, and JetBlue has daily service from Orlando or New York–JFK to Aguadilla. Cape Air flies between San Juan and Mayagüez.

Transfers: There are no airport shuttles in either Aguadilla or Mayagüez. A taxi from either airport into town is about $10, but if you are going any farther, you should rent a car.

Airlines Cape Air ☎ *800/227–3247* ⊕ *www.flycapeair.com.* **JetBlue** ☎ *800/538–2583* ⊕ *www.jetblue.com.* **Spirit Airlines** ☎ *801/401–2200* **United Airlines** ☎ *800/525–0280* ⊕ *www.continental.com.*

BUS AND VAN TRAVEL

No easy network of buses links the towns in the Porta del Sol region of northwestern Puerto Rico. Some municipalities and private companies operate buses and large shared vans *(públicos)* that travel from one city to another, but schedules are loose. But if you're adventurous and not easily frustrated, it's possible to arrange for cheap transportation from San Juan to Aguadilla, Rincón, and Mayagüez, among other towns. Prices from terminal to terminal are set, but drivers may go to another destination if arranged beforehand.

Linea Sultana has vans from San Juan to Mayagüez. They also have service to Aguada, Aguadilla, Quebradillas, and Isabela; the price is about $30 per person.

Contacts Línea Sultana ☎ *787/765–9377, 787/767–5205.*

CAR TRAVEL

You really need a car to see northwestern Puerto Rico, especially the mountain area. The toll road, Highway 22, makes it easy to reach Arecibo from San Juan. Highway 22 turns into Highway 2 just after Arecibo, swings by the northwestern tip of the island, then heads south to Mayagüez. *See also the Ruta Panorámica chapter.*

TAXI TRAVEL

Taxis can be hailed near the main plaza in Mayagüez, but in the smaller towns they may be hard to come by. Check with your hotel or restaurant, and staff there may be able to call one for you.

ABOUT THE RESTAURANTS

If you like seafood, you're in the right place. Throughout northwestern Puerto Rico you'll find wonderful *criollo* (Puerto Rican creole) cuisine. Most local eateries serve deep-fried tapas, commonly called *frituras* (meaning "fritters"). Offering a break from fried food are dozens of foreign-owned eateries that serve everything from sushi and hamburgers to vegetarian and Thai cuisine. Farther south along the coast options are limited, so you may want to ask the chef to grill or sauté your fish. A trip to Puerto Rico is not complete without sampling Puerto Rico's most iconic dish, *mofongo relleno*, made from fried, seasoned and mashed plantain or yuca stuffed with your choice of seafood or meat. Simply head to where locals from all over the island go for fresh seafood—Joyuda. When it comes to beverages, locals usually drink rum and coke or mix it with fresh-squeezed orange or grapefruit juice. You'll also see people sipping on Medalla Light, Puerto Rico's most popular and affordable beer. All restaurants are no-smoking. Tips, normally 15%–20%, are usually not included in the bill, but it's always wise to double-check.

ABOUT THE HOTELS

The western part of the island near Rincón has a variety of hotels, from furnished villas geared toward families to beachfront hotels ideal for honeymooners. Interior design leaves much to be desired, however, as most rooms are decorated with faux wood, sun-bleached photographs, floral bedding, and white linoleum flooring. Fortunately, some of the newer accommodations resemble Spanish villas, a refreshing change from the typical 1970s decor. Surprisingly, the few hotels with Internet access only have it available in the common areas. Smaller beach cottages, especially in Rincón, usually have "adopted" dogs or cats roaming the premises, so guests with allergies may want to inquire ahead.

WHAT IT COSTS IN U.S. DOLLARS				
	$	$$	$$$	$$$$
Restaurants	$8–$12	$13–$20	$21–$30	over $30
Hotels	$80–$150	$151–$250	$251–$350	over $350

Restaurant prices are per person for a main course at dinner or, if dinner is not served, at lunch. Hotel prices are the lowest cost of a standard double room in high season.

SAFETY

Unless you're camping in a recreational area, it's best to go to forest reserves during daylight hours only. Outside metro areas there's little crime, but you should take normal precautions: Remember to lock your car, and don't leave valuables unattended.

For Surfers: The waves in the Rincón area range from gentle, low waves suitable for novice surfers to expert-only breaks. It's a good idea to talk with other surfers about which beaches would be suitable for your skill level. *See also the "Surfing" feature later in this chapter.*

TOUR OPTIONS

The Mayagüez-based AdvenTours offers bird-watching, biking, and kayaking trips. Rincón Vacations offers vacation-planning services; they'll help you book your entire stay.

Contact **AdvenTours** ✉ *1102 Calle Uroyán, Mayagüez* ☎ *787/530–8311* ⊕ *www.adventourspr.com*. **Rincón Vacations** ✉ *Rte. 414, Km 2, Rincón* ☎ *787/632–2889* ⊕ *www.rinconvacations.com*.

VISITOR INFORMATION

The Puerto Rico Tourism Company has an office at the airport in Aguadilla. The Cabo Rojo branch is open weekdays from 8 to 4:30. Rincón's tourism office is open weekdays from 8 to 4. Mayagüez has a tourism office in the city hall.

Contacts Cabo Rojo Tourism Office ✉ *Galleria 100, Calle 100, Km 7.6, Cabo Rojo* ☎ *787/851-7070*. **Isabela Tourism Office** ☎ *787/872-2100*. **Mayagüez City Hall** ✉ *8 McKinley St., Mayagüez* ☎ *787/834-8585*. **Puerto Rico Tourism Company** ✉ *Rafael Hernández Airport, 405 Hangar, Aguadilla* ☎ *787/890-3315* ⊕ *www.seepuertorico.com*. **Rincón Tourism Office** ✉ *Sunset Village, Calle Cambija, next to Balneario de Rincón, Rincón* ☎ *787/823-5024* ⊕ *www.rincon.org*.

RINCÓN

93 miles (150 km) southwest of San Juan.

6

Jutting out into the ocean along the rugged western coast, Rincón, meaning "corner" in Spanish, may have gotten its name because it's tucked into a bend of the coastline. Some, however, trace the town's name to Gonzalo Rincón, a 16th-century landowner who let poor families live on his land. Whatever the history, the name suits the town, which is like a little world unto itself.

The most famous hotel in the region is the Horned Dorset Primavera—the only Relais & Chateaux property in Puerto Rico. It's one of the most luxurious resorts on the island, not to mention in the Caribbean. A couple of larger hotels, including the Rincón of the Seas and Rincón Beach Resort, have been built, but Rincón remains a laid-back place. The town is still a mecca for wave-seekers, particularly surfers from the East Coast of the United States, who often prefer the relatively quick flight to Aguadilla airport direct from New York–area airports instead of the long haul to the Pacific. The town continues to cater to all sorts of travelers, from budget-conscious surfers to families to honeymooners seeking romance.

The pace picks up from October through April, when the waves are best, but tourists can be found here year-round, and many American mainlanders have settled here. Budget travelers will most likely find discount accommodations during August and September, when tourism is slow. Hurricane season runs from June through November, bringing in occasional swells for the surf crowd.

GETTING HERE AND AROUND

Rincón itself is a spread-out labyrinth of unmarked streets without any apparent logic to its layout. Built on a hillside, most streets are narrow and steep, weaving erratically through the intermingled residential-business zones. There are three main routes to keep in mind; Route 115 cuts through the middle of "downtown" (the administrative center) and

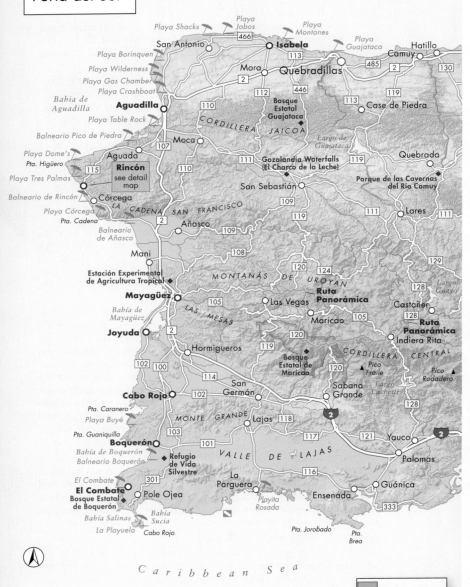

Rincón and Porta del Sol

Playa Shacks

Playa Jobos

466

Playa Montones

San Antonio

Playa Borinquen

Mora

Playa Guajataca

Camuy

Hatillo

Playa Wilderness

Playa Gas Chamber

Playa Crashboat

Isabela

Quebradillas

113

485

2

130

2

446

112

119

Bahía de Aguadilla

Aguadilla

110

CORDILLERA

Bosque Estatal Guajataca

113

Case de Piedra

JAICOA

Largo de Guajataca

Playa Table Rock

Balneario Pico de Piedra

107

Moca

111

Gozalandia Waterfalls (El Charco de la Leche)

119

Quebrada

Playa Dome's

Pta. Higüero

Aguada

Rincón

see detail map

110

San Sebastián

Parque de las Cavernas del Río Camuy

Playa Tres Palmas

115

Balneario de Rincón

Córcega

109

111

111

111

Lares

Playa Córcega

Pta. Cadena

LA CADENA

SAN FRANCISCO

Añasco

119

Balneario de Añasco

2

109

Mani

108

Estación Experimental de Agricultura Tropical

MONTAÑAS DE UROYAN

120

124

129

128

Mayagüez

105

Las Vegas

Ruta Panorámica

Largo Guayo

Bahía de Mayagüez

LAS MESAS

Maricao

105

Castañer

128

Joyuda

2

120

Ruta Panorámica

Indiera Rita

Hormigueros

119

CORDILLERA CENTRAL

102

100

Bosque Estatal de Maricao

120

Pico Fraile

Pico Rodadero

Cabo Rojo

114

San Germán

Sabana Grande

Largo Luchetti

128

Pta. Caranero

102

118

2

Playa Buyé

MONTE GRANDE

Lajas

Pta. Guaniquilla

Boquerón

103

101

117

121

Yauco

2

Bahía de Boquerón

VALLE DE LAJAS

Palomas

Balneario Boquerón

Refugio de Vida Silvestre

116

El Combate

301

La Parguera

Guánica

El Combate

Pole Ojea

Ensenada

Bosque Estatal de Boquerón

Playita Rosada

333

Bahía Salinas

Bahía Sucia

La Playuela

Cabo Rojo

Pta. Jorobado

Pta. Brea

C a r i b b e a n   S e a

0 _____ 6 mi

0 _____ 6 km

connects north to Aguadilla airport and south to Mayagüez airport. Route 413 snakes the hillsides, past villas and local restaurants. The smaller Route 4413 parallels the water, past Punta Higüeras Lighthouse, and ends at the Bonus Thermonuclear Energy Plant.

AIR TRAVEL

San Juan's International Airport is the most commonly used on the island and is approximately two hours from Rincón. The closest airports however, are in Mayagüez and in Aguadilla, only 20 minutes' drive in either direction. A taxi from either airport into town costs around $10, but the best option is to rent a car at the airport.

BUS AND VAN TRAVEL

Amigos Tours & Travel has private transfers from Aguadilla's airport to Rincón and to most hotels in the Porta del Sol for $80 per van (limit five passengers).

Amigos Tours & Travel ☎ 787/826–6418 ⊕ *www.amigostours.net.*

CAR TRAVEL

To reach Rincón from San Juan, take Highway 22, which becomes Highway 2 after Arecibo. Follow it past the northwestern tip of the island, just beyond Aguadilla. Take the 115 southwest past Aguada until you reach Rincón's Route 413, "The Road to Happiness."

TIMING

With a land area of 14 square miles (36 square km), Rincón is easily traversable in an afternoon. Nevertheless, to fully embrace its laid-back surfer vibe you'll want to allocate three to five days for surfing, diving, fishing, or just relaxing at the beach.

EXPLORING RINCÓN

Tres Palmas. On a handful of days each year, this epic wave is one of the world's best, drawing surfers from around the globe. On calm days, it's an excellent snorkeling spot and is home to the Tres Palmas Marine Reserve. From the shore, the sand drops about five feet and gives way to clear waters filled with tropical fish and brain coral. It is a great place to spend the day or watch the sunset. It is on the same road as Steps (*see below*). ⊠ *Rte. 413, north of turnoff for Black Eagle Marina.*

WORTH NOTING

Desecheo Island. For divers, Desecheo Island, about 13 miles (20 km) off the coast of Rincón, has abundant reef and fish life. Protected by the U.S. Fish and Wildlife Service, this uninhabited island is home to lizards, rats, and Rhesus monkeys, first introduced in 1967 from Cayo Santiago. The main draw here is "Candy Land," a rocky bottom sloping to 120 feet that rims the island. Here long tunnels and caverns covered with purple hydrocoral distinguish one formation known as Yellow Reef. With visibility of 150 feet, this is also a popular snorkeling spot. There are other sites with plentiful fish and coral in the more shallow water just off Rincón's shores.

Looking down at Domes Beach from Punta Higüeras Lighthouse in El Faro Park.

OFF THE BEATEN PATH

Gozalandia Waterfalls. About 45 minutes east of Rincón, just north of San Sebastián, are these hidden waterfalls also known as El Charco de la Leche (The Pool of Milk). Though difficult to find, the tiered swimming holes are worth the effort it takes to get there. The first of the three is generally visited by locals, but a five-minute hike upstream will bring you to a second cascade, where the waters are deep enough for diving. A crude rope swing entices adventurers to mimic Tarzan's antics before plunging into the cool spring. Follow the trail about ½ mile (1 km) farther to reach yet a third oasis. From Rincón, take Route 115 northeast to Route 111 east. Near San Sebastián, take the 446 north and continue ½ mile (1 km). Turn right over the bridge and follow the road up about a mile. On the left you will see two gates. One has "No Parking" signs on it and the other looks like an entrance to a park with a cement-paved driveway. Go around the larger gate and follow the driveway down to some mud pathways that will lead you to the waterfalls. ✉ Off Rte. 111, San Sebastian 🚗 $5 parking.

BEACHES

The waves of northwestern Puerto Rico have long served as a siren song for traveling surfers. Spared the trade winds that can limit surf in other areas, the northwest's beaches have some of the best waves in the world, especially in winter. But you don't have to be a big-wave rider to enjoy the beaches of the northwest.

The best beaches north of Rincón are lined up along Route 413 and Route 4413 (the road to the lighthouse). South of town the only beach worth noting is Playa Córcega, off Route 115. As with many other

GREAT ITINERARIES

IF YOU HAVE 1 DAY

If you have only a day to spend in the Porta del Sol, make the drive to **Joyuda** for some of Puerto Rico's freshest seafood. You probably won't be the only ones driving from San Juan for this feast.

IF YOU HAVE 3 DAYS

If you have a few days to explore the region, start in **Rincón**, where you'll find accommodations for every taste, from compact inns to sprawling resorts. There isn't too much to see, other than the lighthouse at Parque Pasivo El Faro, but you will see plenty of beautiful beaches. Most have been discovered, however. If you crave complete solitude, you're more likely to find empty beaches in the communities of **Aguadilla** or **Isabela**. On Day 2, drive south to the coastal communities in the Cabo Rojo. Your first stop should be **Joyuda**, where you can choose from dozens of seaside restaurants. After lunch, continue past **Boquerón** to **El Combate**. This is the end of the line, quite literally. The road ends at the lighthouse that once warned sea captains about the treacherous waters around the island's southwestern tip. On Day 3 you can explore more of this windswept landscape, or head offshore for a look at Mona Island.

IF YOU HAVE 5 DAYS

After spending three days along the western coast, you may be tempted to set sail to one of the islands off the coast. On Day 4, head out on an overnight trip to **Mona Island**, a 14,000-acre paradise known as the "Galápagos of the Caribbean." You'll have to camp on this deserted island, but the view from the 200-foot cliffs on the northern shore makes it all worth it. Trips to Mona Island must be arranged weeks in advance.

6

beaches in the Caribbean, there are often urchins, riptides, undertows, and rocky reefs below the surface. Never swim alone.

Balneario de Rincón. Swimmers enjoy the tranquil waters at this beach. There's a playground for the kids and shelters where families can enjoy seaside picnics. The beach is within walking distance of the center of town. **Amenities:** parking (free); showers; toilets. **Best for:** sunset; swimming. ⊠ *Calle Caubija.*

Domes. Named for the eerie green domes on a nearby power plant, this beach is extremely popular with surfers, with its consistent rights and occasional lefts. On a good surf day, arrive early if you want a spot on the sand. Although not recommended for swimmers because of the rocks, it's a great whale-watching spot in winter. The dirt road leading to the parking area is rather steep and difficult to exit. There are no facilities here, so plan accordingly. **Amenities:** none. **Best for:** surfing. ⊠ *Rte. 4413, north of the lighthouse.*

Maria's. This surf spot, south of Domes, can get crowded when the waves are high. When waves are small, surf lessons are generally taught here. It's popular with locals, as much for its breaks as for its proximity to the Calypso Café. To get here, look for the street sign reading

"Surfer crossing." **Amenities:** none. **Best for:** surfing; sunsets. ⊠ *Rte. 4413, south of the lighthouse.*

Playa Córcega. The long stretch of yellow sand in front of Villa Cofresí is considered one of the best swimming beaches in Rincón. It's the perfect beach for relaxing and stand-up paddleboarding. **Amenities:** none. **Best for:** swimming; walking. ⊠ *Rte. 115, Km 12.0.*

Steps. A set of concrete steps sitting mysteriously at the water's edge gives this beach its name. The waves, breaking on a shallow reef, can get huge. On a calm day, the snorkeling here is wonderful. This is also a good place to find sea glass. It's hard to find—look for the turnoff at a whale-shaped sign indicating "Playa Escalera." **Amenities:** none. **Best for:** snorkeling; sunsets. ⊠ *Rte. 413, north of turnoff for Black Eagle Marina.*

WHERE TO EAT

Use the coordinate (✛ A1) at the end of each listing to locate a site on the corresponding "Where to Eat and Stay in Rincón" map.

$
CAFÉ

✕ **Banana Dang.** "Think, Drink, Link" is the motto of this Internet café, where you can check e-mails while drinking one of the specialty coffees. The fruit smoothies are a local favorite, as are the light breakfasts of veggie paninis, bagels with cream cheese, and pastries like cranberry teacake and carrot muffins. As part of their "green initiative," the owners serve locally grown coffee and utilize compostable cups. [$] *Average main: $5* ⊠ *Rte. 413, Km 4.1* ☎ *787/823–0963* ⊕ *www.bananadang. com* ☿ *Closed Tues.* ✛ *B2.*

$$
GERMAN
Fodor'sChoice
★

✕ **Das Alpen.** Granted, it's not traditional Puerto Rican fare nor does it have anything to do with the local culture, but the authentic German food at this restaurant will make you feel as if you're on a vacation from your vacation. Owner Jacob Elmstrom—of German descent—has gone to great lengths to recreate the flavors of Deutschland. Everything is homemade, including the *bratwurst* (sausage), *sauerbraten* (beef marinated in red wine), and *kasseler rippchen* (smoked pork chops). All the classics are served with red cabbage, bread dumplings, or *spätzle*. The *schnitzels* (there are three types) are ridiculously flavorful, and there are plenty of imported beers to wash down the goodness. As much as locals love the German cuisine, they also come for the Italian dishes like pumpkin ravioli or sausage tagliatelle, all made from scratch. Of course a meal wouldn't be complete without hot apple strudel. If you happen to be in Rincón during the month of October, Das Alpen celebrates *oktoberfest.* [$] *Average main: $20* ⊠ *Calle Muñoz Rivera, Corner of Calle Comercio* ☎ *787/233–8009* ⊕ *www.dasalpencafe.com* ☿ *Closed Mon. and Tues. No lunch* ✛ *B4.*

$
CAFÉ

✕ **The English Rose.** Open just for breakfast, this quaint bed-and-breakfast has a spectacular view of the valley spilling into the sea. House specialties such as eggs Benedict are served with homemade breads and sausages. The BBC, a toasted croissant topped with organic chicken, cranberry sausage, poached egg, and hollandaise sauce, is quite popular. But we can't stop thinking about the Portobello Road, made with roasted portobello mushroom, smoked Gouda, thick-cut Black Forest ham, cherry tomato confit on a fresh-baked croissant. If terrace seating is not available, inside dining is equally charming with the walls colorfully decorated with work by local artisans. Adding to the freshness of the dishes are the herbs grown on-site. During high season, you may wait up to an hour for a table, so reservations are recommended. ■TIP➜ **English Rose is BYOB. Bring some vodka or your favorite champagne to spike one of the fresh juices or make a mimosa.** Ⓢ *Average main: $10* ✉ *Rte. 413, Km 2, Barrio Ensenada* ☎ *787/823–4032* ⊕ *www.larosainglesa.com* ⊙ *Closed Sep. and Oct; Closed Mon.–Wed. May–Aug.* ✛ *B2.*

$$$
CARIBBEAN

✕ **Francisco's Caribbean Local Cuisine @ The Lazy Parrot.** This open-air terrace restaurant highlights the impossibly lush greenery that draws so many people to Rincón. Located on the second floor of the Lazy Parrot Hotel, it catches a breeze even when the rest of the island is stifling in the heat. For dinner there are tropical entrées like fresh wahoo with papaya, ceviche of the day, and plantain-wrapped marinated salmon. Meat lovers will enjoy the grilled *churrasco* steak with rice and beans and *mojo isleño*. You can also head downstairs to Mi Familia's Pizzeria for gourmet, brick-oven pizza. Ⓢ *Average main: $22* ✉ *The Lazy Parrot Hotel, Rte. 413, Km 4.1* ☎ *787/823–0101, 800/294–1752* ⊕ *www. lazyparrot.com* ⊙ *Closed May–Oct.* ✛ *B2.*

$$$
CARIBBEAN

✕ **La Copa Llena at The Black Eagle.** Set right on the beach, La Copa Llena is the newest restaurant to open its doors at The Black Eagle, an iconic property dating back to 1969. For decades, the location has drawn patrons from all over the island for its spectacular sunsets. Today the sunsets seen from the outdoor terrace are just as beautiful as they were in the '70s, and the cuisine, a mixture of French, Spanish, Southwest, and Mediterranean, is well executed. Brendan Basham, former chef of The Tapas Bar, maintains strict standards of quality, so the menu might change, depending on availability of ingredients. Start with the smaller plates like the chorizo and Manchego on toasted baguette or the char-grilled octopus. Move on to the coconut steamed mussels or the fried snapper with sweet papaya salsa. We also tried the BLT on artisan brioche and it was, hands down, one of the best we've ever had. Must have been the house-cured Berkshire pork belly. Don't miss happy hour from 3 to 7. Brunch is served on Sunday. Ⓢ *Average main: $25* ✉ *Rte. 413, Km 1.0, Ensenada, Black Eagle Rd.* ☎ *787/823–0896* ⊕ *www.attheblackeagle.com* ⊙ *Closed Mon. Closed Aug.–Oct. No lunch* ✛ *B3.*

$
THAI

✕ **Ode to The Elephants.** Tucked away on a hilltop, Ode to The Elephants offers a wonderful selection of reasonably priced Thai dishes. The main courses have a one-to-five-star spice rating ranging from mild to very hot. If you choose too boldly, the server will bring over a surprisingly tasty milk-based tea that will magically bring your taste buds back to normal. Most dishes can be served with either chicken, vegetable, shrimp, or tofu. There is both indoor and outdoor seating on the wooden deck. Co-owner Clay Burnsed is a master martini mixologist. His love for the craft shines through in his well-balanced, creative martinis. Choose from cucumber, ginger tea, watermelon, and

6

piña colada. The special during our visit was the mandarin martini with fresh-squeezed juice and passion-fruit rum—a spectacular cocktail! Reservations are not accepted for parties fewer than 10, and weekends get packed. Stop in on Thursday night for $5 martinis. ■TIP➜ For your main dish, go for the daily special. ⑤ *Average main: $12* ⊠ *Calle Vista Linda, Barrio Puntas* ☎ *939/697–8033* ⊕ *www.odetotheelephants.com* ☉ *Closed Tues. and Wed. No lunch* ✛ *B1.*

$ × **The Pool Bar Sushi.** One of only a few sushi restaurants on the west
JAPANESE   coast, the open-air Pool Bar attracts visitors from as far away as San
Fodor'sChoice   Juan. The menu rivals that of any high-end Japanese restaurant, with
★   mango tuna rolls, eel maki, dim sum, and wakame seaweed salads. A house favorite is the Starving Surfer Roll of crunchy shrimp and avocado topped with spicy tuna. They also have an awesome lunch grill menu that serves fish tacos, salads, and burgers. The relaxed setting is especially popular with surfers drawn by the nightly surf flicks projected on the movie-screen backdrop. ⑤ *Average main: $9* ⊠ *Pools Beach Cabanas, Rte. 413* ☎ *787/823–2583* ⊕ *www.poolbarsushi.com* ☉ *Closed Tues. No lunch* ✛ *A1.*

$$$$ × **Restaurant Aaron at the Horned Dorset Primavera.** A pair of stone stair-
CARIBBEAN   ways leads up to Restaurant Aaron's elegant dining room, with black-and-white marble floors, chandeliers with ruby-red shades, and a Steinway piano dating back to 1901. Dessert and after-dinner drinks are often served on the terrace, where you'll hear the constant crash of the waves. The 7-course tasting menu, an extravagant meal with a $125 price tag, might include foie gras with maple berry glaze, pan-seared scallops with asparagus risotto, or poached *chillo* (red snapper) with apricot gnocchi. Adding Caribbean accents to classical French cuisine, the à la carte menu changes weekly but might include roasted rack of lamb and wahoo (a kind of mackerel) in a pistachio crust. Dress is formal by island standards, except in the downstairs "Blue Room" dining area, where a similar menu is served. Lunch is served outside, on the terrace. ⑤ *Average main: $36* ⊠ *Horned Dorset Primavera, Rte. 429, Km 3* ☎ *787/823–4030* ⊕ *www.horneddorset. com* ⌂ *Reservations essential* ☉ *Closed Mon.–Wed. Apr.–Nov.* ✛ *C6.*

$$ × **Rincón Tropical.** Don't be scared off by the cheap plastic tables and
PUERTO RICAN   chairs. What you should notice is that they are almost always full of locals enjoying the area's freshest seafood. The kitchen keeps it simple, preparing dishes with the lightest touch. Highlights include mahimahi with onions and peppers as well as fried red snapper with rice and bean and octopus salad. Fried plantains make a nice accompaniment to almost anything. Stop by weekdays for the affordable lunch special. ⑤ *Average main: $15* ⊠ *Rte. 115, Km 12* ☎ *787/823–2017* ⊕ *www. rinconpr.com/rincontropical* ✛ *B4.*

$$$ × **Saltaire Restaurant.** Saltaire is the newest venture by Executive Chef
ECLECTIC   Christopher Klos, who gained recognition for heading the kitchen at
FAMILY   the Lazy Parrot. Chef Klos prepares gourmet dishes in a casual setting that are seasonally and locally inspired. The fish changes daily, depending on what was caught that morning. The snapper is excellent, as is the octopus salad. The pastas and breads are homemade, and vegan—as well as raw—dishes are available with prior notice. If you

crave suckling pig, call at least three days ahead and put in your order. Don't miss the opportunity to dine at this lovely eatery; you will be pleasantly surprised. $ *Average main: $24* ⊠ *Casa Verde Hotel, Rte. 413, Km. 4.5, Barrio Puntas* ☎ *787/823–3756* ☉ *No lunch. Closed Mon.* ✛ *B1*

$$$ ╳ **Shipwreck Bar & Grill.** This pirate-theme restaurant has a laid-back vibe
CARIBBEAN and a friendly staff that's always ready with a smile or a joke. Don't be surprised to see local fishermen making their way to the kitchen with their still-flapping catch, attesting to the freshness of the food. Main dishes include juicy steaks, grilled mahimahi, homemade pastas, and skewered pork. Although portions are large, lighter-fare options include fish tacos, various wraps, and seared ahi served on a pyramid of mixed greens. Don't miss the daily happy hour from 3 to 7 or the Sunday afternoon pig roast, offered November to April. $ *Average main: $22* ⊠ *Black Eagle Marina, Black Eagle Rd., off Rte. 413* ☎ *787/823–0578* ⊕ *www.rinconshipwreck.com* ☉ *No lunch May–Oct.* ✛ *B3.*

$$ ╳ **Tamboo.** Here is a bar and grill that doesn't fall too far into either
CARIBBEAN category. The kitchen prepares a wide range of unique items, from king-crab sandwiches to baby-back ribs brushed with guava sauce. Despite the laid-back atmosphere, the food presentation is fit for a high-end restaurant. The open-air bar serves a mean mojito. The deck is a great place to watch novice surfers wipe out on the nearby beach. On weekends, you can enjoy live music. $ *Average main: $16* ⊠ *Beside the Pointe, Rte. 413, Km 4.4* ☎ *787/823–8550* ⊕ *www.besidethepointe. com* ☉ *Closed Sept.* ✛ *A1.*

WHERE TO STAY

Use the coordinate (✛ A1) at the end of each listing to locate a site on the corresponding "Where to Eat and Stay in Rincón" map.

$ ⛿ **Beside the Pointe.** This perennial favorite sits right on Sandy Beach,
HOTEL where the waves are big but not too large for novice surfers. **Pros:** Social atmosphere; popular restaurant; great views. **Cons:** Noise from restaurant; not all rooms have ocean views; no elevator. $ *Rooms from: $140* ⊠ *Rte. 413, Km 4.4* ☎ *787/823–8550* ⊕ *www.besidethepointe.com* ⤳ *7 rooms, 2 apartments* ☉ *Closed Sept.* ❍|*No meals* ✛ *A1.*

$$ ⛿ **Blue Boy Inn.** A walled garden that surrounds this little inn makes you
B&B/INN think you're miles away from civilization. **Pros:** gorgeous gardens and pool; use of common kitchen; extremely private. **Cons:** not on beach; some noise from nearby restaurant. $ *Rooms from: $200* ⊠ *556 Black Eagle Rd., off Rte. 413* ☎ *787/823–2593* ⊕ *www.blueboyinn.com* ⤳ *8 rooms* ☉ *Closed Sept.* ❍|*Breakfast* ✛ *B3.*

$$ ⛿ **Casa Isleña.** With its barrel-tiled roofs, wall-enclosed gardens, and
B&B/INN open-air dining room, Casa Isleña might remind well-traveled souls of a villa on the coast of Mexico. **Pros:** beautiful beach; friendly staff; waking distance to great restaurants; daily yoga offered. **Cons:** books up quickly; somewhat dated rooms. $ *Rooms from: $165* ⊠ *Rte. 413, Km 4.8, Barrio Puntas* ☎ *787/823–1525, 888/289–7750* ⊕ *www.casa-islena.com* ⤳ *9 rooms* ❍|*Breakfast* ✛ *B1.*

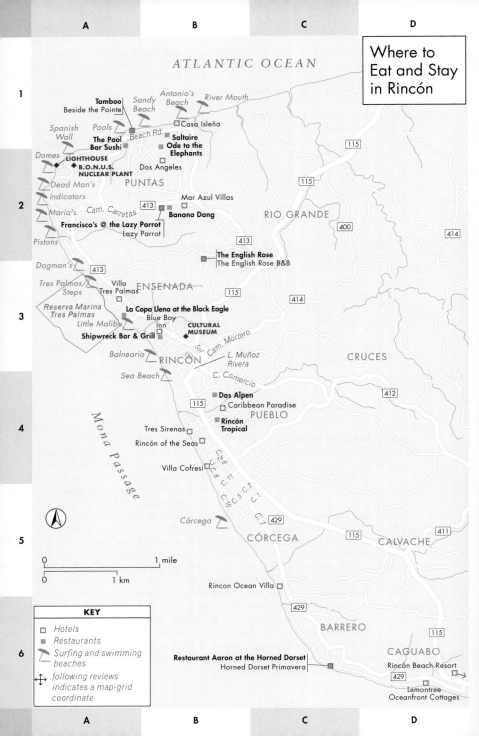

Where to Eat and Stay in Rincón

ATLANTIC OCEAN

A
B
C
D

1

Sandy Beach
Antonio's Beach
River Mouth

Tamboo
Beside the Pointe

Pools
Casa Isleña

Spanish Wall

Beach Rd.

The Pool Bar Sushi
Saltaire
Ode to the Elephants

Domes
LIGHTHOUSE
◆ B.O.N.U.S. NUCLEAR PLANT

Dos Angeles

115

Dead Man's

PUNTAS

Indicators

Mar Azul Villas

115

2

Maria's
Cam. Carretas
413
Banana Dang

RIO GRANDE

Pistons

Francisco's @ the Lazy Parrot
Lazy Parrot

400

115

414

Dogman's
413

The English Rose
The English Rose B&B

Tres Palmas/ Steps

Villa Tres Palmas

ENSENADA

115

414

Reserva Marina Tres Palmas

La Copa Llena at the Black Eagle
Blue Boy

3

Little Malibu

Inn

CULTURAL MUSEUM

Sol Cam. Mortero

Shipwreck Bar & Grill

CRUCES

Balneario

RINCÓN

L. Muñoz Rivera

Sea Beach

C. Comercio

412

Das Alpen
Caribbean Paradise

PUEBLO

115

Rincón Tropical

4

Tres Sirenas
Rincón of the Seas

Mona Passage

Villa Cofresi
C. 14
C. 8
C. 11
C. 10
C. 5
C. 2
C. 1

Córcega
429

5

CÓRCEGA

115

CALVACHE

411

0   1 mile
0   1 km

Rincon Ocean Villa

429

KEY

□ Hotels
■ Restaurants

Surfing and swimming beaches

BARRERO

115

following reviews indicates a map-grid coordinate

CAGUABO

Restaurant Aaron at the Horned Dorset
Horned Dorset Primavera

Rincón Beach Resort

6

429

Lemontree Oceanfront Cottages

A
B
C
D

$
B&B/INN

Dos Angeles del Mar. On a quiet hillside overlooking the ocean, this no-frills guesthouse is about as clean and comfortable as it gets. **Pros:** friendly staff; great breakfast; peaceful haven. **Cons:** morning rooster crows; uphill climb from the beach. ⑤ *Rooms from: $129 ⊠ Calle Vista del Mar ☎787/823–1378, 787/431–6057 ⊕ www.dosangelesdelmar. com ➾ 5 rooms ⧖Breakfast ✦ B2.*

$
B&B/INN

The English Rose. Nestled in the hills of Rincón, this bed-and-breakfast has some of the best views of the Caribbean ocean. **Pros:** excellent breakfast; peaceful setting; hospitable owners. **Cons:** somewhat isolated; no beach; restaurant serves breakfast only; closed September and October. ⑤ *Rooms from: $130 ⊠ Rte. 413, Km 2, Barrio Ensenada ☎787/823–4032 ⊕ www.larosainglesa.com ➾ 3 apartments ☺ Closed Sept. and Oct. ⧖Breakfast ✦ B2.*

$$$$
RESORT
Fodor's Choice
★

Horned Dorset Primavera. This is, without a doubt, the most luxurious hotel in Puerto Rico. **Pros:** unabashed luxury; unmatched meals; lovely setting; pet-friendly; beautiful decor; yoga "treehouse." **Cons:** on a very narrow beach; long staircase to some villas. ⑤ *Rooms from: $770 ⊠ Rte. 429, Km 3 ☎787/823–4030, 800/633–1857 ⊕ www. horneddorset.com ➾ 17 villas ⧖Multiple meal plans ✦ C6.*

$
HOTEL

The Lazy Parrot. Painted in eye-popping tropical hues, this mountainside hotel doesn't take itself too seriously. **Pros:** economy rooms available; tropical setting; microwaves in rooms. **Cons:** not on the beach; stairs to climb; some may consider the whimsical style tacky. ⑤ *Rooms from: $135 ⊠ Rte. 413, Km 4.1 ☎787/823–5654, 800/294–1752 ⊕ www.lazyparrot.com ➾ 21 rooms ⧖Breakfast ✦ B2.*

$$
HOTEL

Lemontree Oceanfront Cottages. Sitting right on the beach, this pair of lemon-yellow buildings holds six apartments named after fruits such as Mango, Cocoa, Banana, and Piña. **Pros:** far from the crowds; on-call massage therapist; spacious balconies. **Cons:** beach is very narrow; you have to drive to reach shops and restaurants; no elevator. ⑤ *Rooms from: $155 ⊠ Rte. 429, Km 4.1 ☎787/823–6452 ⊕ www.lemontreepr. com ➾ 6 apartments ⧖No meals ✦ D6.*

$
RENTAL

Mar Azul Villas. Set in a tropical garden behind Mar Azul Surf Shop, these charming little apartments have all the comforts of home. **Pros:** spotless rooms; friendly owners; walking distance to restaurants; best surf shop in Rincón. **Cons:** limited ocean view; foot traffic from attached surf shop. ⑤ *Rooms from: $95 ⊠ Rte. 413, Km 4.4 ☎787/214–7224, 787/823–5692 ⊕ www.puertoricosurfinginfo.com ➾ 2 apartments ⧖No meals ✦ B2.*

$$$
RESORT

Rincón Beach Resort. It's a bit off the beaten path, but that's part of the allure of this oceanfront resort. **Pros:** beautiful pool area; laidback vibe; children's playground. **Cons:** far from restaurants; decor is slightly dated; halls echo. ⑤ *Rooms from: $260 ⊠ Rte. 115, Km 5.8, Añasco ☎787/589–9000 ⊕ www.rinconbeach.com ➾ 112 rooms ⧖No meals ✦ D6.*

$$
RESORT
FAMILY

Rincón of the Seas. Tucked at the end of a palm-lined drive, this high-rise hotel feels as if it could be in Miami Beach. **Pros:** lush gardens; gorgeous pool area; Wi-Fi in common areas. **Cons:** on a slender beach; loud music blares from pool area all day; rooms need a makeover.

$ *Rooms from: $165* ⊠ *Rte. 115, Km 12.2* ☎ *787/823–7500* ⊕ *www. rinconoftheseas.com* ⤷ *112 rooms* ⦿ *No meals* ✛ *B4.*

$$
B&B/INN
Fodor's Choice
★

▦ **Tres Sirenas.** Waves gently lap against the shores at this boutique inn named "Three Mermaids" in honor of the owners' daughters. **Pros:** in-room massages; spotless and tastefully decorated, discounted rates May through October. **Cons:** usually booked; set breakfast hour; Wi-Fi signal occasionally drops. $ *Rooms from: $230* ⊠ *26 Seabeach Dr.* ☎ *787/823–0558* ⊕ *www.tressirenas.com* ⤷ *2 rooms, 1 studio, 2 apartments* ⦿ *Breakfast* ✛ *B4.*

$$
HOTEL
FAMILY

▦ **Villa Cofresí.** On one of the best swimming beaches in town, Villa Confresí is Rincón's oldest hotel, making it extremely popular with Puerto Rican families. **Pros:** good restaurant; family-friendly environment. **Cons:** standard rooms lack ocean views; not enough parking; lots of noise from pool area. $ *Rooms from: $155* ⊠ *Rte. 115, Km 12* ☎ *787/823–2450* ⊕ *www.villacofresi.com* ⤷ *107 rooms* ⦿ *Breakfast* ✛ *B4.*

VILLA RENTALS

Villa rentals are becoming more and more popular in Rincón. Because many people come here for a week or more to surf, find a secluded spot on the beach, or just hang out, renting a villa makes perfect sense. Guests can make the place their own, without worrying about the noise from the kids bothering the people in the next room or leaving sandy shoes outside the door. In the long run, it might also be a money saver for those who cook at home rather than dine out. There are several local chefs who will prepare gourmet dinners for large groups in private villas.

A few things to keep in mind: If you're looking for a secluded location, you won't find it on this crowded part of the coast. It's likely that your neighbor will be within shouting distance. In addition, few villas are actually on the ocean, and the ones that are go for a premium price. Many are within walking distance of the water, but some will require that you drive to reach the shore. If a beachfront location is important to you, make sure to specify. And where you stay will depend on whether or not you're a surfer. Those who like to ride the waves favor the northern coast, while those who want to snorkel, scuba dive, or swim prefer the calmer southern shore.

Island West Properties. This office can help you rent villas in Rincón by the day, week, or month. The company has been around for years, so it corners the market. ⊠ *Rte. 413, Km 0.7* ☎ *787/823–2323* ⊕ *www. islandwestrentals.com.*

$$$
RENTAL

▦ **Caribbean Paradise.** This two-story house is great for two families traveling together, as each floor has plenty of room, and there is a fenced yard where children can play. **Pros:** on the beach; nearby dining. **Cons:** no pool. $ *Rooms from: $325* ⊠ *Calle 8, Corsega Beach* ☎ *787/823–2323* ⊕ *www.islandwestrentals.com* ⤷ *4 rooms, 3 baths* ⦿ *No meals* ✛ *B4.*

$$$$
RENTAL

▦ **Rincón Ocean Villa.** This 10-bedroom villa has served as a vacation home for the rich and famous, including country star Shania Twain. **Pros:** beautiful pool; sleeps 26 guests; private bath in each room; wait staff included. **Cons:** small gym; courtyard marble gets slippery with rain; this public beach might see weekend traffic. ⑤ *Rooms from: $2,500 ⊠ Rte. 429, Km 1.4* ☎ *787/925-6600* ⊕ *www.rinconoceanvilla. com* ⟿ *10 rooms* ⓞⓘ *No meals* ⚓ *C5.*

$$$$ ⬚ **Villa Tres Palmas.** Not all beach houses are created equal, as Villas Tres
RENTAL Palmas makes clear. **Pros:** full kitchen; near many good restaurants; great location for surfers. **Cons:** only the bedrooms have air-conditioning; not on a bathing beach. ⑤ *Rooms from: $790 ⊠ Off Rte. 413, Playa Tres Palmas* ☎ *787/539-3519* ⊕ *www.trespalmasinnandvillas. com* ⟿ *6 bedrooms, 5 baths* ⓞⓘ *No meals* ⚓ *A3.*

NIGHTLIFE

Rincón attracts a younger crowd, so there are plenty of options for fun after dark.

Calypso Café. On weekends the Calypso Café often has live music. The open-air establishment has daily sunset happy hour and is a good place to grab fresh ceviche, grilled fish, or a juicy burger after you've had your fill of the beach. They have the coldest beers in town. ⊠ *Maria's Beach, Rte. 4413* ☎ *787/823–1626.*

Tamboo. A beachfront, casual restaurant by day, Tamboo Tavern turns into a fun, loud hang out at night. ⊠ *Beside the Pointe, Rte. 413, Km 4.4* ☎ *787/823–8550* ⊕ *www.besidethepointe.com.*

SHOPPING

Playa Oeste. Playa Oeste has an eclectic collection of surf art, jewelry, clothing, and pottery. Paintings and photographs can be shipped directly to your home. ⊠ *Rte. 413, Km 0.5* ☎ *787/823–4424* ⊕ *www. playaoestegallery.com* ☉ *Closed Mon. Closed Mon.–Wed. Jun.–Aug.*

SPORTS AND THE OUTDOORS

DIVING AND SNORKELING

Most of the region's dive operators also run fishing charters around Desecheo Island and whale-watching trips in season.

Taíno Divers. Taíno Divers has all-day snorkeling and diving trips that cost $89 and $129, including lunch. It also offers daily trips to Desecheo Island, winter whale-watching trips, and scuba certification courses. ⊠ *Black Eagle Marina, Black Eagle Rd., off Rte. 413* ☎ *787/823–6429* ⊕ *www.tainodivers.com.*

HORSEBACK RIDING

Pintos R Us. Pintos R Us has two-hour horseback riding tours along the beach to the lighthouse, as well as full-moon tours and riding lessons. The horses are spirited but gentle enough for newcomers. Reservations are a must. ⊠ *Rte. 413, Km. 4.7* ☎ *787/516–7090* ⊕ *www. pintosrus.com.*

6

SAILING

Katarina Sail Charters. Set sail in the morning for a day in the sun, or in the late afternoon for unobstructed sunset views, with Katarina Sail Charters. The catamaran sails from Black Eagle Marina, except from mid-August to mid-November, during hurricane season. ✉ *Black Eagle Marina, Black Eagle Rd., off Rte. 413* ☎ *787/823–7245* ⊕ *www. sailrinconpuertorico.com.*

Rincón Sailing. Rincón Sailing has introductory courses and race clinics that cover handling, strategy, tactics, and tuning. For those who know how to sail, the shop rents Lasers, Sunfish, and Optimists. Four-hour lessons start at $120. Call to reserve a spot in one of their weekly courses. ☎ *787/421–4700* ⊕ *www.rinconsailing.com.*

SURFING

Desecheo Surf & Dive Shop. Desecheo Surf & Dive Shop rents snorkeling equipment, Boogie boards, and a variety of short and long surfboards. The company also has a small shop with swimwear, sandals, sunglasses, and surf gear. ✉ *Rte. 413, Km 2.5* ☎ *787/823–0390* ⊕ *www. desecheosurfshop.com.*

Mar Azul. Mar Azul has Rincón's best selection of performance surfboards and stand-up paddleboards to buy or rent. Paddleboard lessons are also available. This is one of the best surf shops on the entire island. ✉ *Rte. 413, Km 4.4* ☎ *787/823–5692* ⊕ *www.puertoricosurfinginfo.com.*

Puntas Surf School. With more than a decade of surf-coaching experience, Puntas is the only surf school in Rincón with female instructors. ☎ *787/366–1689* ⊕ *www.puntassurfschool.com.*

Rincón Surf School. Rincón Surf School offers private and group lessons as well as surf yoga classes. ✉ *Rte. 413, Km 4.4* ☎ *787/823–0610* ⊕ *www. rinconsurfschool.com.*

MAYAGÜEZ

15 miles (24 km) southeast of Rincón.

"Me encanta" is what most people from Puerto Rico say when you ask them about Mayagüez. But you are likely to be less than enchanted by the grungy city, home to 12,000 university students and several casinos. With more charming communities in every direction, there's no real reason to stop in this traffic-clogged area. But if you have some spare time, the city known as the "Sultan of the West" has some worthwhile attractions. Its tree-lined main square, called Plaza Colón, is dominated by a large statue of Christopher Columbus. On the surrounding streets you'll find the domed Teatro Yagüez, which dates from 1902, and a mishmash of buildings that run the gamut from neoclassical to baroque to art deco. You'll also find the largest shopping mall on the west coast.

Mayagüez isn't famous for its beaches—you'll find better stretches in Rincón, about 25 minutes north—but Balneario de Añasco, also called Tres Hermanos Beach, is 10 minutes north of town via Highway 2 and

Continued on page 263

SURFING
PUERTO RICO

by Marlise Kast

With turquoise waters, sugary sand, hollow barrels, offshore winds, and arching palm trees, it's no wonder the island has been labeled "Hawaii of the Atlantic." This vision of paradise is a magnet for myriad surfers. Whether you're a beginner or a big-wave rider, there's a break to suit your ability—on the northwest coast near Rincón, along the northern beaches, or off the eastern shores.

WAVES OF GLORY

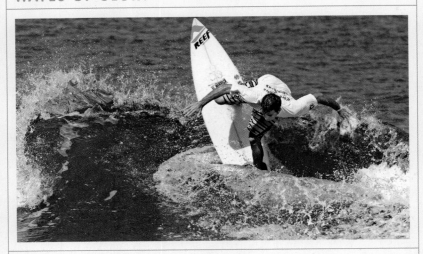

Pro surfer Gabriel Escudero conquers the waves at Domes Beach in Rincón.

Puerto Rico is home to more than 70 surf spots with some of the Caribbean's most consistent waves, breaking anywhere between 3 feet (for beginners) and 20 feet (for advanced/professionals). Along 310 miles of ride-able waters are coral reefs, point breaks, hallow barrels, beach breaks, rights and lefts. The downside of surfing in the tropics are jellyfish and sea urchins that cling onto the rocks. Other dangers include shallow reefs, riptides, and territorialism at some local spots. If you're a beginner, enroll in a surf course and learn from someone who knows the environment. Respect the locals, never surf alone, and remember the unwritten law: never drop in on another surfer.

THE GOOD OLE DAYS
According to local legend, the first surfers to test the northwest waters were Puerto Rico's own Jose Rodriguez, Rafy Viella, and Guille Bermuda. In 1960, American surfer Gary Hoyt opened the island's first surf shop in San Juan. Following in his wake were Johnny Flain and Butch Linden from Malibu, Cali-

fornia, who claim that only fifty surfers braved the waters in the mid 60s. It wasn't until 1968, when Rincón hosted the World Surfing Championships, that word spread of epic waves peeling along the north and northwest coasts. Winter waves and a laid-back lifestyle made the island a haven for American surfers and hippies, who took one look at the coastline and never turned back. Since the 1970s, Puerto Rico's roster of talent has featured such legends as Edwin Santos, Juan Ashton, and Pepe Alvarez. Noted for charging monster waves are local big-wave riders like Alberto Lincha, Carlos Cabrero, and Waldo Oliver

Today, the island hosts dozens of competitions and is home to 25,000 surfers and 30 surf shops.

Cresting a wave at the Corona Pro Surfer event

SURF SEASONS

(clockwise from top left) serene paddle-boarding; a crowded wave at Tres Palmas; competing at Middles Beach

Waves peak during winter, but it's possible to catch one during "off season" due to periodic hurricanes and cold fronts that pass Puerto Rico. Summer is generally flat, except when a hurricane passes (season, July–November) off the coast. The fall is when North Atlantic storms create enough swell to make Puerto Rico a world-class destination. This is when the pros take to the waves, providing a spectacle for beachgoers.

BEGINNER

For a light splash in the whitewash, the summer months (late May through August) offer playful waves.

INTERMEDIATE

In springtime (March to mid-May), swells fade but are compensated with offshore winds that hold the wave's barreling shape, averaging between shoulder-to-head high.

ADVANCED

September through May is ideal for experienced surfers. November through February in particular is when top surfers—mostly locals and East Coasters—crowd the line-up for monster waves that can fire as high as 20-feet.

WHERE TO RENT

Puerto Rico has dozens of surf shops renting everything from foam longboards and boogieboards for beginners to high-performance shortboards and paddleboards for experts.

Offering the best quiver on the island is **Mar Azul** (☎ 787/823–5692 ⊕ www.puertoricosurfinginfo.com) located on Rincón's Rte 413. **WRV** in Isabela (☎ 787/669–3840 ⊕ www.waveridingvehicles.com) is another top spot for beginner board rentals.

NORTHWEST BREAKS

KEY

- Right Break
- Left Break
- Point / Beach Break
- Beginner Area
- Intermediate Area
- Advance Area

Pta. Agujereada · **Jobos**
Wilderness Beach ·
San Antonio · San Antonio · Isabela
Pta. Borinquen · Mora
Gas Chambers · 110 · 2
Aguadilla · 112
Bahia de
Sandy Beach · Aguadilla
Domes · Aguada · Moca
Maria's · Pta. Higüero · 115
Tres Palmas · Rincón · 2 · 110

When the surf is on in the northwest, it's on. This is the best place to capture the scene, as some breaks here experience 40-foot swells in winter. Aguadilla and Rincón are ideally stationed for offshore wind conditions, which hold the waves' shape.

ADVANCED

To witness Puerto Rico's true surfing experience, head north of Rincón to Aguadilla's **Wilderness Beach.** Surrounding jungle landscape makes it worth the drive to this local spot where fast, long rights average 8–15 ft.

Considered the "Sunset Beach" of Puerto Rico, **Tres Palmas** is reserved for kamikaze-surfers who take on the 40-foot waves that only break a few days each year. In summer, however, this deep outer reef is surprisingly calm, making it the perfect place to snorkel.

Head to **Gas Chambers** to watch surfers charge Puerto Rico's most powerful wave. Next to Crash Boat Beach, this spot breaks less than 10 times per year, but is la-

Corona Pro Surfer event, Rincon

beled world-class due to the 15-foot faces and oblong tubes that crash with unbelievable force.

INTERMEDIATE

At **Domes,** a spot named for the nuclear power dome neighboring the parking lot, peaky right-hand waves average 3 to 10 feet. This break is one of the area's most consistent, even on smaller days. Breaking directly in front of Tamboo Restaurant is a sandbar known as **Sandy Beach.** This intermediate spot still delivers on smaller days, but is not as protected from south winds as the neighboring coves. Although generally void of crowds, the rocky shoreline embedded with urchins isn't good for beginners.

BEGINNER

When the waves are between 2 to 4 feet, beginners can head just south of Domes to **Maria's.** This break has some fun right- and left-hand peaks, and offers a pleasant beach for photographing surfers when the swell picks up. Once waves reach head-high (Nov. through Feb.), this spot is best reserved for advanced surfers who can handle the shallow reefs and strong currents.

Popular with beginner and intermediate surfers, **Jobos** in Isabela has 4–10 foot rights that break off a reef in a crescent-shaped bay. This section often connects to the inside waves, making for a nice long ride. Because of the food shacks and shallow waters, this spot is often crowded with beachgoers and beginners learning to surf. Those who prefer to watch the action can photograph surfers from the peninsula on the beach's east side.

NORTH BREAKS

Susceptible to Atlantic storms and their aftermath, the north coast has more than 30 breaks to explore.

ADVANCED

Unless you're quite experienced, you may just want to take photographs from the shores of **Chatarras**. This epic wave breaks on a sharp coral reef, creating hollow left-hand tubes fit for the pros. When the 10+ footers are firing, this spot gets crowded with surfers who will do whatever it takes to claim their wave.

INTERMEDIATE

Near San Juan, **La Ocho**, is a forgiving wave great for intermediate surfers on medium-size days. Working best at 5 feet, this break is long but usually mushy. It's a long paddle to the break so make sure you're in shape before you head to the line-up.

BEGINNER

Near the town of Manati, **Los Tubos** (The Tubes) has a pleasant crowd and is manageable for novices. The best time to come is be-

tween September and April, but beware of sea urchins that line the rocky shore. In the town of Luquillo, **La Pared** delivers right and lefts that break on a soft, sandy beach. On a weekday, you may have all the waves to yourself, except after 5 PM when you might be joined by a handful of locals out for a sunset session. This is an excellent beginner's beach, with friendly 3 to 5 foot waves that break 150 days of the year.

6

IN FOCUS SURFING PUERTO RICO

SOUTH BREAKS

Overshadowed by the north, the south rim of Puerto Rico experiences all types of waves from the Caribbean hurricanes and tropical storms. This is most common between August and October when swells hit the southeastern side from Humacao down to Patillas.

INTERMEDIATE TO ADVANCED

Inches, has the island's longest left-hand barrel. Waves here often peel for 300+ yards. Named for the "inches" separating you from the reef, this spot has powerful waves that spread between three peaks. Trade winds make this the south's most consistent surf break, even in summer when most other spots are flat.

BOARD SHAPES

Longboard: Lengthier (about 2.5—3 m/ 9–10.5 feet), wider, thicker, and more buoyant than the often-miniscule shortboards. Offers more flotation and speedier paddling, which makes it easier to get into waves. Great for beginners and those with relaxed surf styles. Skill level; Beginner to Intermediate.

Funboard: A little shorter than the longboard with a slightly more acute nose and blunt tail, the Funboard combines the best attributes of the longboards with some similar characteristics of the shorter boards. Good for beginners or surfers looking for a board more maneuverable and faster than a longboard. Skill level; Beginner to Intermediate.

Fishboard: A stumpy, blunt-nosed, twin-finned board that features a "V" tail (giving it a "fish" like look, hence the name) and is fast and maneuverable. Good for catching small, steep slow waves and pulling tricks. At one point this was the world's best-selling surfboard. Skill level; Intermediate to Expert.

Shortboard: Shortboards came on the scene in 1967-70 when the average board length dropped from 9'6" to 6'6" (2.9m to 2m) and changed the wave riding styles in the surf world forever. This board is a short, light, high-performance stick that is designed for carving the wave with a high amount of maneuverability. These boards need a fast steep wave, completely different than a longboard break, which tends to be slower with shallower wave faces. Skill level; Expert.

Beginner   Expert

Funboards

Fish

Longboards

Shortboards

Shallow wave faces, easiest surfing   Steeper wave faces, difficult surfing

Routes 115 and 401. Dotted with palm trees, it's good for swimming and has changing facilities and restrooms.

GETTING HERE AND AROUND

AIR TRAVEL

The small Aeropuerto Eugenio María de Hostos (MAZ), just north of Mayagüez on Highway 2, has flights between San Juan and Mayagüez on Cape Air. If you are not flying into San Juan, you can rent a car at the airport. Prices vary from $35 to $65 per day.

Airport Information Aeropuerto Internacional Rafael Hernández ⊠ *Hwy. 2, Km 148.7, Rtes. 110 and 107, Borinquen/Ramey, Aguadilla* ☎ *787/891–2286, 787/890–6075.*

CAR TRAVEL

Driving in Mayagüez can be complicated, especially in the high-trafficked center of town where one-way streets compose the city grid. Nevertheless, a rental car is your best option for getting around town. From Highway 2 you can reach downtown by taking Route 105 (Calle McKinley) or Route 106 (Calle Méndez Vigo). Either route will take you to the heart of the city.

Car Rental Avis ☎ *787/890–3311.* **Budget** ⊠ *Aeropuerto Eugenio María de Hostos, Off Rte. 2* ☎ *800/527–0700.* **Enterprise** ⊠ *505 Calle Post Sur* ☎ *787/805–3722* ⊕ *www.enterprise.com.* **Hertz** ⊠ *Aeropuerto Eugenio María de Hostos, Off Rte. 2* ☎ *787/890–5650.* **Leaseway of Puerto Rico** ☎ *787/791–5900 in Mayagüez* ⊕ *www.leasewaypr.com.* **Thrifty** ⊠ *Aeropuerto Eugenio María de Hostos, Off Rte. 2* ☎ *787/834–1590 in Mayagüez.*

TAXI TRAVEL

In Mayagüez taxis charge flat rates—no meters—by location. Fares to or from San Juan are steep: for example, service is $120 from Mayagüez.

EXPLORING MAYAGÜEZ

WORTH NOTING

Estación Experimental de Agricultura Tropical (*Tropical Agriculture Research Station*). Founded in 1901 on a 235-acre farm on the outskirts of Mayagüez, the Estación Experimental de Agricultura Tropical is run by the U.S. Department of Agriculture and contains a tropical plant collection that has been nurtured for more than a half century. More than 2,000 plant species from all over the tropical world are found here, including teak, mahogany, cinnamon, nutmeg, rubber, and numerous exotic flowers. Free maps are available for self-guided tours. ⊠ *Hwy. 2 at Rte. 108* ☎ *787/831–3435* ⊠ *Free* ⊙ *Weekdays 7–4.*

Teatro Yagüez. The Teatro Yagüez is an extravagant yellow-and-white theater dating from 1902 that's famed throughout the island for its lavish, columned facade and domed roof. The structure, a little over the top, is still the main venue for theater in Mayagüez. ⊠ *Calle McKinley, 1 block from Plaza Colón* ⊠ *Free* ⊙ *Weekdays 8–4:30.*

FAMILY **Zoológico de Puerto Rico.** Puerto Rico's only zoo, the 45-acre Zoológico de Puerto Rico, is just north of downtown. Its 45-foot-tall aviary allows you to walk through a rain-forest environment as tropical birds fly freely above your head. There's also a butterfly park where you can let brilliant blue morphos land on your hand, and an arthropodarium where you can get up close and personal with spiders and their kin. Video monitors are built into the floor to show off the bugs that normally get trampled underfoot. The older section of the park has undergone an extensive renovation, so most of the cages have been replaced by fairly natural-looking environments. One of the most popular residents is Mundi, a female elephant who arrived as a baby more than two decades ago. There are also plenty of lions, tigers—and even bears. ⊠ *Rte. 108, north of Rte. 65, Miradero* 🕾 *787/834–8110* ⊕ *www.parquesnacionalespr.com* ⊠ *$13; parking $3* ☉ *Wed.–Sun. 8:30–4.*

WHERE TO EAT

$ ✕ **Ricomini Bakery.** This popular bakery, open daily from 5 am to midnight, is a good spot to try one of the city's trademark delicacies, a *brazo gitano* ("gypsy arm"). These gigantic jellyrolls are filled with anything from guava to sweet cheese. You can also find another famous local product here, Fido's Sangría, made from the closely guarded secret recipe of Mayagüez resident Wilfredo Aponte Hernández. There are also tasty pastries like flan, *tres leches*, cheesecake, as well as freshly baked bread and a selection of sandwiches. ⑤ *Average main: $6* ⊠ *101 Calle Méndez Vigo* 🕾 *787/832–0565.*

CAFÉ

$ ✕ **Siglo XX.** This busy restaurant has an enormous menu of chicken, steak, and seafood dishes prepared every way imaginable. Meals come in a basket with rice, beans, or plantains. Sandwiches, displayed behind the glass counter, are served lightly toasted with the traditional mayoketchup "secret sauce." Booths at the diner setting are packed with locals, especially during the midweek lunch hour. This Spanish-speaking eatery is a great place to practice your language skills. ⑤ *Average main: $8* ⊠ *9 Calle Peral* 🕾 *787/833–1370* ☉ *Closed Sun.*

PUERTO RICAN

WHERE TO STAY

$ ⊡ **Holiday Inn Mayagüez & Tropical Casino.** Everything seems shoehorned into this big box on the northern edge of Mayagüez—the sound of slot machines is impossible to escape in the extremely popular casino, which is adjacent to the lobby, as well as the bar and restaurant. **Pros:** great staff; pretty pool area. **Cons:** not on the beach; motel-style rooms; free Continental breakfast for executive rooms only. ⑤ *Rooms from: $125* ⊠ *2701 Hwy. 2, at Km 149.9* 🕾 *787/833–1100* ⊕ *www.hidpr.com* ⊸ *141 rooms* ⑩ *No meals.*

HOTEL

$ ⊡ **Howard Johnson Downtown Mayagüez.** Set in a former monastery, this downtown hotel still has stained-glass windows in some rooms and a stone cross on the roof. **Pros:** interesting building; rooms designed for families and business people. **Cons:** far from the beach; on an uninteresting block; Wi-Fi only in common areas; rooms and bathrooms need some TLC. ⑤ *Rooms from: $116* ⊠ *70 Calle Méndez Vigo* 🕾 *787/832–9191* ⊕ *www.hojo.com* ⊸ *50 rooms* ⑩ *Breakfast.*

HOTEL
FAMILY

$$ 🎰 **Mayagüez Resort & Casino.** The center of the city's social life, this old-fashioned hotel is packed with elegantly dressed men and women all weekend. **Pros:** lovely pool area; best casino on this coast. **Cons:** not on the beach; must pay for parking even to visit the casino; guests must wear identity wristbands; time for a renovation. ⑤ *Rooms from: $215* ⊠ *Rte. 104, Km 0.3, off Hwy. 2* ☎ *787/832–3030, 888/689–3030* ⊕ *www.mayaguez resort.com* ⌁ *140 rooms* ❯❮ *No meals.*

HOTEL
FAMILY

THE GOLDEN MILE

Anyone interested in seafood must visit Milla de Oro del Buen Comer, aka the Gourmet Golden Mile. In the small fishing village of Joyuda, this string of more than 15 restaurants serves the best fish on the island. It spans from Tony's Restaurant at Km 10.9 to Parada los Flamboyanes at Km 16. The seafood here is the freshest— caught daily from the Caribbean Sea or from Laguna Joyuda.

SHOPPING

Small stores and pharmacies dot downtown Mayagüez.

Mayagüez Mall. For heavy-duty shopping, Mayagüez Mall has local stores, a food court, movie theaters, and stateside chains such as JCPenney, Wal-Mart, and Marshalls. ⊠ *975 Ave. Eugenio Maria de Hostos* ☎ *787/834–2760.*

6

CABO ROJO

Named for its pinkish cliffs, "Red Cape" was used in the late 18th century as a port for merchant vessels—and for the smugglers and pirates who inevitably accompanied oceangoing trade. Today the miles of coastline to the west and north of this tiny curl of land jutting into the Caribbean are a destination for families. Many small, inexpensive hotels can be found in the communities of Joyuda, Boquerón, and El Combate. Outdoor activities are quite popular, from sailing out of Boquerón to hiking to the lighthouse near El Combate.

JOYUDA

14 miles (21 km) south of Mayagüez.

Known as the Milla de Oro (Golden Mile) because of its string of more than 15 seaside restaurants, the community of Joyuda is a must for seafood lovers. The same can't be said for those in search of a beautiful beach, as erosion has taken a terrible toll, leaving in some places only a sliver of sand. But that doesn't stop hordes of local families from making a beeline to the bit of beach that's left.

GETTING HERE AND AROUND

From Mayagüez, take Highway 2 south to Route 100 south toward Cabo Rojo. Head west on Route 102 until you hit the coastal town of Joyuda. Most of the area's restaurants and hotels are staggered along a 2-mile (3-km) stretch on Route 102, making this a convenient town to explore on foot.

Surrounded by rugged coastline, the Cabo Rojo Lighthouse is best reached by a four-wheel drive vehicle.

EXPLORING

Mona Island. About 50 miles (80 km) off the coast of Cabo Rojo, Mona Island sits brooding in the Atlantic Ocean. Known as the Galápagos of the Caribbean, the 14,000-acre island has long been a destination for adventurous travelers. It's said to have been settled by the Taíno Indians and visited by both Christopher Columbus and Juan Ponce de León. Pirates were known to use the small island as a hideout, and legend has it that there is still buried treasure to be found here. Today, however, Mona's biggest lure is its distinctive ecosystem. It is home to a number of endangered species, such as the Mona iguana and leatherback sea turtle. A number of seabirds, including red-footed boobies, also inhabit the island. Off its coast are reefs filled with 270 species of tropical fish, black coral, and purple sea fans. There are plenty of places to explore, such as the 200-foot cliffs on the north side of the island or the abandoned lighthouse that once protected ships off the southern coast. Travelers must reach the island by boat—planes aren't permitted to land. Several tour operators in Joyuda and Boquerón, as well as companies in Mayagüez and Rincón, offer overnight camping trips to the island; they will help you with the camping permits from the Department of Natural and Environmental Resources. You need to reserve at least a few weeks ahead for an overnight stay. ☎ 787/722–1726 *Department of Natural and Environmental Resources.*

WHERE TO EAT

$$ ✕ **El Bohío.** Watch seagulls dive for their food while you dine on a cov-
SEAFOOD ered deck extending out into the bay. The long list of seafood is pre-
pared in a variety of ways: Shrimp comes breaded, stewed, or skewered;
conch is served as a salad or cooked in a butter-and-garlic sauce; and
the lobster can be prepared just about any way you can imagine. This
restaurant, on stilts above the water, is about the most charming setting
in Joyuda. Ⓢ *Average main: $15* ⊠ *Rte. 102, Km 13.9* ☎ *787/851–2755*
⊕ *www.restauranteelbohiojoyuda.com* ☉ *Closed Oct.*

$$ ✕ **Raito's.** Specializing in croquette-encrusted seafood, this waterfront
SEAFOOD fish house is reminiscent of the '70s with its speckled linoleum floors and
clear vinyl tablecloths. Mozzarella tops most house favorites, including
the baked lobster and snapper. For the seafood-weary, pork chops and
filet mignon are on the menu, but be sure to leave room for the mango-,
guava-, or coconut-flavored flan. Two inviting gazebos overlook the
water, but sadly the view is somewhat obstructed by a chain-link fence.
Ⓢ *Average main: $20* ⊠ *Rte. 102, Km 13.7, Joyuda* ☎ *787/851–4487*
☉ *Closed Mon. and Tues.*

$$ ✕ **Tino's.** The colorful neon sign outside this restaurant touts its sig-
SEAFOOD nature dish of mofongo as: "An earthenware goblet overflowing with
mashed plantains and seafood." It comes in two sizes, but the smaller
one is usually enough to satisfy all but the biggest appetites. There are
plenty of other seafood dishes on the menu, from red snapper in a spicy
sauce to lobster with butter. Although most come here for the fish, the
restaurant also serves beef, pork, and chicken. There's no ocean view,
but the elegant dining makes up for it. Ⓢ *Average main: $20* ⊠ *Rte.*
102, Km 13.6 ☎ *787/851–2976* ☉ *Closed Tues.*

SPORTS AND THE OUTDOORS

DIVING AND SNORKELING

Several reef-bordered cays lie off the Cabo Rojo area near walls that
drop to 100 feet. A mile-long reef along Las Coronas, better known as
Cayo Ron, has a variety of hard and soft coral, reef fish, and lobsters.

Tour Marine Adventures. You can arrange snorkeling and scuba-diving
trips with Captain Elick Hernández Garciá, who runs Tour Marine
Adventures. Trips cost between $35 and $75 per person. He'll also
arrange trips out to Mona Island for around $200 per person. ⊠ *Rte.*
101, Km 14.1 ☎ *787/255–2525* ⊕ *www.tourmarinepr.com.*

GOLF

Club Deportivo del Oeste. Get in 18 holes at the Club Deportivo del
Oeste. Jack Bender incorporated the region's rolling hills in his design
to provide golfers with panoramic views. The nicely tended course is
open daily, as are the tennis courts on the same property. ⊠ *Rte. 102,*
Km 15.1 ☎ *787/254–3748* 🖼 *$50, $25 after 3 pm.*

6

BOQUERÓN

3 miles (5 km) south of Joyuda.

Once a quiet fishing village, Boquerón still has its share of seaside shanties. Its narrow streets are quiet during the week but come alive on the weekend, when vendors appear with carts full of clams and oysters you can slurp down on the spot—wedges of lemon are provided, of course. Bars and restaurants throw open their doors—if they have any, that is. Many of the establishments here are open to the breeze, making this a Puerto Rican party spot where the music (and the people) can be heard until 2 in the morning. Boquerón is also a water-sports center; many companies operate from or near the docks of the imposing Club Nautico de Boquerón, which is easy to find at the end of Route 100.

GETTING HERE AND AROUND

To reach Boquerón from Mayagüez, head south on Highway 2 to Route 100 south. After bypassing Cabo Rojo, take Route 101 and follow the signs southwest to Boquerón. The small town can easily be explored on foot.

BEACHES

Balneario Boquerón. The long stretch of sand at this beach off Route 101 is a favorite with islanders, especially on weekends. This is a Blue Flag Beach, meaning it is recognized for its high environmental standards. **Amenities:** showers; lifeguards; restrooms; picnic tables; playground; parking. **Best for:** swimming; relaxing. ⊠ *Off Rte. 101.*

Playa Buyé. This white-sand beach has crystal clear water lined with swaying palm and almond trees that provide shade. The beach is a bit hard to find and very crowded on weekends so visit during the week or in off-season. During peak season, some kiosks with food and drink are open. **Amenities:** toilets; showers; parking (free) along Calle Buyé, $3 at the Buyé Beach Resort. **Best for:** swimming; walking. ⊠ *Rte. 307, Km 4.8, north of Boquerón.*

WHERE TO EAT

$$
STEAKHOUSE
✕ **Brasas Steak House.** Offering a refreshing alternative to seafood, this is Boqueron's most upscale eatery and serves certified Angus beef, including T-bone, sirloin, and filet mignon. Equally notable are the grilled chicken, pork, and pastas. Set back from the main strip, this restaurant lacks an ocean view but is quieter and more intimate than others in the area. ⑤ *Average main: $20* ⊠ *46 Calle Barbosa* ☎ *787/255–1470* ⊗ *Closed Mon.–Tues.*

$$
SEAFOOD
✕ **Galloway's.** From a covered deck overlooking Bahía Boquerón, you can catch the sunset while enjoying some seafood—caught fresh from local waters, of course. Steak, ribs, chicken, and pasta are available, but the red snapper and dorado—prepared breaded, sautéed, or grilled–are by far the best options. There's a lively happy hour and occasional live music. This place is along the main drag but is set back from the street so you don't have to be a part of the passing parade. One major plus in this traffic-choked town: There's a large free parking lot. ⑤ *Average main: $20* ⊠ *12 Calle José de Diego* ☎ *787/254–3302* ⊕ *www.gallowaysrestaurant.com* ⊗ *Closed Wed. and Oct.*

Locals flock to the pretty beaches of Boquerón on weekends.

WHERE TO STAY

$ **Aquarius Beach Resort.** As Boqueron's largest property, this high-rise
RESORT resort offers one-, two-, and three-bedroom suites, each with a pri-
FAMILY vate balcony. **Pros:** family-friendly; calm beach; prime location. **Cons:**
no Internet in rooms; hotel is often full; blocked double parking.
⑤ *Rooms from: $148* ✉ *Rte. 101, Km 18* ☎ *787/254–5400* ⊕ *www.*
aquariusvacationclub.com ⤳ *88 rooms* ⫶⊙⫶ *No meals.*

$ **Cofresí Beach Hotel.** A favorite with families, this place puts you a
HOTEL few blocks from the hustle and bustle of Boquerón. **Pros:** best value
FAMILY in the area; family-friendly environment; walking distance to many
restaurants. **Cons:** not on the beach; some traffic noise; additional $15
daily cleaning fee; no Wi-Fi. ⑤ *Rooms from: $129* ✉ *57 Calle Muñoz*
Rivera ☎ *787/254–3000* ⊕ *www.cofresibeach.com* ⤳ *12 apartments*
⫶⊙⫶ *No meals.*

SPORTS AND THE OUTDOORS

DIVING AND SNORKELING

Mona Aquatics. Snorkeling and scuba-diving trips are the specialty at
Mona Aquatics. Night dives are available as well. You'll find the crew in
a wooden shack painted an eye-popping shade of blue next to the Club
Nautico de Boquerón. The company also does trips to Mona Island.
✉ *Calle José de Diego* ☎ *787/851–2185* ⊕ *www.monaaquatics.com.*

FISHING

Light Tackle Adventure. You can arrange fishing trips with Captain Francisco "Pochy" Rosario, who runs Light Tackle Adventure. His specialty
is tarpon, which are plentiful in these waters. ☎ *787/849–1430* ⊕ *www.*
lighttackleadventure.8k.com.

EL COMBATE

2 miles (3 km) south of Boquerón.

This is the end of the earth—or the end of the island, anyway. El Combate sits on the southwest corner of Puerto Rico, a bit removed from everything. The travel industry hasn't figured out how to market this place, so they've left it mostly to the locals, who have built small but elaborate weekend homes—some with grandiose touches like fountains—along the narrow streets. On the road closest to the beach, which for some reason is called Calle 3, is a cluster of seafood shacks. The more prosperous ones have added second stories.

If you're wondering about the town's odd name, which literally means "The Combat," it seems that long ago some unscrupulous characters were eyeing the salt flats just outside town. But they were repelled by machete-wielding villagers who were to live forever in local lore. Is it a true story? Residents of El Combate swear it is.

GETTING HERE AND AROUND

To reach the coastal town of El Combate from the 101, take Route 301 south to Km 7.8, where the road intersects with Route 3301. The five-minute drive west on Route 3301 ends at El Combate Beach, where a cluster of restaurants and hotels line the main strip, Calle 3. To reach Cabo Rojo Lighthouse and the salt flats, bypass Route 3301 and continue south on Route 301 until the road ends. This paved road soon turns into a bumpy one with potholes dotting the dusty course. The trek is well worth the effort, however, as jutting mangroves and crystal waters welcome travelers to Puerto Rico's southwestern tip.

It's a good idea to rent a four-wheel-drive vehicle from Mayagüez airport if you are heading to Cabo Rojo Lighthouse, as it is reached via a truly terrible dirt road.

EXPLORING

WORTH NOTING

Cabo Rojo Lighthouse. The area's most popular attraction is the neoclassical Cabo Rojo Lighthouse, dating from 1881. The magnificent structure, built on a limestone cliff has amazing views of the Caribbean Sea. It is open to the public, and you are free to hike around the rugged terrain or relax on La Playuela or one of the other pink-sand beaches nearby. ■ TIP→ **There are no facilities here, so bring water, food, and sunscreen.** ⊠ *End of Rte. 301* ☎ *787/255–1560* 🔳 *Free* ☻ *8–4pm. Closed Wed.*

Centro Interpretativo Las Salinas de Cabo Rojo (*Cabo Rojo Sal Flats Interpretive Center*). The Centro Interpretativo Las Salinas de Cabo Rojo has two-hour guided tours along the nature trails and a small display about the salt flats. (Remember that the name of the town comes from a battle over control of the salt flats.) The best part of the center is a massive observation tower that lets you scan the outline of Cabo Rojo itself. Next to the main building is an audiovisual center where presentations on marine ecosystems and bird migration are offered. ⊠ *Rte. 301, Km 11* ☎ *787/851–2999* ⊕ *proambientepr.org* 🔳 *Center free, tours $3* ☻ *Thurs.–Sat. 8:30–4:30, Sun. 9:30–5:30, tours at 9:30 and 1:30.*

Refugio de Vida Silvestre de Cabo Rojo (*Cabo Rojo Wildlife Refuge*). Home to six different ecosystems, the Refugio de Vida Silvestre de Cabo Rojo has an interpretive center with exhibits of live freshwater fish and sea turtles. You can see as many as 100 species of birds along the trails, even the elusive yellow-shouldered blackbird. The entrance is about 1 mile (2 km) north of the turnoff for El Combate. ⊠ *Rte. 301, Km 1.2* ☎ *787/851–7260* ✉ *Free* ☾ *Weekdays 8–4.*

BEACHES

El Combate. This great beach draws large crowds on weekends to its rustic waterfront eateries and calm waters. You can rent small boats and kayaks here. **Amenities:** At the nearby eateries or Combate Beach Resort. **Best for:** partiers; swimming. ⊠ *At the end of Rte. 3301.*

La Playuela. The crescent-shaped strand is the most secluded and beautiful of the area's beaches. It's commonly referred to as *Bahía Sucia* ("Dirty Beach") because of the blankets of seaweed that drift to shore during winter months. The label is rather unfitting for the white sand and turquoise waters that mark the island's southwestern corner, reachable by way of a dirt road lined with mangroves. **Amenities:** none. **Best for:** swimming, hiking. ⊠ *End of Rte. 301, past the vast salt flats, Cabo Rojo.*

WHERE TO EAT

$$
SEAFOOD

✕ **Annie's Place.** A dining room facing the ocean is a fitting place to try some of the southwest coast's best seafood. You can snack on *empanadillas* (deep-fried fritters), then move on to red snapper with rice and beans or *mofongo relleno* (stuffed with seafood). This place, in an unmistakable lime-colored building on the main drag, has festive music and great views. $ *Average main: $15* ⊠ *Rte. 3301, Km 3, at Calle 3, Cabo Rojo* ☎ *787/254–2553.*

WHERE TO STAY

$$
HOTEL

🏨 **Bahía Salinas Beach Hotel.** With the Cabo Rojo Lighthouse in view, you can wander along the boardwalk or down the garden paths, bask in the sun on a deck or terrace, or relax in the infinity pool at this resort. **Pros:** near interesting sites; good dining options. **Cons:** beach is extremely narrow; stray dogs roam property; sulfur odor from nearby salt flats; service needs improvement. $ *Rooms from: $225* ⊠ *End of Rte. 301* ☎ *787/254–1212* ➽ *30 rooms* ¶○¶ *Breakfast.*

$
HOTEL

🏨 **Parador Combate Beach.** On a quiet side street near the beach, this nicely renovated little hotel is one of the best in the area. **Pros:** good value; quiet neighborhood; recently remodeled. **Cons:** isolated location; patios face the parking lot. $ *Rooms from: $150* ⊠ *Rte. 3301, Km 2.7* ☎ *787/254–2358* ⊕ *www.combatebeachresort.com* ➽ *18 rooms* ¶○¶ *Breakfast.*

$
HOTEL

🏨 **Combate Guest House.** This simple property—across the street from El Combate Beach—is centrally located just off Calle 3. **Pros:** centrally located; good value. **Cons:** noise from beach crowds; cash only; no Wi-Fi; simple accomodations. $ *Rooms from: $80* ⊠ *Rte. 3301, and Calle 2, across from Combate Beach* ☎ *787/254–0001* ⊕ *www.combateguesthouse.com* ➽ *31 rooms* ▭ *No credit cards* ¶○¶ *No meals.*

6

THE NORTHWESTERN COAST

North of Rincón there is a string of beaches that have yet to be discovered. You won't find much large-scale development along this stretch of shoreline, other than the new Royal Isabela Golf Club and Resort. Instead, the area is populated with modest hotels that cater to local families. Many surfers say the waves here are better than those in Rincón itself.

AGUADILLA

12 miles (18 mi) north of Rincón.

Resembling a fishing village, downtown Aguadilla has narrow streets lined with small wooden homes. Weathered but lovely, the faded facades recall the city's long and turbulent past. Officially incorporated as a town in 1775, Aguadilla subsequently suffered a series of catastrophes, including a devastating earthquake in 1918 and strong hurricanes in 1928 and 1932. Determined to survive, the town rebuilt after each disaster, and by World War II it had become known for the sprawling Ramey Air Force Base. The base was an important link in the U.S. defense system throughout the Cold War. Ramey was decommissioned in 1973; today the former base has an airport, a golf course, a university, and some small businesses. As a result of tourism, the north end of town is budding with international restaurants, surf shops, and even an outdoor mall. Additions such as a children's water park and ice-skating rink make Aguadilla a family-friendly destination, too.

Perhaps the town's greatest draw is its surfing at local spots like Wilderness Beach, Table Tops, Playa Crash Boat, and Gas Chamber. Famous for their right-hand barrels, these beaches have hosted a variety of amateur and professional surfing events, including the 1968 and 1988 ISA World Championships and the 2010 ASP World Tour.

GETTING HERE AND AROUND

Most people arrive in Aguadilla either by car from San Juan or by flying directly into Aguadilla's Aeropuerto Internacional Rafael Hernández. United Airlines offers daily flights from Newark to Aguadilla, and JetBlue has service from Orlando or New York. Rental cars ($35–$65 per day) are available from companies operating out of the Aguadilla airport, located at the old Ramey Air Force Base. To reach Aguadilla by car from San Juan, head west on toll road Highway 22, which turns into Highway 2. Continue on Highway 2 until it intersects with Route 111, leading to the center of town.

Airport Information Aeropuerto Internacional Rafael Hernández ✉ *Hanger Rd., reached via Rte. 110 or Rte. 107* ☎ *787/890–6075.*

Car Rental Avis ✉ *Aeropuerto Internacional Rafael Hernández, Hanger Rd.* ☎ *787/890–3311.* **Enterprise** ✉ *Aeropuerto Internacional Rafael Hernández, Hanger Rd.* ☎ *787/890–3732.* **Hertz** ✉ *Aeropuerto Internacional Rafael Hernández, Hanger Rd.* ☎ *787/890–5650.* **L & M Rent a Car** ✉ *Aeropuerto Internacional Rafael Hernández, Hanger Rd.* ☎ *787/890–3010* ⊕ *www.alliedcarrentalpr.com.*

EXPLORING

WORTH NOTING

FAMILY **Aguadilla Ice Skating Arena.** As you might imagine, this is the only ice-skating complex in the Caribbean. ⊠ *Rte. 442, Km 4.2, Paseo Colón, Plaza Plácido Acevedo, Aguadilla Centro* ☎ *787/819–5555* ⊕ *www. miaguadilla.com/index.php/en/empresas/iceskating* 🎫 *$10* ⊙ *Daily 10 am–11 pm.*

La Ponderosa. Along Route 107—an unmarked road crossing through Punta Borinquen Golf Club—you'll find the ruins of La Ponderosa, an old Spanish lighthouse, as well as its replacement, Punta Borinquen, at Puerto Rico's northwest point. The original was built in 1889 and destroyed by an earthquake in 1918. The U.S. Coast Guard rebuilt the structure in 1920. Just beyond the ruins is a local surf spot, Playa Wilderness. ⊠ *Rte. 107.*

Museo de Arte de Aguadilla. Built in 1925, the building that houses this small museum was listed on the National Register of Historic Places in 1985. Inside you will find a collection of oil paintings by local artists. ⊠ *5 Calle Betances, between Calle San Carlos and Calle Corchado* ☎ *787/882–4336* ⊕ *www.museodeartedeaguadilla.com* ⊙ *Mon., Wed., Fri., 8–4.*

FAMILY **Parque Acuático las Cascadas.** Parque Acuático las Cascadas has a large wave pool, giant slides, and the "Crazy River," a long, free-flowing river pool. It's strictly kid stuff. Call ahead for days and hours of operation; they tend to change. ⊠ *Hwy. 2, Km 126.5* ☎ *787/819–1030* 🎫 *$25* ⊙ *Mar.–Aug., weekdays 10–5, weekends 10–6.*

BEACHES

Playa Crashboat. Here you'll find the colorful fishing boats that are portrayed on postcards all over the island. Named after the rescue boats used when the nearby Ramey Air Force Base was in operation, the beach has soft and sugary sand, and the water's as smooth as glass. A food stand run by locals serves the catch of the day with cold beer. Right before you cross the bridge leading down to the beach, a lookout point on your left is a perfect place for a photo op. **Amenities:** food and drink; parking (free); showers; toilets. **Best for:** partiers; snorkeling; swimming. ⊠ *End of Rte. 458, off Rte. 107.*

Playa Gas Chamber. Just north of Playa Crashboat, this beach with big sucking barrels is favored by surfers. There is limited parking and no beach area, just coral. On a good surf day, this is where you want to be to watch the pros charge the waves. **Amenities:** parking; food and drink; toilets (all at nearby Crashboat). **Best for:** surfing. ⊠ *Rte. 107, north of Playa Crashboat.*

Playa Wilderness. This undeveloped beach near La Ponderosa ruins is recommended only for experienced surfers, as it can have dangerous breaks. The long rights, and difficulty in reaching the break, make this popular with locals. It can be reached by way of the Punta Borinquen Golf Club on Route 107. **Amenities:** none. **Best for:** surfing. ⊠ *Rte. 107, north of Playa Gas Chamber.*

6

WHERE TO EAT

$ ✕ **Cocina Creativa.** At first glance, you might mistake this place for a
ECLECTIC vegetarian restaurant with its organic greens, homemade hummus, and
fresh breads. In fact, the menu includes such meat dishes as chicken lem-
ongrass lollipops, jerk chicken with mango chutney, and *churrasco* with
caramelized onions. The chalkboard-inscribed menu changes weekly
but always features the in-house flan, torte, and cheesecake. With a
Bohemian ambience, this is the type of place you could hang out for
a while enjoying the outdoor patio, local artwork, and free Internet,
while savoring one of their fruit smoothies or specialty coffees. $ *Aver-
age main: $10* ⊠ *Rte. 110, Km 9.2, Aguadilla* 🕿 *787/890–1861* ⊙ *No
dinner Mon.*

$ ✕ **D'Rose Chocolate Factory.** This truffle treasure camouflaged in a non-
CAFÉ descript strip mall is acclaimed for having the "best coffee in Puerto
Rico." The owner, José Rivera, refuses to disclose the secret source of
his specialty beans or the technique that produces his mysterious blend.
The aroma of chocolate entices passersby into the sweet shop with its
candy-striped pink walls and chocolate-toned tables. Rotating glass
towers display rich cakes and pastries, while endless rows of candy jars
further tempt the palate. Chocolate-covered strawberries and gourmet
truffles are all made in-house and are served by adorable grandmoth-
ers in their Little Miss Muffet–like uniforms topped with lace bonnets.
$ *Average main: $5* ⊠ *Rte. 107, Km 2.1* 🕿 *787/891–0552.*

$ ✕ **One Ten Thai.** This restaurant, which started with the owner's experi-
THAI ments at home with Thai cuisine, has blossomed into Aguadilla's most
popular eatery. The menu includes lettuce wraps, curry bowls, and pad
thai noodles with tofu, beef, chicken, or shrimp. The owner's passion
for cooking ultimately took him around the world, resulting in such
signature dishes as lime-peanut stir-fry with cilantro and chili sauce
served over your choice of meat. Despite the restaurant's name, the
cuisine is Pan-Asian, utilizing authentic flavors and ingredients. Most
herbs and vegetables are grown on-site or are supplied by local organic
farmers. A next-door microbrew-bar has the largest beer selection in
Porta del Sol. The bar usually has live music on the weekends. Seating is limited, so expect to wait awhile. $ *Average main: $10* ⊠ *Rte.
110, Km 9.2* 🕿 *787/890–0113* ⊙ *Closed Mon. and Tues. No lunch.*

WHERE TO STAY

$$ 🏨 **Courtyard Marriott.** This former military hospital has been transformed
HOTEL into a hotel attracting both business executives and vacationing families.
Pros: near airport; nice pool area **Cons:** airplane and casino noise; no
beach; Wi-Fi in lobby only. $ *Rooms from: $177* ⊠ *West Parade, off
Cliff Rd.* 🕿 *787/658–8000* ⊕ *www.marriott.com/bqncy* ⤴ *146 rooms,
4 suites* ⊖ *No meals.*

$ 🏨 **El Faro Parador.** This family-friendly hotel isn't very close to the light-
HOTEL house from which it takes its name, but it's a good place to keep in mind
FAMILY if you're driving along the coast and need a place to stop for the night.
Pros: reasonable rates; pretty pool areas; children's playground. **Cons:**
no beach; rather secluded location; simple accomodations. $ *Rooms
from: $84* ⊠ *Rte. 107, Km 2.1* 🕿 *787/882–8000* ⊕ *www.farohotels.net*
⤴ *69 rooms* ⊖ *No meals.*

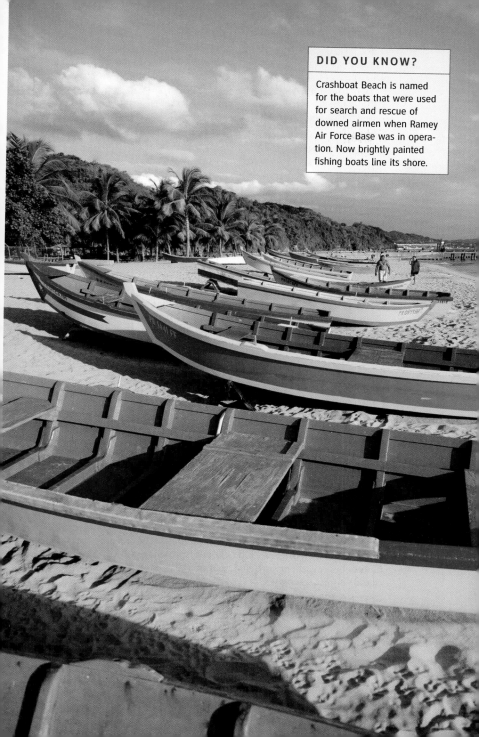

$ ⬚ **JB Hidden Village.** This family-friendly hotel in Aguada, about halfway
HOTEL between Aguadilla and Rincón, has plenty to keep the kids occupied.
FAMILY **Pros:** close to several beaches; good base for exploring the area. **Cons:**
no beach; bland architecture; difficult to locate. ⑤ *Rooms from: $80*
⊠ *Rte. 4416, Km 9.5, after 416 split, Aguada* ☎ *787/868–8686* ☞ *42
rooms* ⦿ *No meals.*

SPORTS AND THE OUTDOORS
DIVING AND SNORKELING
Aquatica. Near Gate 5 of the old Ramey Air Force Base, Aquatica
offers scuba-diving certification courses, as well as snorkeling, paddleboarding, and surfing trips. There's a great selection of surfboards and
paddleboards for rent. For a memorable adventure, try the two-hour
paddleboard tour down the Rio Guajataca. Along the peaceful river,
you'll visit an old train tunnel from 1906. Aquatica also rents bikes.
⊠ *Rte. 110, Km 10, Gate 5, Maleza Alta* ☎ *787/890–6071* ⊕ *www.
aquaticadive-surf.com.*

GOLF
Punta Borinquen Golf Club. The 18-hole Punta Borinquen Golf Club, on
the former Ramey Air Force Base, was a favorite of President Dwight D.
Eisenhower. Now a public course, the beachfront course is known for
its tough sand traps and strong crosswinds. Membership not required to
play. ⊠ *Rte. 107, Km 2* ☎ *787/890–2987* ⊕ *www.puntaborinquengolf.
com* ⊴ *From $20.*

SURFING
Wave Riding Vehicles. Surfboard rentals ($20 for four hours) and one-
hour surfing lessons ($35) are offered through Wave Riding Vehicles,
a surf shop and board factory. They also rent paddleboards and bodyboards. ⊠ *Rte. 4466, Jobos Beach, next to Happy Belly's Restaurant,
Isabela* ☎ *787/669–3840* ⊕ *www.waveridingvehicles.com* ☉ *Mon.–Fri.
10–6; Sat. and Sun. 9–6.*

ISABELA

13 miles (20 km) east of Aguadilla.

Founded in 1819 and named for Spain's Queen Isabella, this small,
whitewashed town on the northwestern tip of the island skirts tall cliffs
that overlook the rocky shoreline. Locals have long known of the area's
natural beauty, and lately more offshore tourists have begun coming to
this niche, which offers secluded hotels, sprawling golf courses, fantastic beaches, excellent surf, and, just inland, hiking through one of the
island's forest reserves.

GETTING HERE AND AROUND
Flying into Aguadilla's airport (BQN) is the fastest way to reach Isabela
and will eliminate the two-hour drive from San Juan. Direct flights to
Aguadilla from Newark are available through United Airlines, and from
Orlando or New York through JetBlue. Several rental-car companies
are on-site at Aguadilla's Aeropuerto Internacional Rafael Hernández,
only 15 minutes from Isabela. If you are driving to the town of Isabela

from San Juan, take Highway 2 west to Route 112 north. The 1120 will intersect with Route 4466, Isabela's coastal road.

Airport Information Aeropuerto Internacional Rafael Hernández ⊠ *Hwy. 2, Km 148.7, Aguadilla* 🕾 *787/891–2286, 787/890–6075.*

Car Rental **Avis** ⊠ *Borrinquen Aguadilla, Aguadilla* 🕾 *787/890–3311* ⊕ *www.avis.com.* **Budget** ⊠ *Rafael Hernandez Airport, 405 Hangar Rd., Aguadilla* 🕾 *787/890–1110.* **Hertz** ⊠ *Rafael Hernandez Airport, Aguadilla* 🕾 *787/890–5650.*

EXPLORING

Bosque Estatal Guajataca (*Guajataca State Forest*). Explore karst topography and subtropical vegetation at the 2,357-acre Bosque Estatal Guajataca between the towns of Quebradillas and Isabela. On more than 46 walking trails, you can see 186 species of trees, including the royal palm and ironwood, and 45 species of birds—watch for red-tailed hawks and Puerto Rican woodpeckers. Bring a flashlight and descend into the **Cueva del Viento** (Cave of the Wind) to find stalagmites, stalactites, and other strange formations. At the entrance to the forest there's a small ranger station where you can pick up a decent hiking map. (Get here early, as the rangers don't always stay until the official closing time.) A little farther down the road is a recreational area with picnic tables and an observation tower. ⊠ *Rte. 446, Km 10* 🕾 *787/872–1045* 🖃 *Free* ☉ *Open during daylight; ranger station weekdays 8–5.*

OFF THE
BEATEN
PATH

Palacete Los Moreau. In the fields south of Isabela toward the town of Moca, a French family settled on a coffee and sugar plantation in the 1800s. The grand two-story house, trimmed with gables, columns, and stained-glass windows, was immortalized in the novel *La Llamarada*, written in 1935 by Puerto Rican novelist Enrique A. Laguerre. In Laguerre's novel about conditions in the sugarcane industry, the house belonged to his fictional family, the Moreaus. Although it doesn't have many furnishings, you can walk through the house and also visit Laguerre's personal library in the mansion's basement. On the grounds is an old steam engine once used to transport sugarcane. ⊠ *Rte. 2, Km 115.9* 🕾 *787/830–4475* 🖃 *Free* ☉ *9–5; no tours Tues. or Wed.*

BEACHES

Playa Jobos. This beach is famous for surfing, especially with beginners. On the same stretch of sand there are a couple of restaurants with oceanfront decks. Down the road, the dunes and long stretches of golden sand are gorgeous for walks or running. Route 466 runs parallel, and there are narrow beach accesses along the road. Parking is along the road. ⚠ **Next to the large rock formation is a strong riptide that drags people out to sea.** The water is only about thigh high, but when the wind changes, the current is like a raging river. There are no lifeguards, no signs, and no roped off areas, so be sure to stay close to shore. **Amenities:** none on-site but nearby toilets and food are available at the beachfront eateries. **Best for:** surfing; walking; partiers. ⊠ *Rte. 466.*

Playa Montones. Not far from Playa Jobos, this is a beautiful beach for swimming; it has a protected natural pool perfect for children.

Amenities: none. **Best for:** walking; swimming. ⊠ *Rte. 466, in front of Parador Villas del Mar Hau.*

Playa Shacks. Known for its surfing and horseback riding, this secluded spot has an area called the Blue Hole that's popular with divers. It has a long strech of sand, expanding for miles in both directions. It is east of Villa Montaña Beach Resort where you can stop in for a great meal at their oceanfront restaurant, The Eclipse. **Amenities:** none. **Best for:** surfing; walking; snorkeling; swimming (conditions permiting). ⊠ *Rte. 4446.*

WHERE TO EAT

$$$
ECLECTIC
Fodor'sChoice
★

✕ **The Eclipse.** The Eclipse is one of the best restaurants on the island, with beautiful beachfront dining, farm-to- table ingredients, and fantastic service. The setting is rustic yet elegant and the view is nothing short of ideal. Executive Chef Jeremie Cruz flawlessly executes dishes full of local flavors and ingredients. For brunch, they offer a wonderful mix of sweet and savory selections that range from coconut brioche French toasts with caramelized bananas and nuts, to an assortment of pizza frittatas. For lunch, they make some delicious classic Neapolitan pizzas crafted from the freshest ingredients and baked in their hand-made brick oven. Try their perfectly marinated catch of the day (from Isabela) ceviche. On top of the already varied dinner menu, Chef Jeremie creates a three-course menu daily that highlights the freshest products he can find. Wine pairings are optional and suggested, given the spectacular wine list. Enjoy live Caribbean jazz on Sunday and Wednesday nights. ⑤ *Average main: $28* ⊠ *Villa Montaña, Rte. 4466, Km 1.9* ☎ *787/872–9554* ⊕ *www.VillaMontana.com.*

$$$
ECLECTIC
Fodor'sChoice
★

✕ **La Casa.** The name of this magnificent restaurant truly embodies how the staff makes you feel . . . at home. They will try to accommodate every request, always with a friendly smile. Many things stand out at this picturesque restaurant: the emerald-green golf course in the foreground, the majestic cliffs on the coast, and the roaring ocean in the background. All the fruits and vegetables from the menu are grown at Royal Isabela's River Farm and Gatehouse Garden; all the fish is caught offshore. The local snapper ceviche is spectacular, and so is the wahoo with watermelon. For the main course, choose from the rack of lamb with acerola mint sauce or the homemade squid-ink pasta with fresh seafood. Caribbean spiny lobster is often a special, cooked to perfection by Chef José Carles. ⑤ *Average main: $30* ⊠ *Royal Isabela, 396 Av. Noel Estrada* ☎ *787/609–5888* ⊕ *www.royalisabela.com.*

$$
CARIBBEAN

✕ **Ocean Front Restaurant.** This seaside restaurant overlooks Playa Jobos, the area's most popular surf break. Outdoor seating is appropriately decorated with surfboards hanging from the rafters and a boat-shaped bar in the center of the rough-hewn patio. To take a break from the salty air, step into the air-conditioned comfort of the more formal dining area. Whatever your appetite, you'll find something to please your palate with a menu offering everything from tropical ceviche and salmon wraps to garlic mahimahi and Porterhouse steaks. Drop by on the weekend to enjoy live music on an outdoor stage. ⑤ *Average main: $20* ⊠ *Playa Jobos, Rte. 4466, Km 0.1* ☎ *787/872–3339* ⊕ *www.oceanfrontpr.com* ☺ *Closed Mon.–Tues.*

$

BISTRO

✗ Ola Lola's. Boasting "the friendliest wave on the island," the owners have maximized their private residence by converting their garage into overflow seating for this garden bistro. With fairy lights, beach chairs, and Latin music, the no-frills setting complements the simple menu of burgers, sandwiches, and signature dips. Flavorful creations include chipotle chicken, the peanut butter burger (just try it!), and for dessert, the grilled banana split. Owners John and Elaine Cosby refuse to reveal the secret of their rum punch recipe, which draws in a large clientele. The Piña Lo-Lada is the smoothest you'll ever taste. For an interesting keepsake, buy one of the souvenir T-shirts from each of the island's top surf spots. Ola Lola's is cash only. ⑤ *Average main: $7 ⊠ Playa Shacks, Rte. 4466, Km 2.1 ☎ 787/872–1230 ⊕ www.ola-lolas.com ▭ No credit cards ⊗ Closed Wed.–Thurs.; no dinner Tues.*

WHERE TO STAY

$

HOTEL

Pelican Reef. Although in need of a face-lift, this place is great for budget travelers. **Pros:** great location; good value. **Cons:** some traffic noise; musty smell in a few of the units. ⑤ *Rooms from: $95 ⊠ Rte. 4466, Km 0 ☎ 347/804–7505 ⊕ www.pelicanreefapartments.com ⟿ 14 apartments ❏ No meals.*

$$$$

RESORT

Fodor's Choice

★

Royal Isabela. One of the area's newest luxury properties, this 2,200-acre paradise is a must for anyone remotely interested in golf. **Pros:** best golf course in Puerto Rico; chefs use organic foods; great views; luxurious accomodations; access to a private beach. **Cons:** casitas are pricey; 15 minutes from other dining options; long walk to beach. ⑤ *Rooms from: $899 ⊠ 396 Ave. Noel Estrada ☎ 949/940–4150 ⊕ www.royalisabela.com ⟿ 20 rooms ❏ Multiple meal plans.*

$$$

RESORT

Fodor's Choice

★

Villa Montaña. This secluded cluster of villas, situated on a deserted stretch of beach between Isabela and Aguadilla, feels like a little town. **Pros:** bikes and playground for children; on a secluded beach; great food. **Cons:** a bit pricey; far from any off-site restaurants; airplane noise. ⑤ *Rooms from: $255 ⊠ Rte. 4466, Km 1.9 ☎ 787/872–9554 ⊕ www. villamontana.com ⟿ 74 rooms, 52 villas ❏ No meals.*

$

HOTEL

Villas del Mar Hau. One-, two-, and three-bedroom cottages—painted in cheery pastels and trimmed with gingerbread—are the heart of this beachfront hotel. **Pros:** laid-back vibe; protected swimming cove great for children; good restaurant. **Cons:** very basic rooms; may be too kitschy for some, 4 pm check-in. ⑤ *Rooms from: $150 ⊠ Rte. 466, Km 8.3 ☎ 787/872–2045 ⊕ www.hauhotelvillas.com ⟿ 46 cottages ❏ No meals.*

SPORTS AND THE OUTDOORS

HORSEBACK RIDING

Tropical Trail Rides. Tropical Trail Rides has two-hour morning and afternoon rides (9 and 3:30) along the beach and through a forest of almond trees. Groups leave from Playa Shacks, one of the region's prettiest beaches. At the end you have a chance to take a dip in the ocean. The company also offers hiking trips to the limestone caves at Survival Beach. ⊠ *Rte. 4466, Km 1.9 ☎ 787/872–9256 ⊕ www. tropicaltrailrides.com.*

SURFING

Hang Loose Surf Shop. For surf lessons, Hang Loose Surf Shop offers a two-hour basic course and has board rentals. Lessons are usually held at Playa Jobos, a great surfing spot where you can reward yourself with a refreshing drink from one of the beach shacks. ⊠ *Rte. 446, Km 1.2* ☎ *787/560–0181* ⊕ *www.hangloosesurfshop.com* ⊘ *Tues.–Sun. 10–5.*

Wave Riding Vehicles. Surfboard rentals ($20) and one-hour surfing lessons ($35) are offered through Wave Riding Vehicles, a surf shop and board factory. They also rent paddleboards and bodyboards. ⊠ *Jobos Beach, Rte. 4466, next to Happy Belly's* ☎ *787/669–3840* ⊕ *www.waveridingvehicles.com.*

RUTA PANORÁMICA

A Journey on the Panoramic Route

The Ruta Panorámica, or Panoramic Route, is an overland journey that reveals rugged beauty and tranquil woodlands not found anywhere else in Puerto Rico. It's an unruly road that clambers its way through the forests of the island's mountainous interior. Towering trees create canopies over the narrow roads, and in their shade pink and purple impatiens bloom in profusion. You'll drive through sleepy colonial villages named for their Taíno ancestors, discover trails leading to secret waterfalls, and behold one breathtaking vista after another.

The grandiose name may lead you to think that the Ruta Panorámica is a highway, but it's actually a network of mountain roads that snakes through the central region, or Cordillera Central. Some are nicely maintained, while others are little more than gravel. But the Panoramic Route certainly lives up to its name, rewarding travelers with sprawling scenery around every bend of the road.

DRIVING THE HIDDEN HEART OF PUERTO RICO

You can explore the Ruta Panorámica in chunks, alternating rural and urban charms. Or you can plan an extended road trip, taking time to fully explore Puerto Rico's interior. Bring your sense of adventure, and on your journey perhaps you'll try *lechon asado*, mouthwatering pork, slow-roasted over open pits. Did we mention that these are whole pigs? You may decide to cool off with a cup of cold *maví*, a local drink made of fermented tree bark. The beaches and city recede from memory here, and you begin to adopt new, unhurried rhythms, allowing serendipity to be your guide. Tropical flora, like birds of paradise, begs to be photographed. On foggy stretches of road, umbrella-sized *yagrumo* leaves laden with water brush the roof of your car. Puerto Rico's highest mountain is tucked into the Toro Negro Forest, and lookout points afford views all the way to the ocean.

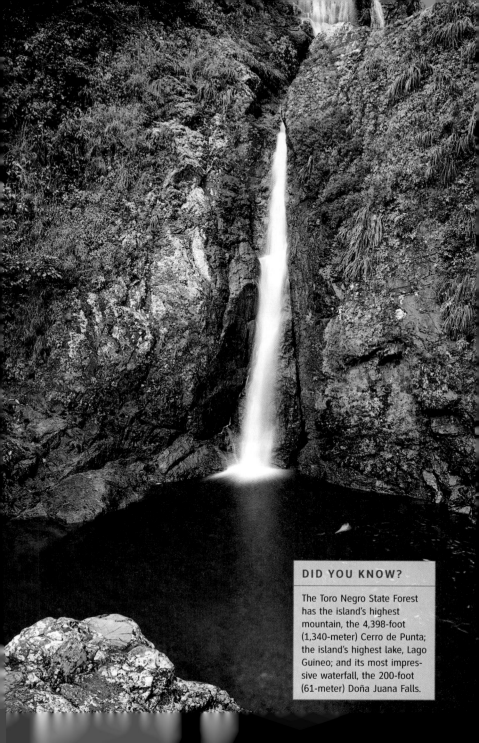

DID YOU KNOW?

The Toro Negro State Forest has the island's highest mountain, the 4,398-foot (1,340-meter) Cerro de Punta; the island's highest lake, Lago Guineo; and its most impressive waterfall, the 200-foot (61-meter) Doña Juana Falls.

THREE JOURNEYS

We've divided the Ruta into three discrete trips, each requiring a full day. Trip 1 takes you from Yabucoa to Aibonito; Trip 2, from Aibonito to Adjuntas; and Trip 3, from Adjuntas to Mayagüez. Put them together for the complete journey, which you can start from the east or the west (Yabucoa or San Juan for eastbound journey; Mayagüez for a west coast departure).

RUTA PANORÁMICA DRIVING TIPS

Rent from a nationally recognized rental car agency. Should you break down on the Ruta or need a tire change, the national chains are more able than local agencies to dispatch assistance or provide a replacement vehicle. Ensure that your rental has a spare tire and a jack and have the roadside assistance number handy in the event that you need it.

Fuel up at each opportunity. There are few gas stations on the Ruta; don't get down to a quarter tank before you fill up.

Avoid driving after dark. The Ruta isn't lit, and driving after dark can be dangerous. Occasional patches of washed-out road aren't uncommon, and they're sometimes impossible to see at night. Also, there are few, if any, food or gas services available once the sun goes down.

Pack drinks and snacks. Because services are limited along most of the route, your options may be limited when hunger strikes. Bring your own drinks and snacks in case you can't wait for the roadside stands, where locals sell just-picked fruits and vegetables from the backs of their trucks. These make a great snack option; just be sure to wash all produce thoroughly.

Invest in a good map. Most hotels have free maps, courtesy of the tourism board; these are highly detailed maps worth picking up. If they don't have one, invest in a good one. Although it may not include all the numbered roads that make up the Ruta, it's better than nothing.

YABUCOA TO AIBONITO

To start exploring the Ruta Panorámica from San Juan, make your way south to the town of Yabucoa, picking up Route 901 Oeste (901 West). Don't be discouraged by all the traffic lights, fast-food outlets, pharmacies, and shops you'll first encounter (in fact, you may want to stock up on supplies here). The road will soon give way to the comparative isolation that characterizes the rest of the Ruta. ■TIP→ Gas up at the

San Cristóbal Canyon near Aibonito

gas station less than a mile into Yabucoa at the start of the Ruta; it's the last service station for a while.

The landscape from Yabucoa to Aibonito is stunning in its variety. From trees typical of the tropics—mango, almonds, palms, and the lush, leafy tree fern—to cedar and bamboo, this stretch offers a preview of the Ruta's diversity.

Don't let your eyes get too carried away by the scenery, though. The Ruta is notorious for its poor signage. Though "Ruta Panorámica" signs are more plentiful on this stretch of the road, they're easy to miss, often covered over by plants or obscured by filmy drippings from the flora. If you're in doubt about your direction, don't hesitate to stop and ask a local. Even if you have road numbers and detailed directions, the Ruta's twists and turns can be puzzling, but going off course and getting back again is all part of the adventure!

Once you're out of Yabucoa proper, there's little more than the flora to capture your attention—that and the road itself—until you reach Aibonito. Legend has it that Aibonito got its name when a Spaniard exclaimed *"¡Ay, que bonito!"* ("Oh, how pretty!") upon seeing the valley where the town now stands. Puerto Rico's highest city, Aibonito is known as the "Queen of Flowers" because flowering plants thrive in its temperate climate. The city hosts a flower festival every year,

THE PLAN

Distance: 48 miles (77 km)

Time: Six hours

Breaks: Roadside fruit stands and roadside restaurants such as El Tenedor Dorado

Yabucoa to
Aibonito Drive

usually in late June or July, and gives awards for blossoms and garden design. Live music and craft stalls add to the festivities. A double-steepled cathedral graces the charming town square, which is surrounded by shops and restaurants. Local guides organize outings to nearby Cañón de San Cristóbal.

ROAD WATCH This stretch of the Ruta is demanding of the driver; with no shoulder for most of the way, there's little, if any, opportunity to stop for a rest or pull over to take photos. Be patient; if you tack on trips 2 and 3, you'll find plenty of places to satisfy both needs.

WHERE TO STAY

$ **Jajome Terrace.** This is the only lodging in Cayey, and it nestles
HOTEL itself cozily into its mountain surroundings. **Pros:** clean, quiet rooms; accessible to Ruta Panoramica and highway. **Cons:** "basic" describes everything here, including limited services; property no longer has a restaurant. $ *Rooms from: $124* ✉ *Rte. 15, Km 18.6, Cayey* ☎ *787/469–3939* ⊕ *www.jajometerrace.com* ⟿ *10 rooms* ⚑ *Breakfast.*

AIBONITO TO ADJUNTAS

Quite possibly the prettiest part of the Ruta Panorámica, the section running from Aibonito to Adjuntas takes you through Puerto Rico's mountain region and the Toro Negro Forest. The views from Aibonito to the midway point of this route open up onto sweeping panoramas of valleys; from the vantage point of your high elevation, the houses below look like tiny dots.

Be sure to stop at the **Mirador Villalba-Orocovis** at Km 39.7 for some of the most spectacular views. This state-run overlook has ample parking and is open from 9 am until 5 pm, Wednesday to Sunday. In addition to the view, there's a playground and sheltered picnic areas. Don't worry if your visit doesn't coincide with the overlook's hours; there's plenty of room to pull over on the side of the road and you can still enjoy the view, surrounded by mountains on either side. It tends to be windy up here at 2,000 feet, so bring an extra layer of clothing.

> ### THE PLAN
>
> **Distance:** 46 miles (74 km) direct from Aibonito to Adjuntas; approximately 19 miles (30 km) for side trip south to Ponce
>
> **Time:** One day without side visit to Hacienda Buena Vista and Ponce; two days for full itinerary
>
> **Breaks:** Mirador Villalba-Orocovis, Doña Juana Recreational Area of the Toro Negro Forest, Hacienda Buena Vista

After the Mirador, the next stop is **Toro Negro Forest**. Climbing to an elevation of more than 4,000 feet, the forest has the distinction of being home to the highest point in Puerto Rico, Cerro de Punta, which tops out at 4,390 feet. Outdoor enthusiasts should stop by the ranger station at Km 32.4 to inquire about trails, request maps, or obtain camping permits. For those who enjoy their scenery within easy reach, pull over at the **Area Recreativa Doña Juana** (Doña Juana Recreational Area). Just a short walk across from the parking area is a natural pool; feel free to dip your feet in!

From the forest, you can drive through to Adjuntas, picking up either Route 10 South or Route 123 South. Both will lead you to Ponce, Puerto Rico's second largest city, after San Juan, but 10 is faster and less scenic. It's also newer and somewhat less treacherous than 123.

If time allows, don't miss **Hacienda Buena Vista**, one of the historic sites operated by the Fideicomiso de Conservación de Puerto Rico (the Conservation Trust of Puerto Rico). This 79-acre property was once one of the island's most important agricultural hubs; today the Fideicomiso maintains the restored hacienda and invites you to explore coffee and cacao production on tours with knowledgeable guides. You'll need to make reservations to visit. Be sure to ask if any special activities—such as the cacao or coffee harvests—coincide with the dates of your visit. Four general tours are offered each day: 8:30 am, 10:30 am, 1:30 pm, and 3:30 pm. Guides also offer a four-hour "long trail" tour Friday to Saturday and two, two-hour short-trail tours Wednesday to Sunday.

7

Caribbean Sea

**Aibonito to
Adjuntas Drive**

0   10 miles

0   10 kilometers

From Buena Vista it's just a 20-minute drive to Ponce. Start your visit at the **Plaza de las Delicias** (Plaza of Delights), Ponce's main square. Here you'll see a historic firehouse, a church, and decorative fountains, all rich with history. Guides and brochures are available at the firehouse. Along the side streets radiating from the square you'll notice Ponce's distinctive architecture, quite different from that of San Juan. If you extend your visit another day, visit the town's cemetery, where many of the island's prominent politicians are buried in elaborate mausoleums. Alternatively, you can scale the hillside for a tour of **Castillo Serrallés**, the former home of the Serrallés family, Puerto Rico's rum barons, and Cruceta La Vigía, a cross-shaped observatory that provides views straight to the Caribbean Sea.

WHERE TO EAT

You won't find much food along this stretch of the Ruta, so it's best to time your meal around your arrival in Ponce, where dining options are abundant. Unless you plan to camp in Toro Negro Forest (and if you do, you'll need a permit), you'll have to detour off this section of the Ruta Panorámica to find a place to rest. Ponce offers many places to stay. *For a complete list of our recommended hotels and restaurants in Ponce, see Where to Eat and Where to Stay sections in chapter 5.*

Take Route 10 North out of Adjuntas to get to Utuado.

Hiking the Toro Negro Forest

$ ✕**Casa Grande.** From the café tables on Casa Grande's towering bal-
PUERTO RICAN cony or deck, you feel as if you've been painted into the landscape.
Lunch is served only on weekends, though you can request sandwiches
in advance during the week. Dinner consists of typical Puerto Rican
dishes, though vegetarians will be pleased to learn that Casa Grande
offers viable alternatives to the meat-heavy local diet. Unless you're
arriving for breakfast or dinner, you'll need reservations for lunch.
⑤ *Average main: $12* ⊠ *Rte. 612, Km 0.3, Utuado* ☎ *787/894–3939*
⊕ *www.hotelcasagrande.com.*

WHERE TO STAY

$ ⛳ **Casa Grande Mountain Retreat.** Here you'll come as close as you can
HOTEL to sleeping in a tree house. **Pros:** unspoiled setting with spectacular
Fodor'sChoice views; accessible for people with disabilities; outdoor activities. **Cons:**
★ no air-conditioning; long drive to other sights/restaurants. ⑤ *Rooms
from: $126* ⊠ *Rte. 612, Km 0.3, Utuado* ☎ *787/894–3939* ⊕ *www.
hotelcasagrande.com* ⇋ *20 rooms* ⧉ *No meals.*

ADJUNTAS TO MAYAGÜEZ

This is a journey through unspoiled nature. There are few places or
reasons to stop from the starting point to the stopping point, but one
exception is **Torre de Piedra** (Stone Tower), an observation tower in
Maricao with breathtaking views. On a clear day you can see almost
the entire western coast of the island from this vantage point.

⚠ This section of the Ruta is perhaps the most treacherous—the road
from Adjuntas to Maricao is in bad shape, pocked with potholes and the

Tram to Cueva Clara, the cave network of Río Camuy Cave Park

occasional sinkhole that's eaten away part of the road—so take it slow. It's also poorly marked; signage is scarce to nonexistent in some areas.

From this section a nice detour is available; veer off the Ruta and steer north on Route 129 toward Lares and Arecibo. This road is no less scenic, but leads through more pueblos until you end up north of Lares at the **Parque de las Cavernas del Río Camuy** (Río Camuy Cave Park).

Fodor's Choice ★ **Parque de las Cavernas del Río Camuy.** The 268-acre Parque de las Cavernas del Río Camuy contains one of the world's largest cave networks. After watching an introductory film, a tram takes you down a trail shaded by bamboo and banana trees to Cueva Clara, where the stalactites and stalagmites turn the entrance into a toothy grin. Hourlong guided tours in English and Spanish lead you on foot through the 180-foot-high cave, which is teeming with wildlife. You're likely to see the blue-eyed river crabs and long-legged tarantulas. More elusive are the bats that make their home here. They don't come out until dark, but you can feel the heat they generate at the cave's entrance. The visit ends with a tram ride to the Tres Pueblos sinkhole, where you can see the third-longest underground river in the world passing from one cave to another. Tours are first-come, first-served; plan to arrive early on weekends, when locals join the crowds. There's a picnic area, cafeteria,

Adjuntas to
Mayagüez Drive

and gift shop. ✉ *Rte. 129, Km 18.9, Camuy* ☎ *787/898–3100* ⊕ *www.
parquesnacionalespr.com* 🎟 *$15* ⊙ *Wed.–Sun. 8:30–5; last tour at 3:30.*

Once you arrive in Mayagüez, you have numerous options. Go north
on Highway 2 toward Rincón, a popular town for surfers and mainland
U.S. expats, or south toward Cabo Rojo, a charming town with lots of
open-air seafood restaurants, houses poised on stilts in the water, and
unfailingly beautiful sunsets. Still another option is to head back inland
toward the town of San Sebastián (a reasonable drive to or from Arecibo or Camuy), where numerous activities await at **Hacienda El Jibarito.**

WHERE TO EAT

$$$$ ✕ **Hacienda Luz de Luna.** This is one restaurant where you can't show
ECLECTIC up unannounced, nor would you ever recognize it from a sign outside,
simply because there isn't one. That's the intrigue of this "underground
restaurant" where guests are invited to dine at the home of renowned-
chef Ventura Vivoni Rivera. In 2008, he had a dream to cook for strang-
ers in the historic hacienda built in 1887. Three weekends per month,
Ventura prepares a 10-course meal for a maximum of 35 guests, served
during two daily seatings (at 1 and 6 pm). Hosted by the chef's father,
Edric, the evening begins with a tour of property, starting at the orchard
where lemons grow the size of coconuts. Sprawling 374 acres is the
family's farm and small factory where soap, jam, candy, and coffee

are produced. Each unique menu (emailed to guests in advance) is never repeated, but might include coffee-crusted pork with mango purée or grilled fish with crunchy rice. This dining experience generally takes up to five hours and costs $75; be sure to reserve well in advance. ⑤ *Average main: $75* ✉ *Rte. 135, Km 73.3, Barrio Yahuecas, Adjuntas* ☏ *787/829–9096* ⊕ *www.restaurartevidaventura. com* ⚲ *Reservations essential* ▬ *No credit cards.*

> **TIPS**
>
> ■ Allow a full day for this trip; the road conditions make for slow going.
>
> ■ Do not drive this section at night.
>
> ■ If it's rainy, call ahead before making the long drive to Camuy Caves. They're sometimes closed during wet weather, as paths can become too slippery for visitors.

WHERE TO STAY

For recommended lodgings in Rincón, see Where to Stay in Rincón, *Chapter 6.*

$$
B&B/INN

⛺ **Hacienda El Jibarito, San Sebastián.** Designated the island's first "agrotourism" inn, Hacienda El Jibarito is an attractive parador hidden in the mountains of San Sebastian. **Pros:** ideal for couples and families; variety of activities; attentive service. **Cons:** distance from off-site services, including restaurants; on-site restaurant open only on weekends. ⑤ *Rooms from: $200* ✉ *Rte. 445, Km 6.5, San Sebastian* ☏ *787/280–4040* ⊕ *www.haciendaeljibarito.com* ⌕ *19 rooms* ⦿ *No meals.*

$
RESORT

⛺ **Parador Villas Sotomayor.** If you're looking for a place to relax in nature and forget about the stress of city life, then look no further. **Pros:** friendly staff; great for kids; gym offers Spinning and dance classes; mountain scenery. **Cons:** tons of bugs; noise from neighboring villas; not very luxurious. ⑤ *Rooms from: $145* ✉ *Rte. 123, Km 56, Hwy. 522 Km 0.2, Adjuntas* ☏ *787/829–1717* ⊕ *www.paradorvillassotomayor. hotelpp.com* ⌕ *35 villas* ⦿ *No meals.*

7

TRAVEL SMART
PUERTO RICO

GETTING HERE AND AROUND

■TIP→ Ask the local tourist board about hotel and local transportation packages that include tickets to major museum exhibits or other special events.

■ AIR TRAVEL

Nonstop flights to San Juan from New York are 3¾ hours; from Miami, 2½ hours; from Atlanta, 3½ hours; from Boston, 3¾ hours; from Chicago, 4½ hours; from Dallas, 4½ hours.

There are dozens of daily flights to Puerto Rico from the United States, and connections are particularly good from the East Coast, although there are a few nonstop flights from the Midwest as well. San Juan's international airport is a major regional hub, so many travelers headed elsewhere in the Caribbean make connections here. Because of the number of flights, fares to San Juan are among the most reasonably priced to the region.

Airlines and Airports Airline and Airport Links.com. Airline and Airport Links.com has links to many of the world's airlines and airports. ⊕ www.airlineandairportlinks.com.

Airline Security Issues Transportation Security Administration ⊕ www.tsa.gov.

AIRPORTS

The island's main airport is Aeropuerto Internacional Luis Muñoz Marín (SJU), 20 minutes east of Old San Juan in the neighborhood of Isla Verde. San Juan's secondary airport is the small Fernando L. Ribas-Dominicci Airport (SIG), also called Isla Grande, near the city's Miramar section. From either airport you can catch flights to Culebra and Vieques, and from SJU you can also connect to other destinations in Puerto Rico and throughout the Caribbean.

Other Puerto Rican airports include Aeropuerto Internacional Rafael Hernández (BQN) in the northwestern town of Aguadilla, Aeropuerto Eugenio María de Hostos (MAZ) in the west-coast community of Mayagüez, Mercedita (PSE) in the south-coast town of Ponce, José Aponte de la Torre (RVR) in the east-coast town of Ceiba; Antonio Rivera Rodríguez (VQS) on Vieques, and Aeropuerto Benjamin Rivera Noriega (CPX) on Culebra.

Airport Information Aeropuerto Antonio Rivera Rodríguez ⊠ *Vieques* ☎ *787/741–8358.* **Aeropuerto Benjamin Rivera Noriega** ⊠ *Culebra* ☎ *787/742–0022.* **Aeropuerto Eugenio María de Hostos** ⊠ *Mayagüez* ☎ *787/833–0148.* **Aeropuerto Fernando L. Ribas-Dominicci** ⊠ *Isla Grande, San Juan* ☎ *787/729–8711.* **Aeropuerto Internacional Luis Muñoz Marín** ⊠ *Isla Verde, San Juan* ☎ *787/253–2329* ⊕ *www.aeropuertosju.com.* **Aeropuerto José Aponte de la Torre** ⊠ *Ceiba* ☎ *787/534–4101.* **Aeropuerto Mercedita** ⊠ *Ponce* ☎ *787/842–6292.* **Aeropuerto Rafael Hernández** ⊠ *Aguadilla* ☎ *787/890–1680.*

GROUND TRANSPORTATION

Before arriving, check with your hotel about transfers: some hotels and resorts provide transport from the airport—free or for a fee—to their guests; some larger resorts run regular shuttles. Otherwise, your best bets are *taxis turísticos* (tourist taxis). Uniformed officials at the airport can help you make arrangements. They will give you a slip with your exact fare to hand to the driver. Rates are based on your destination. A taxi turístico to Isla Verde costs $10. It's $15 to Condado and $19 to Old San Juan. There's a $1 charge for each bag handled by the driver, and depending on current gas prices, you may be required to pay a small fuel surcharge.

FLIGHTS

San Juan's busy Aeropuerto Internacional Luis Muñoz Marín receives flights from all major American carriers. American Airlines flies nonstop from Chicago, Dallas/Fort Worth, Miami, and New York–JFK, Delta flies nonstop from Atlanta,

New York–JFK, and New York–LGA. JetBlue flies nonstop from Boston, Fort Lauderdale, Hartford, Jacksonville, New York–JFK, New York–LGA, Orlando, Tampa, and West Palm Beach. Southwest flies nonstop from Atlanta, Baltimore/Washington, Fort Lauderdale, Houston–Hobby, Orlando, and Tampa. Spirit Air flies nonstop from Fort Lauderdale. United flies nonstop from Chicago, Cleveland, Houston, Newark, and Washington, D.C.–Reagan National. US Airways flies nonstop from Charlotte and Philadelphia.

It used to be that travelers arriving at San Juan's international airport had to transfer to nearby Aeropuerto Fernando L. Ribas-Dominicci (known as Isla Grande Airport) to take a flight to Vieques or Culebra. These days, all the carriers servicing the islands also have flights from the international airport. (That said, if you don't mind changing airports, flights to Vieques and Culebra are much cheaper from Isla Grande than they are from SJU.) Air Flamenco and Vieques Air Link offer daily flights from both airports in San Juan to Vieques and Culebra. Cape Air flies between the international airport and Culebra, Mayagüez, and Vieques. Seaborne Airlines also flies between SJU and Vieques.

Puerto Rico is also a good spot from which to hop to other Caribbean islands. American Eagle serves many islands in the Caribbean from San Juan; Cape Air connects San Juan to St. Thomas, St. Croix, Tortola, Anguilla, Nevis, and Virgin Gorda. Seaborne Airlines departs from San Juan International to St. Thomas, St. Croix, Tortola, Dominica, and Virgin Gorda. JetBlue now flies to St. Thomas, St. Croix, St. Maarten, Punta Cana, Santo Domingo, and Santiago from SJU.

San Juan is no longer the only gateway into Puerto Rico. If you're headed to the western part of the island, you can fly directly into Aguadilla. United flies here from Newark, JetBlue flies here from New York–JFK and Orlando, and Spirit Air flies nonstop from Fort Lauderdale. If the southern coast is your goal, JetBlue flies to Ponce from New York–JFK and Orlando.

Airline Contacts American Airlines ✆ 800/433–7300 ⊕ www.aa.com. **Delta Airlines** ✆ 800/221–1212 for U.S. reservations, 800/241–4141 for international reservations ⊕ www.delta.com. **JetBlue** ✆ 800/538–2583 ⊕ www.jetblue.com. **Spirit Airlines** ✆ 800/772–7117 ⊕ www.spirit.com. **Southwest Airlines** ✆ 800/435–9792 ⊕ www.southwest.com. **United Airlines** ✆ 800/864–8331 ⊕ www.united.com. **US Airways** ✆ 800/428–4322 for U.S. and Canada reservations, 800/622–1015 for international reservations ⊕ www.usairways.com.

Regional Airlines Air Flamenco ✆ 787/724–1818, 877/535–2636 ⊕ www.airflamenco.net. **Cape Air** ✆ 866/227–3247 ⊕ www.capeair.com. **Seaborne Airlines** ✆ 866/359–8784 ⊕ www.seaborneairlines.com. **Vieques Air Link** ✆ 787/741–8331, 888/901–9247 ⊕ www.viequesairlink.com.

▌ BUS TRAVEL

The Autoridad Metropolitana de Autobuses (AMA) operates buses that thread through San Juan, running in exclusive lanes on major thoroughfares and stopping at signs marked "Parada." Destinations are indicated above the windshield. Bus B-21 will take you from Condado to Old San Juan. Bus A-5 runs from San Juan through Santurce and the beach area of Isla Verde. Service starts at around 6 am and generally continues until 9 pm. Fares are 75¢ and are paid in exact change upon entering the bus. Most buses are air-conditioned and have wheelchair lifts and lockdowns.

There's no bus system covering the rest of the island. If you do not have a rental car, your best bet is to travel by *públicos*, which are usually shared 17-passenger vans. They have license plates ending in "P" or "PD," and they scoot to towns throughout the island, stopping in each community's main plaza. They operate primarily during the day; routes and fares are fixed by the Public Service Commission, but schedules aren't set, so you have to call ahead.

Bus Information Autoridad Metropolitana de Autobuses ☎ 787/294-0500 ⊕ dtop.gov. pr/transporte_urbano.

▌ CAR TRAVEL

Several well-marked, multilane highways link population centers. Route 26 is the main artery through San Juan, connecting Condado and Old San Juan to Isla Verde and the airport. Route 22, which runs east–west between San Juan and Camuy, and Route 52, which runs north–south between San Juan and Ponce, are toll roads. Route 2, a smaller highway, travels west from San Juan toward Rincón, and Route 3 traverses east toward Fajardo. Route 3 can be mind-numbingly slow, so consider taking Route 66, a toll road that bypasses the worst of the traffic.

Five highways are particularly noteworthy for their scenery and vistas. The island's tourism authorities have even given them special names. Ruta Panorámica (Panoramic Route) runs east–west through the central mountains. Ruta Cotorra (Puerto Rican Parrot Route) travels along the north coast. Ruta Paso Fino (Paso Fino Horse Route, after a horse breed) takes you north–south and west along the south coast. Ruta Coquí, named for the famous Puerto Rican tree frog, runs along the east coast. Ruta Flamboyán, named after the island tree, goes from San Juan through the mountains to the east coast.

GASOLINE

All types of fuel—regular, super-premium, and diesel—are available by the liter. Most stations are self-service. Hours vary, but stations generally operate daily from early in the morning until 10 or 11 pm; in metro areas many are open 24 hours. Stations are few and far between in the Cordillera Central and other rural areas, so plan accordingly. In cities you can pay with cash and bank or credit cards; in the hinterlands cash is occasionally your only option.

ROAD CONDITIONS

Puerto Rico has some of the Caribbean's best roads, but potholes, sharp turns, speed bumps, sudden gradient changes, and poor lighting can sometimes make driving difficult. Be especially cautious when driving after heavy rains or hurricanes; roads and bridges might be washed out or damaged. Many of the mountain roads are very narrow and steep, with unmarked curves and cliffs. Locals are familiar with such roads and often drive at high speeds, which can give you quite a scare. When traveling on a narrow, curving road, it's best to honk your horn before you take any sharp turn.

Traffic around cities—particularly San Juan, Ponce, and Mayagüez—is heavy at rush hours (weekdays from 7 am to 10 am and 3 pm to 7 pm).

FROM	TO	RTE./ DISTANCE
San Juan	Aguadilla	Rte. 22/81 miles (130 km)
San Juan	El Yunque	Rte. 3/35 miles (55 km)
San Juan	Fajardo	Rte. 3/36 miles (59 km)
San Juan	Mayagüez	Rte. 22/98 miles (160 km)
San Juan	Ponce	Rte. 52/73 miles (117 km)

ROADSIDE EMERGENCIES

In an emergency, dial 911. If your car breaks down, call the rental company for a replacement. Before renting, make sure you investigate the company's policy regarding replacement vehicles and repairs out on the island, and ask about surcharges that might be incurred if you break down in a rural area and need a new car.

RULES OF THE ROAD

U.S. driving laws apply in Puerto Rico, and you'll find no problem with signage or directionals. Street and highway signs are most often in Spanish but use international symbols; brushing up on a few key Spanish terms before your trip will help. The following words and phrases are especially useful: *calle sin salida* (dead-end street), carril (lane), *cruce de peatones* (pedestrian crossing), *cuidado* (caution), *desvío* (detour), *estación de peaje* (toll-booth), *no entre* (do not enter), *no estacione* (no parking), *salida* (exit), *tránsito* (one way), *zona escolar* (school zone).

Distances are posted in kilometers (1 mile to 1.6 km), but speed limits are posted in miles per hour. Speeding and drunk-driving penalties are much the same here as on the U. S. mainland. Police cars often travel with their lights flashing, so it's difficult to know when they're trying to pull you over. If the siren is on, move to the right lane to get out of the way. If the lights are on, it's best to pull over—but make sure that the vehicle is a *marked* police car before doing so.

▌ FERRY TRAVEL

The Autoridad de Transporte Marítimo (Maritime Transportation Authority) runs passenger ferries from Fajardo to Culebra and Vieques. Service is from the ferry terminal in Fajardo, about a 90-minute drive from San Juan. Advance reservations are not accepted. There are a limited number of seats on the ferries, so get to the terminal in plenty of time. This means arriving an hour or two ahead of the departure time in Fajardo, somewhat less in Vieques and Culebra. In Fajardo the ticket counter is in the small building across the street from the actual terminal. In Vieques and Culebra the ticket counters are at the entrance to the terminals. There are food kiosks at Fajardo and Vieques that are open even for the early-morning departures. Culebra doesn't have any eateries nearby.

The Fajardo–Vieques passenger ferry departs from Vieques daily at 9:30 am, 1 pm, 4:30 pm, and 8 pm, returning at 6:30 am, 11 am, 3 pm, and 6 pm. Tickets for the 90-minute journey are $2 each way. The Fajardo–Culebra ferry leaves Culebra daily at 9 am, 3 pm, and 7 pm, returning at 6:30 am, 1 pm, and 5 pm. The 90-minute trip is $2.25.

Information **Autoridad de Transporte Marítimo** ☎ *787/484–0934* ⊕ *www.dtop. gov.pr.*

ESSENTIALS

■ ACCOMMODATIONS

San Juan's high-rise hotels on the Condado and Isla Verde beach strips cater primarily to the cruise-ship and casino crowd, though some also target business travelers and families. Outside San Juan, particularly on the east coast, you'll find self-contained luxury resorts that cover hundreds of acres. In the west, southwest, and south—as well as on the islands of Vieques and Culebra—smaller inns, villas, condominiums, and government-sponsored *paradores* are the norm.

CATEGORY	COST
$$$$	over $350
$$$	$251–$350
$$	$151–$250
$	$80–$150

All prices are for a standard double room in high season, meals not included, and excluding tax and service charges.

Most hotels and other lodgings require you to give your credit-card details before they will confirm your reservation. If you don't feel comfortable emailing this information, ask if you can call it in or fax it (some places even prefer faxes). However you book, get confirmation in writing and have a copy of it handy when you check in.

Be sure you understand the hotel's cancellation policy. Some places allow you to cancel without any kind of penalty—even if you prepaid to secure a discounted rate—if you cancel at least 24 hours in advance. Others require you to cancel a week in advance or penalize you the cost of one night. Small inns and B&Bs are most likely to require you to cancel far in advance. Most hotels allow children under a certain age to stay in their parents' room at no extra charge, but others charge for them as extra adults; find out the cutoff age for discounts.

APARTMENT AND HOUSE RENTALS

Local Agents Island West Properties. Island West Properties can help you rent condos in Rincón by the day, week, or month. ⊠ *Rincón* ☎ *787/823–2323* ⊕ *www.island-west. com.* **Puerto Rico Vacation Apartments.** Puerto Rico Vacation Apartments represents some 200 properties in Condado and Isla Verde. ⊠ *Calle Marbella del Caribe Oeste S-5, Isla Verde, San Juan* ☎ *787/727–1591, 800/266–3639* ⊕ *www.sanjuanvacationpr. com.* **Rainbow Realty.** Rainbow Realty rents studios, apartments, and houses on Vieques. ⊠ *278 Calle Flamboyán, Esperanza, Vieques* ☎ *787/741–4312, 787/435–2063* ⊕ *www. viequesrainbowrealty.com.*

HOTELS

In the most expensive hotels, your room will be large enough for two to move around comfortably, with two double beds or one queen- or king-size bed, air-conditioning, a phone, Wi-Fi or other Internet access, a private bath, an in-room safe, cable TV, a hair dryer, iron and ironing board, room service, shampoo and toiletries, and possibly a view of the water. There will be a concierge and at least one hotel restaurant and lounge, a pool, a shop, and an exercise room or spa. In Puerto Rico's smaller inns, rooms will have private baths, air-conditioning or fans, a double to king-size bed, possibly room service, and breakfast (Continental or full) included in the rates. Most also have Wi-Fi or other Internet access in the rooms, though some have Wi-Fi in public areas only. In some smaller hotels several rooms share baths—it's a good idea to ask before booking. All hotels listed in this guide have private baths unless otherwise noted.

In Puerto Rico smoking is prohibited in public places, including restaurants, bars, cafés, casinos, and hotel common areas.

PARADORES

Some *paradores* are rural inns offering no-frills apartments, and others are large hotels; all must meet certain standards, such as proximity to an attraction or beach. Most have a small restaurant that serves local cuisine. They're often good bargains (usually from $85 to $125 for a double room). You can find a listing of and contact information for all the paradores on the Puerto Rico Tourism Company's website. Small Inns of Puerto Rico, a branch of the Puerto Rico Hotel & Tourism Association, is a marketing arm for some 25 small hotels island-wide. The organization occasionally has package deals including casino coupons and LeLoLai (a cultural show) tickets.

Contacts Puerto Rico Tourism Company ☎ *787/721–2400, 800/866–7827* ⊕ *www. seepuertorico.com.* **Small Hotels of Puerto Rico** ⊕ *www.puertoricosmallhotels.com.*

▌ADDRESSES

Addresses in Puerto Rico, especially in and around San Juan, can be confusing because Spanish terms like *avenida* and *calle* are used interchangeably with English terms like avenue and street. This means that the shopping strip in Old San Juan may be called Calle Cristo or Cristo Street. (And it might just be called Cristo, as it is on many maps.) A highway is often called an *expreso*, and an alley or pedestrian-only street is labeled a *paseo*.

Outside a metropolitan area, addresses are most often given by the kilometer mark along the road. That means that the address for Parque de las Cavernas del Río Camuy, south of Arecibo, is given as Route 129, Kilometer 18.9.

▌COMMUNICATIONS

INTERNET

Internet access in Puerto Rico is as widespread as it is on the U.S. mainland. You can expect rooms in large hotels or resorts to have plug-in Ethernet access or Wi-Fi—or, more likely, both. Many hotels also have business centers; these may be quite sophisticated or merely a computer terminal or two for guest use. In smaller B&Bs and inns, Wi-Fi is occasionally limited to common areas only, but this is the exception rather than the rule. If it's important to you, call ahead to double-check that the hotel you want to stay in can meet your needs. Wi-Fi is also available in many chain restaurants, including Burger King and Starbucks, as well as some local cafés.

PHONES

All Puerto Rican phone numbers consist of a three-digit area code and a seven-digit local number, just like those in the United States. Puerto Rico's area codes are 787 and 939. Toll-free numbers, with the prefixes 800, 888, or 877, are widely used in Puerto Rico, and most can be accessed from North America. By the same token, you can also access most North American toll-free numbers from the island.

Most major American cell-phone companies consider Puerto Rico as part of regular nationwide calling, so it's unlikely that those with U.S. calling plans will incur roaming charges during a visit. Nevertheless, it's always best to call your provider to confirm before you travel. Companies that offer service in Puerto Rico include AT&T, Claro, T-Mobile, and Sprint.

Note that calling from a hotel is almost always expensive; hotels usually add huge surcharges to all calls, particularly international ones. Locally purchased calling cards can help keep costs to a minimum.

CALLING CARDS

Phone cards are widely available in shops, supermarkets, and drugstores, as well as from the local phone company, Claro.

Information Ring Cards ☎ *866/981–2355* ⊕ *www.clarotodo.com.* **Cellular Abroad.** Cellular Abroad rents and sells phones, SIM cards, and Wi-Fi hotspots that work in many countries. ☎ *800/287–5072* ⊕ *www. cellularabroad.com.* **Mobal.** Mobal rents and sells cell phones (starting at $29) and

SIM cards that will operate in 190 countries. Per-call rates vary throughout the world. ☎ 888/888–9162 ⊕ www.mobal.com.

PlanetFone. PlanetFone rents cell phones, but the per-minute rates are expensive. ☎ 888/988–4777 ⊕ www.planetfone.com.

■ CUSTOMS AND DUTIES

Puerto Rico is considered a part of the United States for customs purposes, so you will not pass through customs on arrival if you're coming from the mainland. When leaving Puerto Rico, you must pass your bag through a checkpoint of the U.S. Department of Agriculture's (USDA) Animal and Plant Health Inspection Service (APHIS). The list of organic products that can be transported from Puerto Rico to the States includes avocados, bananas, breadfruits, citrus fruits, ginger, papayas, and plantains.

U.S. Information U.S. Department of Agriculture ⊕ www.aphis.usda.gov.

■ EATING OUT

Throughout the island you can find everything from French haute cuisine to sushi bars, as well as superb local eateries serving *comida criolla,* traditional Puerto Rican meals. Note that the *mesón gastronómico* label is used by the government to recognize restaurants that preserve culinary traditions. By law, every menu has a written warning about the dangers of consuming raw foods; therefore, if you want something medium rare, you need to be specific about how you'd like it cooked. *For information on food-related health issues, see Health, below.* The restaurants we list are the cream of the crop in each price category.

MEALS AND MEALTIMES

Puerto Ricans' eating habits mirror those of their counterparts on the mainland United States: They eat breakfast, lunch, and dinner, though they don't tend to drink as much coffee throughout the day. Instead, islanders like a steaming,

high-test *café con leche* in the morning and another between 2 and 4 pm, perhaps alongside a local pastry or other sweet treat. They may finish a meal with coffee, but they never drink coffee *during* a meal.

People tend to eat dinner late in Puerto Rico. Many restaurants don't open until 6 pm. You may find yourself alone in the restaurant if you eat before 7 pm; from 8 pm onward, it may be quite busy.

Unless otherwise noted, the restaurants listed in this guide are open daily for lunch and dinner.

RESERVATIONS AND DRESS

Regardless of where you are, it's a good idea to make a reservation if you can. In some places, it's expected. We mention them specifically only when reservations are essential (there's no other way you'll ever get a table) or when they are not accepted. For popular restaurants, book as far ahead as you can (often 30 days), and reconfirm as soon as you arrive. (Large parties should always call ahead to check the reservations policy.) We mention dress only when men are required to wear a jacket or a jacket and tie.

Puerto Ricans generally dress up to go out, particularly in the evening. And always remember: beach attire is only for the beach.

WINES, BEER, AND SPIRITS

Puerto Rico isn't a notable producer of wine, but it does make several well-crafted local beers and, of course, lots of rum. Legends trace the birthplace of the piña colada to several San Juan establishments. Puerto Rican rum is popular mixed with cola (known as a *cuba libre*), soda, tonic, juices, or water, or served on the rocks or even straight up. Look for Bacardí, Don Q, Palo Viejo, Caliche, and Barrilito. The drinking age in Puerto Rico is 18.

ELECTRICITY

Puerto Rico uses the same 110-volt AC (60-cycle), two-prong-outlet electrical system as in North America. Plugs have two flat pins set parallel to each other. European visitors should bring adapters and converters, or call ahead to see whether their hotel has them on hand.

Consider making a small investment in a universal adapter, which has several types of plugs in one lightweight, compact unit. Most laptops and mobile phone chargers are dual voltage (i.e., they operate equally well on 110 and 220 volts), so require only an adapter. These days the same is true of small appliances such as hair dryers. Always check labels and manufacturer instructions to be sure. Don't use 110-volt outlets marked for shavers only for high-wattage appliances such as hair dryers.

EMERGENCIES

Emergencies are handled by dialing 911. You can expect a quick response by police, fire, and medical personnel, most of whom speak at least some English. San Juan's Tourist Zone Police are particularly helpful to visitors.

General Emergency Contacts Ambulance, police, and fire ☎ *911.* Air Ambulance Service ☎ *787/977–1585.* Fire Department ☎ *787/343–2330.* Police ☎ *787/343–2020.* Tourist Zone Police ☎ *787/725–7015* for Condado, *787/726–2981* for Isla Verde.

GAY AND LESBIAN TRAVEL

In sophisticated San Juan gays and lesbians will find it easy to mingle. Many gay-friendly hotels, restaurants, and clubs are scattered throughout the city, and beaches in Condado and Ocean Park tend to attract a gay crowd. Many guesthouses here are gay-owned and operated. The bohemian Old San Juan crowd is particularly friendly and—just as in Ocean Park and Condado—many businesses there are

owned by gays or lesbians. However, in recent years the gay energy has moved south to the relatively non-touristy but artsy and increasingly lively Santurce district; take a taxi to get there. One popular gay hot spot in Santurce is Circo Bar.

Some clubs and bars also host a weekly "gay night." On the first Sunday in June, a gay pride parade takes place in Condado and is preceded by a week of events.

Other welcoming areas include Ponce in the south, Rincón in the west, and the island of Vieques in the east, although the local population here is more conservative and it's the large and bohemian expat crowd that is tolerant. Remember that Puerto Rico is overwhelmingly Catholic, which has a strong effect on how locals view gay people. In rural areas and small towns, overt displays of affection between same-sex couples can cause problems.

Connections Travel. Frank Fournier of Connections Travel, a member of the International Gay and Lesbian Travel Association, is a reliable local travel agent for the gay and lesbian community. ☎ *800/973–5550* ⊕ *www.connectionstravelpr.com.*

HEALTH

The most common types of illnesses are caused by contaminated food and water. Make sure food has been thoroughly cooked and is served to you fresh and hot; avoid vegetables and fruits that you haven't washed (in bottled or purified water) or peeled yourself. If you have problems, mild cases of traveler's diarrhea may respond to Imodium (known generically as loperamide) or Pepto-Bismol. Be sure to drink plenty of fluids; if you can't keep fluids down, seek medical help immediately.

Infectious diseases can be airborne or passed via mosquitoes and ticks and through direct or indirect physical contact with animals or people. Some, including Norwalk-like viruses that affect your digestive tract, can be passed along through contaminated food. Condoms can help prevent most sexually transmitted diseases, but they aren't absolutely reliable and their quality varies from country to country. Speak with your physician and/or check the CDC or World Health Organization websites for health alerts, particularly if you're pregnant, traveling with children, or have a chronic illness.

SPECIFIC ISSUES IN PUERTO RICO

While uncommon, dengue fever, a mosquito-borne disease, is a reality of everyday life in the Caribbean. Puerto Rico has experienced several recent epidemics, most recently in 2010 and 2012. Virulent forms of the virus can cause high fever, joint pain, nausea, rashes, and occasionally death, but the most common strain is relatively mild, causing mostly flulike symptoms. Most cases were reported in urban areas far from the usual tourist destinations. As a precaution, the U.S. Centers for Disease Control and Prevention advises the use of an insect repellent with DEET and clothing that covers the arms and legs.

Health care in Puerto Rico is among the best in the Caribbean, but expect long waits and often a less-than-pleasant bedside manner. At all hospitals and medical centers you can find English-speaking medical staff, and many large hotels have an English-speaking doctor on call.

Tap water on the island is generally fine for drinking, but avoid drinking it after storms (when the water supply can become mixed with sewage). Thoroughly wash or peel produce you buy in markets before eating it.

Do not fly within 24 hours of scuba diving.

OVER-THE-COUNTER REMEDIES

All the U.S. brands of sunscreen and over-the-counter medicines (for example, Tylenol, Advil, Robitussin, and Nyquil) are available in pharmacies, supermarkets, and convenience stores.

▌ HOURS OF OPERATION

Bank hours are generally weekdays from 9 to 5, though a few branches are also open Saturday from 9 to noon or 1. Post offices are open weekdays from 8:00 to 4:30 and Saturday from 8 to noon. Government offices are open weekdays from 8 to 4 or 9 to 5.

Most gas stations are open daily from early in the morning until 10 or 11 pm. Numerous stations in urban areas are open 24 hours.

As a rule, San Juan–area museums are closed on Monday and, in some cases, Sunday. Hours otherwise are 9 or 10 am to 5 pm, often with an hour off for lunch between noon and 2. Sights managed by the National Parks Service, such as Castillo San Felipe del Morro and San Cristóbal, are open daily from 9 to 5.

In cities, locally run pharmacies are generally open weekdays and on Saturday from 9 to 6 or 7. U.S. chain pharmacies, such as Walgreens and CVS, are open seven days a week; some are open 24 hours.

Street shops are open Monday through Saturday from 9 to 6; mall stores tend to stay open to 9 or sometimes even later. Count on convenience stores staying open late into the night, seven days a week. Supermarkets often open at 11 am on Sundays, although some remain open 24 hours, seven days a week.

▌MAIL

Puerto Rico uses the U.S. postal system, and all addresses on the island have ZIP codes. The rates to send letters and postcards from Puerto Rico are the same as those everywhere else in the United States.

SHIPPING PACKAGES

Many shops—particularly those in Old San Juan and Condado—will ship purchases for you. Shipping services are especially common at art galleries. Pay by credit card, and save your receipts. Make sure the proprietor insures the package against loss or damage and ships it first-class or by courier. Grab a business card with the proprietor's name and phone number so you can readily follow up with him or her if needed.

Post offices in major Puerto Rican cities offer express mail (next-day) service to the U.S. mainland and to Puerto Rican destinations. In addition, you can send packages via FedEx or UPS. Ask at the concierge desk of your hotel; most have regular courier pickups or can call for one. Hotels that offer business services will take care of the entire ordeal for you. Note that courier delivery and pickup is not available on Saturday, and even "overnight" packages often take two to three days to reach the U.S. mainland.

Express Services FedEx ☎ *800/463-3339* ⊕ *www.fedex.com.* **UPS** ☎ *800/PICK-UPS* ⊕ *www.ups.com.*

▌MONEY

Puerto Rico, which is a commonwealth of the United States, uses the U.S. dollar as its official currency. Prices for most items are stable and comparable to those in the States, and that includes restaurants and hotel rates. As in many places, city prices tend to be higher than those in rural areas, but you're not going to go broke staying in the city: soft drinks or a cup of coffee run about $1–2; a local beer in a bar, $3–5; museum admission, $5–10.

Prices listed here are for adults. Substantially reduced fees are almost always available for children, students, and senior citizens.

ATMS AND BANKS

Your own bank will probably charge a fee for using ATMs outside its network; the foreign bank you use may also charge a fee. Nevertheless, if you're visiting from overseas, you'll usually get a better rate of exchange at an ATM than you will at a currency-exchange office or even when changing money in a bank. And extracting funds as you need them is a safer option than carrying around a large amount of cash.

▌TIP→ **PIN numbers with more than four digits are not recognized at ATMs in many countries. If yours has five or more, remember to change it before you leave.**

Automated Teller Machines (or ATMs, known here as ATHs) are as readily available and reliable as on the U.S. mainland; many are attached to banks, but you can also find them in gas stations, drugstores, supermarkets, and larger hotels. Just about every casino has one—to keep people in the game—but these can carry large surcharges, so check the fee before withdrawing money. ATMs are found less frequently in rural areas, but there's usually at least one in even the smallest village. Look to local banks, such as Banco Popular.

CREDIT CARDS

It's a good idea to inform your credit-card company before you travel, especially if you're going abroad and don't travel internationally very often. Otherwise, the credit-card company might put a hold on your card owing to unusual activity—not a good thing halfway through your trip. Record all your credit-card numbers—as well as the phone numbers to call if your cards are lost or stolen—in a safe place, so you're prepared should something go wrong. Both MasterCard and Visa have general numbers you can call (collect if you're abroad) if your card is lost, but you're better off calling the number of your issuing bank, since Master-Card and Visa usually just transfer you to your bank; your bank's number is usually printed on your card.

Reporting Lost Cards American Express
☎ *800/528–4800 in U.S., 336/393–1111 collect from abroad* ⊕ *www.americanexpress. com.* **Diners Club** ☎ *800/234–6377 in U.S., 514/881–3735 collect from abroad* ⊕ *www. dinersclub.com.* **Discover** ☎ *800/347–2683 in U.S., 801/902–3100 collect from abroad* ⊕ *www.discovercard.com.* **MasterCard** ☎ *800/627–8372 in U.S., 636/722–7111 collect from abroad* ⊕ *www.mastercard.com.* **Visa** ☎ *800/847–2911 in U.S., 303/967–1096 collect from abroad* ⊕ *www.visa.com.*

▌ PASSPORTS AND VISAS

U.S. citizens don't need passports to visit Puerto Rico; any government-issued photo ID will do. Nor is there passport control either to or from Puerto Rico; in this respect, flying here is just like traveling on any domestic flight. Nevertheless, it's always wise to carry some form of identification that proves your citizenship, and we still recommend that you carry a valid passport when traveling to Puerto Rico; it's a necessity if you're making any other trips around the Caribbean, except to the U.S. Virgin Islands, where you will pass through customs but not passport control.

▌ SAFETY

San Juan, Mayagüez, and Ponce, like most other big cities, have their share of crime, so guard your wallet or purse in markets, on buses, and in other crowded areas. Avoid beaches at night, when muggings have been known to occur even in Condado and Isla Verde. Don't leave anything unattended on the beach. If you must keep valuables in your vehicle, put them in the trunk. Always lock your car. The exception is at the beaches of Vieques, where rental-car agencies advise you to leave the car unlocked so thieves don't break the windows to search for valuables. This happens extremely rarely, but it does happen.

We recommend that women carry only a handbag that closes completely and wear it bandolier style (across one shoulder and your chest). Open-style bags and those allowed to simply dangle from one shoulder are prime targets for pickpockets and purse snatchers. Avoid walking anywhere alone at night.

▌ TAXES

You must pay a tax on your hotel room rate: For hotels with casinos it's 11%, for other hotels it's 9%, and for government-approved paradores it's 7%. Ask your hotel before booking. The tax, in addition to each hotel's discretionary service charge (which usually ranges from 5% to 16%), can add a hefty 12% to 27% to your bill. There's a 7% sales tax in Puerto Rico.

▌ TIPPING

Some hotels—usually those classified as resorts—automatically add a 5%–16% service charge to your bill. Check ahead to confirm whether this charge is built into the room rate or will be tacked on at checkout. Tips are expected, and appreciated, by restaurant waitstaff (15%–20%), hotel porters ($1 per bag), maids ($1–$2 a day), and taxi drivers (10%–15%).

▌ VISITOR INFORMATION

In addition to the Puerto Rico Tourism Company's ¡*Qué Pasa!*, pick up the Puerto Rico Hotel and Tourism Association's *Bienvenidos* and *Places to Go*. Among them you can find a wealth of information about the island and its activities. All are free and available at tourism offices and hotel desks. The Puerto Rico Tourism Company has information centers at the airport, Old San Juan, Ponce, Aguadilla, and Cabo Rojo. Most island towns also have a tourism office, usually in the city hall.

Contacts Puerto Rico Tourism Company 787/721–2400, 800/866–7827 ⊕ www. gotopuertorico.com.

▮ VACATION PACKAGES

Packages *are not* guided excursions. Packages combine airfare, accommodations, and perhaps a rental car or other extras (theater tickets, guided excursions, boat trips, reserved entry to popular museums, transit passes), but they let you do your own thing. During busy periods packages may be your only option, as flights and rooms may be sold out otherwise.

Packages will definitely save you time. They can also save you money, particularly in peak seasons, but—and this is a really big "but"—you should price each part of the package separately to be sure. And be aware that prices advertised on websites and in newspapers rarely include service charges or taxes, which can up your costs by hundreds of dollars.

▮TIP➔ Some packages and cruises are sold only through travel agents. Don't always assume that you can get the best deal by booking everything yourself.

Each year consumers are stranded or lose their money when packagers—even large ones with excellent reputations—go out of business. How can you protect yourself? First, always pay with a credit card; if you have a problem, your credit-card company may help you resolve it. Second, buy trip insurance that covers default. Third, choose a company that belongs to the United States Tour Operators Association, whose members must set aside funds to cover defaults. Finally, choose a company that also participates in the Tour Operator Program of the American Society of Travel Agents (ASTA), which will act as mediator in any disputes.

You can also check on the tour operator's reputation among travelers by posting an inquiry on one of the Fodors.com forums.

Organizations American Society of Travel Agents 703/739–2782 ⊕ www.travelsense. org. **United States Tour Operators Association (USTOA).** 212/599–6599 ⊕ www.ustoa. com.

INDEX

316 <

PHOTO CREDITS

Front cover: Danita Delimont / AWL Images Ltd [Description: Malecon, Esperanza, Vieques]. Back cover (from left to right): Jamie18/Shutterstock; Joseph/Shutterstock; Starwood Hotels & Resorts. Spine: SeanPavonePhoto/Shutterstock 1, Katja Kreder / age fotostock. 2, Franz Marc Frei / age fotostock. 5, Franz Marc Frei / age fotostock. Chapter 1: Experience Puerto Rico: 8-9, Katja Kreder / age fotostock. 10, Christian Wheatley/Starwood Hotels & Resorts. 11 (left), Lori Froeb/Shutterstock. 11 (right), John Frink/iStockphoto. 14 (left), Jacom Stephens/Avid Creative, Inc./iStockphoto. 14 (top center), Diueine/Flickr. 14 (top right),Ksaraf/wikipedia.org. 14 (bottom), Jorge González. 15 (top left), Nick Hanna /Alamy. 15 (bottom left), Frank Llosa. 15 (right), imagebroker / Alamy. 17 (left), Jbermudez/ wikipedia.org. 17 (right), MissChatter/wikipedia.org. 18, Danny Lehman/Celebrity Cruises. 19 (left), Tomás Fano/Flickr. 19 (right), Charles Harris/Royal Caribbean International. 20, Hotel El Convento. 21, Museo de Arte de Puerto Rico. 22 (left), Museo de Arte de Puerto Rico. 22 (right), wikipedia.org. 23, Lynn Watson/Shutterstock. 24, The Ritz-Carlton. 25, The Ritz-Carlton. 30, Oquendo/Flickr. Chapter 2: San Juan: 31, Katja Kreder / age fotostock. 32 (top), John Rodriguez/iStockphoto. 32 (bottom), Lori Froeb/Shutterstock. 33 (left), Miguel A. Alvarez/Shutterstock. 33 (right), Adam Bies/Shutterstock. 34, DU BOISBERRANGER Jean / age fotostock. 41, Heeb Christian / age fotostock. 44, Tomás Fano/ Flickr. 48, George Oze / Alamy. 51 (left), Franz Marc Frei / age fotostock. 51 (top right), Lawrence Roberg/Shutterstock. 51 (bottom right), Franz Marc Frei / age fotostock. 52 (top right), iStockphoto. 52 (bottom left), Oquendo/Flickr. 53 (top left), runneralan2004/Flickr. 53 (top middle), runneralan2004/ Flickr. 53 (top right), Franz Marc Frei / age fotostock. 53 (bottom), Prknlot/Flickr. 55, Atlantide S.N.C. /age fotostock. 56, Oliver Gerhard / age fotostock. 59, imagebroker / Alamy. 71, Wendell Metzen / age fotostock. 72, steve bly / Alamy. 86-87, Ken Welsh / age fotostock. 91, DU BOISBERRANGER Jean / age fotostock. 97, Lawrence Manning/photolibrary.com. 98, Craig Lovell / Eagle Visions Photography / Alamy. 99 (top), Pietro Scozzari / age fotostock. 99 (second from top), Julie Schwietert. 99 (third from top), Julie Schwietert. 99 (bottom), STEPHANE - FOTODECLIC / age fotostock. 100 (left), Julie Schwietert. 100 (right), Julie Schwietert. 107, Martin Florin Emmanuel / Alamy. 114, Wendell Metzen / age fotostock. Chapter 3: El Yunque and the Northeast: 119, Ken Welsh / age fotostock. 120, Diana Lundin/Shutterstock. 121 (left), Joseph/Shutterstock. 121 (right), Thomas Hart Shelby. 122, Robert Fried / Alamy. 123 (left), John Frink/iStockphoto. 123 (right), iStockphoto. 124, Doug Schneider/iStockphoto. 125, Joseph/Shutterstock. 126, Luis César Tejo/Shutterstock. 133, Kreder Katja / age fotostock.136, Katja Kreder / age fotostock. 139, Rolf Nussbaumer / age fotostock. 144-45, Ken Welsh / age fotostock. 147, Aleksandar Kolundzija / iStockphoto. 149, Katja Kreder / age fotostock. 156, Larry Lambrecht. Chapter 4: Vieques and Culebra: 159, Katja Kreder / age fotostock. 160 (top and bottom), underwhelmer/Flickr. 161 (top left), plizzba/Flickr. 161 (top right), Jjankechu/wikipedia. org. 161 (bottom), underwhelmer/Flickr. 162, Michele Falzone / age fotostock. 169, Michele Falzone / age fotostock. 171, SuperStock/age fotostock. 173, Frank Llosa. 174 (top), Frank Llosa. 174 (bottom), kayakingpuertorico.com. 175, Starwood Hotels & Resorts. 176 (top), Frank Llosa. 176 (bottom), Sue Braden. 177, Starwood Hotels & Resorts. 185, jasonsager/Flickr. 192, Hector's By the Sea. Chapter 5: Ponce and the Porta Caribe: 195, Ken Welsh / age fotostock. 196 (top), Capricornis Photographic Inc./ Shutterstock. 196 (bottom), Oquendo/wikipedia.org. 197 (top), Oquendo/Flickr. 197 (bottom), Jmoliver/wikipedia.org. 198, Oliver Gerhard / Alamy. 199 (bottom left), Oquendo/Flickr. 199 (top right), Greg Vaughn / Alamy. 200, Oquendo/Flickr. 207, Franz Marc Frei / age fotostock. 211, Greg Vaughn / Alamy. 213, Eric Fowke / Alamy. 216, Nicholas Gill. 224, Julie Schwietert. 225 (left), Museo de los Santos / Richard Holm. 225 (right), Tony Amador. 227, DU BOISBERRANGER Jean / age fotostock. 229, giulio andreini / age fotostock. 232, Morales / age fotostock. Chapter 6: Rincón and the Porta del Sol: 237, Marlise Kast. 238, Hiram A. Gay/wikipedia.org. 239 (top), Oquendo/Flickr. 239 (bottom), Oquendo/Flickr. 240, SuperStock/age fotostock. 246, Juerg Heinimann / Alamy. 257, Marlise Kast. 258 (top and bottom), Eric Rivera Vázquez/Shutterstock. 259 (top left), Marlise Kast. 259 (bottom left), Eric Rivera Vázquez/Shutterstock. 259 (right), Marlise Kast. 260, Eric Rivera Vázquez/Shutterstock. 266, Israel Pabon/Shutterstock. 269, Nicholas Pitt / Alamy. 275, Ken Welsh / age fotostock. Chapter 7: Ruta Panorámica: 281, Nick Hanna / Alamy. 282, Casa Grande Mountain Retreat. 283, Michele Falzone / age fotostock. 285, Robert Fried / Alamy. 289, Nick Hanna / Alamy. 290, Oliver Gerhard / Alamy. 291, Jorge González. About Our Writers: Heather Rodino, courtesy of Pierre Baumann; Paulina Salach, courtesy of Gustavo Antonetti; Julie Schwietert Collazo, courtesy of Francisco Collazo.

NOTES

NOTES

NOTES

ABOUT OUR WRITERS

 Heather Rodino is a freelance editor and writer based in San Juan. She has contributed to *Fodor's Puerto Rico* (6th, 7th, and 8th eds.) and *Caribbean* (2011–2013), among other publications. For many years, she worked in the publishing industry in New York City, but she doesn't miss those long New York winters.

 A culinary and travel entrepreneur, **Paulina Salach** is the co-founder of Puerto Rico Restaurant Week and Spoon Food Tours, a food tour company based in San Juan. She is also a licensed publicist, culinary consultant, event producer, and social media manager. In 2014, she was one of the hosts of the Saborea food festival held in San Juan. Paulina has contributed to *Have Fork Will Travel*, a handbook for food and drink tourism. She is a native of Poland and has lived in Barcelona, New York City, and currently resides in Puerto Rico.

 Julie Schwietert Collazo is a Lowell Thomas Award–winning bilingual writer interested in overlooked people and places, especially in Latin America. She has written about Chinese Cubans in Havana, Generation Y in Colombia, workers' and indigenous movements in Mexico City, and environmental issues in Chile and Puerto Rico. She was one of only a handful of journalists to visit the Joint Detention Facility at Guantanamo Bay in Cuba in 2008. Julie has lived in Mexico City and San Juan, Puerto Rico. She currently calls New York City home. Find her online at collazoprojects.com.